FORTUNATE SON

FORTUNATE SON

My Life, My Music

JOHN FOGERTY

WITH JIMMY McDONOUGH

LITTLE, BROWN AND COMPANY

New York • Boston • London

Little, Brown and Company
Hachette Book Group
1290 Avenue of the Americas, New York, NY 10104
littlebrown.com

First Edition: October 2015

Little, Brown and Company is a division of Hachette Book Group, Inc. The Little, Brown name and logo are trademarks of Hachette Book Group, Inc.

The publisher is not responsible for websites (or their content) that are not owned by the publisher.

The Hachette Speakers Bureau provides a wide range of authors for speaking events. To find out more, go to hachettespeakersbureau.com or call (866) 376-6591.

Unless otherwise noted, all photographs are courtesy of John and Julie Fogerty.

ISBN 978-0-316-24457-2 (hc) / 978-0-316-38773-6 (large print) / 978-0-316-35189-8 (signed B&N edition) / 978-0-316-35369-4 (signed edition)
LCCN 2015943212

10 9 8 7 6 5 4 3 2 1

RRD-C

Printed in the United States of America

For Julie...
I love you more than the sky

CONTENTS

CONTENTS

FORTUNATE SON

INTRODUCTION

Beautiful Dreamer

IT ALL BEGAN with a record. A children's record.

My mother, Lucile, was a teacher at a nursery school about half a mile from our home, down a dirt road. I remember walking there a few times when I was four or five years old. By myself. That's how innocent our town—El Cerrito, California—was then.

One day, at around this time, my mom brought me home after school and gave me this record. It was a small-size children's record, and nearly the first object I would have realized was my possession—mine alone.* My mom sort of made a presentation of it, and we listened to it together.

The sound of it! Like a bolt into my brain. On each side of this record there was, of course, a song. For all I know the artist could've been Fred Merkle and the Boneheads, but I sure do remember the songs: "Oh! Susanna" and "Camptown Races."

---

* Actually, my *very* first possession was a doll. A black baby boy doll. I carried that thing around with me everywhere until I was three or four years old. I've often wondered if that somehow predisposed me to love black music, black culture.

3

And for some odd reason my mother explained that Stephen Foster wrote both of them. He was a *songwriter*. That's just a fascinating direction for my mom to go in. When you're explaining "Rudolph the Red-Nosed Reindeer" to a child, you don't tell the kid that the songwriter was Johnny Marks. But my mom sat me down and explained this to me. A lot of things have happened in my life, but this one made a huge impression. And like I say, I wasn't even four years old.

"Camptown Races" I thought was an odd title, because it sounded like "Doo Dah, Doo Dah." But there was a certain flavor to the song that I liked. "Oh! Susanna" was even better! I liked how they sounded. They seemed *right*. I don't know another way to say it, yet I have that feeling to this day—I feel the rightness of a song when it's tight and works, from the words and music to the heart. I considered them amongst my favorite songs. So Stephen Foster became very important to me.

Just a mom, a kid, and a little record. I am still kind of dumbfounded and mystified by this. I have actually wondered if my mom had some kind of a plan—if she knew the gravity that this moment would have for me, each day deep into my life. The simple act of my mom saying to me, "These songs were written by Stephen Foster," set a tone. Opened a door.

When something hits you that hard, even when you're three years old, you begin to watch for it, to crave it. And every time I heard about Stephen Foster, I took note of the song. "Old Folks at Home" (a.k.a. "Swanee River"). "Old Black Joe." "My Old Kentucky Home." "Beautiful Dreamer." There were a lot of them. Over two hundred, I'd learn later.

The stories, the pictures, the way the songs were told—I really took all that to heart. Foster's songs seemed historic, part of America. It was important—in the same way that Mark Twain became important to me. This stuff all felt like the bedrock of America, like the *Mayflower,* or the way that we grow corn in

Indiana. These were things that I didn't realize as a kid—whatever it was, I just knew I really, really liked it.

So when it was time for me to evolve and be my own artist, there was Stephen Foster. Riverboats and the Mississippi...I mean, "Proud Mary" could've been written by Stephen! And then there was that moment when I realized that when I did that sort of thing, it was *good*. It resonated so strongly when I got it right— not always immediately and sometimes even decades after a song's first inspiration hit me. I began to encourage myself to go deeper in that direction.

Now, if you had told me when I was fifteen and playing for drunks in some dive like the Monkey Inn that I was gonna some- how combine rock and roll with Stephen Foster, I would've told you that you were crazy.

People would listen to my songs and ask, "Where does this come from?" I had trouble explaining that. I hadn't been to Mis- sissippi when I wrote "Proud Mary," nor had I been to Louisiana when I wrote "Born on the Bayou." Somehow it all just seemed familiar to me. Still does.

In recent years, I was fascinated to learn that even though he wrote all these songs about the South, Stephen Foster was from Pittsburgh! I think he wrote "Swanee River" long before he'd ever been to the South. There were other parallels between our lives. Stephen was tricked out of his royalties. And there were parallels that could have been. Foster ended up alcoholic and dying in pov- erty at the age of thirty-seven. A pretty sad but typical tale. And if it hadn't been for my wife, Julie, that would've been me.

I didn't get into music to get girls. Or to become famous. Or rich. Those things never even occurred to me. I got into music because of *music*. I just loved it. It was (and is) a mystical, magical thing. I just wanted to write songs, good songs, *great* songs, ones that

Stephen Foster might not cringe at. "Proud Mary," "Born on the Bayou," "Have You Ever Seen the Rain," "Lodi," "Who'll Stop the Rain," "Green River," "Fortunate Son"—chances are you might know a few of those.

Now, if you're familiar with that last song you might be surprised to see it as the title of my autobiography—*Fortunate Son* has even been used for the title of a biography of George W. Bush!* So how do those two words apply to me? The best way I can illustrate that is by sharing a story about something that happened recently—on Veterans Day.

I was performing on a broadcast called *A Salute to the Troops: In Performance at the White House*. It was hosted by President Obama and the First Lady and shot on the south lawn of the White House, and shortly after being shown on public TV it was broadcast around the world via the American Forces Network.

Being part of this special evening was a big honor for me. The producer of this event was Ken Ehrlich, who also produces the Grammys. Years ago, Ken and I had teamed up for another event in Washington to honor Vietnam veterans. This time, Ken and I and Julie felt that "Fortunate Son" was exactly the right song for the occasion.

Among other things, you could call it an anti-war song, and there was some pushback over my choice—"No, we don't want him to do *that* song." I was very respectful: if the powers that be were too scared and didn't want me to do it, I wasn't going to make a stink, because I was there to play for our veterans, a group of guys and gals I sure have respect for and feel somewhat akin to. It's been a long relationship, you might say.

So everyone was a bit on eggshells—President Obama was sit-

---

* Apparently George W. is a fan of my song "Centerfield"—I've been told it's on his iPod. Which always makes me wonder: has he heard any of my *other* songs? Like..."Fortunate Son"?

ting right up in front, and I'm sure he was wondering, "Have I made the right decision to let this go forward?" When I went to the mic, I said, "I just want to say what a great country we live in, and God bless the men and women who protect us." With that, my band and I tore into the song. I ripped into the guitar riff and all the troops stood up. Here I was, standing there and shouting out the lyric, "It ain't me! It ain't me!," and all these veterans were like frat boys, yelling out the words and just having a great old time. There was a four-star general among them. Even the president was bopping away. It was the coolest thing.

I finished the song to a huge reaction. Returning to the mic, I said, "And I *am* fortunate." I had thought about this—I wasn't sure I was going to do it until the very last moment—but I said those four words and I left the stage. Meaning, "Yeah, that's my song. Yes, I believe every word of it. But look who I am, look at what's happened for me. My dream came true." I was also saying, "What a great country. We do this in America, the land of the free. They don't do this in North Korea." In that way I truly am a Fortunate Son.

We had another introduction all ready to go for this book. It was pretty action-packed, with all the bells and whistles. A lot of razz-amatazz. Cinematic, even. It had Robert Johnson, Bob Dylan, roaring guitars, and a cast of thousands. I think Richard Nixon might've even had a cameo. But you know what? It wasn't me. I'm not a flashy guy. I'm pretty simple and from the heart. And that's how this book should be. Miss Julie pointed all this out.

Julie. You'll see that name a lot in this book. I'm not joking when I say I'd been waiting my whole life to meet her. If you're a friend of mine, you understand that she's the love of my life. You'll be hearing from Julie directly later on. She knows everything there is to know about me. It's powerful to have someone you can be so open with, and by the time you reach this book's last words, you'll know as well as she does that I'm not afraid of the truth.

Julie's a big reason I'm doing this book. She's quite aware of the emotional content in things. In the old days, I tended to not talk about it. I can yak for three days on the subject of James Burton's guitar playing. Meanwhile, something that involves anger or fear or trepidation or uncertainty I wouldn't say two sentences about. In the old days, if I was talking about some conflict or controversy regarding my band, I'd downplay it. I didn't want to sound like a whiner and I really didn't want to throw mud all over Creedence — that was still *my band*.

So I'd end up talking about things in a surface, almost scientific way, not revealing my true feelings. I'd circle around but never get to the heart of the matter. This is my chance to finally set the record straight.

I'm not going to sugarcoat things or make excuses for anybody, especially myself. Hell, I'm not running for president. So I don't have to hide anything. It's very freeing to make up your mind and let it all hang out. Once you shine the spotlight on your own failings, there's little else that can touch you.

I'm just going to tell you my life story the way I see it.

This is the story of a kid from El Cerrito and his musical dream. It came true, and then it turned into a nightmare. His record company betrayed him and so did his band. Worst of all, he was pulled away from his music, from the songs that to this day mean everything.

Stick around, though, because, unlike so many stories about the music business, there's an honest-to-God happy ending.

CHAPTER 1

El Cerrito Days

I WAS DRIVING HOME the other day with my wife, Julie, and our daughter, Kelsy, after a long day out and about. It felt right — all of us warm and comfortable together, content from our day. Suddenly I had a flash of a memory, something that I hadn't thought about in a long time. It reminded me why I cherish these ordinary moments with my family.

My mind was back in a time when I was in the ninth or tenth grade, and I needed to get the homework for that day, which I'd somehow missed at St. Mary's High School. I'd been instructed to pick it up at the house of my friend Michael Still. He answered the door with his younger brother, both of them in nice robes and pajamas, looking freshly scrubbed. My friend apologized for their pj's, saying, "My mom likes us to get our nightly bath over with before dinner so we can relax." *Relax*.

I remember standing there, feeling all that warmth and happiness flowing from their home, thinking about how these boys were really taken care of. Even though I was just a kid, the disparity between my friend's life and mine was pretty clear to me: he was going to stay home and relax, and I was heading home to a cold, empty house and my drab cement basement bedroom that often flooded. There were no dinner plans—my mom was working, and my dad no longer lived with us. And no, I wasn't going to relax.

I was born on May 28, 1945. I grew up in El Cerrito, California. Years ago I made the mistake of filling out some questionnaire that asked where I was born, and since there's no hospital in El Cerrito, the correct answer is Berkeley, which is what I answered. But I didn't live there and I wish I'd reasoned that out, because now when my childhood is mentioned, it's always attributed to a place that's not my hometown.

I am proudly from El Cerrito. And warm predinner baths and robes or not, I dearly loved my early days and wouldn't trade them with anybody. El Cerrito certainly stamped a different view on me than what some hustling street kid in New York City would have gotten, or a songwriter growing up in Nashville. They're more savvy about stuff. Basically nothing came from El Cerrito, although the baseball players Pumpsie Green and Ernie Broglio both attended El Cerrito High School. I do feel really lucky to have grown up in a little town.

Things were unhurried. Everything was close and friendly and familiar, not nearly so fearful as things can seem these days. There was a little row of businesses near my house, with Bert's Barber Shop, the Louis grocery store, a drugstore, a beauty salon, and Ortman's Ice Cream—you could get a slush for a quarter. When I had a paper route, that was a daily thing.

Man, I'm not even that old but I lived in a different time. I grew up before rapid transit. A six-year-old kid could walk around by himself, head over to the market with a nickel in his pocket, and buy an apple. I remember going over to talk to the butcher to get bones for my dog. You could walk to school. I'm sure the class sizes were actually fairly large, but I recall them being intimate. The teacher looked right at me and talked to me. I had some teachers I really liked. My second-grade teacher, Mrs. Fuentes. Miss Begovich, my sixth-grade teacher. She talked about education and intellectual things in a way that mattered. Miss Begovich was inspiring and always gave me a lot of time.

Officer Ray Morris was the local police officer. He rode a three-wheel motorcycle—a memorable thing, for sure. But the reason I know his name is because he was, in a sense, my commanding officer. I was in traffic patrol in fifth and sixth grade—a lieutenant with a whistle and a sweater. And Officer Ray Morris was in charge.

Once I sent away for a siren that you could attach to the front wheel of your bike. I added an old stove timer to that, so when I pulled up to a place, it would go *rooooooowrrrrr DING!* Outasight. One day I'm blazing down Fairmont Avenue, going all of twenty miles an hour, and I blast right through the Ashbury Avenue intersection by the school, revving my siren and timer. And Ray Morris is sitting right there on his three-wheel motorcycle, just shaking his head. He didn't come over and yell at me—the look was enough. He'd show up at our Boy Scouts meetings too. Once, my bike got stolen and it was no time before he got it back. When I look back now, it's remarkable how close and interwoven all that stuff was in my life. It was community.

Children—I prefer their world even now. I'll bet I have every episode of *SpongeBob SquarePants* committed to memory. Same with *Hannah Montana* and the Wiggles' TV show. I sit and watch the shows with my kids. A child can sit and think about one little thing for eons. Adults can seem short and snippy to them. They don't dive into things. They're in a hurry. Kids are aware of that other, grown-up place, and they think, *It's okay—if I don't do anything too bad, they'll leave me alone.*

So you wander around in your own little world, mostly unfettered by what the grown-ups do. I know I did. At the drugstore near my house, there was a soda fountain. I'd put my ten cents on the counter, they'd take some syrup and fizz water and make you a soda fountain drink. There was a little moment one time when I was sitting there, staring at the Green River soda label on the syrup bottle. It's an old-timey illustration of a yellow moon over a river between two banks—now it reminds me a bit of the Sun Records logo. It really struck me, like, "Wow, I'd like to go there." Green River—I saved that title in my brain, filed it away. Why did I care about that? I was eight. But I was absorbing everything, everything I thought might be important for later in my life, even if I didn't know why. That's what you do as a kid. Everything matters.

El Cerrito had a drive-in movie theater. We always called it the "Motor Movies." When we lived at 226 Ramona Avenue I had the room over the garage and the top bunk of a set of bunk beds. I could watch the movies from my bed. I remember watching *Gentlemen Prefer Blondes* and, I believe, *Moulin Rouge* through my bedroom window. And various monster movies that my mom wouldn't let me go see!

Us kids would ride bikes on the grounds of the drive-in, and I regularly climbed up inside the screen to the top. Next to the drive-in was an old adobe building called the Adobe Restaurant. My mom told me that the place used to have slot machines, and I learned it may have been a "house of ill repute" in the '30s and '40s. Strangely, when they closed the drive-in and a shopping mall was about to be built, an arsonist destroyed the Adobe (perhaps clearing the way for that property to be included in the new mall). I remember going through the ruins and finding square metal nails from the early 1800s.

There was a really cool place to play that was not too far away from our house. It was called Indian Rock and it was just a big bunch of boulders. There were a couple of passageways you could squeeze through. A great place to play hide-and-seek.

Of course, the ultimate play place had been the high school itself when I lived across the street on Eureka Avenue. It's a wonder any of us kids survived. I remember all these big pipes that were one and a half to two and a half feet in diameter. We were little, so we could crawl inside those things and shimmy down to the other end and hide. Kind of like in the movie *Them!* Jeez! It would have been so easy to have gotten sealed up inside there. No one would've found us...ever. Then there were the piles of sand and gravel—I guess they made concrete out of that. And ropes hanging everywhere that you could climb up and slide down. I think the jig was up when we found a whole bunch of glass. It was probably meant to be windows for the classrooms, but for us aspiring baseball players it made a perfect target! Busted...

One sunny morning me and Mickey Cadoo had a day for the ages. I was about four years old. First we had climbed some small apricot trees and stuffed our pockets with green (unripe) apricots. Then, after eating a few of these, we decided to "climb to the top of the high school." They were still framing the building up on the top floor, and there was a lot of exposed wood crisscrossing and not nailed down. Somehow we managed to get all the way to the top level and stand up on the frame. There was nothing but sky above us.

I had seen cartoons where guys slip on a banana peel, so to make it even more dangerous, I untied my shoelaces, letting them dangle. There was a long, thin board that was just lying across the two sides of the framed space, maybe ten feet from one side to the other. The board was about six inches wide and perhaps one inch thick. So as I stepped out onto this board, it began to bounce up and down. Right about this time, I noticed my dad down in the front yard of our house, which was just across the street. There I was, fifty feet in the air, calling down to my dad, "Hey, Dad, Dad—look at me! I'm up here!"

Well, my dad looked up and saw me there, and his heart must

have stopped. I remember that he started jumping up and down, almost like dancing, arms waving in the air. And after a few shocked exclamations, he began to say, "Don't move, Johnny! Stay there, stay there. *Do not move!*" Somehow I stayed put and my dad clambered up the structure and got us to safety. Whew.

I lived in the El Cerrito area until I was forty. In 1986, long after I'd graduated out of traffic patrol, El Cerrito declared July 15 John Fogerty Day. That little ceremony was very small and sweet, the mayor spoke, and a few fans came from far and wide. Usually when somebody gets these things it's because they invented something or cured a disease. In my case, the official proclamation mentioned songs: "Whereas Mr. Fogerty has written 'Proud Mary' and 'Down on the Corner'..." Not everybody has a day set aside by their hometown, so being honored in that way is pretty untouchable to me. Whatever happens for the rest of my life, I will always remember that fondly.

I loved the song "Shoo-Fly Pie and Apple Pan Dowdy," and when I was a kid I sang it everywhere. Apparently, one Sunday morning at church I became filled with the spirit and broke into the song. I started dancing, and to illustrate the lyric I made my eyes bug out while I rubbed my naked tummy. The folks in church got a big kick out of this bouncy, diaper-wearing baby belting out "Shoo-Fly Pie." The more my parents tried to shush me, the more my "audience" laughed. I'm told I created quite a scene. Two years old and already on the road to perdition!*

I can remember riding in the car in the dark back then. Nighttime. And my parents were singing to each other. With no accom-

---

* My parents converted to Catholicism when I was two. They had me baptized, and yes, I remember it. I did *not* like it. Somebody held me while the priest poured water on my forehead. I thought, *You trying to drown me?!*

paniment. They would sing a lot of old American and Irish standards, like "By the Light of the Silvery Moon," "Shine On, Harvest Moon," "Little Sir Echo," "Danny Boy"—things like that. They weren't singing to the radio, they were just singing with each other. They'd do one song they called "Cadillac"—"Cadillac, you got the cutest little Cadillac." I asked my parents about that one. I thought it was odd that somebody would write a song about a car. They explained to me that it was actually a song called "Baby Face," and they had changed the words. When Little Richard's second album came out, he had both "By the Light of the Silvery Moon" and "Baby Face" on there for the parents, and this made total sense to me.

Listening to my folks sing was really nice. I realized even then that it sounded full. I'd sit between them and sometimes sing along. If one of my parents sang a different note that complemented the melody of a song that I knew, like "Jingle Bells," I'd get curious—"That sounds good, but what are you doing?" They told me they were *harmonizing*. My parents were very good at it.

So that's where I first heard about harmony: sitting in the front seat in that old car with my parents. A little later, in public school, probably about the fourth grade, Mrs. Gustavson would come in and teach music for an hour once a week or so. That's where I first learned "The Erie Canal Song" and "This Land Is Your Land." There was some American songbook we were learning from. Sometimes there would be a piano accompanying us, and sometimes we were just doing this a cappella. And I always looked forward to it.

Everyone was singing in unison, all singing melody, and I'd sit there and start singing harmony. I really had fun finding a note either over or under what the class was singing. And because there were forty kids singing *their* part and only me singing *my* part, it felt pretty safe to experiment. I was drowned out a bit, but I could hear it. If it was wrong, I could quickly change before anybody heard. Both my regular teacher and my music teacher would take note that I was somehow harmonizing—and knew what sounded right. Without being told. One day we were singing "Come Now and See My Farm for It Is Beautiful," and Mrs. Gustavson looked over as I was singing away, and I said, "Is that okay?" She said yes and smiled.

Sound was one thing and lyrics another, and I have cared about both practically forever. My dad and I were in the car once, talking about the song "Big Rock Candy Mountain." We liked that song and he was explaining it to me. It seemed like a really fun place. Then we got to that "little streams of alcohol" part. I asked my dad, "What does that mean? What's 'alcohol'?" He said, "It's something grown-ups like to drink. That would be fun—a whole river full of it, like if there was a whole river of soda pop!" It's ironic: here I was, asking a guy the meaning of "alcohol" when I would eventually learn that he consumed far too much of it. And so would I.

There's certainly a lot of musical influence from both of my parents, but probably more so my mom because I was around her a lot more. My mom played what was called stride piano: her left hand would play a bass note and then a chord, and the right hand would be doing melody and also some syncopation. It was cool, kind of like boogie-woogie. And she was appropriately sloppy. It sounded kind of barrelhouse.

My mom would play the piano and sing "Shine On, Harvest Moon," and sometimes I'd sing along. This was after my parents split up. When you're a kid who's a little rambunctious and rebellious, sometimes you join in, sometimes you act like it's corny and not cool at all. But "Shine On, Harvest Moon" is still one of my favorite songs. One of the best versions is Oliver Hardy singing it in a Laurel and Hardy movie, *The Flying Deuces*. That version of "Shine On, Harvest Moon" was truly inspiring to me. Laurel is dancing, doing a kind of soft shoe, and Hardy is singing. It's a thirties musical arrangement, but Oliver is more bluesy. And he sings really good! Even though it was slapstick for the rest of the movie, this was serious. Nobody laughed at this. At least that's how I took it: they were presenting art.

There were five boys in our house. We were pretty rough-and-tumble, it's a wonder we didn't all end up in San Quentin. It would've been so easy to fall in with the wrong kids. None of us had any trouble that way, really. My parents—especially my mom—kept my brothers and me on a fairly wholesome path. Whenever I got too close to the edge, my mom would pull me back. I'd call us lower middle class.

My mom was a social person, kind of gregarious. After my parents divorced, she got a teaching degree and dealt mostly with emotionally and even mentally challenged young people. She knew an awful lot about that stuff—I say "that stuff" because us boys really didn't know a lot about my mom's work. Her job was across the bay in South San Francisco, so she left pretty early in the morning and didn't get back until almost dinnertime. That's a lot of day we had to ourselves, and we turned out all right.

I don't know how my parents met. They came to California, to the Bay Area, from Great Falls, Montana. Lucile—my mother—was born there. That's a cool place to be from, Montana. I can remember my parents talking about the mosquitoes being so big they could open the screen door and let themselves in. Around 1959—either before or after I was in the ninth grade—my dad took my brothers Dan and Bob and me on a trip to Montana. We had stopped at a railroad crossing, and my dad pointed and said, "John, look at that train. Trains are really beautiful. And they're going away." I think he said it was a steam engine. He got the message across—that this was important and it was too bad the steam train was going away, and more so an era. My dad had quite an affection for trains. I have a feeling he spent some time riding the rails. The folklore in our family is that my dad hoboed all the way to California.

My father, Galen Robert Fogerty, came from South Dakota and grew up on either a ranch or a farm. My dad was Irish. The way I heard the story is, either my dad's dad or his grandfather had escaped the potato famine in Ireland by moving to England. Our family name used to be "Fogarty," but there was a lot of prejudice against Irish people in England, so to disguise that fact, they changed the spelling to "Fogerty." To my mind, that's kind of like changing the spelling of "Smith" to "Smythe."

England proved unsuitable too, so they came to America. I grew up feeling very strongly about being Irish—leprechauns, the pot of gold, the Irish whiskey—and I took note that the Irish are pretty good at sitting around a pub and putting down a pint.

My mom's roots go all the way back to the *Mayflower.* Her distant relative was William Gooch—he was English, and the first governor of Virginia. George Washington was born in Goochland County. I liked the fact that we had roots going way back in our country. Family legend has it that we were related to Daniel Boone. Another story I'd heard was Davy Crockett.

My dad worked at the *Berkeley Gazette.* Speaking of appreciating trains and beautiful things going away, he was a Linotype operator, setting type for the paper each day. Then he took a second printing job, so he was not only working an eight-hour-a-day job, he was working after that. In other circles, other times, he would've been called a man of letters. Well-read. Even though I believe that my dad graduated from college back in Montana, in our lifetime, it never really translated into a better job, into making more money or offering any change to our station in life.

That may sound selfish, but I don't mean it that way.

My dad was a dreamer.

He wrote stories. My dad had a movie camera in the forties, for taking movies of our family. I still have some of that film (and even use it as a backdrop in my show). And he would sit and edit different pieces of it on this editing contraption that he had. But he also had some stories that were filmed about a character named Charlie the Chimp. My dad wrote a story about the discovery of Pluto. I think it might've appeared in *Reader's Digest*. I believe that was the biggest thing he ever got published. In later years, my dad really identified with Ernest Hemingway: he had the white beard, white hair. There were a few manuscripts lying around the house. I think my dad really had the goods as a writer, but he was never able to get it across. There are many people in this world like that: they're artistic and yet they don't know how to meet the right emissary, that person who's going to publish their work and get it out there. Dad wasn't able to pull off being a famous writer. Or even one who gets paid for his work.

He was always on the fringes, smart and in the moment. He had invented a little game that I had when I was three or four. It was an educational toy: little round cardboard disks, each disk had a letter and a number, and every disk was a different color. There were shapes, colors, letters, and numbers—that's how I learned my alphabet, how to count, and the names of colors. It was a cool idea! Looking back on it, why couldn't he have made a million dollars with that? He never hooked up with the right people, I guess—maybe never even tried—so we just had it in our house.

Like I said, Dad was a dreamer. I tried to write a song about it I don't know how many times. The way I felt about it even as a fourteen-year-old kid was, "Dad isn't practical. He doesn't bring that dream into the real world. He doesn't do something about it." Being a dreamer, I know that can be a good thing. But when it came to my own life, the idea was, "Don't be just a dreamer. *Do* something." The lot of the dreamer is, he gets to hold bricks made out of mud. He never finds the gold mine. It's always some turkey like Rupert Murdoch. Or Saul Zaentz, for that matter. For me, I wanted to do both. I wanted to dream and I was going to try to be more successful.

Now, my dad was successful in so many other ways, like exposing us kids to nature. He loved camping and the outdoors. I didn't really learn to fish from him, but I think I wanted to know how to fish *because* of my dad. He also read stories to us when we were really little, stuff that was cool and informative to his family of five boys. "The Shooting of Dan McGrew" and "The Cremation of Sam McGee" by Robert Service were favorites. Tales of the Yukon and gold-mining camps. One of the greatest scenes in "Sam McGee" never left me, the part about this guy who was really cold and died. He froze to death. Well, firewood was scarce, so they threw him into the incinerator, right? Then a little later in the story they open the door to throw in some more logs and the guy they threw in there goes, "Hey, would you put another log on the fire? It's getting cold in here!" That was just cool to me.

Sometimes we'd visit Davis or Dixon or other small towns up in the central valley of California. I remember being in Dixon for the Fourth of July one year. There were fireworks and jungle gyms, swings, a lot of green grass....Further up Interstate 80 were the Giant Orange Stand (which was shaped like a big orange) and the Milk Farm Restaurant. It was a really warm, happy, cozy feeling. My parents liked to go to places like that. And they transferred that love to me. I really have a love of interesting little American towns—it's an idyllic way of life, at least to an outsider. Almost like a Norman Rockwell painting.

Some of my happiest memories are of Putah Creek. It was a wild creek up near Winters, in Northern California—"going to Winters," my family called it, and every summer we went. In my childhood we went to Putah Creek five or six years running. Putah was a picturesque, slow-moving little creek. We stayed in a small cabin. I remember that cabin fondly—it had a wooden, green screen door. I don't know why that's important to me. We rented it from a guy named Cody who was around seventy-five years old, tall, very thin, wore a hat. I was told that he was a direct descendant of Buffalo Bill Cody.

Not far from the cabin was a rope that hung down from a tree, over a little shallow spot in the creek that was ours when we were there. There's home movies showing my brothers swinging out and dropping in the water. My dad helped us kids make slingshots out of Y-shaped twigs with elastic bands cut from an old car tire's inner tube. We didn't hear talk about, "Well, you can put somebody's eyes out" or "Don't break those windows over there." There was so much open, free space. It was woods and brush, hardly a car anywhere—you really had to go far to see any people. All day long we could wander around. Once I even found an old, decrepit abandoned house.

The air was fresh up there, but when I breathe deep and think back, it isn't of grass and sky. My dad had a canister attached to a pump that he'd use to spray for mosquitoes. It had a certain sort of smell, kind of like paint thinner. I remember that smell fondly. It brings it all back.

I learned how to swim in Winters—when my older brothers, Jim and Tom, dared me to stick my head underwater. One day I learned how to float on my back. I was up early and the rest of the family was asleep. I floated across to the other side of the creek. I think it got deep enough in the middle that I couldn't stand up. When my dad came out of the cabin and saw me on the other side he just freaked out. I was a little afraid he might whack me.

Once in a while my dad would go with us into the actual town of Winters. There was a little grocery owned by this one family that owned the liquor store and the gas station too. My dad would give me a dime or a nickel to get a soda, usually a Nehi Orange. Or cream soda. Or lemon-lime.

Boy, I looked forward to Putah Creek. One time, when my brother Bob was a baby, there was some discussion about going to

Los Angeles instead. My dad said, "We'll have the baby decide."
He wrote down "Winters" on one little piece of paper and "Los
Angeles" on another piece. They put baby Bobby down and let
him go. For a while he was crawling toward the "L.A." I remember I didn't want that. Finally Bobby went over to the "Winters"
piece of paper and we all went "Yay!," so happy that we were
going back to Winters.

After we stopped going, I'd think back fondly about our trips,
even as a kid. I was possessive about Winters and Putah Creek. In
my memory, they were *mine*. My vacation place, my special little
spot. I always felt really good there. Number one reason, I think,
is because my parents were relaxed there, as they used to be when
they'd be singing songs together.

Things change and sometimes they change a lot and leave just
bits of what mattered behind. Sometimes the best things stay
around only in our heads. At one point back in those days, Dad
drove us in the car high up on a hill, and we were looking down at
the little town of Monticello, and he said, "One day that will all
be underwater." I had no idea what that could mean. How could
that be? Are people going to walk around underwater?

I think Dad was saying good-bye to our idyllic Putah Creek. In
fact, they did dam up the creek. Now it's called Lake Berryessa, a
big man-made lake. I drove my motorcycle up there in the seventies and I think I found the spot where the cabin would've been. It
was all overgrown, just bushes, remnants of wood. I couldn't find
the actual cabin. I think even then it had long since fallen down.

CHAPTER 2

The D Word

FOR FIRST GRADE, my mom enrolled me in a Catholic school in Berkeley, the School of the Madeleine—or the School of the Mad, as us kids called it. It was a few miles away—which doesn't sound too far, but all I know is it took a half hour or more in the morning and many's the time I ran out of the house to catch the bus and missed it.

Our teacher was a twenty-year-old named Sister Damien, who was in her first year. She was just a kid. And throughout that year she had several unhappy episodes. Sister Damien was overwhelmed. In the end we heard that she had a nervous breakdown. One time she was mad at the class and kept us all after the bell. "You can't leave. You have to stay in your seats and not a peep out of you." And this little second grader comes in, he's got his rag, and he dutifully starts polishing up the platform that Her Majesty's desk is sitting on. He's busy and doesn't turn around to see the whole class sitting there. Suddenly Sister Damien just slaps him across the face—*wham!* That was indicative of the atmosphere.

To get to school, I would leave my home alone and walk two blocks to catch the 67 Colusa Avenue bus across from the Sunset

View Cemetery in El Cerrito. Then I'd ride all the way to the top of Solano Ave, in Albany, and get a transfer from the bus driver. From there I would catch the F train, which went into Berkeley and passed behind the School of the Madeleine. The conductor would let us off behind the school. Mind you, I'm in the first grade doing this—six years old! Every morning at eight o'clock the students would assemble in the playground and then march into class to the music of John Philip Sousa. If I missed the 7:05 bus, I was going to be late to school, which happened many times. There was a chain-link fence surrounding the playground, and they locked the gate at 8 a.m., so I would have to climb the fence and run to class.

By this time I've been away from my home for maybe an hour. And at around nine thirty or so, something would happen. And it would happen over and over again, okay?

I'd raise my hand and say, "Sister, I have to go to the bathroom."

"Not now," she'd say.

After that, she just ignored me. Again, this isn't, like, one time. It was enough times that it was a normal occurrence.

I'm sitting there in my uniform, blue shirt / salt-and-pepper corduroy trousers, taking my pencil and poking the cracks and crannies in my desk. Oh, I'm squirming. I'm like Alan Shepard in the space capsule. "Houston?" "Yes, Alan." "I gotta go wee-wee. Is it okay?" "Uh, wait. We'll get back to you." You're holding it, you're holding it, and then you can't anymore. Finally, you give up all rules of social convention. It's too late.

And then you're hoping nobody will notice. But Kenny Donaldson noticed. "Sister Damien! John Fogerty has a puddle under his desk." And even then she wouldn't call on me. So I had to sit there until there was a break, and then I had to clean it up. And sit in my moist clothing for the rest of the day. This happened probably two dozen times over the course of the school year. I'd get detention after detention for wetting my pants—I guess they figured if they punished me enough, I'd stop having to pee.

So one day at lunchtime I found myself looking at the water fountain. It had a white porcelain trough and three faucets. Now, fresh in my mind is getting detention, because I drank water and then had to pee. Under the trough, I see the knob to turn off the water and I'm thinking, *Oh, I can help everybody here.* I turned off that fountain. *Wham!* When they found out I was the dude responsible? Another detention and a note home to my parents. At the end of the year, the rest of the class was being rewarded with a trip to the circus. Not Johnny Fogerty. Because I was such an uncontrollable little wild man, I had to stay home. I was a bad boy.

The next year, my mom put me in Harding Grammar, a public school two blocks from my house. I could walk to school! And things were normal. I thrived. I really loved it there.

Okay, so how many of you have had the "flying dream"? For me this was a common occurrence as a kid. In the movie *E.T.: The Extra-Terrestrial* there is a scene where a bunch of kids are following E.T. Suddenly, they are all up in the air (flying!) and then they "fly across the moon." That scene made me cry and I still don't know why.

There was a period from about the third grade to about the sixth or seventh grade where I had this flying dream a lot. It was almost always the same. Every night, I would fly around my little town, just above the trees and telephone wires, looking down at the houses and people. I was accompanied by a "friend" who seemed to be acting as a guide. As far as I can remember, we always saw the same stuff. Looking back at this from many years later, I find there is just enough room in my head to believe that perhaps this was an E.T. encounter. *O-o-o-o-EEEE-o-o-o.*

One day in sixth grade Miss Begovich noticed an odor in our classroom. "What is that smell?" she said. Most of the kids didn't seem to notice it and couldn't identify what it was or where it was coming from. Suddenly, this kid Fred blurts out, "John Fogerty smells." Of course, now everyone is looking at me, and I start to go into confused mode. *Like...huh?* But Fred is adamant—"Yes, it's John, he *smells!*"

So Miss Begovich gently says, "Well, John, maybe you should go to the bathroom and figure this out," or words to that effect. I stand up and start to head to the washroom, not really understanding what I should do. Suddenly, Kathy, a girl I'd known since preschool days, stands up and says, "It's me! *I'm* the one who smells!" Now my emotions are completely topsy-turvy.

Kathy insists to the teacher that she is the one who should go to the washroom, and of course this whole scene is being played out in front of the entire class. My head is spinning. *Whoa...this girl is taking a bullet for me.* I'm filled with emotions that are hard to describe. I realize that she is a very brave person, a very *good* person, to do something like this. It is such an honor to have somebody do that!

Finally, Miss Begovich decides that we should both go to the washroom, thereby defusing some of the guilt, I suppose. I went to the washroom not really knowing what to do, so I peed, washed my hands, and headed back to class. In the hall, I ran into Kathy and I thanked her. This is one of those times in life where I wish I could go back to that person and really express how amazing that made me feel.

After school a few days later, a couple of us kids were working on an extra school project. This one kid, Yvonne, had been absent for more than a week with an illness, so Miss Begovich asked us to clean out her desk so we could send some books and schoolwork home to her. Among the books and papers, we found a dead bird—in her desk. *Y-e-e-o-o-w!* We were kinda grossed-out. Miss Begovich said, "That was probably the bad smell from the other day." The next day she quietly explained it to the whole class...

*   *   *

So much of the flip side—the good side—of those years was rooted in music. I was born with the gift of curiosity, and if I heard music I liked, I just had to find out all about it. I got into the blues at seven. It was really because of doo-wop. There was no rock and roll yet!

My two older brothers were listening to rhythm and blues, and KWBR in Oakland was mostly doo-wop and R & B, meaning black music.* They played records like "Gee" by the Crows and "Ling, Ting, Tong" by the Five Keys—we'd try to decipher the crazy Chinese references. It all seemed so exotic. Later, it was "Death of an Angel" by Donald Woods and the Vel-Aires—he's talking about his girlfriend dying, but it was so cool! Kids love death! (Much later I found out that the Catholic Church *banned* "Death of an Angel" because their position was that angels can't die. Even cooler!) Thirty years later, when Ozzy and all those guys were shouting at the devil? Same kind of deal: it was something forbidden, behind a veil and unspeakable, and therefore music that parents don't like. A lot of the music I was hearing was pre–rock and roll, but it had so much of the vibe.

Intermingled there on KWBR was some real blues—urban blues, even some country blues. I remember hearing Muddy Waters in the early fifties, and then Howlin' Wolf came along with that *voice*. I loved that voice—"Wow, listen to that guy. And the name!" I'd listen mostly by myself. Bouncin' Bill Doubleday was the deejay from three until six, and then Big Don Barksdale had a show at night. On Sunday they played gospel. That's where I first

---

* One of the major sponsors on KWBR was a product called Dixie Peach Pomade. I imagine that in those days it was used by young black guys to straighten their "do." I rode on a bus all the way to Swan's Drug Store in Oakland to get this stuff. It was great on a "flattop" or on longer Elvis hair. Plus, it smelled good!

heard the Staple Singers, "Uncloudy Day." The sound of that guitar—God, what a cool thing. That vibrato: *bewoowowow.* Even as a kid I could identify that sound right away. Pops Staples was doing all that. I loved that sound. The Swan Silvertones might've been my favorites. It was spiritual, church stuff, but I was mostly interested in the music.

By the time I was eight years old, I was using my mouth (and my body) to imitate the R & B records I was hearing. Every day I'd walk a couple of blocks from my house down to Harding School. There was that time to be alone, that precious time. I spent a lot of it thinking about music. I'd make the sounds of the band that I was hearing in my head. I'd go along and imitate Ernie Freeman's "Lost Dreams" or Bo Diddley's "I'm a Man"—*daaaaah daaaaah da dummmm.* Sometimes I'd snap and clap and all that, but mostly I just did it with my mouth. Or my throat. Or hummed it. Grunts and hums and noises. Sort of...guttural sounds. Probably sounded like I was coughing to the outside world, but I loved making the sound of the bass and the kick drum. Nobody I knew of was doing anything like this, but I was quite comfortable with it. That was my way of making music.

It would hypnotize me, walking to school doing that. I even had a little friend who walked with me sometimes who called me Foghorn Fogerty—that's what he thought I sounded like when I made my noises. I still do that, actually. I hear music in my head and I make those guttural sounds to catch the vibe.

I even invented a persona, a group called Johnny Corvette and the Corvettes. It must've been right around 1953, because the Corvette had just been introduced and every kid loves sleek, sexy lines and a big, fast motor to die for. Everyone in my mind's band had matching jackets, like the Turbans or the Five Satins or the Penguins. I was Johnny, and we were black. I meant no disrespect— I was just a kid fantasizing about what he loved. So in my mind, the grown-up version of me and my group was black.

*   *   *

The first house we lived in was right across the street from El Cerrito High School, at 7251 Eureka Avenue. That house stayed cool in the summer. I have good memories from there.

But we moved about 1951, and I turned six in the new house, at 226 Ramona Avenue. I remember that time being less happy. My parents split up in that house.

I think working two jobs got to my dad. I remember my mom actually saying a couple of times that he was working way too hard. I think my dad went kind of crazy.

He had a nervous breakdown and was up in Sonoma or Napa, where we went to visit him, and I'd think, after seeing him, that we were all getting back together.

I didn't see most of the fighting personally, but as I understand it, my parents had a long, messy split. One night we all went to the drive-in to see a Bob Hope movie called *The Lemon Drop Kid.* When we came home, I went to sleep. My brothers Tom and Jim were awake and our mom and dad were fighting over something. I only heard about it the next day.

Apparently my dad was pointing his finger angrily at my mom and she bit his finger. And there was blood all over the place. Luckily, I didn't see that particular fight either. I can tell you I never went to see *The Lemon Drop Kid* again. When it comes on TV, I'm still, like, *click!* "Sorry, I ain't watchin' that." There was something in that movie that caused bad stuff to happen.

The whole idea that my parents had separated and then divorced was upsetting and very traumatic for me. It really cut like a knife. It was something I couldn't actually even talk about. The *D* word. And nobody else was talking then either—there were no divorce jokes on sitcoms. Though I'm sure divorces were everywhere, I didn't know any other kids whose parents had divorced.

At school, if there was some kind of paper I had to fill out

29

answering "Who do you live with?," where I had to state that I lived with my mom—*only* my mom—I was mortified. Because that initiated the inevitable questions: "Where's your father? Has he joined the...foreign legion?" That's a phrase I heard more than once. It was a shameful thing, having only one parent. I took it really hard. Almost like it was my fault.

When my mom and dad finally divorced is hazy. When I was near the end of the third or fourth grade—I can't quite remember— we were all going to move to, I think, Santa Rosa. I was about eight. So I informed all my pals that I'd been with pretty much since kindergarten that we were moving. But I know I didn't seem to be that upset about it—the way you see kids being torn apart from their roots. I just remember that I kind of explained it to everybody. Then come next fall when school started, there I was, back again! And there were all my friends that I'd already said so long to.

"John, what happened?"

"Well, my dad moved."

I remember just feeling unworthy and kind of like, "I gotta slink home and never talk about personal things." I didn't quite know how to approach the subject, because I don't think I really understood.

The main issue for both of my parents was the fact that they were both alcoholics. Believe it or not, I had a real aversion to alcohol as a young person. Seeing my parents in a drunken state and hearing them talk in an incoherent way? It was repulsive to me.

I really used to kind of rag on my mom. I was a typical kid, dissatisfied with my parents. There was one meal we hated, liver and onions, because the liver would never be cooked. All us boys would just be repulsed. My mom would kind of be in her cups, acting funny—and we didn't know why, because we never really saw her drink. I think she hid it in a cupboard or something. That was part of our lifestyle more than I care to admit, and far more than any kid should ever know about. I used to say I got negative examples from my mother. What *not* to do.

I'm a lot more forgiving now, especially with my mom. And that's not just because I realize the good she instilled in me from when I was real young. It's because, man, human beings are fragile. We break easily if things go wrong, especially if you feel hopeless. Oh God, that's the worst thing for any of us. Frustration is a very powerful and almost insurmountable thing. I'm sure my mom had a lot of heartbreak. She had five boys that were quickly turning into five men that she had to deal with and try to raise right. On her own. I think my mom tried valiantly. God knows she tried.

So I want to do right by my mom. I worry about disclosing so much—always have. In the world I grew up in, you didn't reveal things that you considered nobody's business. Now that she's gone, I'm really just trying to tell the story, to get to the truth of her experience and mine.

In many ways my mom was remarkable. She educated me on many subjects, exposed me to a lot of music, and showed up for things in my life. I'm very grateful for all that.

And I see the whole situation a little differently now—not nearly so much from the point of view of what I was missing, what I didn't get. Because these days I have so much, because of Julie. I see both of my parents almost as tragic figures. It's a shame that for so much of her life my mom probably felt unloved, that she wasn't taken care of. My dad certainly never found love after the two of them split. That was all a waste. The real tragedy? Before all the economic struggles and alcohol started ruining everything, I think my parents actually loved each other.

We had a record at home called "When You Were Sweet Sixteen" by the Mills Brothers, an old 78. My dad and mom used to sing that together. God, what a song. Beautiful. It breaks my heart to hear it now. I was just a kid watching his parents divorce and this was their song!

*   *   *

I remember us boys stuck in some courtroom. All five of us, without our parents, being called into a room where an official person, I assume a judge, asked each one of us directly: which parent do you want to stay with?

I think we had all agreed we wanted to stay with our mom. I don't know if we had gotten our stories synchronized, but I know that in our hearts we all felt like that was the best solution. But it was really scary that this even would happen, being asked this question by a grown-up, a stranger.

It was difficult to have to think about that. Mainly I just wanted to stay with my brothers. We wanted to stay together.

My parents were continually arguing over all the manifestations of divorce. There was one Saturday morning when us boys had been camping overnight in the backyard in our sleeping bags, when suddenly the police arrived. Here we were, just kids in our own backyard, being awakened by the police. Apparently we were supposed to be with my dad that Saturday and Sunday.

My dad was being pushy by sending the cops. And he was supposed to pay alimony, but he wasn't doing it. I don't know if he had a job or not. And my mom was basically withholding us. I'm sure my mom was within her rights. She would make comments like, "Well, y'know, I could have him put in jail, but what good does that do anything?" It wasn't going to change our situation.

All I know is, I was being woken up at eight o'clock on a Saturday morning by the police saying, "You have to go with your father." Maybe I didn't even want to go with my father.

I didn't see my dad much after that. One period it was one weekend a month. We'd go to a movie. Those kinds of things are just so awkward, at least in our case. It kind of petered out to where I really didn't see my dad at all. For years.

*   *   *

A few years later, when I was in the eighth grade, my civics class—which was all the kids I knew in junior high and a lot from before that—went on a field trip to Richmond, the county seat. They drove us down in private vehicles—a couple of station wagons, not a big school bus. And we went to the courtroom.

We all file in and sit down, maybe twenty of us. There's a case going on. A divorce case, ironically enough. I heard one teacher tell another afterwards, "Y'know, I'm not really sure that was something the children should've seen."

Both parties were there, the husband and the wife, and it's the wife who's wanting to leave the husband, not the other way around. The wife testifies a little bit, and she's fairly matter-of-fact. I don't want to say cold—just straightforward.

Then we watch this poor man talking about his family, his wife. And he's being grilled by the wife's attorney. This moron lawyer is pointing an accusatory finger at him. He's like a bulldog and he is just *killin'* this guy. We're watching, dumbfounded. It's like television, but it sure ain't *Father Knows Best,* y'know? Finally the husband, who is now very emotional, says, "Well, perhaps my wife would consider a reconciliation. Maybe we could get back together." He's made himself so vulnerable in front of everybody. Like a little boy. That was unexpected. I'm a twelve-year-old kid who had never imagined such a thing before. I don't know anything at all outside my parents' divorce. At that point I didn't even have a serious girlfriend yet. I'm thinking, *That's real sad.* I was shocked and hurt and everything else. It's hard to revisit this, even now.

But their case is done for the day. Because the husband can't go on. I see the attorney look over at the woman and she's got her arms folded. She's a tough one. And the husband's broken down, just blubbering. So the judge goes *boom, boom,* with the gavel. "We'll adjourn until two weeks from now."

We're all just sitting there, and the clerk comes up to read the next case—this is God's honest truth. He says, "This is the case of Galen Robert versus Edith Lucile Fogerty. Can we hear the case? Are either of the participants present?" Well, that's my mom and dad, of course. It had been four or five years and they hadn't finalized the divorce.

They say the name Fogerty twice, and the judge asks, "Are any of the parties here?" And somebody says, "No, your honor, they're not here." And the judge says, "Okay, we'll continue this at a later date."

But the damage has been done. I thought, *How in the world did that spaceship ever land on me? I gotta be in court and hear that? With my classmates?*

So we get back in our vehicles for the trip home and I remember that Sandy, one of the girls, said to me, "The Fogertys they named in court—is that your parents?"

And I said no, tryin' to act cool. I got real...stiff. Not myself. They had *no idea* that it was my family. I pulled it off...or maybe I didn't.

The kids were all jumping up and down in the back of the station wagon and I was acting kind of weird. Not like a kid. Obviously I was in shock. The others thought I was kind of snooty because I wasn't laughing. And somebody made the comment, "Oh, yeah—he's too mature for us." Kids can be so unaware of how much, and how little, they know.

My dad stayed angry 'til the end. Late in his life he lost a leg to diabetes. He was in and out of the hospital, and we were over there to move him out of his apartment. All the brothers got together to help.

There was his old television, from way back in the day, in a metal case made to look like wood grain. And the metal had all these big dents in it, and in some places even perforations. I recognized that from before. When I was a kid my dad would get so pissed trying to make the picture come in he'd give the TV a few whacks.

Back then we had taken a trip to Montana and had rented a trailer and hitched it to the back of our '56 Buick. A little trailer with a kitchen and a couple of beds. There was a little compartment over each wheel with a door that hung down and locked. This was where they stored a hose for filling the water tank in the trailer and other small essentials. We noticed that the door had several dings on it, almost like it had been hit with a sharp instrument. Well, a week or two later we were deep into our trip, perhaps in the middle of Yellowstone National Park. The car was overheating, so my dad would have to use the hose to siphon water from the trailer into the radiator. He parked the car and we all went back to help. The door was open and the hose was gone. We were screwed! Apparently, the latch on the door was faulty and wouldn't stay closed. My dad got really angry and started hitting the door with a hatchet. Then it dawned on us kids: those marks we had noticed on the door were the same marks my dad was now making with the hatchet. Apparently, the last poor guy with this trailer had gone through the exact same thing.

Now Dad started to kick the trailer. There were a couple of expletives coming out of his mouth. He may have even had the hatchet in his hand. There's my dad, just kicking the crap out of this trailer. Most of the time my dad was very thoughtful and peaceful and calm. I was kind of shocked—a kid watching his dad lose it. This was a whole nother guy—a guy that, truth be told, was a lot like me. I've had a temper since I was very young. I can remember another kid coming up to me during kickball and saying, "You know, you're gonna have to learn how to control your temper." It was noticed by my teachers in grammar school too.

So years later, when we were moving my dad, there's that old banged-up TV. This was some time after Creedence had broken up, and it wasn't like I was livin' on Happy Street. But I looked at that TV and realized that my dad was seventy and he was still that way. I thought to myself, *I don't want to get old and die being so ornery, so angry.**

Being a teenager has to be the toughest time for almost everyone. Especially if there's anything you perceive as wrong in your world. I felt put-upon, unworthy. Behind the eight ball. Divorce was an immense failure to me. Huge. It just didn't happen to good families.

There was an overall aloofness that I would have. The fact that our economics really went downhill after the divorce certainly made it worse. I felt that I was at the bottom end of the social totem pole. I sure wasn't as bad off as some guy living in a shack in Mississippi with no plumbing and no electricity. But somehow I felt poor. Between that and my parents' divorce it was almost too much to bear.

After I'd been at St. Mary's for ninth grade and half of tenth, one of the teachers said to my mom, "John seems so sad, reserved. He's just really quiet. Is there something wrong? Is Johnny okay?" And my mom would try to say, "Oh, no—he's just thoughtful." Even I would say it. Most all of the pictures of me as a kid show that thoughtful, pensive side. I'd always have my eyebrows knot-

---

* Happily, my mom was able to find love after all this turmoil. She met a wonderful guy named Charles Loosli, and they got married on June 11, 1977. I got to spend time with Charles and Mom in later years. We all loved Charles.

ted together. Sadness may not be quite the right word, but if that's not the one I don't know what is.

I was ashamed of the house we lived in. The furnace never really worked right—it was run-down. This was a middle-class suburban neighborhood, but we had the worst house on the block. Around the seventh or eighth grade, I moved into that concrete basement that flooded every winter. There would be an inch and a half of water on my floor, and I got to laying two-by-fours so I could get from outside my room to my bed without stepping in the water.

I had a clock radio. My first radio had been one of those art deco plastic ones—a funky color, bluish gray, a Philips or an Emerson. Then, with my paper route money, I upgraded and got a clock radio that plugged in and was supposedly going to get me up—it had an alarm. At some point the knobs came off. I liked to take things apart, so I was probably to blame, but now it had no knobs—just metal posts. One morning I was standing in the water and decided to turn on the radio. When I grabbed the metal posts, I got quite a jolt. I'm lucky it didn't kill me.

I liked to listen to the radio before school, so when the alarm went off, dang it if I didn't figure out how to propel myself forward from the bed, stand on the little wooden sill on my closet to avoid the cement and water, turn off the alarm, and fall back to bed listening to the music. Every morning that was my little dance. Directly above my bed there was a metal grate for the furnace, so when my mom was leaving for work in the morning, she'd stomp on that grate and go, "Oh, John! Oh, John! Wake up!" *Thump, thump, thump.*

You know that Brian Wilson song "In My Room"? It's the *truth.* Your room is your sanctuary. That basement room was my place to be me—"I'm not hiding, but I'm *in my room.*" Upstairs with the family was a bit chaotic, challenging, whereas in my room I had Duane Eddy, Elvis Presley, Bill Haley, the Coasters. They were in the windows — literally. We didn't have window shades for the basement, and if people in the next house were in their garage, they could see right into my room, so I put my record albums up to cover the windows.

Music was my friend. I absolutely loved to listen to it. I surrounded myself with it, thought about it all day. I think my interest only intensified after my parents split. There was joy in music. And for some reason, I don't know how or why, that joy only confirmed what I'd known since I was small: that it was for me.

CHAPTER 3

My Influences

BY THE TIME I got to the fifth grade, I thought, *I need to be able to earn some money.* I think my mom was giving me a quarter for an allowance. At that rate, I was never going to get anywhere.

The *Oakland Tribune* had to be delivered at 4 a.m. on Sunday, but you needed an adult to take you around in a car, and my mom wasn't going to do that. So I got a paper route at the *Berkeley Gazette,* the small paper where my dad had worked, and they didn't deliver on Sundays. The place to pick up the papers was only two blocks from my house, right by the cemetery up at the top of Fairmont Avenue, and my route was just down all the streets across from Harding Grammar School.

My route was only about thirty-five papers. If things were okay, I'd make twenty, twenty-five dollars a month. But it turned out that some people were unscrupulous. I had thirty-five customers, but sometimes I'd get stuck with forty newspapers. Those were called extras, yet you were financially responsible for them. You had to get on it, call the *Berkeley Gazette* and say, "You're givin' me five extra papers. I don't have forty customers—I only have thirty-five." I think they did this sort of routinely, because it kept happening to me. This went on for months. They'd stop, and then they'd start again.

Finally I'd had enough. I turned the tables on them. I'd receive thirty-one papers for thirty-five people. Then I'd go right to the front of the Louis store, where they'd have the papers for sale in a little stand. Customers would take a paper, drop their ten cents in the box. Honor system. Well, I'd go over there and take the four I needed and go off and deliver them. I did this until I got my money back, not a cent more.

I was really mad. But my paper route money allowed me to buy things, and the things I liked to buy were records.

Forty-fives were the coin of the realm. If there was a hit song you liked, you bought the single. The very first time I ever bought 45s, it was the Platters' "The Great Pretender" and "At My Front Door" by the El Dorados. They were Christmas presents for my brothers Jim and Tom. Tom and I shared music even pre–rock and roll. There was a song called "Billy's Blues" by Billy Stewart. Tom really liked that song. This was before the Internet days, and man, you could not find that record anywhere. So I went to my mom-and-pop record store at the mall, Louis Gordon, and even though it was a year and a half late, I got them to order that record, and I gave it to Tom for his birthday. I knew it was precious, better than a million dollars, because you just couldn't get it.

I can hear and see the little record player I'd bought with paper route money as if it were yesterday. It was red and white and had three speeds. That was a boon to guitar players, because you could slow down 45s to 33 and try to learn the solos. The record player had a funky speaker. Certain records, like "Susie Q" by Dale Hawkins, really skipped, so you'd have to put a quarter or a battery on top of the tonearm. I liked to put the first Elvis album on when I took a shower.

I first saw Elvis on the Dorsey Brothers' TV show in January 1956. He had that whole juvenile delinquent thing that kids love. I was a kid, so I was drawn to the danger of it. I don't think I was playing guitar yet. After the first or second time I saw him, I was standing there in front of a mirror with a broom, practicing the sneer. I was hypnotized without even realizing why.

It was the other side of "I Want You, I Need You, I Love You" that really grabbed me. I was up visiting my dad, and we were in some little grocery store with a jukebox when I heard "My Baby Left Me." I went, "*What* is *that?*" I ran over there to see. "It's Elvis!" "My Baby Left Me" is one of the greatest rock and roll records ever made. That guitar was just…so…great. Man, it had attitude and attack. It was a big part of what made the record special. Scotty Moore *invented* rock and roll guitar. Even though I didn't know his name and I wasn't a musician yet, I just knew right then: "Whatever *that* is, that's what I wanna do."

I tried to buy the first Elvis album while I was at my dad's house in Santa Rosa. I had four dollars and fourteen cents. I walked all the way to the mall and they were sold out. I ended up buying Bill Haley's album *Rock Around the Clock*. The guitar playing on the song "Rock Around the Clock" was way ahead of everybody else. It was kind of jazzy—Danny Cedrone was older, more advanced than your average rock and roll guy. It's only been in the last dozen or so years that I can play that solo!

A week later, I got that Elvis album. That and the Bill Haley album I knew backwards and forwards.

I saw Elvis at the Oakland Coliseum in 1970, when he was just speeding through the songs—the whole Vegas thing with the karate moves. Elvis had recorded "Proud Mary," which, of course, was a tribute and an honor, but it seemed like he hurried through it. I guess if I were more tactful I wouldn't say that. Yes, it was great to have your idol do your song, but you just wished that he had killed it. I never got to meet Elvis, and I really wish I had. Elvis got crazy, but he just lost his way. And we have all done that, whether a little or a lot.

I took Elvis very personally. Even as a kid, standing there at the record store, paper route money in hand, I was really thinking about value. I thought about buying an Elvis 45, but Elvis was in the "Big Hunk O' Love" / "Doncha' Think It's Time" phase. And I was already thinking, *Yeah, but Elvis isn't really rock and roll now.* This was in 1959, still the beginning of Elvis's career! In my mind I had noticed a kind of softness, a pop ethic in Elvis, and if I'm going to a desert island, I better have rock and roll. So this time I bought "Red River Rock" by Johnny and the Hurricanes instead.

Still, Elvis was Elvis, and in the fifties you had Elvis and you had Pat Boone. Elvis was obviously cool, but Pat Boone just... wasn't. Now, don't get me wrong: Pat Boone made records that I actually like. "Bernadine." "Love Letters in the Sand." "Moody River" was outstanding. Then there are the really sappy ones, like "April Love." I used to hear that song in my head at the oddest moments. Much later in life, I'd be hunting up in Oregon, climbing up a long, long ridge uphill, I'm sweating, out of breath, and I'd take that first step onto the flat ground on top, and suddenly there it would be in my head: *dumdumdum DUM* ... "Aaaaa*april love!*" I'd go, "Where did *that* come from?!" Like it had been waiting to happen — my own personal soundtrack.

Pat seemed like a really decent fellow, but he was almost *too* nice. And so was his music. I sure didn't want to be sappy, but I didn't want to be a bad guy either. In those days, it was, "Do you wiggle like Elvis or do you croon like Pat? Which gang are you with?" I struggled with that. Well, not really.

Through Elvis I discovered more Sun records. "Ooby Dooby" by Roy Orbison and "Blue Suede Shoes" by Carl Perkins. As an eleven-year-old, I had the same exact connection with Carl Perkins that the Beatles did. There were times when I actually thought Carl was way higher up than Elvis, because Carl could play *and* sing *and* write songs. That combination made a big impression on me. In baseball, Willie Mays was what they called a five-tool player. To me, Carl was the musical equivalent.

Go back to the "Boppin' the Blues" / "All Mama's Children" and "Blue Suede Shoes" / "Honey Don't" singles, and listen to that twangy thing in Carl's voice. His singing is killer! Those two singles are still, like...perfection. I bought "Blue Suede Shoes" three or four times because I was wearing them out! I'm still astonished at how great "Blue Suede Shoes" sounds. There's so much air. And the groove of the band, that country boogie thing—whew. Just untouchable.

I met Carl in Memphis on my 1986 tour. It was like meeting God. He said the nicest thing. Chips Moman, the producer, was with him, and Carl said to Chips, "The way this guy writes, imagine what Sam would've done with him if he'd walked into Sun." Here's somebody I idolized, *Carl Perkins,* giving *me* some cred? Talking about Sam Phillips and Sun Records and me? What a dream. I just ate that up.

Years later I was doing a fund-raiser for Bill Clinton, and out of the blue, Carl showed up. He mentioned that he was making a record with Tom Petty. I wasn't going to let this opportunity go by. I just looked at him, my face a question mark, and I said, "*Well...?*" And he looked at me and said, "Well, John, I'd love it if you'd come and do 'All Mama's Children' with me." Carl knew that was my favorite.

Our version is not as good as his original—how could it be? But I'm glad I got to do it. Especially because of this memory: While we were recording, I came back from the powder room to find Carl sitting there with a Stratocaster, and he was just rippin', playing this really mean, nasty stuff. Just vicious guitar. I was taken aback. He was sixty-four, he'd already had some surgery and a heart attack, and I was thinking of him as older, vaguely fragile. And here he was, just slayin' it, in tone, vibrato, and attitude. For a moment I could not believe it.

Then my mind did this little double take: *Well* of course *Carl can play like that—he's one of the two or three guys who started it all. He was right there. Why should I be surprised that he sounds that way?*

Carl passed in 1998. And to this day, I still have his number in my phone.

・ I've mentioned hearing the blues at age eight. As I was growing up listening to KWBR, it was a flood: Muddy Waters, Howlin' Wolf, B.B. King, Elmore James, John Lee Hooker. Wolf had a gigantic influence on my singing—"Big wheel keep on *toinin'*." But I didn't realize it at the time. It just seemed natural to me.

Fast-forward to August 1968, and Howlin' Wolf is opening for Creedence, which mystifies me even now. I stood in the audience and watched Wolf's whole set. He was a big guy, and he'd point that finger at you. I think he was sitting down most of the time, but this was not some old guy going, "Blah, blah, blah"—this was life and death. Hubert Sumlin was on guitar, a 335 Gibson, and he was badass. He had a youthful look, like Floyd Patterson when he won the heavyweight championship. We got to go in the dressing room, and I felt like a little kid. The Wolf smoked Kools and so did I at the time. We shared a smoke. I'm sure he was amused. He looked at me like he was going to reach down and pat me on the head.

There's a handful of guys you keep coming back to, and for me, a lot of them are the kinds of guys who can't be copied. Why has no one *ever* done Jimmy Reed since Jimmy Reed? *No one* has been able to do it. Jimmy had a bunch of harp solos that were really high. Jimmy played up there where nobody else went. And he's not in a hurry on the guitar. There's a couple of funny notes here and there. That's his signature, those notes. Because he does them all the time! I listened to "Honest I Do" about three times the other day. Man, it's just such a feel. Everything is for a reason and a purpose. That band is *locked*.

I saw him only once, at the Berkeley Community Theatre in 1964. Jimmy was drunk. *Drunk*. His guitar was out of tune, and he was sitting down. I remember after three songs that were kind of incoherent, someone in the audience yelled, "Tune up!" In those days, we were all prim and proper—to do that to an icon, it had to have been pretty bad. I was so sorry to have seen that. Later you find out he'd gotten screwed out of his record royalties so he's pretty bitter, and he's an alcoholic. Oh, really? Even though later I went through the same stuff, I think seeing all this as a young guy was informative, in that it made me not want to end up there. I was no better—don't get me wrong. It's just that I saw tragedy in it.

The music that was new when I was a kid was *hot*. I bought Bo Diddley's first album. In my eyes, Bo was like Elvis. That was the first fight I had with the guys in my band. We got paid, like, twelve dollars total for a gig, and instead of buying new strings, I took my four bucks and twelve cents and bought Bo Diddley's album. "*What?!* Why did you do *that?!*" "Because there are several songs on there I think the band should learn, like 'Before You Accuse Me.'" Much later we recorded that one. I rest my case.

That first Bo album was just chock-full of stuff. "Who Do You Love?," with its human-skull chimney and cobra snake for a neck-tie....I was fascinated by the imagery. Many times I've said there's a part of my writing, my imagery, that's kind of spooky and weird and about dark places. Well, I walked into that room through Bo Diddley's door. The song "Bo Diddley" is probably my favorite. Spooky as all get-out. That whole child-rhyme thing—if that ain't the most primitive mumbo jumbo! Yet it sounded so full on the radio. I don't even know if there is bass on that record. It doesn't matter. Then you have Bo doing his thing on guitar, especially the solo. It's just hypnotic. Bo magically fell into a thing that was just

so hot because of the deep drums. The tom-toms, the maracas—
it's really tribal. Even now, that drum is so big—*bum da bum da
bum*. A lot of bands have come down through the years trying to
do the Bo Diddley beat and haven't come close.

Man, I was *lucky*: I saw Ray Charles live several times right
around the "What'd I Say" time. He had that old beige 120
Wurlitzer (later I got one myself). He played saxophone—that
was amazing. The big album for me was *Ray Charles in Person*.
Has a better live album ever been made? It was recorded with one
microphone in the audience by a deejay from a local Atlanta station. It was an outdoor summer show, and because of the acous-
tics of the space you can almost hear the hot air. God, the sound
of the instruments. Obviously they didn't have echo machines. It's
live. It's natural. "The Night Time Is the Right Time"—Ray's
version is way more soulful than Creedence's, which is more rock
and roll, screamin' guitar. That live album has "Drown in My
Own Tears." Everything is just so slow. He's wrenching every last
ounce of feeling out of that song. That album had a huge effect on
me, and its influence still lingers.

Little Richard is another one whose influence on me is total,
complete. We played together at the Grammys in 2008 and I
finally got to tell him, "Richard, man, I've loved you since I was a
little boy." He's probably the greatest voice ever in rock and roll. I
really mean that. His performances on those classic rock and roll
records are perfect. "Lucille," "Keep a Knockin'," "Good Golly,
Miss Molly," "Send Me Some Lovin'." They are like textbooks of
how a rock and roll singer should sound. A couple more that have
always meant so much to me—"Long Tall Sally" and "Slippin'
and Slidin'." Like they say, "It don't get any better than that!"

Even as a kid I loved dissecting a recording. The music behind it
all was just as important to me as the vocal. I thought Gene Vin-

cent was *great*. His records were like instrumentals to me. "Lotta Lovin'," "Woman Love," and of course "Be-Bop-a-Lula." I'd sit and play him on my record player, and in my mind I'd block out the vocal. Because there was all this *great stuff* going on back there. *Man!* That was an education to me: *Without the singing, it's like an instrumental.* And as you'll soon see, that's how I presented the songs and the arrangements to my guys in Creedence. Gloriously, I grew up in an age when there were instrumental rock and roll records with lots of guitar. They were very important to me as a kid, and a great way to learn.

Like "Honky Tonk" by Bill Doggett, from 1956. That's an incredible record. It was big-time important to me as a kid. Side one of the single is the guitar side, side two the sax. Both are incredible. It's just that groove. As a kid, I decided one night that I was going to learn "Honky Tonk." I put the record on and practiced. By the way, I played it in F, like the record. That's hard, because it means you're fretting every single note. In recent years I've checked out some of these online forums, and lo and behold, there are guitar nuts talking about playing "Honky Tonk." Comments like, "If you're gonna play that song, be a man and play it in F!" If you play it in E, it's a lot easier. The Ventures did that and turned it into more of a rock and roll song.

"Hide Away" was another song that just killed me! A Top 40 record, it wasn't just on the R & B station. Freddie King was a huge influence on my guitar playing and my musical knowledge in general. He's playing a shuffle, but the piano player is kind of straight, and the drum is somewhere in between. It's the coolest feel, especially in this age of computer music, where everything's locked together in a really boring fashion. My first band, the Blue Velvets, played almost as many Freddie King songs as we did Duane Eddy. One of the songs we always played was "Just Pickin'."

This might surprise people, but "Flying Home" by the Benny Goodman Sextet is one of my favorite records. It's got a great feel and I just loved that melody. My mom talked about Benny Goodman, so as a kid I just went ahead and got my own copy of the 1938 Carnegie Hall concert. I don't know much about the other big band guys, but I figured out everything I could about Benny Goodman. Once I discovered Charlie Christian's guitar on that record, I became interested in him and wound up buying and collecting everything of his that I could find. I've listened to hundreds of hours of Charlie Christian.

I'd say there's a whole lot of Charlie Christian in how I play. Just the feel of that swing, the way he riffs off the melody. Parts of "Keep On Chooglin'" are referencing Charlie. In my head, when I go Americana, and I hear that soft shoe happening, like "Shortnin' Bread" or "Down by the Riverside," and I'm trying to keep things just real simple, I'm probably in some way referencing Charlie Christian. Not that I'm as good as Charlie!

Speaking of that feeling you have when you make music that clicks, when I was a kid there was a lot about the record *Rumble* that was absolutely right. The guy's name was *Link*. Link Wray. Oh my God. That record was really important. The song sounds like the title: "Rumble"! *Blang blang blang.* It's so...menacing. When that was a hit on the radio, all kids were tuned in to it—not just me. Everybody understood: *Man, that's so cool.*

Some guys rightfully become known as guitar gods, and Duane Eddy was a huge influence. James Burton was behind Ricky Nelson, Scotty Moore was behind Elvis—that was usually the way. But Duane was his own front man. The name on the record was his. "Rebel Rouser" *killed* me. Real melody, that honky sax, and those guys back there modulating every twelve bars—what made him *do* that? It's just cinematic.

"Three-30-Blues"—as a guitar player, "Three-30-Blues" was a high moment. I used to practice that with my band, and I still play that song. Some people might say, "Oh, that's a simple blues." But it's a *mighty* simple blues. I heard Duane play that at the Oakland

Auditorium with B.B. King on the bill. Fantastic. I heard later that B.B. sidled up to Duane and said, "I sure like that 'Three-30-Blues.'" Only Duane Eddy sounds like that. He means every note.

I learned so much from his early albums. The thing I noticed was that all of his songs had these great titles, like "Forty Miles of Bad Road." Cool song, but I realized he could've called it anything—it didn't matter, because there's no words. Duane came up with these descriptive titles that created a mood to match the feel of the music: "Rebel Rouser," "Cannonball," "The Lonely One," "First Love, First Tears." This was instructive to me as a songwriter. I was learning what went into a good song, and Duane helped me see that having a great title was a big part of it.

I think influences can come from anywhere. The sound of a bee's drone or a truck's Doppler effect as it drives further down the road. And of course the TV. I became aware of Ricky Nelson through *The Adventures of Ozzie and Harriet*. I was already watching the show like the rest of the world. Rick was doing the cool things that teenagers did, like washing his jeans in the shower. They sprung his recording career on us in an episode where Rick plays football—which Ozzie likes—and plays music, which is what Rick likes. Rick did "I'm Walkin'," and the next week he did "A Teenager's Romance," singing with his eyes almost closed, eyelashes fluttering. He was sixteen years old and impossibly good-looking—no flaws! By "Stood Up," the fourth single, Ricky had shanghaied a young guitarist named James Burton from some country band. When I heard James going *dangadangadanga,* oh man, I knew something had changed. This was rock and roll ground zero. I was totally on board! When I saw them do the song on TV, this cool dude was playing guitar behind Ricky. During traffic patrol in sixth grade, a girl asked me if I liked music, and I said, "I like that guitar player with Ricky

Nelson. He's really cool." I didn't even know his name. I didn't even play guitar yet!

The main music coming out of Rick Nelson was rockabilly, as opposed to Frankie Avalon or Fabian or Bobby Rydell, or even Elvis by then. I was lucky enough to get to posthumously induct Rick Nelson into the Rock and Roll Hall of Fame in 1987. Sam Phillips was sitting right down there in the audience. I looked at him and said, "Sam, he gave you a run for your money." Ricky Nelson was doing rockabilly—pretty urgent, even dangerous, stuff. Even when he did "Lonesome Town," he just killed it. That was a slow ballad, but it wasn't sappy and dumb: it was rock and roll guys playing a ballad.

I remember listening to his version of "My Babe" over and over and over. That guitar was like, "Oh, *yeah!*" In some ways that record was better than Little Walter's original. It was *James*. James just shines and sparkles, and Ricky clearly knew this, because there was always a James moment on those singles. Listen to "Believe What You Say." There's the greatest guitar solo you ever heard. Basically, the world stopped. Ricky was letting everybody know there was this wild genius in town. Scotty Moore, James Burton, and a few others in the world at that time were inventing cool rock and roll guitar. And James was all of eighteen!

I thought Ricky seemed like a very normal teenager. A nice guy. I liked that a lot. Elvis was spending his money recklessly, buying big rings and Cadillacs—I worried. I just thought that was really extravagant. Ricky was just a kid living at home. He seemed like a good role model. I never heard about temper tantrums, anything scandalous—he struck me as mild mannered, not showy, not crazy. I know that sounds boring, but to me that was an admirable trait. I'll go to my grave saying this, although lots of folks would disagree: you don't have to be crazy or a lunatic to make good rock and roll. I know guys who make really great music and they're solid dudes and family oriented. They value that sort of thing. Like Bruce Springsteen and Dave Grohl.

Rick wanted me to produce him back during my long, dark time. It was 1978 or '79. I was in no shape to handle that. I couldn't even produce myself, let alone one of my heroes. At least I got to meet him. The very last time I saw him was in Memphis, recording a tribute to Sun Records in the eighties. He was singing along on one of my songs, "Big Train (from Memphis)."

An interesting bit of musical history (at least to my mind) is connected to that solo in "Believe What You Say." One of my favorite records of all time is a song called "Party Doll" by Buddy Knox and the Rhythm Orchids from 1957. Starting with this song, I became a very big fan of Buddy and the sound he was making. The drum part on this record became very influential, as it was maybe the first rock and roll song to feature a "two-one" backbeat. I was fortunate enough to meet Buddy Knox in the late eighties, and I mentioned the drum part to him. He was proudly aware of the milestone and immediately responded, "Yes, but it's reversed" (which it is).

Anyway, Buddy had another big hit that year called "Hula Love," which I also had as a boy. Then he seemed to disappear. To a kid, a few weeks is an eternity. Anyway, time passed, and suddenly here was another Buddy Knox song called "I Think I'm Gonna Kill Myself." I *loved* that record, but you couldn't get it. I had to order it at my little record shop and wait for weeks. Apparently, the subject matter of the song had gotten it banned in some places.

So now to the point: "I Think I'm Gonna Kill Myself" featured a guitar solo that sounded exactly like the solo in "Believe What You Say," and I was certain of that for years and years. After hearing it recently, I can now see that they are not the same. They are, however, in the same key and played in the same very high register. Back in the late fifties, the Telecaster was just about the only guitar you could reach those notes on. I thought about the mystique of these two solos many times over the years, so when I met Buddy Knox I asked him about it. His answer was "I don't know if they're the same, but it sure was some great playin' by Cliff Gallup." Man, was I excited by that answer. Only us guitar geeks care, I suppose, but Cliff was the guy on "Be-Bop-a-Lula." And *he* disappeared too! (By choice.)*

In the summer of '57 I was working up at the Russian River in Healdsburg, California, and "That'll Be the Day" was all over the radio. They had a big outdoor PA blasting that song. I just went crazy. Rockin' guitar, rockin' drums, harmony singing, the lead guy's voice—I just knew them as the Crickets then. And that riff! It all sounded so damn right.

Every artist had a band, but the focus was usually on the singer: Elvis, Ricky. With the Crickets, it was presented as the Crickets. It was *the band.* This was just a different approach, and their debut album, *The "Chirping" Crickets,* had that picture. Four guys in suits, all four holding the two guitars, but they're looking straight into the sun! There's Buddy trying to smile, but the sun is shining right in their faces, so they're all squinting. You can tell these were not rich guys. They ran up on the rooftop of a big building in New York City to take that shot. It's a fairly unflattering picture. That picture told a story, though. One that the Beatles would only refine. The wisdom of keeping it a singular image, not being ragtag—like, for instance, the Grateful Dead. Being a little more showbiz about it.

I had made up my mind that Buddy Holly was one of those people that I was going to follow for his entire career, buy every

---

* The Rhythm Orchids had quite a year in 1957—"Party Doll" and "Hula Love," both million sellers by Buddy Knox, and another million seller, Jimmy Bowen's "I'm Stickin' with You," *plus* Jimmy's "Warm Up to Me, Baby." I bought all four of them.

record he made. I had already gotten the first album and a few singles. I still had a paper route in the eighth grade, and getting the papers one day I saw the headline that Buddy Holly, the Big Bopper, and Ritchie Valens had died in a plane crash. So years later, when Don McLean's "American Pie" came out and he talks about delivering papers with the news "the day the music died"? I thought, *Wow, I actually* did *that*. That was a sad day for rock and roll.

I got ahold of a Buddy album in 1965 or so, on some off label, and there were unreleased versions of songs, one of which was "That'll Be the Day" in the wrong key. It's nothing like the version that became the big hit, and I was quite sure Buddy was rollin' over in his grave. Maybe collectors enjoy all that, but as an artist, I cringe at the idea. The artist goes through a process of evolution to get to the recording that he wants to present to the public, and the rest is not presentable. It was meant to stay behind closed doors. I knew I didn't want that to happen to me, so I would always destroy my outtakes—for instance, an earlier unrealized version of "Mystic Highway," or the first version of "Wrote a Song for Everyone." They can't put it out later if it doesn't exist!

There were a few records from the rock and roll era that seemed to be in another place from everything else. I obsessed over these:

"Deep Feeling" by Chuck Berry
"Lost Dreams" by Ernie Freeman
"Honky Tonk" by Bill Doggett
"Blue Moon" by Elvis Presley
"For Your Precious Love" by Jerry Butler and the Impressions
"Little Boy Blue" by Bobby "Blue" Bland
and more recently:
"Island Style" by John Cruz

*   *   *

I think I first heard country music on television. I was four years old. There was a show called *The Hoffman Hayride* that was big in our house. I remember seeing Jimmy Wakely and liking the way he looked. He was a cowboy and had this great big blond guitar. Later he teamed up with Margaret Whiting. Now when I listen to them it sounds pretty schmaltzy, kind of like a country Nelson Eddy and Jeanette MacDonald, but the outfits were great!

One of the most startling things I remember seeing on early TV was Johnny Cash. This is back about '56. Most variety shows had a big chorus line of girl dancers, like the June Taylor Dancers. They'd form a circle and would be shot from above. The shows were big and glittery, with a cast of thousands like a Busby Berkeley movie. Right amongst all that Johnny did "I Walk the Line." It was really stark. There was his face, behind him only shadow. Way back there you could see one guy going *plunk, plunk* on a guitar, but most of the time it was just Johnny, shot from the side like someone on Mount Rushmore. I just sat there with my mouth open because it was so powerful. This wasn't the June Taylor Dancers. This was dark. Strong. And this guy—whoa. Commanding.

Hank Williams I loved, of course. I'm sure I heard about him as a kid, because I remember "Jambalaya" and "Kaw-Liga" almost as nursery rhymes from the early fifties. But the moment I actually became aware and curious about Hank was when I bought the Jerry Lee Lewis single "Great Balls of Fire." When I turned the record over there was a version of "You Win Again" that is for the ages. One of the all-time great rock and roll songs. And there, just under the title, it said, "Hank Williams." I had to learn about that guy, so I began to find more and more great music by him. Songs like "Lovesick Blues," "I'm So Lonesome I Could Cry," and "Your Cheatin' Heart" just slayed me. Hank became one of my biggest influences and is still up there on the mountaintop.

Another at the top of my country list would be Lefty Frizzell—I always wanted to record a version of "Long Black Veil." I loved Webb Pierce. There are many great songs, but it's enough that he did "I Ain't Never." Whoever played that guitar...! I recorded that on my *Blue Ridge Rangers* album. I loved Chet Atkins. He was such an inspiration. I don't know if any musician ever practiced more hours than Chet. Ever heard "Yankee Doodle Dixie"? That's pretty doggone advanced. The guy had all his fingers on both hands working. There's been a couple of those guys in the history of the guitar. It must have taken thousands upon thousands of hours of practice. Or maybe there's another race of humans that are wired differently. I used to wonder if that wasn't true, because it took me such a long time to develop as a player. But then there's always the question about how much you can learn versus how much you have inside of you.

Merle Haggard is one of those artists who hit me really hard way back when and continues to have a profound influence on me all these years later. I guess it starts with that amazing voice of his. But through the years he's just made so many great records. Then there's the writing. Merle has such a thoughtful, intelligent, humble, fun-loving, badass view of the world! Truly one of the giants of music. I think it's not an accident that so many of these guys that I listened to are great writers.

As a teenager, I heard an awful lot of Buck Owens on the radio. "Tiger by the Tail." "Together Again." "Crying Time." Those records were very important to me. That twang, that energy. Don Rich, playing all that Telecaster. When the Beatles covered Buck Owens with "Act Naturally," that was not odd to me. George Harrison's whole style, playing hybrid with his fingers—listen to "Help!" That's a country guy. There was good pickin' in there.

I didn't really meet Buck until kind of by accident at the Bay Area Music Awards (a.k.a. the Bammies) one year in the eighties. He just showed up in a country sports coat and a cowboy hat. We got to be friends. He gave me one of his red, white, and blue guitars. Buck melted me when he told me that Don Rich really loved Creedence.

All this time, while I'm listening to blues, rock, and country, the folk music boom—some called it a scare—was building slowly all through the fifties, starting way back even before the Weavers and Pete Seeger. All this stuff was bubbling in coffeehouses, and then the Kingston Trio did "Tom Dooley" in 1958, and it just took off. There were a lot of folk hits during that time, so they started having festivals, which my mom so kindly took me to. When I asked her later why she didn't bring my older brother Tom, she said, "Oh, he wouldn't come." I was at the right age. I was twelve and Tom was sixteen, so Tom was into girls and cars, and hey, I was...serious.

The folk festivals on the campus at UC Berkeley were put on by a wonderful guitar teacher, Barry Olivier, who also gave me my first guitar lessons. I saw Pete Seeger, Jesse Fuller, Mance Lipscomb, Lightnin' Hopkins, Sam Hinton, Alan Lomax—these weren't just concerts: they were an education. I was enthralled by the whole thing. These folk festivals were hugely rewarding—just bedrock for me. And not just musically. I'm certain that folk music has a lot to do with my entire belief system in terms of how the world should work.

In the daytime, the festivals would offer many different workshops. Pete would talk about the style of banjo he was playing, or things like how a lot of the bluesmen such as Lead Belly liked the Stella guitar because it was built so stoutly. Pete Seeger spoke with such affection and reverence—and Pete had film! Of Lead Belly! I mean, oh my God—I'm seeing Lead Belly playing this big ol' Stella twelve-string, and then five minutes later Pete picks up a Stella, puts on some finger picks, and plays "Midnight Special."

I'd heard my mom sing "Goodnight Irene" way back when I was little. Watching a film of Lead Belly doing it—well, it sounded like what I was hearin' on the radio! Like Muddy Waters or Howlin' Wolf, except *they* had drums and electric guitars. But at these folk events it was almost like, "Shhhh, don't talk about that." I was learning about the folk police. They didn't like any commercial stuff. After "Tom Dooley," all the folk purists were raggin' on the Kingston Trio—"Who are *they?* They're just some college kids. They never picked cotton!" Gee, they took a song and *rearranged* it, and that's a bad thing? You mean like, uh, Lead Belly doing "Midnight Special"? I tucked things like that away in my brain. The folk people were just in their own little world. They didn't want to acknowledge Gene Krupa.

Seeing Lightnin' Hopkins was incredible. He had this huge hit, "Mojo Hand"—one of the coolest records ever made. It had that secret, forbidden, cultish thing—stuff that's just really hidden from the white man. I had to pay attention and try to figure it out. A mojo hand was actually a monkey paw. Whoa! I actually met Lightnin' Hopkins at the folk festival. This was within minutes of meeting Pete Seeger. Lightnin' was very gracious. I gave him a little piece of paper and a pen and he made a very shaky-looking *X.* That was his autograph. If I had been an adult he probably would've said no because he wouldn't have wanted to reveal the fact that he couldn't write. I kept that piece of paper in the drawer with my socks for the longest time, but it went missing. But I can say that the memory is better than any piece of paper. I met Lightnin' Hopkins.

Pete Seeger is the greatest entertainer I have ever seen. An incredible musician. He'd be talking, telling a story, that skinny body of his rocking, and his head would go back and out would come "Michael, row the boat ashore..." You were there in the boat with Pete. Then he'd get everybody in the whole audience to sing along in three parts. It's like, "Damn. How did we all just do that for an hour?" I've never seen anybody else do that—ever. I've tried it myself a few times! I've witnessed the Franks, the Sammys, the Dinos, the Elvises, but Pete Seeger just had the magic, the showmanship. It was authentic and it was effortless.

And right around the time I'm watching him, the House Un-American Activities Committee was flailing Pete. He was taking a stand by saying, "I have the right to believe what I believe." And these kinds of thoughts and ideas were helped along through music. That resonated a lot more with people than a stuffy old speech, especially with some unsuspecting kid like me. There were people fighting and even dying for an idea that in the end actually was good for me? And if enough people didn't stand up and do that, I wouldn't get to be free? That really spoke to me.

I loved Pete. I learned so much from him. He liked to present songs that had ideas, but he never lost sight of just singing and having fun. There was the big folk music canon to perform, and it wasn't all doom and gloom.* So even though I was a rock and roll kid, I just ate all of this up and thought it was the best. Though I didn't realize it at the time, Pete's influence on me was probably greater than any of the rock and roll guys.

Folk, rock, blues, country—I didn't make distinctions, wasn't separating them. "This is R & B. This is country." I was young and open to all of it.

I'm still that way. Get me going and it's tough to stop. I haven't mentioned records like "The Slummer the Slum" by the 5 Royales, or "I Confess" by the Four Rivers. I covered that one in the eighties—had to lower the key. We can't do everything we want

---

* I had wanted to cut the Joni Mitchell song "Both Sides Now" with Creedence. I really loved that song and thought, "Man, with my style, a rock and roll band on it, that would be a really cool thing." Never got around to it.

to do. Only maniacs know that record, and yeah, I'm a maniac. That was a real dashboard-banger. Or "Henrietta" by Jimmy Dee and the Offbeats—that's a frantic rockabilly record. The Offbeats—that's just so wacky in the right way. Very punk name: "We suck! Ugh, stab me!" It was on Dot Records, 1958. The name, the label, the album cover, the sound, and the way the songs came in a certain order, on a certain side—all those little details were so important to me as a kid. They gave an album more mystery, not less. Pulled you in and got you hooked. It was all there to unfold, and that's one thing missing from music now.

Which brings us to Mrs. Starck's class.

In seventh and eighth grade at Portola Junior High, I was in Mrs. Starck's music appreciation class. There was some music history and some hands-on playing of instruments—rhythm instruments, mostly. I really, really loved that class. Mrs. Starck kept her hair in a ponytail and sported beads; she was slightly on the beatnik side, and she was amazing. We learned about Mozart and Beethoven—the idea that Beethoven was deaf was very intriguing to me—and even a little bit about boogie-woogie. Meade Lux Lewis and Albert Ammons—those guys. Mrs. Starck talked about all of it like it was important. Like it was real music, to be mentioned in the same breath as Beethoven. Which was way cool. We even learned some about the music business, how contracts were important and often unfair. I shoulda paid more attention.

One day, Mrs. Starck said, "John, you collect records. Why don't you bring some of your favorites, and we'll play them in class and you can talk about why you like them." I thought she was so cool for doing that. I know I brought "I'm Walkin'" by Fats Domino. I just loved Fats and how that record took its time. I'm pretty sure I brought "Boppin' the Blues" by Carl Perkins. I might've brought "Henrietta" just because I knew that it would probably make Mrs. Starck anxious. She was very tolerant.

Mrs. Starck was a great inspiration. Rather than thwarting me when I went over to the piano to bang out some rock and roll—which I'm sure sounded pretty awful—she encouraged it and acted like it was the coolest thing in the world.

My last class of the day was phys ed, right down the stairs from her classroom, so one day I just wandered back into her room. This was in the eighth grade. I don't know where I got the gumption to sit down and play. I think there was nobody around. I'm a pretty shy person, really.

Next thing I knew, there were a couple of kids standing there. I could do a few things I was learning at home: "Do You Want to Dance" and a couple of instrumentals that I was playing on the black keys in F sharp, kind of bluesy boogie-woogie. After a few days of doing that, there was a crowd of people. One day Doug Clifford was there. And he started talking about playing drums—he even said he had a drum. We decided to get together.

When I went over to his house, I saw a snare drum sitting on a flowerpot stand and a cymbal. That was it. Later, Doug got a hi-hat from a guy named Rich Knapp, who'd made it in metal shop. It was homemade, but it worked.

So we began to play. We started making music—me with my little Sears guitar and amplifier and Doug with his flowerpot snare and cymbal.

CHAPTER 4

"There's Somethin' Missing,"
Says R. B. King

I REMEMBER A TRIP to Montana with my father in the summer of ninth grade. I had my Silvertone guitar and I'd sit in the backseat of the car and play. I was trying out "Red River Valley" in a minor key, kind of making it blues or folk. My dad took note. It was so frickin' hot that the plastic pickguard would swell up like a melting candle. It must've been 115 degrees out, but I didn't care. I had my guitar and I was in a magical world, connecting with the shaman's secret path. I don't know how else to say it. I have the exact same connection to music today.

I came out of the womb whistling. I knew I wanted to express myself musically, that I had to, or else I wouldn't be whole.

The first guitar we had in the house was an old Stella built like a '48 Ford. Us kids used to play baseball inside the house, and the Stella was our bat! But I don't know if it was my dad's or my mom's, since nobody played it. My dad might've known some chords. By the time I was serious about it, my dad hadn't been around for a few years.

My mom and I would bring the Stella acoustic to the lessons with Barry Olivier and take turns playing it. Barry suggested a nylon string guitar, and that made things better. Learning music in a group, all adults except for me, two sessions of about six weeks each—that was a godsend. Barry was such a charismatic person and very sincere about it all. And I was a sponge.

Either my mom or Barry Olivier had told me to get ahold of *The Burl Ives Song Book*. In the back were a whole bunch of chords. "Oh, that's how you make a D chord?" That really helped a lot.

One night on our way to folk lessons my younger brother Dan was in the car. I played "S & J Blues" on the guitar. Dan said, "Wow, you're sounding *professional*."

We had an old piano in the house, so naturally I tried to play it. The piano was certainly out of tune. Sometimes I put tacks on the hammers to make it sound honky-tonk. I can't imagine a kid these days being patient enough to do that. We had a 78 of "Bumble Boogie" by Jack Fina. I played the record at slower speeds to figure out what he was doing. Slowly I learned, "Oooh, there's some mathematics to this." I just stayed at it and stayed at it until I could present a pretty plausible version of "Bumble Boogie." It was probably while I was in high school that I spent the most time practicing and playing piano. I never got real, real good with keyboard, although I could play "Great Balls of Fire" and "Whole Lot of Shakin' Going On." The intro to that song is still one of the coolest-sounding piano parts ever.

I saw jazz pianist Earl Grant doing "Fever" live on TV in 1958 or so, and I bought the 45. Little Willie John had done the song, and Peggy Lee, but as a piano song it was as fresh as "What'd I Say" and "Whole Lot of Shakin'." The song started with a cool riff. When the show ended, I went over to the piano and played it the best I could remember. I didn't know what key he was in, but I played it pretty much on the black keys, maybe in the key of B or F sharp. To get in between notes, he'd hit two notes—a trill or something. You try and hit a blues note—you can't bend a note on a piano. I hadn't heard that before. I had one of those orgasmic musical moments with "Fever." For an hour and a half I played it over and over and over, until I really couldn't reap any more emotion out of it. I was in another land.

Nowadays a kid could do it all on a computer, but way back in the analog world, you just sort of figured it out. A lot of early rock and roll was so simple guitar-wise that you could pick a song apart and learn how to play it. I was really learning from records— what a band did, what parts they played. It sounds obvious, but before this time in my life, when I really had my hands on instruments, the music on the radio was all just sort of coming at you. I had to learn what the mystery of it was, why and how the guy played certain notes.

I remember trying to play Ernie Freeman's instrumental "Lost Dreams." That drum just sounds so forceful. It could've been made yesterday. I had an electric guitar that Tom had rented at Leo's Music. I'm sitting at the piano, playing the melody with my left hand, hitting one or two guitar strings with my right hand, playing the backbeat with one foot on Doug's homemade hi-hat, obviously enjoying myself. It was a way to make that "Lost Dreams" sound, but it was *me* playing instead of listening to the record. Then, for an instant in time, I got to realize how, say, Jerry Lee Lewis must have felt when everybody told him, "Jerry Lee— you're just crazy! *What are you doing?*" That's exactly what happened to me.

I'm sitting there playing that song on three instruments and my mom comes in the front door and says, "*Oh, Johnny!* What *are* you doing?" Like, "You're just crazy!" I said to myself, *Yeah, okay. This must be right!* My mom wasn't wild about rock and roll. She thought Elvis was kind of crude. I think she wondered if it was respectable or not. One time she went to the Monterey Jazz Festival with a couple of girlfriends, and when she got home, she couldn't stop talking about a song one of the jazz guys did — "I think it was called 'Give Me One More Time.' " I didn't have the heart to tell her, "Mom, that was Ray Charles's 'What'd I Say,' and that was rock and roll!" But you know what? I was in the house, banging away on the piano, and she let me. She didn't second-guess it.

My brother Tom was four years older than me, so he was able to move in circles I was too young for. And that included being with musicians who were a little beyond where I was, talent-wise. "Do You Want to Dance" by Bobby Freeman — that song got absorbed into our Fogerty brothers mythology. It's a very simple record: just piano, some bongos. There might be a little bit of upright bass in there and some guitar, but that's all — there's no real drums. It's a great performance, a cool rock and roll arrangement. Plus Bobby was a Bay Area guy, and Tom knew the piano player, Richard Dean. Tom's voice sounded just like Bobby Freeman's, and for some reason we had a set of bongos around, so Tom would play the song on the piano and sing, and I'd play the bongos. Tom had been playing for a few more years than I had, us alternating at the piano every chance we could get, and I learned to do that song just like the record. Bongos are pretty easy, right? Tom would sing that song deep into the night, even at two in the morning, and as good as he was, our neighbor would object. It was cute.

Tom had a really sweet, mellow voice with a high range like Bobby Freeman's or Ritchie Valens's. He was perfect for that stuff. Tom could've been in the front of a white doo-wop group like the Crests or Randy and the Rainbows, singing something like "Sixteen Candles." At some point he hooked up with this band Spider

Webb and the Insects—older guys with a sax player. They came over to the house and did a song with Tom: the Ritchie Valens hit "Donna." I wish there was a record of that. I can still hear it in my mind—Tom singing, the sax player playing the guitar filler parts. Even my mom thought it was cool. The Insects brought these gals with them—rock and roll gals dressed alluringly in tight clothes, enhanced attire for men. Mom didn't like that, and she let the guys know afterward. Even being younger I could kind of tell there was something up with these chicks. My mom was embarrassed for me, I guess.

The musical times with Tom were really magical. I remember we were in his red and white '56 Bel Air station wagon a little later, when he was married and had a couple of kids. We're driving along and the riff for "When Will I Be Loved" by the Everly Brothers came on the radio, and we just looked at each other with that I-just-died-and-went-to-heaven look. We did that exact same move the first time we heard "Satisfaction." We're in the car and along comes that riff: *daaah daaah da da daaaa*...There was a lot of that sort of thing.

Tom and I both loved music, and shared it as brothers. I don't think Tom had much of a cross word for me then.

The inevitable course was to get an electric guitar and play rock and roll. When I was twelve or thirteen, I bought my first guitar at Sears—a $39.95 Silvertone Danelectro (with one pickup—two cost more)—and a $39.95 five-watt amp. My mom cosigned for me. I promised to pay with my paper route money, which I did. The guitar had a cardboard case with an alligator finish. Later I sold the Danelectro to a classmate for five bucks. I think he paid me. I should've held on to that guitar.

Once I had played around with a couple of chords, I guess I had enough gumption to risk embarrassing myself (even though no one else was around) by trying to play Jody Reynolds's "Endless Sleep" on the Silvertone. That's one of my favorite songs of all time, and one of those spooky records loaded with attitude—"Wow, 'endless sleep': he's talkin' about *suicide!*" There's that *bumm-mmm bummm bowwwm* on that record—it's the bottom note of the guitar's range, a low E that really can't go any lower. I deduced that the sound was made with either a whammy bar or a bass sliding up. I had neither of those but figured out how to hammer on an E chord. The minute I started doing that, it was, "Oh, that's like 'Endless Sleep.'" So I sat there in my house and played it. I did that over and over on the Silvertone for probably an hour, because for the first time in my whole life I had performed a song on electric guitar. It was like, "This is *workin'!* I like this! I'll just do it *again.*"

The Silvertone's public debut was at a Christmas program in the eighth grade, when Mrs. Starck allowed me to play a little backup on one or two songs. I can't remember what I played—something Christmassy. I recall a D minor chord and a G. At the time, it was revolutionary for a school to present a program for the parents where some kid got up with an electric guitar. But no worries, parents: I wasn't very loud yet.

That's the guitar I had when I met Doug. I'd go over to his house or he'd come over to mine, and we'd jam. I liked his enthusiasm. Doug had energy and he was likable. It was casual and easy—we both liked rock and roll. Economically, we were kind of in the same place, and his mom and dad split up at around that time, so he went through the same thing I did.

I could play songs like Roy Orbison's "Ooby Dooby" and the single's other side, "Go Go Go," and we worked up a repertoire. Sometimes I'd sing a little—"The Battle of New Orleans" or maybe "Hully Gully." I started thinking about other kids I knew who played—to fill out the sound! We finally settled on Stu Cook for piano. Doug knew Stu, and when I was playing the piano in

Mrs. Starck's class, he mentioned him. Stu was smart and liked the same kind of music as Doug and me. He didn't know much about piano at the time, but he was willing to learn. So Doug and I decided to try him out.

Doug, Stu, and I were all pretty clean-cut, mainstream. Stu was the only one who was wealthy by our standards. He lived in a house up in the El Cerrito hills. He had a rumpus room with a piano. And he had a dad at home. Stu's dad was a lawyer with a great big firm that represented the Oakland Raiders, amongst others. Doug lived down near where I lived, down in the flats. It was all kind of middle-class territory.

At El Cerrito High there were three fraternities: Delmar, the 49ers, and the Saxons. Delmar was very clean-cut, preppy. The 49ers leaned towards jocks. Then the third one, the Saxons — those were not only the greasers, but the naughty boys, the bad boys. By the time I was a junior, I was lucky enough to be asked to join Delmar — at that point I had straight A's. Stu and Doug were in Delmar, but there was a big scandal where Stu jumped ship and became one of the Saxons. Stu went and got a tattoo, which was pretty far-out in 1962. I think he later tried to get it taken off.

The thing that came up with Stu was that at some point he would get impatient. And he would get — what's the word? — *difficult*. Stu would get in a tither about stuff and be pissed off. I made a speech about it after it happened one day. We were down in Stu's rumpus room rehearsing, some idea came up, and he wasn't even willing to try it — "That's *no good,* that's not gonna *work,* blah, blah, blah." Basically, he couldn't play the part, so he was yelling at the part he couldn't play rather than yelling at himself for not being able to play it. Finally I said, "You're that guy on the sidelines at the football game who's not even gonna try. He's not the coach, he's not playing in the game, he's just some dude standing on the side going, '*That'll* never *work*. Why did you try *that?!* Man, this *stinks!*'" I made that speech more than once, because over the years, that was Stu. He was that guy in Creedence. Stu could get in somebody's face. I was too shy to do that—or too polite.

I came up with the name the Blue Velvets for our band. And I was the bandleader, although I say that kind of comically. When Doug and I were first talking, I remember thinking, *Am I joining his band?* Then, *No—he's joining* my *band!* Along the way it became very clear. I was steering the direction. I had more music in me. And I wrote quite a few instrumentals. The Blue Velvets were an instrumental band—that was the whole premise. Every now and then I'd sing something like "Hully Gully," but mostly we did instrumental hits: Duane Eddy, Bill Doggett, Link Wray, the Ventures, Freddie King, Johnny and the Hurricanes.

The Blue Velvets were just a trio—guitar, drums, piano—so it wasn't a band with a lot of oomph, but back then there were a lot of little bands that weren't really fully formed. Johnny and the Hurricanes had a bass player, but you rarely saw that at a local level. And besides, we were the only rock and roll band in our school. Doug, Stu, and I played together as a band all the way from the eighth grade right through high school. Nobody else had the bravado to do something like that—"We're a *band!*" We were really considered kind of cool, but also kind of strange. After the Beatles hit, there were a hundred bands in our school, but for now we were it.

I believe the very first time the Blue Velvets played anywhere was at a sock hop at Portola Junior High at the end of 1959. We might've done five instrumentals. I know we played at least one song I'd written—a slow song, kind of an instrumental version of doo-wop, with those kinds of chords. Another of the songs we played at that first gig was a song I heard in the car on the way to the sock hop—"Bulldog" by the Fireballs. I just heard it on the radio and then when I got to school and had a guitar in my hand, I said, "Just follow me. It's a twelve-bar blues." I'm not made that way, to spring something unknown on people, let alone my own band, but that one time we did it—at our first gig! I was fairly practical. I wasn't trying to show everybody I'm Duane Eddy. It was, "What's my function here? They're hiring me to play for a dance. I better play danceable music." That remained my directive over the years, even as I got on the big stages of the world. I went for music that made you shake your body.

As we kept playing, opportunities started to open up, and this guy, Bob—I cannot remember his last name—took the Blue Velvets under his wing. He was with the El Cerrito boys club. We got to do shows all over the Bay Area—places like Pleasanton, San Leandro, and Oakland—representing the boys club. Because we were kids, Bob would drive us and bring our equipment. He was a really good guy, and he helped us. I've never been able to track him down, but I wish I could.

So the Blue Velvets got great exposure and the opportunity to play a lot. It was good discipline. We worked up three, four songs and went far and wide. We were playing somewhere in Northern California when James Powell first approached me.

He liked my little band. He said, "Well, I'm gonna make a record and I need a band to play on it." I was only fourteen. Unlike some musicians, I was always driven. If something lands in your lap, you're supposed to say, "Yeah, man—I'll do it!" Right? Nowadays every kid can make a record on his iPhone. So it's not such a romantic notion anymore. This was, "Mom, we're gonna make *a record!*" This was out in the world, making a recording. Just to be able to *say* it! How cool is that?

James was a black guy and a pretty doggone good singer. I think he was about twenty-five or so. He had a song he wanted to record called "Beverly Angel," a classic doo-wop. Really cool song. And he had others—every song was a girl's name. We rehearsed. I don't know how many times he came to either my house or Stu's rumpus room. James knew a guy named Joe Jarros who had a little company called Christy Records. He was a small businessman, and on the side he had a tiny label—the innocent side of the old-time rock and roll record business.

We were basically backing James, but to do that right, we needed a bass player on the record. Now, they had a string bass in Mrs. Starck's music room. A couple of times she let me play it. Mrs. Starck had made chalk marks on it so I could see the finger placements and play whatever song she wanted. Hey, it's like a guitar, only bigger.

So I decided I'd play bass on James Powell's session. I couldn't use the school bass, but on my paper route there was an older fella who played bass in a country band. They had a weekly gig in Oakland, broadcast on local TV. I always loved when he was home because we would talk about music for a while, and he was always full of encouragement for me. A cool guy.

So one day as I was delivering the paper, I told him we had this opportunity to make a record. He responded, "The heck you say! Really?" He was enthusiastic, so I asked to borrow his stand-up bass. "Sure, man. If I'm not home, just come tell my wife. The bass is in the garage."

James had rented a trailer. A string bass is huge. That's why they invented the Fender Precision—so you didn't have to go through this! I show up at the guy's house, and he's not there. His wife looks at James, she looks at me—I'm just some kid with a paper route. I'm not sure she understood the situation, but she let us take the bass. Lord, we drove across the Bay Bridge, with that big string bass in the open-air trailer, to Coast Recorders in San Francisco.

We'd already made a little demo record with Tom at a place called Dick Vance Recording Studio. The room was so small we actually had to open the window so Doug could sit on the sill and play his drums. I think we cut two songs there, with Tom singing.

All we got was a shellac copy. The guy just cut it right on the spot, and that's it—that's the only copy you have. I know for at least part of the song Tom had to manipulate the volume control on my Silvertone so it could sound like a vibrato. I just played and Tom turned the knob.

But Coast was a real recording studio. We walked in and I saw Monk Montgomery, the brother of Wes Montgomery. Monk was, like, the first jazz bass player to go electric. I thought, *Wow, the big time!* Walt Payne was the engineer. Years later he was the engineer on "Susie Q" for Creedence. Doug, Stu, and I did the music with James singing, and then I overdubbed bass, which turned out fine. James also overdubbed harmony with himself—an advanced thing for its time.

"Beverly Angel" is not quite "Earth Angel," but it's close. It sounds pretty good. It's got a big echo and a real ending—it doesn't just fade out. "Beverly Angel" didn't sell any copies that I know about, but that record eventually got played on the radio. Feature that: I made a record with my band at fourteen years old—a record that got played on the radio. Even weirder, it was an R & B record, a black record played on a black station—my *favorite* R & B station, KWBR!

I was pretty proud. I mean, I didn't assume, "This means I'm headed to Carnegie Hall." But get this: Stu took electronics with Mr. Thomas at El Cerrito High, and the project was to make a radio. Well, Stu made his radio, and the story goes that when he first fired it up, "Beverly Angel" came wafting out. Can you imagine that? "Hey, Mr. Thomas—it's my record!"

There were some times in my life where I went along with the crowd and was dishonest. When I was about eight years old, a little group of us kids started stealing stuff out of stores—the five-and-dime store, the hardware store. Y'know, just walk out with something under your shirt. Then we would try to sell the stuff door-to-door. Well, that's how we got caught. What's a little kid doing with a spatula he's trying to sell to some mom at her door? It still had the tag on it from the variety store. I was caught. Plus I was ratted out. This one kid, Billy, thought he was such a tough guy. He's the same one who pushed me over on my tricycle when I was about four years old. I rolled over. I was crying. Billy was that edgy, ornery, smokes-and-swears-a-lot kid — a bully. Billy ratted us out. Not so tough as when he pushed four-year-old me over in the crosswalk. That sure wasn't funny at the time. I hope Billy turned out okay.

There was a point when I would steal a record, take a 45. I didn't have what I perceived to be enough money, even though I had a paper route. I believe I had been in the record shop when I saw another kid steal a record. My eyes got real big — I think there was some thrill in doing it, although I hate to say that, and surely there was also some pressure to pull off this kind of stuff. I'm not saying this for bravado, and I'm certainly not happy to be saying it at all. But it's a part of my story from those times.

So here I was, stealing a 45 here and there. I had taken many singles over a period of a year and some months. And I literally looked at this one day and said, "Music is the thing you love. Why are you doing this? This is terrible. It's the thing you love most, and you're breaking your own strongest rule. You know what honesty is. What else do you have besides your word?" I was messing up the thing I loved, putting bad feelings and guilt all around it — to the point where I struggled with the idea of coming clean with the store so I could be free of this bad thing I'd done. But no, I never was that brave, I hate to say.

If anything came of it, I guess you could say I became a real stickler about honesty. To the point of silly things, like when you're driving, there's a roundabout in the road and you're supposed to go around it, but you *could* cut through it. My kids will be going, "Dad! Dad! Cut through!" And I'm like, "Nope, even if it hurts! The sign says this way."

Because it's a slippery slope. One day you do that little thing, and the next day...Obviously, none of us is perfect. As you may have guessed, I'm a fallible human being. But honesty is still very important to me. The idea of being truthful. Moral.

That wasn't the only experience that made me this way.

In eighth grade I stayed home from school. My mom stomped on the furnace grate—"Oh Johnny! Wake up!"—and off to work she went. It was October of 1958 and the World Series was on. "Wow, I'd kind of like to see the World Series." In those days, it was played in the daytime. So I stayed home from school. To watch the series and play my new Silvertone. And I stayed home the day after that. My mom wasn't around to know. Nobody was.

Weeks later I was doing my paper route after school when Mr. Noricaine, a phys ed teacher, went by in his '49 Ford, and I thought, *Oh, my day is comin'*. A few days later, I was busted. My mom confronted me. She'd gotten a call from the school, and after having lost so many credits that year, I got four Fs and a D minus. I used to tell people, "That's what I get for concentratin' on one subject."

So I was in trouble, and deep. I had to go to summer school— twice. The second time was my last hope if I wanted to graduate with my class. Kids don't quite get what the consequences are until the consequences are due. Summer school this time was over at Richmond High—not even my own school. But whoa, there was Mrs. Starck, my music teacher from Portola Junior High! Rather than being a punishment, summer school was a revelation. It was great to be there!

And there was this girl in class. I never really knew her real name, but everybody called her Plookie. She was kind of a heavy-set black girl, and Mrs. Starck allowed her to bring her music to school. Plookie played a Supro guitar through a Supro amp with vibrato. Plus someone played tambourine. Plookie and a couple of her friends did some gospel stuff, and it was *so* good. She might've known only one or two more chords than me, but it was more about attitude.

This was the music I listened to on the radio, but I didn't know anybody doing it firsthand. I'd hear this spooky stuff like the Staple Singers, and I'd sit down and try to do it, and it would come out like the Ventures. Plookie had that thing, she had that sound, and she was...great. Absolutely great. And she was my age! This was really an eye-opener. Because instead of being way off in the clouds, something I dreamed about down in my little room, this was something tangible, right in front of me. It pointed me in a direction towards something I could do, rather than being forbidden, or being too dangerous for my mom, or being too embarrassing to attempt. It was, "This is what I like. This is what I'm gonna do."

Plookie took the time to show me what she was doing with the vibrato, and her cool amp. I had a dinky little five-watt amp, and hers was probably twice as big or more. So I got myself a Supro guitar. First an Ozark model and then a top o' the line Res-O-Glas from the Sears catalog. That Ozark was my main guitar for years. I got short-scale guitars because I thought my hands were small, and I noticed that I could really just bend those strings by putting light-gauge strings on my little Supro.

The light-gauge string thing started when Tom and the Blue Velvets had some band pictures done at a little photo studio in Oakland. They were moody black-and-white pictures, and we were dressed up in suits. Just sitting there at the photo shoot was a Stratocaster guitar. It had that sunburst look and was all curvy. For a long time that was the only good guitar I'd ever held. But what really caught my eye was the fact that it had slinky strings, lightweight and really bendy. Like rubber bands.

I picked it up and went, "Wow, what's goin' on here?" I was

using Black Diamond strings, and positioned in their normal places they're pretty rigid, taut. Holding that Strat just made me think, *How can I do that?* So I would go down to Louis Gordon Music and, along with my normal set of strings, I would buy an extra high-E string. I would put the first E string in its normal first-string position. Then I'd put the other E string in the second-string position and move all the other strings down one spot lower than intended, making them all lighter gauge.

Later I found out that James Burton did the same thing, but he was using a banjo string for the high string. I didn't have enough knowledge for that move. But fairly early on I was into the light-string thing. It was a fortunate coincidence that I picked up that Stratocaster. It showed me that I could really just bend the heck out of those strings, which became an essential part of what I did.

Around the time we made the record with James, we would get together with Tom and do stuff. We were the Blue Velvets, his instrumental backing band. When I was in the ninth or tenth grade, we were at some guy's makeshift studio near Vallejo. It was the Blue Velvets plus Tom. He was singing. This guy had a couple of reel-to-reel tape recorders. Something was going wrong with his equipment, so we took a break. At one point he was fixing something on the tape recorder with a crescent wrench. Like a guy from an auto shop working on audio equipment. It was funny.

I don't know where Tom disappeared to. Stu went off to buy some smokes and Doug went with him.

"John, you wanna come?"

"No, I'm gonna stay here."

"Why?"

"Because I might learn somethin'." How often do I get to be at a recording studio?

So I'm just watching this guy with his wires. And he says,

"Y'know, when you're recording this stuff, remember: it's kind of like a glass of water."

"Huh?"

"You guys are making all this racket, but you're gonna have to put the singer on there."

"Yeah, okay."

"And you gotta put the lead guitar on there."

"Yeah. You mean it's like, 'Is my glass half empty or is it half full?' "

"No, no, no—not that way. You got a glass of water—that's your record, the thing you're trying to capture on tape. Remember that you can only fill the glass with so much water. After that, it all spills out. It's not going to be on your tape anymore—it's wasted. It's a mess, and ugly things happen. So if you're going to have something at the top—like a vocal—other things have to be less, so it doesn't overflow."

Analog tape saturates in a beautiful way—the old blues records, Bo Diddley and Chess Records, rock and roll in the golden age, Manfred Mann singing "Do Wah Diddy Diddy." If you sit right there on the red and everything's calibrated right, that's where rock and roll lives. The great engineers learn how to manipulate that. We don't stop where it starts to go into the red—that's the holy grail.

Digital can't do that. When you're recording in the digital world, you're backing off from that, wimping out. It can't go into the red. To paraphrase that wise old guy, the glass is overflowing, and it's ugly. Digital breakup is not a pretty sound.

So what this guy taught me that day stayed with me the rest of my life. When the guys came back, they were snickering—"Well, did you learn anything?" Later I tried to talk about it. They laughed.

My bandmates didn't really desire to know that stuff. I had to kind of drag them along, kicking and screaming. Sometimes they were in it; sometimes they'd go off with a girlfriend or to a party.

And I was left there—"Oh. Yeah, okay." Stu actually told me a couple of times, "Well, music isn't my whole life!" In Stu's case, it wasn't. In my case, it was. I'd caught it, and it had caught me.

I was the guy who always wanted to learn. I thought, *I'm gonna research this. I'm gonna scratch at it until I can figure it out.* It was about *learning*—learning what it was and how to do it. This was way more mental than, "Oh, poor me, I can't do it because I'm in a crappy recording studio." The great thing about rock and roll was that most of it was coming out of garages on some little label that said Del-Fi or Sun. They were making not only okay records but *the best* records.

Even though we were all very, very young musicians, I was always ahead of the other guys musically—and therefore, right from the get-go, I was the guy showing them what to play. Doug kind of knew that the foot went on one and the snare beat went on two, but that was about it. It was up to me to really study songs on the radio, discern what people were playing, and how that worked within that arrangement of that song. I was the translator. I could decipher. Most other people just hear music as one big sound coming at you. When I heard music, I heard the parts.

Hearing music live went a huge way towards my understanding, and the shows I saw at the Oakland Auditorium were another big influence. Those big revue extravaganzas where each artist got a half hour—James Brown, Jackie Wilson, Duane Eddy, Ray Charles. At all the shows that I saw at the Oakland Auditorium I was in the front row. I was in the front row for every one. I remember standing in line with Doug and Tom—Tom was the transportation, the wheels. We would get down there at three o'clock in the afternoon and be the first ones in line, so when the doors opened a few hours later we'd haul ass and sit front and center. That's how I could see so much detail.

I saw James Brown when I was fourteen. There was such precision. He'd sing one song—"Please, Please, Please"—and then, suddenly, *pow!* James goes down on the ground with the splits. Then he's up on his feet and into another song. *Bam!* His legs are going crazy. Another song! *Bam!* He might've been on for twenty minutes, but he and the band did twelve songs. The idea was to explode in a very short period of time. Energy! At the end, everybody's mouths hung open—"Whaaaa happened?" I loved that.

Larry Williams jumped off the stage with his guitar, and all these girls surrounded him. *Bam!* When they pulled away he was naked to the waist. They had shredded his shirt. Jackie Wilson came out in a tuxedo and all the women totally lost it. White girls, black girls—didn't matter. Jackie was movie star good-looking, with moves that were graceful, effortless, like a panther. Deejay Bouncin' Bill, the emcee, came out and told the women, "You've got to get back in your seats, back in your seats," because of the fire marshal. With Jackie Wilson it just kept happening. The cool R & B backing band we saw there several times had a song called "Spunky Onions" (it had started out as "Funky Onions"), and the guitar player hit what I now know is an augmented chord. Tom turned to me and said, "You should really watch what that guitar player is doing." He wasn't telling himself that—he was telling me. I wondered about that later.

There was one show at the Oakland Auditorium that turned out differently than all the rest. As usual, we had gotten there in the afternoon so we could be first in line. Well, they opened the doors as usual at six or six thirty. Then we sat there for the longest time with nothing happening. The time for the show to start came and went. Still no word....By now the auditorium was full and everyone was ready for the show. It got later and later and nothing was said to the audience. People started to murmur and were getting a bit upset.

Forty-five minutes to an hour after showtime, there began to be a stirring coming from the back of the auditorium. As we turned to see what it was, a few guys came walking down the center aisle on the main floor. They proceeded to walk right past the front row of people toward the stage. A couple of guys had dry cleaning bags over their shoulders, and slowly the audience began to realize that these guys were musicians—part of the show. As they got to the stage—which was raised up from the floor maybe four feet—they each hopped up onto it.

The audience relaxed a bit, thinking that now the show would begin. One of the guys sat down at the grand piano and started to play the opening of Ray Charles's "What'd I Say," which was a current hit on the radio. When he got to the part where the right hand does a little break and then the verse-ending riff, he fumbled and couldn't do it. He tried that riff a few times but could not play it cleanly. Well, the other guys had gathered around the piano, so one of them pushes this guy off the seat and sits down and tries to play the riff. He also fails and gets pushed away by yet another "player." I think five or six guys had a go at it. Finally, I believe Bouncin' Bill—the emcee—came out and scooted them backstage. Watching this scene, I said to myself, *This isn't right. It seems so amateurish*. I made a vow to myself that I would never let this happen at "my show." I was fourteen years old.

I believe it was later on in this same show when I got some more "showbiz instruction." Bouncin' Bill announced the next act, the audience cheered, and...nothing. No one came out. He announced them again, and still nothing. After a couple more times, Bill went backstage, and suddenly a whole bunch of guys came flying out onto the stage, all dressed in matching suits. Bouncin' Bill was obviously pissed at this bunch, so he went to the mic and said, "Somebody had a royal flush and he wasn't gonna come out until the hand played its course." That was another lesson—as in, "Gee whiz, don't treat your audience like crap—they've come here to see *you!*"

In spite of that, we saw a lot of good presentation, good professional showbiz at the Oakland Auditorium. What I learned at the knee of James Brown and Jackie Wilson was how to *entertain*.

My mother sent me back to Catholic school in the ninth grade— St. Mary's, where my older brothers had gone from ninth through twelfth grade. There wasn't a whole lot that worked out for me there, but they had a boys' glee club at St. Mary's. Now *that* was awesome. One of the songs we learned was "There Is Nothing Like a Dame" from *South Pacific*— "We got mangoes and bananas..."

When music is all you've got going, you cling to it. When I first started up at the school, the dean was this guy named Brother Neil. He let me know right away, "I had both of your brothers. I got an eye on you. I'll see you in detention." And he did.

After that year, Brother Neil ran off with the receptionist, quit the order, and got married. Some of my friends were getting hit on by this brother or that brother. We were kind of disgusted. For me it was another slat gone out of the white picket fence that is the Catholic Church.

At one detention I was supposed to write something a thousand times—some sentence like "I will not chew gum in class." Well, my pen ran out of ink. And in detention you're not allowed to talk. I couldn't tell anybody or get up or raise my hand. So I filled in all the rest with the empty pen. If you looked close at the paper, you could see the imprint of the inkless pen. The brother looked at it and said, "Are you crazy?" Of course, I should've known— back when I was born I had inherited original sin from some guy millions of years ago. I should've known that you'd better not run out of ink, right?

One time when I was staying after school, this brother, an older gentleman, had a talk with me. I was having a hard time in school, so coming to class wasn't necessarily something that made me go, "Whoopee!" So the brother was giving me this talk. Now remember, these are religious people. You're not really supposed to be talking about sex, except that you're dealing with teenage boys with absolutely raging hormones, meaning they may go twelve seconds without having sexual thoughts, if the thoughts haven't already knocked them unconscious. And at some point the brother asked if I thought about sexual things, and I said yeah. And he says, "Well, maybe your underwear is too tight." I sure remember that phrase. I don't even know how I responded. And I'm thinking, *Oh, here we go. I got a brother hittin' on me.*

Music—thank God. We had formed a little musical group at St. Mary's. Baynard Cheshire played guitar alongside me. Baynard had a little National electric guitar, and sometimes I'd swap and let him play my Silvertone. Ron White, a guy who could really play, was on drums, and John Tonaga played piano. I don't think we had bass. I can't remember if the band even had a name, although we might've made one up on the spot. I know I brought those guys over to play once at El Cerrito High.

When our little group played at St. Mary's, the principal was Brother Frederick. He was a little short in stature. (I only noticed because he seemed to be overcompensating. We learned the phrase "Napoleonic complex.") At the time, I had been listening to Elmore James, and he'd inspired me to learn a vibrato technique that involved holding down three notes in the key of E, like the high part in Link Wray's "Rumble." You just hit it once or twice, and shake like crazy to imitate Elmore's slide. So there we are in the gym at St. Mary's, playing some fast rock and roll instrumental, and I start doing that E thing. I'm shaking, and the sound is coming out *BEEEEEEEOOOOOOOOOOW!* The kids are all digging the rock and roll. If you want to say "in a frenzy," I won't argue.

And suddenly it just goes quiet. Someone pulled the plug! I look up and there's Brother Frederick, frowning, and suddenly it becomes apparent that I have committed the sin of all sins, because my body was shaking while I was playing. I didn't even know! I still don't. It's rock and roll—that's what you do! Brother Frederick had turned it into plenary indulgence, Hail Mary perversion: "This insidious music is going to be the ruin of the whole school!" Right then I think I lost all heart for finishing out at St. Mary's. I thought, *God, this guy's such a jerk*. Right out of *Bye Bye Birdie*!

Halfway through the tenth grade they took me out of St. Mary's. I don't know if the school just said, "We don't want him here anymore," or what. But I was relieved. I got to start fresh at El Cerrito High. My grades and attendance certainly improved, but it took me a while to get my bearings. On my first day the biology teacher called on me to answer a question, so I stood up to answer as I had been trained at St. Mary's. There was sort of a murmur in the class. I sat down and the teacher said, "That's a wonderful answer—and by the way, you don't have to stand up here."

For a second I felt embarrassed, but then I looked over at this girl who was smiling at me in an unthreatening way. She was a cute girl with glasses, and she asked my name. I was like, *Wow, there's girls!* Everything was so friendly and easy. Man, I loved El Cerrito High!

When I was sixteen, having a car was definitely the thing. I wanted to get a learner's permit and a license, but my mom resisted. My older brothers had gotten tickets and she didn't want the hassle. I had gotten a job at a gas station when I was fifteen—Tom had worked there; I'm sure that helped—so I saved my money and finally, at seventeen, I went and bought a car and just put it in our driveway. And I said, "Well, Mom, I probably oughta get a driver's license now that I have a car."

It was a green 1948 Ford Fastback, forty-eight thousand miles on it. It was a great car—the upholstery was perfect. I'd bought it for a hundred dollars—I'd tried to talk the guy down to ninety. This car had a Motorola radio with a little electric motor that went *grrrrr* over to the next station when you pushed a button. I put in toggle switches so the radio would jump between my favorite stations, KEWB and KDIA (formerly KWBR). I wanted to build a hot rod and screwed the car all up by taking it apart. What I didn't know was now the battery wasn't charging, so I was forever in situations where the car wouldn't start. I'd have to push the friggin' car down the road and pop it into gear. Because of my own foolishness that car gave me some intense, interesting moments in life. I ended up selling it for forty bucks to a guy who worked at the gas station with me. He still owes me twenty.

My first real girlfriend was a straight-A student and kind of insisted that I be one too. There's nothing like that kind of girlfriend to give you incentive to turn into a good student. I was fifteen; she was a year younger. She left me for a guy named Fred. I had an old lady car; Fred had a hot rod—exposed engine, a lot of chrome. He was a year older than me. He was in auto shop; I was in geometry. I guess my girlfriend liked the rugged, rough-and-ready thing at that point in her life and said, "Yeah, I wanna be in *that* car." That was a harpoon in my side. Talk about a broken heart.

I put that teenage emotion into a song I wrote, "Have You Ever Been Lonely." You know how there are these little signs that there's something wrong, and there's some other guy who seems to be pretty friendly with your girl, and you're the last to know? I wrote that song on piano. It had a little of the vibe of Arthur Alexander's "Where Have You Been (All My Life)" or Ron Holden and the Thunderbirds' "Love You So"—Tom would sing that one and I'd play piano. I play a piano solo in "Have You Ever Been Lonely" that's in the same style.

We cut the song in 1961 for Wayne Farlow, who had a little

label called Orchestra Records. We had already done one single for him. The label said "Tommy Fogerty and the Blue Velvets." When we were rehearsing the song in my living room, Wayne said, "I can't hear the solo. Play it in a higher register." So I moved it up one octave. Now, we could've just turned up the solo when we made the record, but this gave the song a different character *and* it made the solo stick out from the rest of the music. That's called arranging, and it was very good advice—a lesson to keep in mind for the future.

Tom sang, Doug played the drums, and I played the piano, not Stu. I don't think he was on that one, unless he played— *brrrrring!*—that opening chord on guitar. When I was writing it, I sang it a little harsher than Tom did on the record, with a few more hiccups in the vocal. Tom sang it pure and sweet. It's still really cool. Mom liked "Have You Ever Been Lonely." That was a pretty good song. I actually sent away and got that copyrighted and joined BMI.

With hindsight, it's funny and pretty sad that way back then I somehow knew how to do this at sixteen.

Around the tenth grade I hooked up with Bob DeSousa, who ran a studio called Sierra Sound Laboratories in Berkeley. I just looked it up in the phone book. I called and said, "I want to get into recording." Bob let me come over, bring my guitar. And experiment. I had to take the bus to get down there, and it became a regular thing. Bob knew how to do slapback echo with a tape machine and he enjoyed trying to come up with sounds. I hung out at the studio quite a bit, got in a lot of hours of experience. A lot of it was fooling around. I'd bang around on the piano, trying to figure out where you mic it so it sounds good. I was Bob's guinea pig. Bob seemed pretty amazed that I was able to just jump in and add harmony parts to the background vocal parts and even a bit of guitar.

And he let me experiment with the equipment. The Blue Velvets recorded a little Floyd Cramer–type instrumental called "Happy Little Thing" there. I think Doug Clifford named that one. And a guitar instrumental called "Bittersweet." I also remember a mournful instrumental called "Last Man on Alcatraz"—the idea being that the prison forgot about one of 'em when they closed the place down. Once Bob saw that I could play the piano a little bit, he even hired me for a session or two as a country guy, playing Floyd Cramer licks. I really liked Bob because he didn't look down his nose at me, all of sixteen years old.

Given how into recording I was, you won't be surprised to learn that I had been fascinated with tape recorders from an early age. Bob Carleton and I were a little team in grade school. We had started out imitating Stan Freberg records, lip-synching "Christmas Dragnet" for our class, one of us in a trench coat and hat like a cop, the other playing the interviewer. I still remember the words to that. In 1956, Buchanan and Goodman had this comedy record, "The Flying Saucer," where they told a story intercut with little bits of rock and roll hits. To do some stuff like that, Bob and I used this Wollensak recorder that Tom had brought home. One skit was called "The Daytime Ghost." The ghost was out of sync with Halloween because he appeared in the daytime. Bob and I wrote the story together and chose the songs. We both knew our records, but I was that kid who knew every line of every song, and I did all the talking.

I got a Sony add-a-track recorder in the tenth grade. It allowed you to overdub onto the original track. I had spent the previous summer babysitting my younger brothers at my dad's house in Santa Rosa to buy the recorder, which I had seen at Louis Gordon Music. My dad reneged on the deal, and you can bet I was really angry about that. But if he wasn't going to help, I was going to do it the right way. I think I finally bought it with paper route money.

Les Paul had inspired me with his overdubbing. On his recordings where Mary Ford was the singer, she harmonized with herself. Sometimes she harmonized with a whole vocal group: on "Vaya con Dios" or "How High the Moon." Mary was the vocal group; Les was the band. They sounded amazing.

The Sony add-a-track was a gray-tweed-and-vinyl-covered thing. It was a revelation for me, since I could now capture what I was hearing in my head. I used it exclusively from then on. All through high school I'd be down in my bedroom recording. I even used the bathroom as an echo chamber. I spent hundreds of hours harmonizing with myself, and then adding guitar tracks. I learned an awful lot about what sounds rock and roll, what sounds true. I guess you could say that was the beginning of my one-man-band deal.

I managed to do a lot of recordings that were very much like the Ventures, with little harmony lead parts. I did folk songs, like "I've Been Working on the Railroad." I remember being down there in my room recording "Can't Help Falling in Love." We had a small house, and you couldn't do anything without everybody else hearing you. Mom later made a comment: "Gee, what is that you're doing?" "Oh, that's an Elvis song." "That's wonderful!" It was great to get some feedback.

In 1963, the Blue Velvets were playing a high school reunion for the class of '53. At some point in the night, we played "Green Onions." And this fellow comes up, R. B. King. He happens to be a black guy. I only make reference to this because there was a feeling—especially among white kids—that the more soulful stuff came out of black people. And he starts talking to us about "Green Onions"—immediately after we played it, I think. This is only worth mentioning because what he told us was the truth—the truth like a glass of ice water in your face.

For years and years I have said that Booker T. and the MGs were the greatest rock and roll band of all time. Obviously most people are going to say the Beatles, but it's what R. B. King was talking about: no one ever had it like Booker T. and the MGs. I'm talking about soulfulness, deep feeling, especially in between the beats. How to say a lot with a little: that's one rule that will always work—in music, on records, on the radio. Was Steve Cropper scaring Chet Atkins? No. But I daresay, between the two, most people would want to be Steve Cropper, and we adopted Booker T. and the MGs as our idols. Even after we were pretty famous and selling millions of records. The solo in "Proud Mary"? That's me doing my best Steve Cropper.

When R. B. came up, he got right to it and said, "Well y'know, when you're playin' that 'Green Onions,' there's somethin' missing." He said that phrase two or three times—"somethin' missing." I'm thinking, *Well...we're young, we're just a trio, and of course we don't play as good as Booker T. and the MGs.* He didn't say, "You white boys *suck*." But R. B. King, in his gentle way, was saying, "There's somethin' in between the notes."

Allow me to explain. Compare the Hank Ballard and the Midnighters original first recording of "The Twist" to the Chubby Checker version.* Ballard's has that *feel*. Many years later, I sat in with Hank in some New York City club after his induction into the Rock and Roll Hall of Fame, and I mentioned to the bandleader

---

* Chubby Checker's version of "The Twist" is a great record, and I love it. What Chubby had done was to "straighten out" the beat, making it more rock and roll—and much more accessible to the masses. I was thrilled to meet Chubby onstage at the Rock and Roll Hall of Fame ceremony in 1986. Chubby made it a point to say to me [about my Creedence work], "Those are *your* songs...you should play those songs!" Chubby Checker belongs in the Rock and Roll Hall of Fame. Now!

how the Blue Velvets could never pull off that rhythm. His face lit up. He said, "Oh—you mean sand and Vaseline." I thought that was the greatest way to put it. And that's what R. B. King was trying to tell me in the gentlest way.

Some people can play a shuffle and some people cannot. I hate to say it's as simple as a cultural or racial thing, but more often than not, it's the white people who can't do shuffle. I've found there are exceptions: Chris Layton, who was with Stevie Ray Vaughan, is one of the all-time great shuffle players in the world. And I'd like to think I've been able to do it pretty good over the years. So later I tried to explain what R. B. King was talking about to Doug and Stu—particularly Doug—and I used that phrase all through the evolution of the Blue Velvets: the shuffle beat. But it's so much easier to play than to explain.

A few years after the R. B. King incident, the night before I was going on active army duty for six months, we're playing at a club outside Sacramento—I believe it was the Trophy Room. I'm not in the happiest of moods. I'm fairly nostalgic and down, leaving the next day. Who knows what's going to happen?

We're about to do a song, and I turn around to Doug and I say, "Play a shuffle beat."

And he says, "What's a shuffle beat?" *What's a shuffle beat?* It was like I'd been punched in the gut. You might as well have said, "What's a guitar?" This was 1967. I had used that phrase—"shuffle beat"—since 1958. I was speechless.

I must say, I avoided shuffle like the plague for years and years and years, as much as I needed it around. I'd be in rehearsal with the Creedence guys, and there it would be again: the shuffle problem. No sand and Vaseline. Sometimes I'd get frustrated and angry, particularly at Doug. Young musicians tend to rush. If it's a fast song, they tend to get excited and be a half block ahead of the beat before everybody else. Or they drag, especially on slower, funky things. I could almost see the ghost of R. B. King going, "There's somethin' missing here."

There's a couple of times when Creedence did play a shuffle beat more or less pretty good. One was our cover of "Before You Accuse Me." It's not Bo Diddley, but for some guys from El Cerrito, it's pretty good. We did this little two-sided narrative for the fans called "45 Revolutions per Minute (Part 2)," and it included a song in the background called "Thank You, Mr. J" that had a shuffle beat, and that was pretty tight.

I was pretty hard on Doug. I still am. Timing. In the eighties I was hunting up in Oregon. This was long after Creedence had broken up. And I had this dream. Our tent was on Miller Creek, and to get across it, you had to step on a path of rocks and logs — otherwise you'd land in the water.

So in my dream the rocks are representing the beats in music. I'm in the woods with Doug Clifford, and I step on all the rocks and get to the other side of Miller Creek. Then here comes Doug, *ker-splish, ker-splash,* missing the rocks and stepping in the water.

And I'm going, "No, no, no, you step *on* the rock. *On* the beat." And I woke up. My dream was about timing. About being on beat. There was so much of not being on the beat in the early days. What I'm trying to get at is, all was not lost, but it took a ton of effort, a ton of persistence, to get there.

CHAPTER 5

The... Golliwogs?

MY SENIOR YEAR I almost didn't graduate. My job at the gas station really interfered. Somehow I scraped through. I had been accepted at the University of San Francisco but didn't have the money to go there. Contra Costa College, a community college, was the only road that looked open—to me, anyway—grade-wise and money-wise. I followed the crowd from El Cerrito High to Contra Costa College, those that weren't going off to Stanford or Harvard or anywhere else.

At some point in my life, I thought I might somehow pose as a history teacher. I still love history. But I hadn't even set junior college up to be very good, and it wasn't. I wasn't pushing, fighting to be there. When you're young, you need assistance and advice, a little nudge to get going. You can't just sit around and stare at the wall. I didn't really get guidance. I didn't even have it together enough to get the official dropout W, like you're supposed to, so it doesn't count against you. I just stopped going.

That's why I try so hard now to help my kids. One of my boys is at the University of Southern California, and another is at CalArts. I say that with a lot of pride. They're succeeding in a world where

I didn't. (Shane has since graduated from USC and Tyler will graduate in the spring.)

When I say things like this, my wife, Julie, grabs my hand and goes, "I think you did okay, John." But to me? Some big part of me still feels unworthy. Feature that. Wow.

In March 1964, the local PBS station ran this special, produced by the *San Francisco Chronicle* music critic Ralph J. Gleason, called *Anatomy of a Hit*. It was about Fantasy Records, a dinky little company in the Bay Area having its first hit record despite having been in business since the forties. It followed the rise of Vince Guaraldi's "Cast Your Fate to the Wind," which I loved, and this was a look into all the personalities involved. This TV special was in three installments running a week apart, so there was time to talk and think about it before the next episode. Tom and I considered Fantasy a jazz label and didn't think it would be a place that we should even knock on the door. But after seeing this program, we talked some more, and I decided, "Well, I'm just gonna go over there."

San Francisco was always a bit of a mystery to me as far as navigation. I was eighteen years old, and I'd probably gone once or twice by myself and had been there a few times with my mom. That was the big city, and you didn't just venture over there casually, even though it was only across the bridge from El Cerrito.

Once I found the address on Treat Avenue, I pumped myself up and went over. I pressed the buzzer, went up a little flight of stairs, and there was an office with a counter and some machinery and a typewriter, and somebody standing there talking to one of the guys I'd seen on the TV show, Max Weiss.

I had some manners, so I waited. I listened to the guy talk about all his big songs and all the places he'd been, dropping names like Johnny Mathis and Andy Williams. And Max keeps saying, "All right, Colonel...All right, Bright Eyes." And I'm thinking, *If you know all these people and they're all into your songs, why are you standing here?* It sounded like common show-business puffery.

When the other guy left, I introduced myself. And somewhere in the next ten minutes, Max called me both Colonel and Bright Eyes. He did that for the rest of our relationship. It was his way of treating the high and mighty and the low and full of it equally. Max was the resident hipster. He had a beard and sometimes wore funny Russian hats. I think he even had a fez. I guess I thought of him as a beatnik. Three Weiss brothers owned Fantasy: Max, Sol, and Milton, the bookkeeper. Saul Zaentz was the sales manager then.

Max took me into another office and listened to some of the instrumentals that I had brought. After three or four, he said, "Do you have any songs with words?" I'd been writing songs with words since I was eight. So I said, "Well, sure!" Max said, "Songs with words do a lot better than songs that don't have words." And he opened up a copy of *Billboard,* and the first five songs on the chart were all by the Beatles. (Yes, it was *that* historic week in April of 1964.) So we made another appointment, and I came back with songs with words.

We started recording songs for Fantasy Records. Later we signed a contract with the label in a very dark and noisy Italian restaurant. I couldn't read the menu, let alone the contract. I was underage anyway. All of us were, except Tom.

I also worked at Fantasy as a shipping clerk. I had to box up the records and call a delivery service, and a big truck would come and take our three boxes of albums. Maybe three hundred records a week were going out that door. It sure wasn't a lot. They had a shed with all the album cover stock—people like Mongo Santamaria and Korla Pandit. Fantasy clearly didn't have a clue about rock and roll. I know we went to lunch with Max a few times on

Saturdays, and he'd write down on the check "Vince Guaraldi." I think it was a tax write-off.

Fantasy had an R & B label called Galaxy, with songs like "Part Time Love" by Little Johnny Taylor. Little Johnny struck me as one of the old-fashioned stars—he'd call Saul Zaentz "Mr. Saul." Rodger Collins, who had the hit "She's Looking Good," was more my friend. Rodger was an entertainer. He'd make a guitar talk like it was asking a question. He played a Strat and had a Fender Super Reverb amp that was big and loud. He was a guy I was watching, because he was further along down the path than I was. I heard his record at the rifle range when I was in the army. To jack everybody up, get them happy about shooting targets with real bullets, they'd put on "She's Looking Good."

Fantasy recorded us in this lean-to out back. A big, open room. I think it had been a storage shed in the past and was connected to the main building. The tape recorder was right next door, in the warehouse where they kept the record albums. The doorway between the tape machine and the lean-to was a strange deal. They had cut out a hole in the drywall about the size of a normal door but had left the wooden struts, the frame, in the open space. It was explained to me that they would have to pay higher taxes to have a real door there (I have often thought about that syndrome— either you're in it or you ain't...). Because of that cheap-ass attitude, we were forced to squeeze between the two-by-fours with our instruments. There were no windows and you couldn't see the engineer—you just yelled. We kind of ragged on the whole setup. I remember recording "Fight Fire" when Doug was playing the maracas and hit the microphone right in the middle of the take. Things were just so funky.

By early summer of '64, we had recorded some songs. Max, the mad Russian, acted as our mentor and our engineer. We had all just graduated from high school, and Stu wasn't there for those sessions. I don't know how many songs we recorded, but we ended up concentrating on two of them: "Don't Tell Me No Lies" and "Little Girl (Does Your Mamma Know?)." Tom was the singer then. I remember overdubbing some tambourine and some tuned-down guitar that was supposed to sound like bass since we had no bass player.

Tom and I cowrote the songs, like nearly all the songs that came pre-Creedence. We hadn't joined forces as songwriters until after Lennon and McCartney. Before that, if he wrote a song, it was his song, and if I wrote a song, it was my song. On "Have You Ever Been Lonely," the writing credit is "Johnny Fogerty." The Beatles hadn't happened yet. Then we both got the idea: "Oh yeah—they write together." Tom's writing alias was Rann Wild. I really liked the singer Dobie Gray, who had the hit "Look at Me," and I liked the name Toby, so I became Toby Green. We were Wild and Green—songwriters.

Rock and roll was in a weird place before the Beatles came along. I had gotten so disenchanted, hearing the Singing Nun or the fifteenth rehash of "Can I Get a Witness," and I'd gotten restless down on the farm. So much so that around Christmastime in '63, I was down in Oakland, shopping, and I realized, "Oh my God, I'm listening to KSFO!" That was the "easy listening" station: you'd hear John Gary crooning "Once Upon a Time," and then they'd play Bing Crosby. Early that year, in May—I think it was on KFRC—I heard this song, "Please Please Me," by the Shields—at least that's what I thought they had called them. I heard the song every day after school for a week in my senior year, driving to work at the gas station. I thought, *Yeah, that's pretty cool.* Then they turned the record over and played "From Me to You"—*dahr dahr dahr dahar dar dar.* I was gone. I went, *God, what* is *that?* That record killed me. Then they disappeared. Nothin'. All gone.

The next January, suddenly they're playing the Shields all over the radio. They're gonna be on Ed Sullivan. It's not Elvis: it's a group, a whole band, and by now I know what they're really called. And girls are screaming for a...band? I was eighteen when that happened. I thought, *Man, this is the coolest,* and went down to the store and bought every record with "Beatles" on it. They were seamlessly going from this music to that: Arthur Alexander, Carl Perkins. People forget that part. They were coming from the heart of rock and roll.

I can tell you I didn't feel jealous—"Hey, they're taking our music!" We needed a shot in the arm in the USA, and they were shaking things up. That whole burst of energy. All of a sudden there's all these people who are really, really good. One after another: the Stones, Kinks, Searchers, Billy J. Kramer, Gerry and the Pacemakers. Remember: two months before January of 1964, Kennedy had been assassinated. When JFK died, it really punched me in the gut. I loved the Kennedys—all of 'em. For all their very human failings, it seems to me that they wore their wealth and their position of power in a much different way than almost anybody else that's ever been powerful and political. They had ideas that were very much for the good of the common man, and for the good of America as a society. And it cost them all very dearly. I was in the lunchroom at Contra Costa College when they announced Kennedy's assassination. I was stunned, in shock. Then here comes the Beatles. Thank God for the Beatles.

Put it this way: there were some little shows I did—with my band or just with pickup guys at a party—where I'd actually wear a Beatles wig and do three or four of their songs. I remember some older person saying, "Tell John he doesn't need to do that," as if I was going to be an Elvis impersonator for the rest of my life. It was fun, because *they* were fun. Quick, instant, like sea monkeys— put the wig on and "Yeah, yeah, yeah." We knew all their songs, and songs they never did, because you could kind of do 'em like the Beatles. I was, as you'd say, totally down with it.

*   *   *

A lot of things happened while we waited for our Fantasy single to come out. At this point, the band was not really meeting all that often other than for recording. I don't know how many times I played with Doug and Stu in our high school senior year—once, maybe twice. It wasn't a lot. At some point, Doug and I did a spate of frat parties. That was just for fun—half the time I'm sure the music wasn't very good because Doug and I were drunker than skunks.

When we got to the frat house to set up, the frat president would always say, "Hey, we wanna hustle the chicks, so you guys keep it slow. You just keep playin' slow songs."

"Oh, you mean like 'In the Still of the Night'?"

"Yeah, perfect! Like that!"

Right. Then we'd start, and maybe in the first half hour we'd play one slow number. After that, no more slow songs. Nobody really wanted that. We'd play "Wooly Bully," "Wipe Out," "Louie Louie," "Money," and "Twist and Shout" over and over. That's what they really wanted—a big, drunken howl. Doug and I had a running joke at those shows. As one of us was coming back from a pee break, we'd surprise each other with the house fire extinguisher. *Blam!* It would be all over me. I'd look like a flocked Christmas tree.

That summer of '64 I went up to Portland, Oregon, with Mike Burns and Tom Fanning, who were both in architecture school at UC Berkeley, and stayed there for about a month. I had met these two earlier that year, and I believe we had played a couple of parties together. They were great guys and good musicians, but I think they were on a career path to design buildings. Mike had the idea for us to go up to Oregon, audition a couple of local musicians, and get a job playing music for the summer. We ended up getting a gig at a club called the Town Mart. Mike named that band the Apostles. He had these beige shirts made that had big puffy sleeves — vaguely British Invasion–looking — and we had longish hair. In fact, when we got to Portland that summer, we walked into a diner and it was like we were terrorists. We were just going to sit down at the counter, get some pancakes and bacon. Except for the jukebox, you could have heard a pin drop. Then the jukebox stopped, and you could hear people saying, "Oh, they think they're the Beatles. Look at those juvenile delinquents!"

Mike played Farfisa organ. That was my first experience being in a band with one of those cool things. I was a real fan of that cheesy organ. "She's About a Mover," "Do Wah Diddy Diddy," "96 Tears" by Question Mark and the Mysterians. That song is one of those oddities — it's really awful *and* it's really cool. It held both positions! What an awesome song. Mike and Tom were really fun to be around — really good guys.

Portland was just an adventure. I liked the Northwest bands. The Sonics I loved. "The Witch"? I'm *still* going to do that song one of these days. Hell, yeah! We saw Paul Revere and the Raiders — they were still up there, not big stars. One night we were driving down the street in the dark, drinking beer, and saw the Kingsmen loading their gear. We shoulda stopped. Somebody in the car went, "The Kingsmen, man," and I went, "Wow."

Mike sang a few of the songs, like "Louie Louie." He was also tone-deaf. Mike literally had to count "One, two, three, four. One, two, three, four" in his head to make the chord changes. That's what he told me, anyway. I was determined to work on my singing and evolved into being the main singer of that little band. I took the add-a-track recorder on that Portland trip. I could record a whole set on one side of tape at the slow speed. We played from nine maybe until two, and then went back to the house where we were staying and spent another three hours drinking beer and listening to ourselves on tape. I was concentrating on my vocal, really going to school on that, because I desired not to be lame. And y'know, what I heard so far sounded kind of lame.

I'd sung in different situations but never thought I was killer. I did "Hully Gully" once at a dance for KYA at the El Cerrito armory. I had a little harshness in my voice, and people said, "Oh man, that was really cool," but that was only two minutes and thirty seconds. Maybe I had to get away from home to be free enough to do it. I knew in my head what I thought I should sound like, but what came out of my mouth didn't match that. I wanted to have a tougher sound, like the guys who really had an edge: James Brown; Wilson Pickett— "I Found a Love"; the Contours— "Do You Love Me"; Don Gardner and Dee Dee Ford— "I Need Your Lovin' "; the Sevilles— "Charlena"; and, of course, Little Richard, the best singer in rock and roll.

That's where I was trying to go. Have that alpha thing. So after listening to the tape, I'd go back the next night and try to make my voice sound a little harder, a little more rock and roll. I'd say words funny, in my own style. I'd try to do a scream going into the solo.

Portland was also the first place where I played harmonica. We were going to do a number— "Louie Louie," I think—and Mike was going to play the harmonica. Remember: this is the guy who's tone-deaf. A moment came where I just said, "Gimme that thing! No, I can't play it, but God, it's got to be better than *that*." I was never Little Walter, that's for sure. But it was rock and roll. It fit the occasion.

When we came back from Portland, Mike Burns called with a gig at this place in Berkeley, the Monkey Inn. Since the drummer we had used in Portland stayed back, I convinced Mike to use Doug. It was a typical college crowd, mostly UC Berkeley students. They had shuffleboard, and sawdust and peanut shells all over the floor. Peanuts and a pitcher of beer—for five dollars you could have one heck of a night. And that's all I was being paid, anyway. I think we got twenty bucks—for the band, not apiece—and all the beer we could drink. So you know what we leaned heavy on.

Tom Fanning and I played guitar, Mike was on Farfisa, and Doug was on drums. That lasted for a few months, and then it just kind of dissolved. I convinced the Monkey Inn's owner that I knew some other guys who could play. This would've been about 1966. We were making our records, but we still weren't really hanging together. Stu was busy at college or busy at frat parties down in San Jose, and he didn't come up that often, or he'd show up late in our set. This is when my brother Tom came in.

We had started out the other way: with Tom playing piano or singing with that beautiful voice. But now I was trying to include my brother in this new musical thing—my thing. I had to broach it to Doug and Stu. The first thing one of them said was, "Well, Tom can't sing." In fact, they had both said that way back at Dick Vance studios, which might've been the first time we were all at a recording studio. I was sticking up for my brother. (What's so funny about this is that later they went the opposite way. They would make it me versus Tom, with both of them on Tom's side.)

This was the fragile way our quartet started. Slowly we were evolving into the template for a rock and roll band as laid down first by the Crickets, and then by the Beatles: two guitars, bass, and drums.* There's no odd man out, no singer that doesn't do anything but sing and play tambourine. In a band, four is perfect. It's an even square, a beautiful shape in geometry. It's not six and a half people, which is too many, or three, which is too small.

With the British Invasion, I was beginning to see that those bands had certain instruments, and it had to be a certain way. The Beatles, the Stones, and the Kinks had all arrived fully formed,

---

* Of course, the very first rock and roll band had this lineup—Elvis on rhythm guitar, Scotty Moore on lead, Bill Black on bass, and D. J. Fontana on drums.

with a bass player. They looked professional, and we just weren't. It's not going to be rock and roll if you go out there with a tambourine and a triangle and a fiddle. To be a real band, we needed a bass player. Up until then, Stu was playing piano. One night I said, "Look, I want you to get a bass. Just get a cheap bass"—I think he got a St. George—"and we'll grow up learning this thing together. I'll show you what to do, and when you master that, I'll give you more bass lines to play, and we'll get there eventually."

Once Tom was in, he started just playing tambourine. Besides Stu learning bass, Tom was learning guitar—he literally couldn't play a bar chord, so it all had to be cowboy chords. It doesn't take forever to learn how to play rhythm guitar in a rock and roll band. Later we could really laugh about it. At one of the early Monkey Inn gigs, this drunk guy was standing in front of the stage, and he looked up at Tom and his tambourine and screamed, "You're *useless!*" It was drunken affirmation, a badge of honor that Tom could stand up there and be useless.

There was a lot of beer drinking at the Monkey Inn. In the back of the bar there was a partial wall, and over the top of it you could see the people playing shuffleboard. And whenever we played "Blue Suede Shoes," a fight would break out. You'd see the light over the shuffleboard swinging back and forth. Then the bartender would have to run back there and get everybody calmed down. Until we played "Blue Suede Shoes" again. We did it for our own amusement.

Talk about formative places. There's a habit I developed at the Monkey Inn that I had for the longest time: singing to the side, away from the audience. I had this cheap little mic plugged into my guitar amp, so I could use it for my PA as well as for my guitar. Sometimes watching the people would make me crack up, so I would look over and stare at the wall, singing sideways into the mic. Even in Creedence, I'd go up to the mic and sing sideways like that. It took me a long time to break that habit.

I played my cheap Supro guitar at the Monkey Inn. I didn't have a very good guitar or amp. My equipment was not professional. But somehow I sensed that this little gig at a dumpy little bar was a great opportunity for the future. Rather than just enduring the time spent there or using it as an excuse to party, I saw it as a way to gain experience for myself—and more importantly, a way to transform my little group of musical tourists into *a band*.

Throughout my two or three years at the Monkey Inn, I was learning an awful lot about how to play in front of a live audience. How to talk to a crowd. How the music affects the mood and energy of the audience. If you played the wrong song, it could really deflate the atmosphere. But if you chose the *right* songs, it would make the place soar, and the feeling could be magical. I learned to string songs together, to "take a journey with the music." Ah, man, the power of rock and roll!

During my growth as a guitar player and while thinking about style, I began to wonder about what Lead Belly had done with a twelve-string tuned down to D. That was so amazing. It was just... *the sound*. Rock and roll guys learn to play the E chord pretty quickly. A lot of great songs have been in that key. The Lead Belly sound is a whole step lower than that. You didn't hear it very often. And still don't! And the key to that basically was a guitar tuned low.

In about the ninth grade, I bought a cheap twelve-string guitar and tuned it that way. An acoustic guitar—I think it was a Harmony. It wasn't amplified, so I got a special sound hole pickup—I think it was a DeArmond—a big fat thing, and I'd play maybe one song. I can't recall what, but I'll bet it was closer to Lead Belly than the Orlons.

By the time of the Monkey Inn, I was using that guitar as a feedback thing. I had a volume pedal. Sometimes it had a separate amp, and sometimes it was the same amp my guitar was plugged into, the idea being that I could step on the volume pedal and activate the twelve-string, which is just sitting there tuned to a D chord, or maybe just tuned normally but down a whole step. And it would start to feed back instantly, because there's a drum beating and all this resonant stuff going on. The volume pedal cranked it louder—*AooOOOooOOO!* It was in that rock and roll tradition: a hellacious cacophony of sound. Where people go, "What *is* that?"

It had that kind of effect, like in a Little Richard song where Richard lets out a *"WAAAAAAH!"* just before the sax comes in. "Be-Bop-a-Lula," one of my favorite records, did that. There's a break and the drummer just *screams "WAAAAAAA!"* Much later, I learned that when Owen Bradley recorded that song, the band was making such a racket that they moved the drummer farther and farther away, and finally he was in the doorway, but they could *still* hear him screaming. Owen Bradley turns to the engineer and says, "Why does he have to do that?!" The answer: "Because he's fifteen years old!" And Bradley let it be that way. That's the thing in rock and roll: it's wacky, but it makes sense. Feedback was my way to plug into that.

I also invented my own fuzz tone with a set of World War II army surplus headphones. There were two earpieces, and each one could function either as a speaker or a microphone. So I stuck the two earpieces together, wrapping them in duct tape, tin foil, and a piece of my old flannel pajamas, and put this inside a small coffee can. I wired one to an "input" jack and the other to an "output" jack mounted on the can.

To make this work, I would plug my guitar into an amplifier with the output of the amp going to the "input" on the coffee can. As I turned up the amp, that headphone would distort like crazy. The other earpiece would act like a microphone, sending that distorted sound to the "output" on the can. I could then plug that sound into a normal guitar amp, and voilà: distorted fuzz tone guitar. I had that for three or four years. Nowadays you just plug into a box to get that sound, but back then it was a revelation (although I listened to "Walk on the Water" recently, and if that's what I used, it's pretty awful and shrill—I had nothing to compare it to then).

There was nothing like the Monkey Inn for experimentation. We could develop as a band and there wasn't a lot of pressure yet. We just had to present fun. They were having a fight back there anyway. I still chuckle when I hear "Blue Suede Shoes."

For the longest time, the single we recorded for Fantasy just didn't come out. It was a lifetime to us kids. Finally, in November of 1964, Max told Tom, "Come on over. We have your record." At that time we were still the Blue Velvets. Either Max didn't like "Blue Velvets" or, now that we were a quartet, he wanted a new group name. So we called ourselves the Visions, right? Which to me always sounded like that guy in "Earth Angel" who sang "da vision." As in math. So for, like, five minutes we were the Visions.

Tom, Doug, and I drive over to San Francisco. "Where's our record? Where's our record?" Max gives us a box of twenty-five singles. Now, we're expecting our new name to be on the label: the Visions. But we pop open the box and the label says...the Golliwogs. We say, "Oh man, somebody really screwed up here!"

Max tells us he didn't like our new name, the Visions. It wasn't interesting enough. So in a stealth, surreptitious move of intrigue, he had named us the Golliwogs. "We're trying to have you guys be like the British Invasion here. So we wanted to give you a hip-sounding name. Mod. It's mod."

"Yeah, Max, mod. Okay. But what is a golliwog?"

"Well, way back during a war that England had with some other country during the colonial British Empire days—"

"Yeah, Max. What's that got to do with us?"

"Well, the British soldiers would interact with the people of the country that they were actually trying to conquer. So the people in that country made these little dolls that had fuzzy hair and black faces—kind of like a voodoo doll."

"Oh, okay."

"The British soldiers got to calling these dolls wogs. Like a golliwog. And sometimes they even called the people golliwogs or wogs. So this little voodoo doll is a really important thing in British history. See, we want you guys to seem like you're British—part of the hip, British musical invasion!"

"But Max—we come from El Cerrito."

So we went home very disgruntled. And dozens of times later, we would find ourselves reenacting this rationale as we had heard it in Max Weiss's office.

"John?"

"Yes, Mom?"

"I thought you guys were the Blue Velvets?"

"Yeah, see, Mom, they named us after this doll..."

For the rest of the time that we were the Golliwogs, we had to explain the name to every single person that ever heard our music. And everybody's telling you, "Well, that's dumb!" So you might say it was a very self-limiting—and perhaps self-fulfilling—prophecy. If you have to explain a marketing device, then you're barking up the wrong tree. Kind of like Edsel.

We hated the name. We felt helpless. And our first single came and went. My goal was to somehow figure out how to be a great band and make a great record. Max was no help. I'd be at the microphone hearing all these things Max was telling us, things that were about as applicable as that Golliwog doll: "How about you put on a British accent?" Or "Put on a 'Yeah, yeah, yeah.'" Or "Get that sound on your guitar that George does." Just weird, from-left-field advice from an older person.

I was feeling frustrated. We were desperately trying to figure out how this works. And I'm realizing some of the shortcomings of our sound and our approach. At one point I remember looking across the microphone at whoever was there and saying, "Well, I guess Phil Spector's not gonna come down here and produce us."

What that really meant was, I'm going to have to figure out

what producing is. And do it. I was expressing it out loud. I said it for my compadres in the room. Because I was only pulling for the band. I never ever thought of myself any other way through all the years I was in it.

So after that, I was a producer. I didn't get credit for it, of course. Max got some kid and named him our producer, ha ha. But what this really meant was that I began to think of the finished record at the moment of conception. I learned to envision the sound of the instruments and the style of the arrangement as I was writing the song, sometimes letting that vision guide the writing process. This is quite different from how a singer-songwriter creates. Usually, the writer is preoccupied with words and melody and his focus is on completing the song. He leaves the record making to someone else.

This syndrome of recognizing a needed service or function — and then assigning that task to myself — happened over and over on our journey through showbiz.

I finally got to tell Phil Spector that story, by the way. In the eighties I had gone to one of the Rock and Roll Hall of Fame's secret inner sanctum meetings to try to get my hero Duane Eddy included. And who should happen to be sitting next to me but Phil Spector. I told him my Golliwogs story. He got a big kick out of that. As a matter of fact, two or three years later it was Phil who called to tell me that Duane Eddy had gotten into the hall of fame.

Tom sang lead on our first single, "Little Girl (Does Your Mamma Know?)," and I sang harmony with him on the other side, "Don't Tell Me No Lies." On the next single, "Where You Been," Tom sang the lead again, and on the B side, "You Came Walking," I harmonized again. We weren't quite good enough to pull that one off — with a little higher level of musicianship and a George Martin behind us, I think it would've been cool. One side of our third single was "You Can't Be True." The other side was "You Got

Nothin' on Me." I sang lead on both of these. They were bluesy, edgy—more like me. More like how I had sounded in Portland than this sweet, mellow thing that Tom was always doing.

I had never heard Tom sing rough. But by the time I had come out the other end of that trip to Portland, I wanted my music to have more of an edge, be more raw. There seemed to be an audience for a more bluesy approach to rock, and we kind of got into that— certainly the Stones had more of that. It was less doo-wop and a lot more growl from Mick Jagger and the boys. You'd see these other British bands, what they were doing—I thought we should follow that path, rather than bongos and tambourines. There seemed to be a model for us to grab on to and push forward with.

So I sang our next single, "Brown-Eyed Girl," and went in that direction. I just thought it was a much more viable style than that other Bobby Freeman kind of sound that we'd done with Tom, which I felt was dated, passé. "Little Girl," the piano, doing doo-wop...it just seemed old-fashioned. And when you're a kid, that's fatal—"Whew, that's *two years* ago!" I was trying to catch up... or get ahead!

"Brown-Eyed Girl" was a regional hit. It was big in California's Central Valley, starting in San Jose. And it enabled the Golliwogs to actually start getting some local musical dates. We'd work Turlock, Merced, Roseville, Modesto, Marysville, playing school dances and National Guard armories.

We'd have these jobs way up in the northern part of central California or way down south—Tom and me in one car, Doug and Stu in the other. Later we graduated to a Volkswagen bus that had been owned by the Du-All floor company—it was still painted that way. Our gig would be over at one or two in the morning, and we'd drive home in the night listening to Wolfman Jack on XERB. Wow, what great memories I have of that! Wolfman Jack was so great. He was broadcasting on a radio station from Mexico, and I guess the normal U.S. transmitter regulations didn't apply. His transmitter was something like 250,000 watts (or more), and you could hear that station all over the United States.* The Wolfman played R & B–leaning rock and roll, and it was presented with much urgency. Kind of like you were peeking into a hidden vein of music that no one else knew about. Records like "Mystic Eyes," "It's All Over Now, Baby Blue," and "Gloria" by Them; "Up in Heah" by Junior Wells; "You're Gonna Miss Me" by the 13th Floor Elevators; "Are You Lonely for Me" by Freddie Scott; "Keep On Running" by the Spencer Davis Group; and "Try a Little Tenderness" by Otis Redding. When he got really excited, the Wolfman would do kind of a pep-talk rap and then play the werewolf howl. It was frantic and *great!* Tom and I really looked forward to those rides home.

Now that we were doing some real concerts, we needed clothes. The four of us went somewhere, maybe the Haight-Ashbury. Max from Fantasy was probably there too. We were young people with no real experience buying clothes, trying to dress currently. And Max was telling us what was hip. In one store there were these big, shaggy, white fur hats—Himalayan yak hats. Hard to say now who they were for—women? Bald-headed guys? Sherpas? But we bought 'em.

When we'd come out wearing our big white hats, some would snicker and laugh. "Here's the Golliwogs!" We were *those* guys. Always going to be a local band. Later on there'd be a point of just ripping that furry hat off and throwing it in the audience, or at somebody. I think at least one of us threw his out in the audience. I know I don't have mine. Because I hated it.

---

* I sent away for a Wolfman Jack photo that you could iron onto a T-shirt. When it arrived I was disappointed. It was a cartoon drawing of a hipster wolf.

But something was working, and we opened for Sonny and Cher at the Memorial Auditorium in Sacramento. That's the place where Keith Richards got knocked unconscious when his guitar made contact with a wrongly wired mic. (When I stood in that exact same space, I always got shocked there as well.) Sonny and Cher were the big time: "I Got You Babe."

So we do our set, and by God, there's such cheering going on that we're going to get to do an encore. Outstanding! They open the curtain. We come out doing "Walking the Dog." We did it more funky, like Rufus Thomas. We're rockin' away when suddenly—*whoosh!*—the curtain closes again! *What?*

It turned out that "Walking the Dog" was Cher's very first number, the first number of Sonny and Cher's set. Ixnay! I'm sure it would've been all right—she's Cher and we're not. But no, they used the big hammer. Our moment was stolen from us.

How does a band survive that kind of crap? You keep on. Our ragged "Brown-Eyed Girl" was progress, a step up. "You Better Get It Before It Gets You"—I like that one a lot. "Fight Fire" was another. Man, I don't know how I sang so high. The maracas on that record were inspired by the Bell Notes song "I've Had It." We saw the band on TV, and the drummer played them. I loved that record. "Fight Fire" is a pretty cool little song. That's our best British Invasion imitation.

Sometimes we'd take a step back because our ambition was too grand, or maybe we went left a little bit, doing something off character, but it seemed like things were getting better and better as we moved along. The guys were learning their instruments a bit as we played more and more. And our songs—the ones we wrote and the covers we played our own way—were starting to sound like "us," getting closer to that thing where it sounds "right."

Now, I'm not saying the Golliwogs were very good—it was not a real band yet, commanding a stage. We were lightweight, thin. We were just kids. But hey, we'd gotten the hook opening for

Sonny and Cher! And it was a fun time. It was so innocent. We're not making it, we're not hitting the big time, but maybe, just maybe, we... *could*.

There were big changes in my life at this time. In 1965 I got married. I had met Martha Paiz while I was working at the gas station. She'd come in with her sister and her sister's boyfriend. I started talking to Martha that way. We were children when we got married. I was twenty years old. Martha proposed to me. I don't remember the exact words—"We should get married" or something like that. I had a typical male response: "Uhhh... okay."

There really ought to be a law. Probably one out of ten of those marriages is going to work. At eighteen, Tom had left home and married his high school sweetheart, so there was some precedent in my immediate family. I was also tossed out of my house by my mom—"Just go there!," meaning over to Martha's. She wanted to be done with raising a feisty boy.

My mom even declared that I had to pay rent if I wanted to stay at home. That's something Julie and I have vowed not to say to our kids. Both of our parents booted us out.

My mom and I had sort of an estranged relationship after that. I think she saw Creedence only once, in Oakland. (Although Mom was the one who told me that Chet Atkins played "Proud Mary" with the Boston Pops. I detected that she was proud of that—and so was I!)

Martha's family was very much a family. She had a whole bunch of brothers and sisters, a large family, and when I'd go over and hang at their house, it was a real warm and happy feeling. There was this sense of closeness, whereas my house had just been depressing. So that had a lot of appeal to me. I moved right out of my home and into married life.

And then I got drafted.

CHAPTER 6

Dirty Little Wars

IN 1966, VIETNAM was on every young person's mind. The draft loomed large. We'd start to talk about it and ask each other, "Well, why are we in Vietnam?" And we'd go around and around and around and never really have a good answer.

In the early stages of the conflict, I was more gung ho, thinking that's what America should do. But the reasoning started sounding more and more flimsy. Most of it was just a sham: a couple of egocentric politicians too full of themselves to listen to their own people, and who had the incredible arrogance to send our young kids off to die. My generation just thought it was the most sorry, useless exercise that our country could be involved in, and we were powerless to stop this stupid thing but trying our darnedest through protests, music, and all the rest.

At the time, I really didn't understand all the implications, but as I got older, I began to feel that the war (and probably most every war that's ever been fought) wasn't actually about the flag: it was about a very small group of rich, powerful people, usually men, who were able to bamboozle a nation to go to war for some myth that they had created. This gets shrouded in patriotism, but it basically comes down to money. Making a profit. Vietnam was surely about that.

Regrettably, it's become a familiar story: the powers that be prey on the patriotic feelings of our youth, young people who have very noble ideals and want to go out and do what they assume are good things. But in situations like this, they're just being manipulated. That's the part that really makes me mad—even now, because I believe that the wars we're in are not for the good of America or the American people. Just for some businessmen to make a lot of money.

To use American citizens—basically kids—to fight and die for big corporations so they can make billions of dollars is just shameful. And to present it as if it's some patriotic thing, when it's just because a gas company wants to monopolize the market in another part of the world, or some big steel company wants to build all the buildings and bridges there—to have people die for that?

But I wasn't thinking about this back before I was drafted. I wasn't even going to be drafted—I was classified 4-F, meaning unfit for service. That was a good thing. I know a lot of people would say, "God, how unpatriotic. You're supposed to go out and fight for Uncle Sam." I'm sure in some quarters there are folks who will have strong feelings about what I'm saying. It'll strike some as vaguely un-American, even cowardly. I get that. Now, had I been around in the wake of Pearl Harbor, I'm quite certain I would've felt differently. But Vietnam was something else. Most of us felt that if you got drafted, you were going to Vietnam. And if you went, you were probably going to die. It didn't feel like, "Oh, here's my chance to be a hero for my country!" Being drafted, you could just immediately see the other end of it. So I received my 4-F classification, and I was smiling.

A couple of months went by before they sent a letter saying,

"Oops! We made a mistake. You've been reclassified. You are 1-A." And after that I got my draft notice.

I lost my job at the gas station because I told the manager the news, and he still said, "John, you have to come into work today." I said, "Al, I just got drafted! In thirty days I'm gone! I have to go out and see if there's anything I can do." So I was fired.

I went out looking at the Army Reserve and National Guard in the Bay Area, but they were full and couldn't take any more people. I came home from one of those days a little distraught, and my wife, Martha, told me she had called a reserves unit. There must've been something in her voice talking to that sergeant down at the Army Reserve, because he told her, "You just tell him to come on down here." I told him my story and he signed me up. He must have put a certain date on my papers—perhaps a date that was earlier than when I received my draft notice—so that I had officially signed up *before* I got my notice. I was now in the Army Reserve. I never actually got to thank that guy again. He was an awesome, soulful person.

The first time I went on active duty was at a two-week summer boot camp. One sergeant in particular just liked the sound of my name. "Hey, *Fo-ger-ty!*" "Where's *Fogerty?*" I got...noticed. And I didn't like it. There could be a group of fifty guys standing there, and you'd hear, *"Hey Fogerty!"* It was horrible. I was called every time.

So when I went on my six-month active-duty boot camp, I had learned my lesson. Don't do anything where you're straggling behind, don't do anything where you're stepping out ahead—just be in the group. Man, be somewhere in the shadows. Try to be invisible. Once the sergeant snags your name, you're toast.

So that's what I did. I became a model of responsibility. Unlike many other times in my life where I had been a flake (such as playing hooky for weeks), I remade myself into the company man. They had all this stuff you have to do: have your bunk made the right way, have all your clothes exact, your uniform spotless. It's good training, good discipline. And I did it exactly right—all of it. I was on the A-list.

After a couple of weeks, I got assigned as a barracks leader and was put in charge of a row of bunks. The guy over us noticed that I was getting it done, and by putting me in charge, he had a lot less to do. So I would be after my guys: put your toothbrush away, your shoe-shining kit, your underwear. Everything had to be in a specific spot, and I made sure it was.

I'd have all my ducks in a row. I was terrified of being caught, frankly. I didn't want them to ever notice me again. Which I think was a good philosophy, but the other guys got to calling me Ma Fogerty. It was with some affection and respect, but they might as well have called me Old Man Fogerty. They thought I was acting like somebody's parent! But it kept us out of trouble. We were all twenty years old, kids, and liked rock and roll. There's that whole sense of, yes, you're in the military, but you're twenty, not fifty. But I didn't want to be snagged. Once you're on the shit list, you're not coming off. I learned my lesson the first time.

When I came back from active duty, I still had my once-a-month reserve meetings and, every summer, two-week boot camp obligations. All of that was going to last another four or five years. And I kept having conflicts. My monthly weekend meeting was in Richmond. I'd have to be there at 7 a.m. after doing a gig four hours north in Roseville the night before. I overslept a couple of times and the sergeant called me up: "You want me to send you to *Vietnam?*" That was the threat they held over you. I knew I couldn't let it happen again or they'd send me.

I very earnestly tried to work something out. I wanted to come in during the week and I wanted to have long hair. I was the quartermaster supply clerk, and I could've easily done my job during the week. And of course the answer came back, "*No*, we can't have any of *that*." They were pretty rigid.

At certain times in my life I can get pretty tough mentally—it's just a matter of focusing, I guess. Once I really had the door slammed in my face by the army and realized that they weren't going to entertain some other approach, I decided that I was going to resist, go against the grain. And try to get myself removed from the reserve. But in the calmest way possible.

I started fasting. Like prisoners on strike or Buddha fasting under a fig tree. During this time, the Golliwogs played a show at the Claremont Hotel, and I was on my fast, hardly eating anything. I remember staring at a table of lemon meringue desserts, but no—I didn't take one. I had a brain of steel. This was a very volatile time in America, with all kinds of confrontation and conflicts and philosophies floating across the cultural windscreen. People chaining themselves to government buildings. If I had to chain myself to an army building, I was prepared.

I wrote honestly about my plight to my congressman, Jerome Waldie—yes, I brought it to Jerome—and he was pretty helpful. That carried a lot of weight. He started kicking tires around the Army Reserve unit. That got their attention. They don't like the people's representatives peeking in the window at all their shit.

I became skinny as a rail, and because of the stink I was raising, the army made me go to the Presidio in San Francisco for an evaluation. My friends in the band gave me herbs to imbibe, supposedly to calm me down and make me weird. I was not a big pot smoker, yet there I was, driving across the Bay Bridge, smoking a joint on my way to be evaluated by the army. All I can say is, it wasn't my idea and the Big Lebowski would have been proud.

I told the evaluator that I was very upset and didn't agree with the war. I didn't sleep very well. By now Martha and I had an infant son, and I had experienced a couple of dreams where I was literally stabbing babies with a bayonet. I told the evaluator I'd lost a lot of weight. He said, "Well, how's your libido?" I didn't know what that meant. I looked at him and said, "What's a libido?" I think the fact that I was that stupid—and that I didn't have a big, long, over-the-top scenario, wasn't really there with a prepared case—might've swayed the day a little in my favor.

I saw a lawyer. I remember writing to various causes, even the Black Panthers. I was trying anything I could think of. I even showed up at boot camp with a syringe. Just planted it in my stuff, waiting to be found. I might've got it from Martha's mom because she worked in nursing. It was new, unused, and I didn't have what went with it. It was more just to be scary—"What's *this*, Private Fogerty?" If they had actually said, "Okay, tell us what you do with that," I wouldn't have had a clue!

The head of our reserve unit was this guy, Lieutenant Ritzman. He was a second looey—typical military guy. I think Ritzman was in the reserves, just like me, but he took it way more seriously. A real brownnoser. We had this big meeting, almost like a social get-together, semicasual, and he's doing armyspeak. A pep talk. We're kids—he's late twenties, I'm barely twenty—and he starts by quoting *Laugh-In*, I guess to be hip. Then he says, "America has a counterculture and the army has to tread carefully. As you folks know, there's been a lot of demonstrations, protests. Civil disobedience. Unruly crowds. Where we will have to control the situation, not let it get out of hand. So when we arrive, we don't want to be doing our formations out in the open. We will go around to a side street..."

Slowly it's dawning on all of us that he's talking about using the U.S. Army (and perhaps our reserve unit) to keep protesters in line, keep people down. The idea was to get into formation, out of sight from the disturbance, and then come around the corner in full force as an organized show of military muscle. At the time, I think it was illegal to use the army for that. We have a National Guard for internal domestic emergencies. He kept talking like this for fifteen minutes.

Finally, I raised my hand and stood up. I'm feeling somewhat cynical and sarcastic. We've all seen pictures of Red Square. You know, the Soviet Union parading its military might around the Kremlin for all to see and be intimidated. So I said, "Why don't we just have the military parade all our rockets and tanks down the main street of every major city, y'know, like, once a month? Just show 'em the army's muscle, our might. I think that would keep people in their place." I sat down.

You could see the steam coming out of Ritzman's ears. After that, I showed up at my reserve meeting with my gray Peugeot 403 plastered with signs I had made. "Warning—the Army Is Coming!" "The Velvet Glove Is Off, the Iron Fist Is Revealed!" Well, they noticed.

"Susie Q" was already happening, and with the guys in tow, I took the same leaflets down Macdonald Avenue, the main street of Richmond, near where we lived, and started taping these things onto telephone poles and streetlights. We get about two blocks and a cop car pulls up. We get arrested and taken to the Richmond city jail. It's illegal to post signs on the light fixtures. The officer could barely contain himself. He was a patriot; we were long-haired hippie types. They held us there a few hours. I think our one phone call was to Al Bendich, the lawyer at Fantasy.

These activities started to weigh in my favor. Eventually I saw this guy, Mr. Legere, at the Presidio. He was on the army base and part of the military, yet he was a civilian. And Mr. Legere was a good guy. The first time I sat in his office and told him my tale, there was one thing he said that blew my mind: "Wow, it's rather like a story by Camus." I'd been in the army awhile and had never met anybody like that. I could sense that Mr. Legere was willing to help because I think he respected how I was going about it. I wasn't a wacko. Even though I was against the war—I think he was too—I was clearly just trying to support my family. He could sense that I was trying to do right, trying to find a way to work within the system.

This process went on for several months. I was never sure how it would all turn out, but I kept trying everything I could think of. Of course, I had to keep going to reserve meetings and treading carefully through these treacherous waters. I believe I met with Mr. Legere at least one more time at the Presidio, and we spoke by phone several times throughout this ordeal.

It was starting to get near summertime, and they were going to send me to camp again, this time to Camp Roberts. I was even skinnier now. Mr. Legere seemed to think we were getting close to a discharge for me, and we were feeling hopeful about that. But one day he tells me, "I think it would be a good idea if you could get a medical to avoid that camp this summer, because you know what's going to happen if you go."

He was right, of course. There was going to be a great *big* bull's-eye on my back—"There's that wimp that's trying to get out of the reserve. Let's get him."

I went to my doctor at Kaiser Permanente. They needed to do all these blood tests. I hate shots and having my blood taken, but I sat there like a good soldier while they took vial after vial of my blood. They needed to take thirteen vials, and I thought they were done, but I had miscounted. Feeling a little woozy from losing blood, I heard them say, "Oh no, we're not done—we need to take *one* more..." I just sorta crumbled onto the tabletop and lost consciousness. At that point, I think I weighed 129 pounds.

Turned out I had a mild form of dysentery. The report said, "If you turn this guy loose in the camp, it's not so much what it's gonna do to him, it's what he's gonna do to everybody else! You're all gonna get sick. This thing will spread like wildfire." Thank you, Mr. Legere. Sometime in midsummer of 1968 I received my discharge, and as far as me being in the army, that was that. My army days were over.

There was a time when I could barely talk about Vietnam. Since I was lucky enough to get into the reserve, I wasn't sent to Vietnam. I wasn't in combat. There was such an anxiety in those years over whether or not I was ever really going to go. I managed not to. But I was and still feel very much a part of that generation, and the whole thing that was going on all around us. Yeah, maybe I looked like a hippie wacko, but as a guy in a rock and roll band who was exactly the same age as those soldiers, I tried to represent the cause as best I knew how. It would just bring me to my knees, it was so sad and very real to me. I must admit that practically every time I'd think about the guys, our vets, I would cry. I'd hear "Where Have All the Flowers Gone" on the radio and would lose it. Because it was just so senseless.

I know of so many people whose lives were ended or ruined, families that lost a kid. Let alone all the broken lives that came home—"Why is Daddy so fucked up?" People having flashbacks who can't talk about it, won't talk about it. All that carnage and fear. I know how I felt about Richard Nixon grinning at me through the damn TV screen like some kind of clown, calling the protesters at Kent State "bums." Where was Richard Nixon when our soldiers were out in a rice paddy? Those soldiers were pretty much just thrown out there on their own to improvise. Hopeless. I still feel sorrowful about those times.

I remember that day in 1974 when it came on the radio that we had ended the war in Vietnam—well, we were withdrawing. The thing we had been telling Nixon to do for five years: just *leave*. He didn't want to be the only president who had ever lost a war, so the damn fool had said to push on (just like in the song). Now it was finally over. I was driving in my jeep and had stopped at a light, and I can remember just shaking my head and going, "Let's just make damn sure we never do somethin' that stupid again." As I looked through the windshield, this thought formed: *Y'know, I still don't know what we were fighting for.* Down through the years, I've wanted to have that be the last line of a song: "And they've still never told me what we were fighting for."

The real answer is, we were fighting for businessmen, fighting for guys to get rich. Not for me, not for my friends out there in the field, but for the guys who own companies wrapped up in military contracts, the guys paving the roads, building the buildings, making the bridges, and finding the oil—all that crap. Those people who want your kid to die so they can get rich. And if you look at our kids today, that's still pretty much what they are fighting for.

The Vietnam generation is aging but has remained soulful. In the nineties I was helping with a benefit for the Berkeley Hall School. This is where all our kids went to school. It was a sweet little place, and Julie and I tried to support it in whatever way we could. They were having an auction, and she decided that something special I could contribute was some autographed handwritten lyrics. So I wrote out the words to "Bad Moon Rising" and signed them. I usually print, since my handwriting is horrible, plus my signature's a mess—I don't have the John Hancock gift. So I worried about it.

The event arrives and we attend. I wonder how my little contribution turned out, so I go to have a look. It's been framed, and I'm standing there reassuring myself: "Okay, John, it's not that bad." And I feel the presence of somebody beside me, someone I don't know. He looks at the lyrics and says, "You're John, right? That's your song, 'Bad Moon Rising'?"

"Yes, sir," I say.

He says, "Your song means a lot to me."

"Really?"

"Yes. Can I tell you a little story? I was in Vietnam."

Now he's really got my attention. Nice-looking guy, dressed well, looks good.

"I was in a little group. We called ourselves the Buffalo Soldiers. We had a little encampment, and every night our assignment was to go out into the jungle, find Charlie, and engage Charlie."

The wheels are spinning in my head now.

"So we called ourselves the Buffalo Soldiers to kind of brace ourselves up. We had a little PA system and lights. Every night, just before we'd go out into the jungle, we would turn on all the lights in our encampment, put on 'Bad Moon Rising,' and blast it as loud as we could."

I'm looking at him, thinking, this was crazy—suicide. "Why did you do that?"

"Because we were about to go into the jungle."

"And you're announcing it?"

"Yep. 'Here we come.'"

And I thought to myself, *How profoundly courageous and fatalistic*. They knew they were doomed. Whose crazy idea was this assignment? Sometimes all is lost and all you can do is be brave. No matter how you feel about it, there's no other choice. These guys were being brave to the nth degree.

"Anyway, John, I just want to thank you, because your song really helped a lot of us in what we had to do over there."

I shook his hand. I wish I could remember his name. He had done what was asked of him and didn't cry or whine about it, as opposed to me. He had done something I didn't do, something I'm not sure I could've ever done. And he certainly had my respect.

In his heart he has a connection with that song and me. And to hear from others like him that my music helped them in some way, helped GIs endure what they had to go through? You feel a little sheepish in the presence of something like that. I sure wasn't taking any bows.

I just looked at him and said, "I'm really glad you made it through."

You could say that one good thing happened to me in the army. It was 1967, and I went on duty right at the end of January and didn't get out until July, one day before I would've qualified for all the benefits that the government can give you—"Okay, let's get his butt outta here. Otherwise he's gonna get the GI plan."

They drafted millions of guys and didn't know what to do with us. They're trying to keep you busy from the time they wake you up at five thirty in the morning until you finally get off at seven at night. They're keeping you moving the whole time. So you're marching, marching, marching every day.

I was sent to Fort Bragg, Fort Knox, and Fort Lee. By the time I got to Fort Lee, summer was raging. They had this massive, mile-square parade field made out of asphalt. The heat coming off that black asphalt felt like an oven, and you've got on your army fatigues, boots, and rifle, and you just march, march, march. You could go for miles. It was endless.

I started to get delirious. In the military, you try to make the toes of your boots shine like glass. Black glass. Shiny like an expensive car. You could see yourself in them. Spit shined. As I'm marching along, I imagine that there's this one smudge. This stinkin' smudge. I go to shine it, and it keeps moving—"I'm over here!" I'm rubbing it, but it moves and won't go away. I'm a little crazy at this point: delirious, rubbing, rubbing, rubbing. And somehow this evolved into thinking about music.

I started thinking about a story—a character from the wrong side of the tracks, sort of a put-upon guy, whose dad was frowned upon in the community because he may have stolen something, committed some kind of crime. It was me, but it wasn't me. Not specifically my own life, but enough of me in there. It could've been a Tennessee Williams play.

I kept doing this, day after day. I'd kind of click on the station in my head, and the same story would start to play. It was comfortable...soothing. "Okay, I'm going there. Okay." March, march, march. Grunt, grunt, grunt. At some point I became self-aware. At first it was like you're swimming in a stream — your mind is so busy that you don't realize what you're doing. You're just trying to survive. "The army thinks they have me but they don't. They don't have *what's in my mind.*"

I thought, *Man, you're onto something here. This is better than "Have you ever been lonely, have you ever been blue, boo, hoo, hoo,"* and all the teenage angst songs I had known. This was more meaty, it had some serious stuff in it, and it resonated with how I *felt.* And I realized, *I'm writing a song.* It was music. That song eventually became "Porterville."

I think more people listen to "Porterville" and identify with the guy who feels like he's on the wrong side of the tracks than with the mob that came and took his dad away to serve his time. They probably don't want to be the lawmen. They probably don't want to be the dad in the song. In other words, the character telling the story — he's the common man. A perspective. How I look at the world. Which runs pretty much throughout all the songs I write, or at least the good ones. Because "Porterville" really is how I look at the world, and have for a long time. That's where I'm comin' from, as people say. It isn't made up, it isn't a fairy tale, it's not fake. I might take poetic license describing a situation, but the personal truth, the truth of my station in life, is in there.

You'll notice I never say "Porterville" in the song. I wanted it to be a small town. I could've named it "Merced." Or "Turlock." I just wanted a certain feel to it and eventually found Porterville, and that sounded *exactly* right.

So this thing I did while I was marching in the army really became my first narrative song. Something was coming into my head—it was above me, it was above anything I had done before. It had a scene in it, a place that felt right to me, an emotion about why something is right or wrong. It was *about* something. I hadn't done anything like this before.

It's one thing the army did give me that will last a lifetime.

It was a new way of looking at a song.

CHAPTER 7

Susie Q

WHEN I CAME off active duty in the summer of 1967, the band had a different frame of mind. Before I went into the army, we weren't great, particularly with the timing issues—"What's a shuffle beat?" Before that, practicing was something we did to learn a new song or when we were getting ready to record. Now we were going to be more serious. We decided—all four of us— that we wanted to start getting good. So we made a regimen of practicing every day. This was maybe going to be our last fling at this big dream.

Doug and Stu had moved in together, kind of out in the country, in El Sobrante. They had rented a little house that was actually painted pink. And because of a certain book, they called it the Shire. I remember rehearsing "Good Golly, Miss Molly" there, and "Ninety-Nine and a Half (Won't Do)." And, of course, "Susie Q."*

Every day Tom and I would drive out together. We'd sit, drink

---

* Later we rehearsed in Tom's garage. The El Cerrito police showed up because we were so loud. Then we moved to a little shack behind the house, where Doug lived with his wife. I remember working on "Midnight Special" there. Eventually the cops showed up there too.

coffee for half an hour, and talk—most of it about music, a little about politics: Eugene McCarthy, the Vietnam War, Nixon. That was good, motivational.

And we'd talk about records we'd heard. One album that had come out while I was in the army was Albert King's *Born Under a Bad Sign*. Here was Booker T. and the MGs, my favorite band, backing this guy that I hadn't heard much about before. Albert was so awesome on that record, and the band played with such command. We all loved it. I bet that happened countless times— musicians my age taking note of *Born Under a Bad Sign*. Cream certainly did. We kind of adopted that as a high-water mark. Unbelievably enough, a little over one year later Albert King would be opening for us at the Fillmore.

We were deep into a pretty healthy time for the band. We were gung ho. Tom made a statement: "John is our leader. When John says, 'Jump,' we should say, 'How high?'" It was acknowledged that I seemed to have a clearer idea of what we should be doing musically, because not only was I able to sing, but I understood the music enough that I could teach. This was different from a bunch of guys showing up who could already play. It was clear that I knew how the instruments should sound. My arrangements of songs and my own playing and singing had become more focused too, and I was having more visions of the future. Because with everybody trying, I had the belief that we could actually achieve our dream. All this is happening within months, really.

In August, I started telling the band, "Something's gonna happen in October." Now, I had no clue. I didn't have any inside information. But the notion just kept coming to me and I kept saying it: "Something's gonna happen in October, and it's gonna change things."

And what happened was this: Saul Zaentz, along with some backers, bought Fantasy away from the Weiss brothers. Saul called us to a meeting at his house in early October 1967 and said,

"I have just purchased Fantasy Records, and I want to sign you guys." Saul seemed like our friend. He had been the sales manager at Fantasy. Whenever we would come in, we'd see Saul at his desk, and he struck us as less crazy than the others. He seemed to be our ally. Now Saul was going to be the guy in charge, and he wanted to give us a real shot.

So the first thing out of our mouths was, "Can we change our name?" And that is the way it happened, because there is no other way. I've read that Saul takes credit for that. We said it to him first, because we *hated* being Golliwogs.

So Saul said, "Yeah, of course."

We asked, "Can we finally go and make a real record in a real studio? Not in the lean-to?"

And he said, "Yeah, I think that'll be all right." Then he added, "I want us to have a new contract because I'm gonna be the new owner, and I don't want the Weiss brothers saying you're under contract to them."

We all looked at each other. We felt like we had been working a lot harder now. Our intent wasn't to keep doing it the way Max Weiss had done it. We wanted to change our name and make a living at this. We were all still poor as church mice. The idea of actually "making it" was such a faraway concept that nobody even knew what that would mean — but it might have meant getting a song on the radio. Or making enough money off a record to buy a new car. Y'know, like a hit group! Like the Beatles or something!

Doug Clifford said to Saul, "What if we make it, and we're successful?"

Saul said, "I will tear up that contract and we will get a new contract."

I'm sure Doug remembers that to this day, because it was kind of addressed to him. And us. That was Saul's response: we will tear the contract up. I think he added, "We all share equally in this thing." We felt that Saul was our partner. He was penniless, broke, driving a five-year-old station wagon, and operating Fantasy out of that car. So the way Saul explained it to us was that we were part of the business. We were not just that stupid group called the Golliwogs; we were now partners making this business go. That's how we all felt, this group of five people. All for one and one for all. We *were* Fantasy Records. There was not another living soul there. We were it.

Almost instantly, we started trying to think up a new name for the band. All I can say is that most of them were pretty dreadful. We'd sit around at these coffee sessions: "How about...?" I remember Stu called me up one day and suggested the name Hardwood. I think Doug came up with Gossamer Wump and Gumby.

Tom was the one who suggested the word "credence." Our friend Jerry lived in an apartment building where the custodian was named Credence Nuball. He was South African—it was his real name. So Tom suggested we name our band Credence Nuball and the Ruby. I thought of the name Whiskey Rebellion, and for, like, a minute I liked it. It had a kind of funky sound to me, obviously reflecting my love of history—especially American history. Also, I really liked the idea of our band having a renewal, a resurgence. Whiskey Revival? That wasn't any better than the rest. If some guy comes up and hands you a lug nut, it's up to you to say, "No, I'm not going to be a lug nut." I knew I'd know the right name when I heard it. So for almost three months we kept coming up with names and rejecting them.

Then, on Christmas Eve of 1967, I was watching TV and this commercial for Olympia Beer came on in glorious color. The image was this wonderful enchanted forest with a bubbling brook, everything green and mossy. Their motto was "It's the water." I'm pretty sure it was the Beach Boys singing beautifully in the background. The very next thing that came on was a black-and-white public service announcement for clean water. An antipollution commercial—a concept that was just starting to fly in America. It showed a stream full of cigarette butts and Styrofoam cups, and on the screen it said, "Write to CLEAN WATER," and it gave a Washington, DC, address.

Even though it plainly said "clean water," my mind turned it into "clear water." *Clearwater.* Wow...I liked that. It sounded kind of Native American. I had a great love for their lore and history, and for figures like Geronimo, Sitting Bull, Crazy Horse, and Chief Joseph.

Right there I went back to the word "revival." Clearwater Revival. That just wasn't quite...unique enough. This was all happening in a nanosecond.

Suddenly the word "Creedence" came to me. "Creedence" meant credibility, belief—it had a spiritual sound. "Clearwater" instantly had a *positive* vibe, a point of view, a sense of history, culture, Americana. My mind was racing, a million thoughts at once. Somehow the words "Creedence" and "Revival" were swirling around in this tumbling torrent of thoughts. I'm not sure in which order the words were first connected, but I do remember that I had to juggle them around a bit. Was it Clearwater Creedence or Clearwater Revival? This was all happening in a matter of a few seconds, maybe a minute or two. Suddenly it just popped: Creedence Clearwater Revival. I *loved* it. But I thought, *Wow, that's a mouthful.* It sounded even more American. It told you this was an American rock and roll band, and it was unique. So that's how it all kind of clanged together in my head.

Then I had to sell it. I knew the personalities in my band well enough to know that I had to not take ownership of the name. It had to look like it was in the air and just happened. The other guys were not all that sure. I'd write it out—"See how that looks?" I think Tom might've convinced them. No more Golliwogs. We were now Creedence Clearwater Revival.

I remember telling the guys at the time, "The name is better than we are." We were a Top 40 band playing clubs. Playing more distinctly than we had a year ago, but still kind of messy. Not organized, not powerful.

But by February I had come up with the idea of recording "Susie Q."

In January 1968, we signed the new contract with Fantasy Records that Saul Zaentz had requested. Sometime after that October meeting at Saul's house, he gave me the contract and I took it back to the band. We had agreed that in Creedence every band decision had to be a unanimous one. If one person said no, the matter was vetoed.

Now, I wasn't the most sophisticated guy in the world, and I knew that I could read that contract until the end of time and not know what it meant. We didn't have any legal representation—it was just us four guys. Stu was a business major, and his dad, Herman, was a prominent Bay Area attorney. So we all decided to give the contract to Stu so Herm could look it over.

One thing I've learned over the years is that when you are trying to make a deal with another entity, there is back and forth dialogue over the contract. You negotiate—it's expected. They propose something; you send it back with a counteroffer. The lawyers haggle, hopefully with input from you, and an agreement is eventually reached. I didn't know that then, but a prestigious attorney like Herman Cook certainly would have. That's the very reason we asked Stu to take the contract to him. So that should've been done for us. It wasn't. We were too dumb to know anything about that—all of us. I mention this because in the years since, Stu has been in the press talking about what a terrible businessman I was, and how I messed it all up for the group—*Boy, did John ef up*. Ironically, it was business major Stu who was supposed to get input from his lawyer father. Herm's only supposed advice was that it was okay to sign—no additions, no revisions, nothing.

Over the years, I have often wondered if Stu even showed the contract to his father.

About two weeks later, the band was at the Shire, loading up equipment for a show that night, and we were passing each other, carrying guitars, amplifiers, and drums. I remember this scene vividly, as I have replayed it many times in my mind.

One of us said, "Hey, Stu!"

Stu said, "Yeah?"

"What did your dad say?"

"What did Dad say about what?"

"What did your dad say about the contract?"

There was a pause. "He said, 'It's okay.' "

"Okay what?"

"It's okay to sign."

"Yay!" we all cheered. We were very happy.

Now, I certainly take responsibility—at least a quarter share!—for signing that contract on January 5, 1968. I've never said, "I was drunk!" Or "They pumped me full of morphine!" At the time, we thought Saul was our friend. He wasn't going to screw us, right?

But this contract would become infamous. And it would have a much more devastating impact on my life than it did for the rest of the band. Yes, it was terrible for all of us financially—our royalty rate (paid out of net sales, not gross) was 10 percent, increasing gradually to 12 percent over a few years—but for the creator of the material, there were long-reaching implications. Saul owned the copyright on all our songs, lock, stock, and barrel.

Fantasy was also now owed a number of songs per year, and if we didn't record them, the obligation would carry over to the next year. And the next. The grand total (which was actually upped in our second, June 1969, contract) amounted to 180 songs over seven years—and if not completed once that period ended, they'd *still* be owed. In 1969, Creedence's best year, we recorded three hit albums, but that only amounted to twenty-six songs. Besides me, nobody wrote songs in Creedence that amounted to anything, so when we broke up, the other guys were all set free. Not me. Fantasy Records had not only chiseled me out of a fortune, they still owned my future. I was enslaved.

That was all in the dark future, though. Right now we were four guys in a room with a dream. And Saul was in the same boat. How innocent it all was.*

I didn't hang out in San Francisco a lot—maybe went over to Golden Gate Park occasionally, headed to the Fillmore to see a few shows. But when I got off of active duty with the army, it was the Summer of Love, 1967. And there was a lot of attention being given to San Francisco culturally, musically, politically. I liked the politics. Because that's the way Pete Seeger talked: Be responsible for yourself and help your fellow man. Don't be a burden. Live and let live. Don't try to control everybody. I still feel that's the best way.

I always felt that I had everything in common with the other bands that way, and I liked that bands rather than record companies seemed to be controlling the thing. And the San Francisco scene seemed to be outside the regular music business. It definitely wasn't Los Angeles.

I felt connected with the San Francisco scene, but there were times when we'd see something there that would always bring home how different Creedence was. We went as a band to see Otis Redding at the Fillmore. To me he was so much better than almost anything else you could see there. Otis commanded that stage.

---

* Back in the nineties someone wrote a book about Creedence. I've always thought it was wack, even though I've never read it. How good could it be if the guy wrote a book about Creedence but never *talked* to me?

On the other hand, I remember going to Winterland—I can't remember if it was to see Jefferson Airplane or the Grateful Dead. Everybody was stoned. Somebody started to play and went into a guitar solo, and that was the whole set. Forty-five minutes of guitar solo. I was so frickin' out of there.

I reacted against that. What I had learned from James Brown and Jackie Wilson was how to *entertain*. When you're performing, it's a presentation. Watching Hank Ballard at the Oakland Auditorium, there was so much energy. There was competition, each act trying to outdo the other. The way the Grateful Dead and bands like that performed just seemed so sleepy. "And now, from San Francisco, the Grateful Dead!" They'd come shuffling out and everybody went to their amps—*bring, bwang, bwing*. They'd *tune up* for ten minutes. What?! Don't let them announce you until you're ready! "And now...*again*...the Grateful Dead!" When the Dead would jam, it seemed like they'd go off the path right away—and then *stay* off the path. Either you like that or you don't. In my world, I couldn't have my music be as unstructured as that. It makes me uncomfortable. They'd announce Creedence, and we'd tear out there, plug in, and *go!*

I think what I took most umbrage with was the stoned part, and that made me different from many of the San Francisco musicians. You dare not be stoned playing music around me. Not in *my* band. No. I talked about it then and I'll talk about it now. How are you going to do your best work stoned? Look, it's not that I'm anti-pot, especially in those days. It's a recreational deal. But when you're working, you're supposed to be working. I didn't want to see a drunk Dean Martin up there singing sloppy ballads either. Potheads always thought they were superior to the alcoholics. For one thing, they'd have a picture of a marijuana plant on their wall. My dad never had a picture of a Budweiser can on the wall. I sure as shit didn't want to see that. This was just an unhappy addiction to me.

Timothy Leary? What a jerk. A buffoon. I thought what he was doing was damaging. Lots of kids did stuff and probably hurt themselves because some official-looking guy like Leary told them it was okay. You'd be backstage at the Carousel Ballroom, and there'd be some guy who hadn't taken a bath in ages handing out greens or yellows or blues—yeah, it's free, but it might be arsenic. I didn't want any part of that, whatever it was. People were walking around with mystery pills. This scared me. LSD? I didn't want to jump out a window.

I could probably count on one hand how many times I smoked marijuana in my whole career. Okay, I'm exaggerating, but not by much. In the early days of Creedence, I remember sitting around the Shire stoned, and we were going to solve all the problems of the world...

As I mentioned, we had begun to practice every day, and we talked a lot about being more serious. There were many pot-smoking sessions at night where we discussed things like writing songs and being better on our instruments.

At one point we even adopted a pseudonym, "T. Spicebush Swallowtail," which was going to represent the songwriter on the tunes we would all write together. About this time, I went and got my little songwriting notebook. And I began to write songs, titles, ideas, etc. There was a lot of talking and a lot of pot smoking...a lot of being stoned and talking about doing this or that. This probably went on for a few weeks.

Every day we would meet at the Shire to practice. We would jam a bit and, after some time had passed, I would ask, "Does anybody have anything, any new songs?" And there'd be a silence and some mumbling. There is a quote from Ernest Hemingway about working on Hollywood movie projects that resonates with me. To paraphrase: "After all the talking, sooner or later someone is going to have to get down to the business of writing." So I would show the band what I had come up with on my own.

Things went on like this for a time, until it evolved into me just showing the band some songs and musical ideas. After a while I stopped asking if anybody had anything.

But the subject really remained open. It was not as if I had said, "Okay, you guys can't write any songs. I will write *all* the songs from now on." I simply got very busy and worked feverishly to come up with music for the band. I really did *not* want to go back to being an obscure band. If at any time the other guys had come up with a great song, I'm sure we would've jumped on it. But instead of actually doing the work, they contented themselves with grumbling about it...from the sidelines.

This is something that really ticks me off, in showbiz and in life. You know, people who complain about how they should have gotten this break or that part.... "They" stole my idea....I coulda been a contendah. But these same people never do the work, never come up with anything of substance. We ended up using T. Spicebush Swallowtail for only one single: "Porterville" / "Call It Pretending." I wrote both songs—by myself.

So there we were at the Shire, stoned, and we were gonna solve all the problems of the world. And the next day everything went right back to where it had been before. I guess we're not all gonna write "Strawberry Fields Forever." At some point the drugs wear off.

I don't mean to be on a soapbox or sound preachy. I wasn't a prude, and I didn't think I was above it—I just thought, *man,* be yourself while you're trying to make a record or perform in front of people. They want to see you at your best. I always viewed a live performance as kind of like a prizefight. Meaning you have to be in shape for this, give the most that you can to your fans.

I never wanted to feel that I let one get away from me, to have a show where I'd just gone out and been sloppy and awful and stupid. In the Jackie Wilson era, there seemed to be a sense of honor, a sense of duty, like, "I'm lucky to have this job. You should take it seriously, or pretty soon they're not going to let you *do* that job." I still feel that way.

I was always making this speech to the band. I had to be the general and I wanted us to rock. I didn't appreciate hearing, "Maybe it would be better if we're stoned." I think there were some instances later when the guys in the band tried to put one over on me because I was such a square. They tricked me a couple of times and did it anyway. And then blamed it on the Grateful Dead: "They put LSD in the coffee!" (Hell, you can blame *anything* on the Dead.) I thought we were better than that. I'm not going to say "smarter"; I'm going to say "better." Meaning that we were a band, and that for us, music was the most important thing.

What many British groups—even some American ones—had done when they first started out was show the world how well they played classic rock and roll. The Stones had "Not Fade Away," "Around and Around," and "Carol"; the Beatles did "Money," "Kansas City," and "Twist and Shout." They had their feet planted firmly in the tradition of rock and roll. With that in mind, I liked the idea of doing an old song instead of trying to come up with a new one. The point in my mind was not to worry about writing a new song, because we'd done that and it wasn't working. I said, "I'm gonna take a song I already know is a good song." And so I settled on "Susie Q."

We were all listening to KMPX, the cool underground FM station. It was counterculture, really outside the mainstream, but more and more people were gravitating toward it. Tom Donahue was the main deejay. They played the Dead, Jefferson Airplane, Quicksilver—all the happening San Francisco bands, but we'd also noticed that these guys were playing some songs that weren't actual released records. Unreleased tapes like Janis Joplin's "Hesitation Blues," and I think a tape by Kaleidoscope. There were a few of them. The deejays would play them and talk about them—on KMPX, that was as valid as hearing "Mustang Sally" or "Nights in White Satin." Instead of doing a whole album and going through a record company—I think we still weren't so sure about Fantasy Records anyway, and whether we'd ever break out of that recording shack—covering a classic song seemed like the quickest way to go.

I loved the 1958 Dale Hawkins record "Susie Q." Tom did too. I remember hearing it in my mom's car and just bangin' away on the dashboard. It has a great riff. *Great.* You'll notice that James Burton's name is not among the names of the people credited with writing "Susie Q." That's a crime. At least half of the song is that lick. It was somewhere during the Monkey Inn period that I sat down and said, "Y'know, I have to actually learn how this really goes. What's James doin' here?" His unique hybrid guitar picking was far ahead of its time, especially ahead of the Telecaster country pickers. James used a flat pick plus one metal finger pick. It gave "Susie Q" an edge. I thought, *I gotta figure out a way I can do that, but still use my regular flat pick so I don't have to change anything. I'm not Elmore James or Grandpa Jones—I'm a rock and roll guy.* I came up with a way of using two fingers and a pick. It was a cool thing. Nowadays they call it hybrid picking.

I'd been playing that song forever—with the Blue Velvets and at the Monkey Inn. We'd do the song every once in a while, and once we did it at some club, we'd play it for a couple of nights, and then stop. We were playing up somewhere in the Sacramento area in the beginning of 1968. Some club, people just milling about, and we could experiment and no one would care. I'm thinking about "Susie Q," and I turn to Doug and say, "Let's try somethin' a little different." I wanted it to have a gospel feel, but I didn't dare say to him "shuffle beat."

I said, "Try to get this feel: *doom chick, doom doom chick*." Doug starts imitating that. I go, "Right," and start playing the "Susie Q" riff. But I say, "Let's don't change—let's jam. We're not gonna play the song. Just stay in E." Stu's going, "Well, what should I play?" "Just stay in E, no pattern." That was the start of it. It was by no means what it became, but it was the format. At that time you had British Invasion, psychedelic music, folk rock. "Susie Q" stood out as a gutbucket, country blues thing. And people liked it.

"Susie Q" is a pretty simple song. After *Sgt. Pepper,* rock and roll grew up and everybody got all brainy and highfalutin and introspective and impotent—I mean important. Some people looked down on what made rock and roll what it is in the first place: fun. Loud, in-your-face, rebellious. Full of attitude. Definitely not "I have a dissertation that I must explain." I'm a guy who admires "Wooly Bully" as much as "The Times They Are a-Changin'."

We spent weeks preparing for the recording. We rehearsed the song out at the Shire, making it longer and longer in the solos. I remember saying to the other guys that it sometimes felt like I had an out-of-body experience playing "Susie Q." I'd actually forget where I was. When the song was over, I'd look around and realize, "Oh." And then we'd look at each other and play it again. There was a lot of playing that basic song as a four-piece band. But I was also making them settle down, instead of just jamming like at the Monkey Inn.

There were no defined musical parts yet. That was my job, because I could see what was missing. Clear as a bell. From "Susie Q" on, I realized that my job was to arrange everything, period. I'd been doing it somewhat before, arranging Golliwogs singles to sound vaguely like the Beatles, the Stones—and they did. With "Susie Q," I was going into new territory.

I had seen an old movie on the late show, *The Glenn Miller Story.* Miller's band has been struggling to find their identity, and they're rehearsing a make-it-or-break-it gig. The trumpet player busts his lip on his music stand, and all is lost. Miller stays up all night rewriting the lead for clarinet, and it changes the music. Everything falls into place—"That's the sound!" Having the right individual parts blended together. This made a big impression on me, and that's how I approached arranging.

In the sixties, everyone thought rock was free-form noodling. But look at the Beatles. Or more so the Ventures—it's even more obvious with them because their records are so bare. It's textbook how to play rock and roll. Listen to those records: it's very clear what each guy's role is. With the Ventures, you have a lead guitar, a rhythm guitar, a bass, and a drummer—there's not even a singer. Everything is planned out to sound a certain way together. Everybody is playing arranged, specific parts.

The idea of jamming was cool to me—challenging—but the point was that it had to be great, not one-note meandering, and none of that nobody-knows-what's-gonna-happen-next philosophy. I could not let that happen in my band. Be it "Susie Q," "I Heard It Through the Grapevine," "Commotion," or "Keep On Chooglin'," there was a structure. It was organized. There were parameters for how far out the song could go. I had to know darn sure what was going to happen, because I didn't want people falling asleep—the audience or the band. The difference between our jams and, say, the Dead's? In my band, there was an *arrangement*.

I'd tell the band, "Just try stuff. It's okay. When it's good, I'll smile." All through Creedence it was me either smiling yes or saying no. Even if they didn't know the parameters, I did, and if they got outside that, I would let them know. I always tried to explain why. I didn't just mysteriously say, "Here's your notes. Play them." Really, it was a friendly thing. But what you hear on the records is what I controlled.

I'd say, "When doing the drum fill, Doug, it should be this type, this style." I'd be right there working on a backbeat. Each instrument had a role to play, so the rhythm guitar had to be in a specific place, the bass in another. Or I'd be thinking to myself, *What's the bass part gonna be? I know it's gotta be* that *feel*. I would literally do it on the guitar, or in my mind. As Stu was playing it, I'd go, "No, no, no — lose that note." Whatever bass part the Dale Hawkins band was playing on the original "Susie Q" had to be changed to fit KMPX, a place where they played the Dead.

That was how I approached the jams. If we were learning a two and a half minute single, frankly, it was, "Here's how it goes and this is what you play." In Creedence, the learning curve was there each and every new song. By the time "Susie Q" was recorded, we would play it live, and it sounded pretty good. Then I'd start to show them a brand-new song, like "Born on the Bayou," and we'd sound like amateurs again! I'm not saying that as any kind of slam. It was just a weird phenomenon: the stuff we did out on tour was manly, authoritative, and then we'd go in to learn a new song, and it sounded like the Mickey Mouse Club.

Most of the time, when I rehearsed the band I didn't sing. I'd work out all the music ahead of time and then teach it to the band as an instrumental. It had to have a musical hook without any singing. And the guys learned the song without hearing me sing it. Because I didn't want to sing in front of them. I was a little shy about that. I still get a little funny when I'm going to show my band a song, even now. But *especially* then.

On the music side, I developed a formula: I would choose two songs for the singles and we would rehearse those two for six weeks. Of course, those six weeks started with just a snippet of a rhythm idea, trying many variations of chord structure and drum patterns. In this way, I could test-drive many different approaches of presenting the song until I felt I had arrived at the absolute best arrangement. There were dozens of little musical intersections along the way where you had to make a choice about which beat or note was best for that particular song. That's how you refine an arrangement and make it great. That is also how you get the musicians used to performing the music, so that after six weeks they are playing the thing like it's second nature.

Along the way, we'd work on the album cuts. So when we went into the studio to do "Up Around the Bend," "Run Through the Jungle," all the singles, take one would be awesome. It was, "Well, all right—maybe we can beat that." And certainly take three was about it. That was all you needed. Done! There was no point in doing any more. We had rehearsed it and we were ready.

I've heard Stu take credit for making "Susie Q" a "psychedelic" jam. No way. In spite of what Stu says, it is *not* a psychedelic jam. That recording was all planned out on paper. I did it by myself on the kitchen table. I don't know how to read music, so I sat down and taped pieces of binder paper together with Scotch tape because no one piece of paper was long enough, and I made a road map of the song showing what would happen *here*, and *here*, and *here*... all the way through. I turned music into pictures—that's how I took "Susie Q" from here...to there. It was, "I'm gonna take a journey with this song."

To me, a record is a presentation. It is not cinema verité, and all that other artsy crap that people were doing in the early seventies. No: a recording is a presentation. You've thought all about it, the arrangement, the mix—that's why you can hear the singer a little louder than the drum or the bass. You've *prepared* this. You need to have the music be a bed for your song, so it can *present* your song. One of the huge secrets of Creedence was that this music was brain-numbingly simple, but it's the *right* simple. I always said, "There's only one right way."

I feel like I was given the gift of having a very clear understanding of what to do. That might've been the greatest gift of all. You have to have a leader, and in that band, as in all bands, you need a purveyor of taste. If I was not the sole judge, I was certainly the final judge—"Now it's ready." Then we went and recorded it.

Call me a perfectionist? Guilty. I haven't been as anal about that process since Creedence—where I had that level of intensity with an arrangement and kept developing it before we recorded. "Susie Q" was the first time we ever worked on something that way. And that was the way it stayed—until the mutiny at the end of 1970.

We didn't record "Susie Q" in Fantasy's lean-to—I took us back to Coast Recorders and Walt Payne, the same guy who had engineered James Powell's "Beverly Angel" when I was fourteen. After we set up, it was our practice to jam and get comfortable, play some blues. Then we counted off "Susie Q" and recorded it—first take, *boom*. There was no take two. I had to go back another day and sing the vocal. When I got there, Walt said, "Well, Bing Crosby was here this morning singing through that mic, so I figured that would probably be all right for you." My mom loved Bing, and so did I. "Wow—*yessir!*" In the mix, part of my vocal was put through this thing that Walt called "the telephone box," which they would use on radio dramas when someone called on the phone.

There's a lot of little tricks going on in "Susie Q." I knew the song would start with the drums fading in. I tried other things. If you listen to the rhythm, there's something going *shhhhusha shusha*—that's me. It turned out Doug really couldn't keep that beat going on the sand blocks, so I played them. It's a big addition to the groove. It's a pretty cool beat, almost that sand and Vaseline thing. There's some backwards guitars, some tambourine backbeat, and an open piano where I held down the sustain pedal, dissonant notes, sort of a disturbing ambient sound but nestled pretty far back in the track. And the backing vocals—"fine"/"mine," "moon"/"June." We sat in a circle with a mic dropped between us, and I would strum a chord really quietly and we'd go "fiiiiiiiiiine...

miiiiiiiiine." We did that all by itself and then I inserted it into the mix. I knew what I wanted to do with it. I was kind of poking fun at Tin Pan Alley, how they'd use all these simple words that rhymed.

I distinctly remember being in the studio with the whole band the day we were preparing all the tracks for "Susie Q." They were sitting in front of the console down below, where the window out to the studio is. I've got this thing that I've mapped out. I've worked on this for weeks—it's my baby. I'm putting the different pieces together, the "fine/mine/moon/June" stuff, and I hear Stu: "That'll never work!" I was getting more and more annoyed. Some guys never recover from negativity like that. They're not strong enough to go, "Y'know what? Screw you!" I was trying to mix this. I knew what I was doing—I had a map! Even though my actions may have looked selfish at times, I was doing this for my band, what I thought presented us in the best way possible. My heart was in Creedence, and it stayed that way for a long, long, long time. Trying to be protective of the band, sometimes maybe in spite of itself. After "Susie Q," I never allowed them to be in the studio again when I was mixing. I didn't need that distraction.

People told me later that "Susie Q" was cool because it had so much guitar. I had another guitar and amp by then. While I was away in the army, Tom had taken my Mustang and maybe my Supro and traded them in. Those two were worth one short-scale Rickenbacker 325. That's the kind John Lennon played, and there seemed to be a trend in getting that kind of acoustic-electric sound. I also had a new Kustom K200 amp. Saul advanced the money for that: $1,200. We'd asked for money to get an old van and an amp. He would only give us money for the amp. Of course, I ended up paying for that amp out of royalties.

The Kustom was solid-state, with transistors. Everybody prefers tube amps, including me. I learned to pull everything I could out of that Kustom. God, I got a great sound out of that amp. "Susie Q" was practically a demo of what that amp could do. It has to be the right guitar with that amp. The Kustom was really, really loud, and it had a great, clean guitar sound—you can hear that on "Bad Moon Rising." Not *perfectly* clean, the way other transistor amps were—there's a little bit of grit, warmth—but it's not out of control. That amp had the killer vibrato of all time— listen to "Born on the Bayou," which came a bit later.

At Coast, they had one knob that we could pan from left to right. I remember Walt explaining that to me during the mixing of "Susie Q," and I thought that was the coolest thing. It's sort of irritating for me now, the way the drums are and how one guitar's way over here and the other guitar's way over there. Everything is on the left or the right; nothing sits in the middle. It's not real stereo.

I didn't know what stereo was then. I had never heard it. I didn't have a stereo radio, didn't have any stereo records, didn't have a stereo player. Then I got to Wally Heider Studios, and they had all kinds of knobs! Like, eight of 'em! I found out why. "Oh...they call that stereo."

When I was working with the guys on "Susie Q," one of them actually said, "Well, John's got an eight-track recorder built into his head." I already seemed very familiar with the whole record- ing situation. It was a compliment, but they were also talking about something they didn't have.

Despite all that, with "Susie Q" I really felt that we had hit the mark. I remember coming back after that session to play it for Saul in the old Fantasy offices on Treat Avenue. I said, "That's great." Saul goes, "Well...it's very good." I said, "No—that's *great.*" In my heart, I knew that we had transcended to another level. The other song we recorded at that first session was Bo Did- dley's "Before You Accuse Me," and the arrangement was not great. I call that the Jefferson Airplane version because it was kind of like "Somebody to Love." After it was done, I thought to myself, *Nah, I'd rather do it more like Bo's version. Who needs this?* We later rerecorded it. (That first version actually stayed

undiscovered until Fantasy decided they wanted to put out everything, down to me picking my nose.)

I knew that "Susie Q" was it, and when we took the tape to
KMPX, they loved it. They started playing it a lot. I would hear it
at least three or four times every day. Awesome. We split the song
into two parts for the actual single, and it became a Top 40 radio
hit. I think we all knew this was really it.

A funny thing happened. We played a week at a place called
Mousy's, in Davis, typical small college-town bar. "Susie Q" was
new, still just a tape and not on the radio in Davis. We were jamming on it. I thought we'd played a pretty good version—we were
really getting into it. As we neared the big finish, some guy from
the audience laid a piece of paper at Tom's feet. It said, "Hey, you
hippies—you're trying too hard!" Like, "That's not a normal
song. You played the guitar too long. Knock it off!" We all got a
big chuckle out of that.

Creedence had gotten a steady gig in San Francisco at a club called
Dino and Carlo's—another residency like the Monkey Inn, but
with an older, more professional crowd. One thing that happened
there I'll never forget. At the time, I was broke, living with a wife
and baby on literally twenty dollars a week. That was my allowance from Tom. We trusted him to dispense the money: he was the
older person with a job. The rest came from whatever few dollars
we got from playing somewhere. We managed one credit card,
which we always maxed out. It was a kind of socialism—we had
this much money, and each of us got what he needed. I got twenty
bucks a week, which covered food and diapers. Plus I smoked Kools
with filters. One time I walked into a Safeway and looked longingly
at a newspaper and a candy bar. I remember thinking that the mark
of a successful career would be, "I can afford a Hershey bar."

There weren't a lot of groceries at home. Late one night, I found a can of kidney beans and put them in a saucepan. The aroma woke Martha up. I was caught sneaking beans! I felt like the guy on the lost ship who's secretly hoarding all the food.

One night at Dino and Carlo's we were loading our equipment in, and some guy, a fan, reached out his hand and it's got twenty dollars in it. Well, you might as well have given me a cool million. I asked, "Should I split it with the band?"

He said, "Swing with it."

"You wanna hear a certain song?"

"No—swing with it."

The rest of the guys let me keep it. It was such an act of generosity. I might as well have won the lottery!

Another night, Saul came by and watched a couple of sets. We were doing "Susie Q," "Ninety-Nine and a Half (Won't Do)," "I Put a Spell on You," "Good Golly, Miss Molly," and "Hi-Heel Sneakers," most of which ended up on the first record. Saul said, "I think there's enough there that you can make an album." That was a step forward. Besides "Susie Q," we had already recorded "Porterville," which had come out as the first single under Creedence's name on Fantasy's subsidiary label Scorpio, because Saul hadn't quite taken over yet.* "Porterville" is very reflective of mid-sixties rock, British influence, psychedelic—stretching out, playing a little long. That guitar sound is like the Airplane on *Surrealistic Pillow*, although I didn't have any good equipment. Clean with a bunch of echo on it. I'm pretty sure we took that single to KMPX too. I don't know how often they played it, if ever. The flip side, "Call It Pretending," I considered pop in our old style, so I didn't even put it on the album.

We'd been doing "I Put a Spell on You" live, but not for long— I might've done it at the Monkey Inn. I loved the song, and loved

---

* "Porterville" had actually come out as a Golliwogs single. After we became Creedence it was rereleased.

Screamin' Jay Hawkins's whole thing. It was so out there and all by itself— *"MYUHAHAHAHA!"* Back in the fifties, he'd get wheeled out in a coffin and it would take him forever to open it and jump out. I've got to do something like that! Do they have plaid burial clothes?

That sustained drone solo in Creedence's version of "I Put a Spell on You"—that's the Rickenbacker and the Kustom. The weird sounds you hear at the beginning were done later in the mix. Those are my son Josh's baby toys. We had a jack-in-the-box, some pull toys, and one of those tops that hummed once it started spinning—*whoosh whoosh whoosh hummmm.* We recorded them, and then played them back at different speeds. The song fades out with that. It sounds like a spaceship—it's supposed to be the other dimension. On my five-cent budget, I was trying to come up with things that were cool, and it worked. We did all the overdubs at my other old haunt, Sierra Sound. Tambourines and maracas— that's what I remember.

On "Gloomy," I wanted something ominous, so we took boxes with gravel inside and marched on it like soldiers. That didn't turn out to be as cool as I'd hoped.

Saul actually asked to put his name on the first album as producer—"I want people to know that Fantasy is under new management." After that I made darn sure I got credit: "Arranged and produced by John Fogerty." I'd gotten that from Chet Atkins records, which is funny because many of his productions are just Chet and a guitar (but sound as full as any record with two hundred musicians). I liked the phrase "Arranged and produced by" because it was the absolute truth.

That first album—*Creedence Clearwater Revival*—came out on May 28, 1968. My first album on my twenty-third birthday. I've seen other dates listed, but sorry, Charlie: they got it wrong. I remember because I was on the radio with deejay Tony Pig, playing the album for the whole world. The liner notes were written by Ralph J. Gleason—that's where he says, "Creedence Clearwater Revival is an excellent example of the Third Generation of San Francisco bands." Meaning we weren't quite as good as the Grateful Dead or Quicksilver Messenger Service. If you look at the cover of our fifth album, *Cosmo's Factory*—which is a shot of the band hanging out in the rehearsal space–office we called the Factory—you'll see a handwritten sign pinned to the top of one of the posts in the room: "3RD GENERATION." That was for Ralph.

As I mentioned, we had decided that everything in the band had to be voted on, and it had to be a unanimous decision. If one guy said no to whatever was being decided, then that was it: we didn't do it. And if something was voted on and came to pass, it stayed that way. It didn't change later unless we voted unanimously to change it. This is the way Creedence operated, and continued to operate for years and years, even after we broke up.

We also agreed that if the group ever broke up, we wouldn't allow one or two of us to run off and call ourselves Creedence Clearwater Revival. We had seen other groups do this over the years, like the Platters or the Diamonds, where some fraudulent version would be out there with one or maybe none of the original members. We agreed that either we were all in the band or else it just couldn't be.

And I gave the other guys equal share in the songwriting income. As I've mentioned, for a very short time the band used a pseudonym that referred to all four of us as a songwriting entity: T. Spicebush Swallowtail. (Doug knew a little bit about the world of entomology, and a spicebush swallowtail is a species of butterfly.) It's used on both sides of the "Porterville" single. In the all-for-one spirit of Creedence, we were going to use that for all the songwriting credits. Early on, we didn't know that I'd be the guy writing all the songs—but now that the first album was done (and

I was already writing songs for our next album), I began to realize that the credit wasn't fair. It was a matter of pride. I felt that if I had written the song, it should have my name on it.

Now, I didn't want to keep changing the agreement the way the white man did with the Indians, so what I said was, "I will share all the songwriting money equally until the end of 1969." So the guys got royalties for songs they did not write, on four albums that each sold well over a million copies by the end of 1969.

I did that so the other guys would not feel anxious about the money. I was sharing, being generous, because this was my band. The only thing I was counting on was this agreement of unanimity in the group. We were blood brothers, and we gave our word. That's still the law to me.

Creedence was starting to make a stir. You could see we were comers. But we weren't there yet.

Just as the first album came out, we played this weird pizza place near the Stanford University campus. It was a college hang, a daytime gig, small potatoes. We're setting up and I overhear two guys in the audience talking. I was dressed very casual for this gig, and this guy sees my white canvas sneakers and says to the other one, "Oh man—I thought these were, like, *cool* guys." Meaning my wardrobe sucked, and this was a great big hole in his vision of the band. Instead of being crushed or remaining oblivious, I knew exactly what he was talking about. You want to see what you hear. When I first heard the Animals, I said, "We've had the Beatles, we've had the Stones. The *Animals,* man: what are they gonna look like?" I figured it would be guys in loincloths and bones going, *"Aaarrrrh!"* They were the *Animals.* Then they come out and they all had these neat little suits on. It was a bit underwhelming.

So this guy staring at my sneakers was absolutely right. That changed immediately. I never wore those to a show again. Because how I look ought to go with how I sound: cowboy boots, Levi's, plaid shirts. Basically, my vision of myself. Image is important, however offhand it might seem. Even offhand is a thought-out thing.

But cool guys or not, good things were starting to happen to us. The very first time we went to Hawaii was in September 1968. This was a Dick Clark show in Honolulu, opening for Vanilla Fudge. We each got an airplane ticket and a hotel room—I think it was the Driftwood Hotel.

I get to my room, haven't been there but five minutes, and decide I'm going to go see Doug—maybe we can go for a walk. I go down to Doug's room. I'm knocking. No answer. I know we all just got to our room, so I knock again. Nothing.

"Hey, Cosmo, it's John."

I hear shuffling, some muffled voices.

"C'mon, Doug. Let's go to the beach. We gotta see Waikiki."

More shuffling. A mumbling voice. "No, I don't wanna go."

"Doug, what's goin' on?" He's not acting like my friend anymore.

I hear what sounds like another voice in there.

"Shit, Doug—you got *a girl* in there with you?"

I was shocked. We had not been in the hotel more than ten minutes. And what was going on in my psyche was, *Aw, are we gonna be like* that? *I didn't know we were gonna be like* those *bands. Really?*

Over the next few years, Doug certainly earned a reputation. Before anybody else had dropped their luggage on the floor, Doug had something going. He was the Rooster. And the whole world was his barnyard.

Now, I'm no saint, but at the time, I'm just a kid from El Cerrito, a little Boy Scout. And I'm feeling like, I'm amazingly disappointed. I guess you could say I'm not the guy who got into music to get girls—I was there for the music.

"Susie Q" was what I was into. Man, that song—the first piece of music we did that was in the major leagues. We'd finally stepped up out of the sandlots where the Golliwogs and the Blue Velvets were, and I knew it. *I knew* what to do. It was clear.

I was not afraid. I was superconfident, as a matter of fact. The only thing I was afraid of was the so-called sophomore jinx. The one-hit wonder. History is littered with the wreckage of all the one-hit wonders who failed on that second attempt. And I wanted to be the one that didn't. We had our one hit, and by God, I wasn't going back to the car wash. I didn't want to be a Golliwog again.

So I was ratcheting up the game and trying to inspire the people around me to do the same thing. With the guys in the band, I was able to talk a pretty good college rah-rah pep talk. I kept saying, "We have the spotlight! It's on *us!* And it'll stay there if we do something good. Otherwise, guess what?" When I looked at Fantasy Records and Saul Zaentz, I saw that they were clueless when it came to rock. We weren't on Columbia Records, that's for sure. I was on the smallest label in the whole world, and the advertising budget was fifteen cents. Saul wasn't going to spend any money—as Stu always said, "Saul's idea was, 'Spend pennies, make millions.'" We didn't have any machinery behind us, nor did we have anybody that understood that we needed that machinery. We didn't have a manager. We didn't have a publicist. So I took a hard look at all of this and said, "Well, I guess I'm just gonna have to do it with music."

The more music I do that's great, the more it'll overcome all those things that we don't have. I had to put on a work ethic like nobody ever saw before. I saw a musical career as something to work at. *Work.* I was really driven, and I'm proud of that. You might think that it's a curse or some kind of disease—it certainly isn't something you should keep on doing all your life, every day, forever. It's not healthy for yourself and those around you. But if you have a specific goal, a short-term goal, and you believe it's reachable, that's how you do it.

That meant I had to be a whirling dervish. My family and I were living on Kains Avenue in Albany, right outside El Cerrito. I had started to write songs for the next album, and I was putting a lot of thought into it. I had the luxury of a few months to write—time hadn't gotten compressed yet. We were living in a little apartment. In a lot of ways it was better than the house I had grown up in. It was new, and it had the cottage cheese ceiling, which I thought was cool then. At first we couldn't get a TV because I didn't have enough credit. I could barely write a check, with my twenty dollars a week from Tom and the little bit we'd gotten from our gigs.

There were no pictures or art on the wall—just a plain beige room. And I would sit on a little chair halfway between the "kitchen" and the front room, writing. I had my yellow pad of paper, and my little songwriting book. I would stay up every night into the wee hours, writing songs and arranging songs—it was literally all I thought about. For every good song there were twelve I rejected. I'd just sort of stare at the wall. I was slowed down, very much with my own thoughts. I discovered that I would kind of go into a trance, drinking coffee and smoking cigarettes. There were things that were not at hand, but in my mind, they could become very real to me. I was not stoned or drunk or anything like that, but as I concentrated, I would go deep.

I was trying to come up with something new. I was thinking, *Where's this thing going? What's it going to be?*

CHAPTER 8

I Guess I'm Just Gonna Have to Do It with Music

SONGWRITING IS A tricky thing. You have to get real quiet, allow yourself to be alone. At least I do. Set aside time, or you'll never get to it. We're all very busy in our lives, and there's a lot of noise: the TV and your kids and their homework and your dog's barking, paying your bills, returning that crap you ordered because it doesn't fit—all the stuff of life. And songwriting is really much more in the opposite direction: it's about solitude and being quiet, because that's the only way that hidden stuff in your soul can finally be heard. You have to say to the world and to yourself, "I'm going to go to my room. I'm going to be quiet. I've got a guitar in my hand, a blank sheet of paper, and now here is the deal, right there."

Every writer will tell you: you sit down and face your blank sheet of paper. It is the most freeing thing in the world...and the most terrifying. You see, that blank page is a window to infinity. You can go anywhere, do anything, create something that has never existed before. It is curiosity and imagination, all mixed up with a lot of luck and pixie dust...while you pray for inspiration.

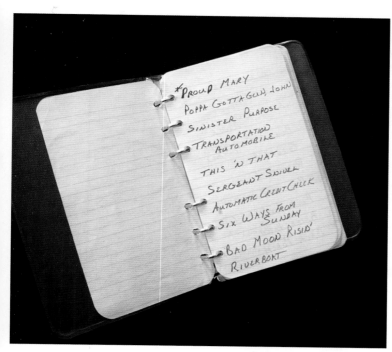

This is the little songwriting notebook I bought in the fall of 1967. The first entry was "Proud Mary."

My mom saved quite a bit of my work from when I was little. Here is the beginning of my writing.

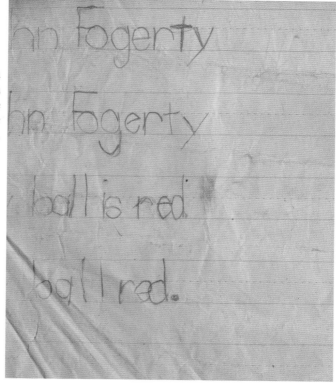

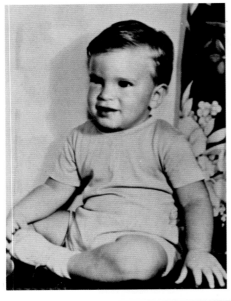

Baby shot of me.

Me as a little boy. I was playing the game my dad had invented.

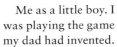

My dad and me at Putah Creek. Those memories turned into the song "Green River."

My mom, Edith
Lucile Fogerty.

My dad, Galen
Robert Fogerty.

Five boys. My
poor mom.

My report card from Mrs. Starck.

RICHMOND UNION HIGH SCHOOL DISTRICT

Summer School | Student's Report

Student _Fogerty_ _John_
Last Name | First Name

Subject Teacher _Sue Starck_ Summer School 19 _61_

Subject _Chorus_

Scholarship Mark	_A_		MEANING OF MARKS
Times Absent	_2_		A—Excellent
			B—Good
			C—Average
			D—Barely Passing
			F—Not Passing

Indicate school student will attend in fall semester _El Cerrito_

Fourteen years old, playing at the county fair.

Tommy Fogerty and the Blue Velvets. All of us are pretty young. That's the Strat with slinky strings.

That's me at the Monkey Inn with Mike Burns (left) and Tom Fanning (middle). (Courtesy of James R. Bagnall Family Archive)

Here's a shot of me in the army.

Martha Paiz, my first wife. Met at nineteen. Married at twenty. Just kids, not ready for marriage.

I kept a scrapbook in the early days. This was a shot I had in the book from the beginning of what would become CCR.

Me with my mom, grandma, and son Josh.

The Golliwogs.

Me at the Factory.

Lost in thought.
Stayed up all night
writing songs (again).

Making
records.

The process.

At the mixing board.

Catching up on
the latest.

Just putting my thoughts
together.

The Factory. I
am having a
meeting with
Jake Rohrer.

Creedence with Saul Zaentz.

ROCK and ROLL!

CCR as a trio.

The house in Albany, California, that was my studio/office. I spent many years here learning to play all the instruments for *Centerfield*. It was a somewhat dark place for me, as I surely didn't feel so good during this time. Now I hear it's a preschool. It makes me happy that it turned into something sweet!

Flying lessons.

Working on *The Blue Ridge Rangers*.

Seymour Bricker helped me sign a new deal with Asylum Records. I thought I was getting away from Fantasy. I was still a recluse.

One of my favorite pastimes.

Hunting in the wilderness near Troy, Oregon. I loved the time I spent there. There is nothing like being out in nature. It just makes everything bad go away, if only for a while.

Our home in the woods.

Early 1970, at the Oakland Coliseum. Over the long years, this shot always looked like "good-bye" to me. Sad...Happily, today I am playing my songs, and Julie picked this shot to promote my tour. I am grateful to my family and fans, because now I can play my music full of joy. (Iconic Images/Baron Wolman)

The happiest day of my life, April 20, 1991. I married Julie, the love of my life!

Our wedding day.

One moment you have nothing, but the next moment you could have a masterpiece! It's just plain *scary*.

You have been telling yourself all year—all your *life—I'm a writer*. And maybe you even got some feedback. An award, or you wrote a song that did well or got some notoriety, so you can actually stand in front of a group of people and be thought of as a songwriter. "Here he is, *a songwriter*." So now you're stepping up to the plate again, your big bat in your hand. You sit there with your blank piece of paper. Okay, songwriter, write something. And you're back to being just a guy with a blank piece of paper. Like nervous Ralph Kramden on the *Honeymooners*: "Humina, humina, humina."

Monday I may be sitting there with a guitar, a couple of pretty lame ideas. Then I get distracted. And I start fiddling with some old musical ideas, and then it's Tuesday. There I am sitting there, I've got a ham sandwich, and it's afternoon. And then it's Wednesday. Well, you can see what is coming.

It gets to be Friday, and I'm starting to have a bit of concern. I haven't written one word and I have to record next Monday. The slot is booked, the band will be there. And what are we going to do? I have had a couple of thoughts, but those thoughts have been a little lame. They're not giving me that feeling that they're right. And if there is any one thing that a good songwriter knows, it's when stuff is good, and when it's crap. If you don't know the difference, you are going to have trouble doing this as your life's work. Because we all are capable of doing both.

The real trick is knowing when you've got crap, because then you've got to start over. And if you do enough of that crap, at least with me, that's when I get to the good stuff. I can't skip the pages where the crap is. Every single time I start on a new song, it's always a bunch of pages of crap first, and then finally something good will happen. Out of nowhere, a phrase will go through my head, like "train of fools," and I'll start writing a song. This is the beauty and the magic and the mystique of songwriting.

So maybe you get a breakthrough, finally get the main thrust of a song, but it's not complete—at least it works that way with me. All songs gestate over a period of time, and they need to be cooked through. And with an album, they'll *all* be bubbling on the stove. You're doing a whole meal. You don't just do the gravy.

In the process you may write a cliché. Once one person has said, "I see my unborn children in your eyes," the next guy who says it is in for a lynching. So that drippy, drug-induced, overly fatigued stuff doesn't fly with me. I thought the idea here was economy. Especially in rock and roll. Don't use a lot of words when you can say it with two. That whole "first thought, best thought" school is not for me either. I rewrite. I edit. If I have an image in my mind and write a line trying to capture it, and over time I realize that I could say it better, make the image even clearer, and make it a cooler line? I don't think Woody Guthrie would flinch. It would be a better song. That's craft. I certainly try to do that.

Songwriting peers I admire include Lennon and McCartney, Bob Dylan, Bruce Springsteen, Elton John and Bernie Taupin, Brian Wilson. Of the old guard, certainly Leiber and Stoller. Every song was a cool story: "Young Blood," "Smokey Joe's Café," "Shoppin' for Clothes." Elton and Bernie have a weird method: Bernie writes a poem and sends it to Elton. Brian Wilson has a cowriter most of the time—he'll write the melody and get somebody to do the lyrics.

There were a few songwriters from the days before rock and roll that I admired.

Hoagy Carmichael, Harold Arlen, and Johnny Mercer. When I was a teenager, I read a book about songwriters and I think these guys were interviewed. One of the writers said something that really hit home with me. He said, "When you are working on a song and something is not quite right, a little bell will ring in your head. You have to pay attention to that bell and fix the song. Otherwise, the bell may not ring for you anymore."

With me it's almost always melody first. I'll start with melody and then get an idea—what's it about? I'll have an unfinished melody and unfinished words. They have to cohabitate at some point.

To my mind, if I'm writing a song, it probably means there's going to be some work to it. "Fortunate Son" was written in twenty minutes, but darn few are like that. And I'd probably been thinking about everything that was in that song for three or four years. I didn't know it would start, "Some folks are born..."— that came from nowhere. But the thought process had been going on for a long time, and after a lifetime of being a songwriter, I never expect, "*Blam!* There it is." If it's a brand-new song, I expect the line that I get right now—if indeed it's a good one— might not even be in the first verse.

It might end up at the end of the lyric. It might end up in another song, or living alone inside a notebook for years. That's the journey. I must say, I do hear a lot of songs that sound uned-ited, not worked on. Everything's so...plain. I think, "You could've said that better." In my mind, that's the job. You're *supposed* to say it better. Hopefully there's a point of view you want to present, an opinion. Otherwise, why should I listen? All good songs engage you because they get you to feel something.

After I got out of the service, I decided to start collecting and writing down phrases that would help me with songwriting. This was part of concentrating on music, being serious about it. In earlier times, I'd feel an inspiration to write a song every so often. Things would occur to me, and then a week later I'd try to remember it. And it was like, "Doggone it, I had the map to the Dutchman's gold. He told me *exactly* where to go, and now I can't remember what he said." So I decided I'd get a little notebook and write it down.

I was a kid with no money, so I had none of the things that an adult has in his life, like a pen. Or paper. I just didn't have any of that kind of stuff lying around. So I went down to the local drugstore and bought a cheap little vinyl notebook and a little package of three-ring-binder paper and a pen. This was my songbook. Sometime soon after I brought it home, I made the very first entry: "Proud Mary." For some reason that phrase had come into my brain, and I thought it was a good song title. It sounded cool. But I had no idea what it was about. Proud Mary? I didn't know what that meant.

It could've been about a person. I remember thinking, *Maybe it's about a woman who's a domestic. She lives in a humble, small house. She has to put on some kind of uniform, like a cleaning lady. Has to ride a bus. Gets off the bus and goes over to the big rich people's house. Maybe that's who Proud Mary is.*

Then one day in the summer of 1968, when "Susie Q" is on the radio, I walk up to my apartment and I see, on the steps, a big white envelope with a government seal. I'm not really expecting any mail, so I ignore it. It was like the phone I never answered or the doorbell I didn't respond to. I'm still that way.

After about three days of stepping over it, I finally look down close and notice it's got my name on it — "Private John Fogerty." I say, "Holy mackerel! That's for me!" I open the thing and it looks kind of like your high school diploma. My honorable discharge from the army. This is a big day! I read it again to make sure. And I run over to this little patch of lawn and I actually do a cartwheel.

I ran right back in the house and picked up my Rickenbacker. I'd been working on these chords, and now I had such a rush of energy and good feeling, like a weight had been lifted off — it was just, *whewwwww*. And out came the first line: "Left a good job in the city." I went, "Yeah, that's kind of what just happened." The idea that I just felt so…free. Open. I started to get some words together.

I got into it. And I got more into it. That riff came about from messing around with Beethoven's Fifth. My mom referenced that when I was growing up: while pregnant with me, she went to a Beethoven concert and I was kicking up a storm. Playing Beethoven's Fifth led to that riff, which sounded like a paddle wheel to me. When I get onto something good, I'll play it over and over and over again, because number one, it feels good. But you start to get little offshoots, more sparks happening. "Big wheel." "Yeah, yeah — the big wheel! Wow, what is this about?" You're not self-aware. You're just going with the thing.

By this time maybe an hour has passed. I go to my notebook and there's "Proud Mary." That title jumped off the page. Oh my — you mean this song is about *a boat?* Without saying anything, it said everything. It was female — ships are female. Proud. Wow, there it is! Proud Mary! At some point along the way I'm singing, "Rollin', rollin', rollin' on the river." Finally, when I realized I had a verse and a chorus — it wasn't every word, but it was mostly there, and in other words, I had a song — I knew I had entered the land of greatness.

Pardon me for not sounding humble. This thing had landed on me and I recognized that this was truly great, far above me. Far above anything I had ever even thought about. I had grown up with my mom talking to me about Irving Berlin and Hoagy Carmichael, how they wrote standards. I knew, "Man, this is a *standard.*" Meaning it was like "Stardust." Or "White Christmas." I had never even brushed up against anything like that.

I had always wondered what that would be like. Before this ever happens, you're planning on having a musical career, you love music, you've studied all these other people. You don't know how it feels, how they felt when they got something that right. I hadn't sat in my room saying, "Someday this will happen, so how will I act? Well, I'll put on my hat and grab my cane and I'll go skipping down the lane." No. I didn't have a clue. You've been outside the fence your whole life. Then one day your mind takes a couple of fortuitous turns and you're *inside* the fence. And you have a sense that you're gonna stay inside the fence.

I was right on the cusp of my birthday, twenty-three years old, all alone in this pretty low-rent apartment, and it was like a space-ship had landed. I never assumed I was the pilot. More like, "You're *allowed* to see this." It's *given* to you. It really does feel that way. You're looking at this shadowy, cloudy shape, you start to go in a direction, and *whump!* The veil is lifted and suddenly there's a song, a *great* song. It was like being struck by God. I was sitting there quaking with this paper in my hand. I really, really knew—I just did. I was literally shaking, just jittery: "Oh my God..." I'm going on and on about it because that's how special it was.

Happily and luckily, it wasn't the last time I got to feel that way.

We recorded "Proud Mary" later that year, down in Los Angeles at RCA Studios during the *Bayou Country* sessions—it was October 1968. We'd recorded one more time at Coast, but being sort of naive I didn't specify an engineer, and instead of Walt Payne they gave us this young kid, and it wasn't anywhere near the magic of "Susie Q." So I convinced Saul that we needed to go to a better place, and he had a relationship with RCA because they pressed Fantasy's albums. Well, that was Elvis's studio! Sure!

We were fortunate enough to get an engineer named Hank McGill, a funky, cool older guy who lived on a boat* and had a lot of experience. We weren't getting the suit and tie here; we were getting a guy who loved music. We recorded in a room big enough for a symphony orchestra, but we just ignored that. Hank set up

---

* We later gave Hank a life preserver that said "Proud Mary" for recording the song.

some soundproofing gobos and made a tiny little room within the room for us to record in.

When I showed "Proud Mary" to my bandmates, I felt that they really didn't see any difference between this song and anything else we had done. I got the sense, "Yeah, it's one of our songs." Well, *I* didn't feel that way. Which is why I was so precious about recording it. A good song but a bad recording was a combination that had happened to us a lot, and at this point I wasn't going to settle for that.

Now, I had been in the award-winning a cappella group at El Cerrito High for two and a half years, a choir of fifty voices. I had heard doo-wop since 1953, where the bass sang real low— *"Bow bow bow,"* all that kind of stuff. There were variations, but basically the bass guy was following what a bass player would do— follow the root note most of the time—but the other guys were staying in one place and just adjusting a little bit. You might call it the core chord, and it didn't go *wooo* up there with the melody: it just stayed right down here, and the melody went around, over it. That's what I adopted as a teenager back in my bedroom with my add-a-track tape recorder—and that's what I adopted later on with the Creedence records when I sang all the background parts myself.

One of the big parts of "Proud Mary" came from paying very close attention to male gospel harmonies. The "Rollin', rollin', rollin' on the river" has to explode. You don't just go "Rollin', rollin', rollin' ": it's "RRRROllin', RRRROllin', RRRROllin'." You're slurring up to the note real quick, and your vocal energy happens all at once. You have to *explode.* Well, when you have three or four voices all doing that at exactly the same time, you get what I heard the good vocal groups do, especially male gospel groups: the Swan Silvertones, the Sensational Nightingales, the Five Blind Boys of Mississippi. That stuff really stirs my soul, and I wanted that sound on "Proud Mary."

Up until that time, when a song required background vocals, some or all of us would sing them. But after our album had been out awhile, I really found fault with the sound of the background vocals on "Porterville." They fit in more with punk, that whole attitude. They had a snot-nosed, bratty sound to them — "I don't care! I don't care!" Kind of ragtag, and I didn't like it.

After the music track for "Proud Mary" was done, it was time to put on those background parts. I'd rehearsed it with the fellas for weeks, teaching them harmony by doing folk songs or sing-along songs like "Row, Row, Row Your Boat" and "I've Been Working on the Railroad," and by practicing the "Rollin', rollin', rollin' on the river." So we recorded it. What I heard back sounded as rough as "Porterville." Angular, unsettled, abrasive. Amateur. Not smooth, not musical. Nor experienced. Or classy or elegant.

The voices just didn't blend, and my heart couldn't let it stand that way. Somebody had to be brutally honest and say, "This isn't gonna get it. This is probably gonna get us laughed at." And there wasn't anyone else but me to say it. "Proud Mary" was the best song I had written up to that point. I knew it was really, really special, and I wasn't going to settle for less. I had done that as a Golliwog and it just hadn't worked. When I was very critical about each element of the song and the performance, it was better, and I wanted us to be very, very, very good. I wanted us to make something for the ages. To be *great*. Like the Beatles.

So I told the guys I knew what to do — "I'm going to sing all the parts, overdub them myself. And I will *make it* sound that way." Well, the other guys were really upset over that. They weren't upset because it would be *better;* they were upset because they weren't doing it. *I* was doing it. There were a lot of angry words, a lot of tension. Tom, Doug, Stu — they were all mad at me. I stood my ground. The other three guys left the studio, so I proceeded to do exactly what I knew how to do: sing all the background vocals. That became "Proud Mary." That's what you hear on the record.

When I was done with the background parts, I went and joined the other guys, who were having dinner at a restaurant called Two Guys from Italy. I ordered spaghetti. I remember, because I played this scene over in my head for years and years, even in my time far away from show business. This was my band, my brother and my friends that I had grown up with, and there was all this friggin' tension.

I made a speech, the heart of which was, "It doesn't matter who in this band does the work. What matters is that this band makes the best record that it possibly can make, because it's us against the rest of the world." I thought my speech calmed things down for a couple of years. But in reality, the fuse had been lit. It was years later that Julie fully explained it to me: they were jealous. That "Proud Mary" incident was a pivotal point in the history of our band. I may have been doing arrangements before, but now I was doing almost everything. A time bomb was now ticking.

After the dinner we went back to the studio and Hank played back "Proud Mary." The guys were standing around. Our friend and road manager, Bruce Young, was there, and he heard the background parts and went, "Sounds like the Ink Spots!" I wish he'd said the Mills Brothers, but the sentiment was exactly right!

How the band acted was very telling, because this scenario played out again and again. It was almost as if they did not know it was great and had to be told by someone else.

That song. In the mid-seventies, I was on a moose-hunting trip with a couple of buddies up above Athabasca, Alberta. At that time I was far away from show business. We were all in some Athabasca bar the night before leaving for the hunting camp, and the band there did "Proud Mary." I was about ten feet away from the stage, but I had a mustache and glasses, so nobody recognized me. Basically, I was in the Arctic Circle, the North Pole, the end of the earth. And here's some Eskimos singing "Proud Mary."

Those Creedence songs I created—every guy in every bar can play them and sound just like the record. Even with medium musical ability, it sounds pretty dang good. The music is so easy to imitate. You don't have to be a Berklee College of Music graduate or have a $10,000 guitar. It's almost folk music, it's so simple.

"Proud Mary" was one of those songs where I had actually melded into mainstream polite society. President Gerald Ford and his wife, Betty, danced to "Proud Mary" at their inauguration. I was like, "Wow. Eat your heart out, Bob Dylan."

I actually did that song at my own wedding to Julie. I got up and said, "Everybody else has done this song at a wedding. By golly, I'm gonna sing this at *mine!*"

"Proud Mary" was the first of our two-sided hit singles. Usually a somewhat lesser song goes on the flip—the B side. But I didn't want to do it that way. There was a lot of discussion with Saul. People said, "You're going to get split airplay. You're wasting it." But I didn't want to cheap it out. Elvis had many double-sided hits. Same with the Beatles. Instead of, "I'm gonna hold this one back until three albums from now," the idea is, give 'em as much great music as you can—now! The fans will know.

"Born on the Bayou" was the other side of "Proud Mary." I first got the inspiration for the song during sound check at the Avalon Ballroom in San Francisco. There was a long bill and we were last. When you're last on the bill, you play first. Everybody else had done their sound check and was long gone. They wanted us to get ours over with and leave our stuff there because they were going to open the doors and get us up on the stage and then out of there.

So we're doing the sound check and I'm playing my Rickenbacker, hearing my cool Kustom amp with the vibrato doing its thing. I think I was doing "I Put a Spell on You"—that sound in the key of E. And with the guitar warbling, doing the tremolo, I got struck by a bolt of inspiration while playing that vibrato E chord. I just started going *"Mmmmmmm nahrnahr,"* and suddenly I'm yelling out a sound, not even words, and I turn around to Doug: "Doug, just give me this *'Doom dat doom bap.'*" I say to Stu, "Just play in E! Play in E!"

I'm screaming nonsense vowels and consonants— *"AEEEEew-waaaaAAAaaaaaAAA."* Random words and sounds lead me into something, and every once in a while it sounds like an actual word. I always tried to pick words that were really cool-sounding to sing. That's a lot different from the way many songwriters write, but it's because I'm the singer too. I'm a rock and roll guy. There are words that are really just cool-sounding to sing, and I'd find that word. "Puppy," "doggy," or... *"hound dog"*? "Shazam"— now there's a cool word. This was an important ingredient, along with pronunciation of the word itself, which was almost like a musical instrument to me.

So I'm there at the Avalon, singing my nonsense words, and I start to hear a melody. I'm inspired, really turned on, just ignited. This was just the coolest thing. Because it means it's going to turn into *a song.* This I know. Suddenly everything stops. "Hey—what happened?" I turn around and my amp has gone dead. The stage manager has pulled the plug.

He says, "You gotta get outta here. Let's face it: this is a waste of time. You're not goin' anywhere, anyway."

And I glared at him and I said, "Oh yeah, buddy? You give me one year and I'll show you who's not goin' anywhere!"

Look, he could've said that to any one of nine other bands that were there, and he'd probably have been right. But he said that to *me.* And that's not what I believed.

Well, a year later we couldn't even play that place. They couldn't afford us.

*　　*　　*

A few days after that night, I'm home, it's late at night, and I'm sitting in my chair, staring at that spot on the wall. Thinking about the bayou. This is right when Robert Kennedy was assassinated. By now we had a nineteen-inch Sears TV and I watched the coverage live. With the sound off.

It was a sad time in America. And one of the craziest times in civilization ever. Later that summer was the Democratic National Convention in Chicago, the youth clashing against Mayor Daley and the gestapo police. At times I was totally removed. I was thinking about the bayou.

I can't really tell you why. I was quite taken with the world of Mark Twain—*Tom Sawyer, Huckleberry Finn.* The same way I loved Stephen Foster. It resonated with me, seemed familiar. Warm and friendly. Like Twain was somebody I knew. Or like it was me in the story. And old movies like *Swamp Water* with Walter Brennan. That inspired me a lot. Something just possessed me to write about these places I'd never been to. I actually didn't even have a guitar in my hands when I wrote "Born on the Bayou." I could come up with a verse and play it all the way through in my head. I can still do that.

People ask me where I get that influence, because I'm certainly not from the South. Well, the first ten inductees into the Rock and Roll Hall of Fame are all from the South, and they all really influenced me. That process—it's a mystical journey. You go from a time when you're honoring other people, the influences you love, and then you begin to discover things you can do that are new and fresh. You begin to have your own personality—you're not just borrowing or copying from somebody.

Maybe you can chalk it up to reincarnation. I mean that quite seriously, but also in a humble way. I take no credit for it. It came so naturally. And it just *kept* coming. I mean, where in the world did all that really come from? I've had guys from Louisiana tell me, "We used to argue over whether you're from Thibodaux or the next town over." Was it a past life? Maybe. There's a lot of room in my head to believe in that sort of thing.

We'd recorded "Born on the Bayou," and just as Hank was playing it back, he went "Oh my God!" because he had erased the first piece of Tom's rhythm guitar—about eight bars, I think. It was really weird that it happened that way. We just decided to leave it. It sounded great as was. I wanted some atmosphere at the start of the song, so I held down an E chord and faded in the volume pedal...*breeeeeeoooowwwriiiin.*

Hearing that come over the radio was just the coolest thing. I sure was inspired when I flew back down to L.A. to sing the vocal. There was some magical trickery going on. Hank used a Fairchild limiter on my vocal (and something else we've never quite been able to pin down), but it gave that vocal track an unusual, cool quality.

Long after the song came out, I was standing in a Vegas casino. I had my hat on, incognito, or so I thought. I was playing a slot machine, and out of nowhere, somebody sidled up and whispered, " 'Born on the Bayou'—best recorded vocal of all time." Then he disappeared. Awesome.

That two and a half year Creedence period when I was just in the zone had already kicked in. Finding a great-sounding word to sing and doing some kind of sympathetic guitar part—it would all roll around in my head at the same time. The thought behind *Bayou Country*'s "Bootleg" was, why is it that those things that are really bad for you—candy, ice cream, alcohol—taste so good? Why is it that the things that we can't have we want even more? That song starts with an acoustic and goes on into electric. Pretty cool. That's Tom on acoustic guitar. We tuned down a Fender

Kingman because it was the only acoustic we had, and I showed him how to do that. Even though it was so new that his hand would still cramp up, Tom could really play by *Bayou Country*. He had great rhythm—in the same way that Elvis did, if you listen to those early records. Tom was like that. "Susie Q," "Proud Mary," "Born on the Bayou"—he always had great rhythm. Solid.

Another reason *Bayou Country* jumped out at you was my guitar sound. At around this time, I decided that in order to do songs with the guitar tuned down, and to avoid tuning up in front of the crowd, I had to have another guitar; be ready for the big time. I went to the Sherman Clay music store in San Francisco and bought a Gibson 175 Sunburst, a big jazz box like the one Scotty Moore used. At that point I was making a choice between Fender and Gibson, and Gibson had the big hollow bodies with humbucking pickups. I wanted to get as much of an acoustical thing as I could, but I didn't want to stick one of those sound hole pickups in the middle of it. When I plugged in the 175, I went, "*Oh!* I recognize that!" It was that *boink boink* "Diddley Daddy" sound. That guitar is most notable on songs like "Proud Mary," "Bootleg," and "Graveyard Train." That was a direct result of me seeing Pete Seeger talk about Lead Belly and his D tuning way back when.

That odd, blurry cover picture for *Bayou Country* was an unexpected gift. We'd gone up to Mount Tamalpais with a photographer and his assistant, Basul Parik. He took the picture while the zoom lens was moving. Was it an accident? When I was writing the album, I had tried to envision the cover, and that photo captured the mood I was seeing in my head. That was actually taken before we recorded. Saul wanted to call the album *Swamp Fever*. I thought that was the corniest title of all time. I thought, *If the kids see that title I'm gonna be a Golliwog again.*

I was at RCA, working with Hank on overdubbing congas and cowbell for "Born on the Bayou," when Tom came by. He had come up the stairwell and I believe we were using it for echo. Tom came in and said, "Man, that sure sounds good when the cowbell comes in." The second Creedence album is a lot better than the first. It's a huge step up. There's a maturity, a sonic difference. We really grew. It's a funny thing with bands, how they evolve. You're a listener, and there's this one song you like. Then they put out another album, you hear it, and you go, "Oh man, that's what they're aspiring to? *That's* what they dare to be?" It's actually beyond the thing that intrigued you in the first place—and that's where you hear greatness. I'm sure people did that with Pink Floyd, with the Beatles. Hopefully they did that with Creedence.

By early 1969, Creedence was on top of the world. That was *fast*. "Proud Mary" came out in January and went to number two on the charts. By March, we'd gone from daytime college gigs to four consecutive nights at the Fillmore. We did four encores every night. Sixteen encores total. The place was packed to the gills. They were going crazy.

Working out our fee with Bill Graham was kind of like playing chess. I stuck to my guns over the money, but I really respected him. Bill seemed a bit gruff at first, but he wasn't demeaning. He was a character, a real showman—"Go out there and give them their money's worth. Don't be silly and don't be stoned." Meaning we're professionals here, we're not stoned slobs or drunken hippies—he was against all that "Hey, I get paid to throw up onstage" stuff. He was the kind of guy that I could appreciate. He said it as much for the guys in the band as for the audience— "We're all gonna do this together."

Even though he'd paid us quite fairly, Bill went and got gold watches for each of us afterward *and* paid us a whole bunch of extra money. That was the type of guy he was. A guy who deserved loads of respect, because he brought a lot of credibility to rock and roll—when maybe some of the bands didn't deserve it. Bill Graham really was the best person I met in show business. Years later I'd turn to him for help in trying to settle things with Saul Zaentz.

The Fillmore was just the start. We flew to New York to appear on *The Ed Sullivan Show* that March. That was the big time—for me, that meant Elvis, the Beatles, Topo Gigio, and Señor Wences. Ed was very nice. He talked to Tom and me during rehearsal, and one thing he told us was that he had a twin brother. By the way, he was in his undershirt. It was just strange to see Ed so comfortable. Before the show, Ed would sneak off to his favorite restaurant and belt a few—I think it was Campari. The show was live, and every Sunday at six minutes to eight, everybody would be in a panic because he wasn't there. He'd waltz in at the last minute, all dressed up, and go right into being Ed Sullivan: "Well, tonight we have a reeelly beeg shoe." (Translation: "really big show.") The staff went through that ritual every Sunday for twenty-three years. Ed was awesome.

The first time, we were on with Jerry Lee Lewis and Moms Mabley, who did "Abraham, Martin and John." The second time was with Norm Crosby—"I resemble that!" We had a lot of fun with Norm. He was just happy to be alive. The second time we were there, we were waiting to go on, and right in front of where I was standing, on the reverse side of one of the backdrops, somebody had scrawled in pencil, "Vietnam is the Edsel of society." Whoever wrote that was one mighty philosopher...

"Proud Mary" / "Born on the Bayou" had been out a couple of weeks or so when I started thinking, *Better get something ready to go on the radio.* I had two new songs, but I wasn't sure that either of them was as good as "Proud Mary." I was even telling the band I considered them B sides. But I needed to record the next two songs or there was going to be a vacancy. I had to get us back on the radio.

"Lodi" was just a title for a long time. The inspiration was those trips with my dad to those small towns in central California, a place that I felt very warm and special about. I had already started to transfer my feelings about that place to the mythical Louisiana swamps I'd been writing about. It was also childhood. I was moving place and moving time, going back to when I felt really special and good and homey. It felt like me.

Somehow I got the idea of a traveling musician, probably a country guy, but older. A guy whose career is in the rearview mirror. The kicker is, "Oh Lord, stuck in Lodi...again!" That "Oh Lord" tells you how he feels. I was twenty-three writing this song, a very young man who'd just had a million-selling single all over the radio. That has nothing to do with the well you are drawing from when doing your craft.

One of the people I love is John Steinbeck and the rural world he created, especially *The Grapes of Wrath*. When you're a kid, you're doing what you do; you don't say your name in the same breath as those gods. You're just a punk kid trying to do a new thing. What's funny is, passing through Salinas I actually wrote down some of the street names in case I ever wanted to touch on all that. I was fascinated with that literary territory, but that research came out not in a specific but in an emotional way—it came out in things like "Lodi."

"Bad Moon Rising" was a title in my songwriting book; I believe it was on the first page. Hippies would be walking around asking, "What's your sign?" It was the lingo of the time—"I'm a Virgo with Libra rising," all this kind of stuff. And after hearing those things I wrote down, "Bad Moon Rising." It was a good image. I was up late at night trying to write, and I started thinking about this old movie, *The Devil and Daniel Webster,* about a farmer who sells his soul to Mr. Scratch—the devil—for good fortune.

The part that really made an impression on me was when this cyclone comes down and the farmer is cowering in the barn while all hell breaks loose outside. When he wakes up the next morning, all the neighbors have lost their crops to the storm. Thanks to the devil, our hero's crops are untouched.

What was important to me was the storm, the devil, and the way this guy had been—at least for the moment—protected. So I started writing about a natural disaster. Pretty unusual thing to write a song about, and what was more unusual was the snappy melody I gave it. Here I am talking about a horrible disaster and the devil taking your life, and it sounded as jaunty as Guy Mitchell doing "Singing the Blues." I thought the song was foreboding and dark, and it was only much later that people pointed out how happy it sounded. "And besides, what is this 'bathroom on the right'?" People made a joke out of mishearing the lyric, but I didn't take offense, like some persnickety language nerd might. It became such a thing over the years that half the time *I* sing that now.

I knew "Bad Moon Rising" was good before any singing happened. We were out back at Doug's, rehearsing, and one of the wives kept saying, "I like the one that goes...," and she'd hum the chord change. The lick on "Bad Moon Rising" is a big part of the song, and it's certainly borrowed from the Scotty Moore guitar lick on the Elvis record "I'm Left, You're Right, She's Gone." In places it's exactly the same. I didn't make the song *out* of his lick, but I used it. I wasn't hiding it—that lick was so great! I was honoring it.

One of the best things that ever happened to me was in 1986 or so, at one of those awards get-togethers. I was standing there, just looking at a lot of cool people, and somebody comes up behind me, puts his arms around me, and says, *"Give me back my licks!"* I turn around, and it's Scotty Moore! I hadn't really met him before and I just gushed. I told him, "I stole everything I know from you!" What a great memory.

I was planning on recording these songs with the Gibson 175

that's so key to the *Bayou Country* sound, but fate intervened. One day we'd been rehearsing at Doug's, and afterwards I went over to Fantasy's office in Oakland. I left my 175—plus a Tremolux amp I'd had since the tenth grade—in the backseat of a new Peugeot I'd bought with some of my first advance money from Fantasy. When I came out, the window glass was broken, my guitar and amp were gone, and there was a brick on the floor of my car. Right in front of my record company. (That should've told me something right there.)

I had to get a new guitar, and fast. I drove straight to Jimmy Luttrell's music store in Albany, looking for a Les Paul. I'd heard about all these English guitar guys playing Les Pauls, so I walk in and ask Jimmy, "Do you have any Les Pauls?" He points to a guitar up on the wall, but it's not a sunburst—it's black. A Les Paul *Custom.* Kind of high-end, maybe five hundred bucks. They had a Fender Twin amp sitting there. Powerful. I say, "I want to retune this." Jimmy didn't quite get it, but he said okay. So I tuned the guitar acoustically—down to D.

"Let's hear it," I say.

We plug it in and I just hit what would normally be an E chord, but what's coming out of this guitar now is a low-tuned D chord. And I go *brrrrrring.* That was the holy grail. Clean, with just a little bit of grit in it. That was *it.* It's *still* it.

That sound was a revelation. That new Les Paul was all ready to go and I bought that guitar on the spot. If I have done anything unique in rock and roll at all, that sound is it. I figured out how to have a great-sounding guitar. Listen to the opening of "Midnight Special." When I play that song live, everybody already knows. They sing that chord back to me! It was better than my stolen 175.

We went back to RCA to cut "Bad Moon Rising" and "Lodi." I remember flying down to L.A. to sing the vocal for "Lodi" and worrying on the plane because I was sitting next to the jet engine.

The rest of the *Green River* album was cut at Wally Heider Studios in San Francisco.* Russ Gary was the engineer who came along with the studio—a good addition to our team. It was Russ who told me that Elvis's guitar player was Scotty Moore; before that I didn't even know Scotty's name. Russ liked that music and understood the vibe. If I said, "Give me a little slapback echo," he knew what to do. And we would experiment a bit in the studio, especially at mix time.

The recording process at Heider's went like this: we'd record two basic instrumental tracks in four hours, and retire for that day. The next day or so, I'd go back alone and overdub lead guitar, cowbell, piano, or whatever was needed. Then I'd do the vocals—background vocals first, and then the lead. After that I'd go from the live studio into the mixing room, where the console was, and mix the songs. Russ and I would rehearse our moves for the faders, and between our four hands the song was mixed in twenty minutes. There was no sitting there going, "Hmm, I think that one syllable needs a bit more brightening." Nope—this was straight-ahead, get-it-done rock and roll. I had a strong work ethic—Ma Fogerty.

We'd finish a whole album in a couple of weeks, and on a very tiny budget. The first three albums were made for five thousand dollars total. This was before people started spending months and years in the studio. The first I heard about that was when we were in the studio and somebody mentioned that the producer for the 5th Dimension's "The Age of Aquarius" had been mixing for eleven hours. I just went, "Whaaa...?" Little did I know...

---

* The first thing we cut at Heider's was a pair of instrumentals, "Glory Be" and "Broken Spoke Shuffle." That was a test to check out the studio, which was new. Fantasy has since put them out on a special edition of *Green River,* but they really had nothing to do with the album. I was toying with the idea of having an alter ego, putting out records under another name.

*   *   *

Green River is my favorite Creedence album. I felt like that one hit the bull's-eye at the center of my soul. It's not that the other records aren't me; *Green River* just seemed to be my favorite place musically.

"Tombstone Shadow" comes from a story of the very early days of Creedence. We played a show in San Bernardino, and right across the street from our hotel was a fortune-teller. I was hoping I'd walk in and it would be like an old Universal horror film, with Maria Ouspenskaya from *The Wolf Man* as the gypsy. But it was just some guy in a green bowling shirt with a TV in the background blaring *Treasure Hunt* with Jan Murray. I gave him my five bucks. First he looked at my palms and said, "That's bad. You shouldn't fly in airplanes." Then he had me cut the cards, and he lifted two cards up: both red, a seven and a six. Thirteen. He says, "You're gonna have thirteen months of bad luck." I go, *Oh, great. Now he tells me*. I'd already signed Saul's contract!

There's a thread in a lot of my songs: I'm kind of ill at ease with what we call civilization. The TV blaring, computers, the fast pace of traffic, iPhones that turn on your porch light from Italy and operate a drone over some town in the Middle East. I'm kind of anti that. I'm seeking some sort of peace—or, to use another word, clarity. Instead of confusion, I'm into having things make sense. "Commotion" is railing against all that confusion.

"Sinister Purpose" was another title in my songbook. That's about the concept of the devil—the unspeakable dark force, he who is most evil. *That* guy. It was an interesting idea to have the devil talking directly to you, not pleading his case so much as handing you his business card. The guy in "Cross-Tie Walker" is from the same town that "Green River" is set in. "Cross-Tie Walker" is a phrase I invented. It's about hoboes catching trains. There was a hobo camp outside Healdsburg, one of the towns where I had a summer resort job. You'd poke around and see cans of beans strewn about, burned-out fires.

"Wrote a Song for Everyone" was based on a real thing that happened. It was a Sunday afternoon in 1969, and I was hell-bent to keep the music coming. Every day I was writing. There was some urgency in my mind—"Strike while the iron's hot, because it could all be over in the blink of an eye." I was home, had my guitar and amp and a little recorder, and I was working away. My wife, Martha, probably had other ideas for the weekend and made some remark like, "Is that all you're going to do today?" I was a bit aloof, off in my world, and didn't realize we were in the midst of a discussion. And she said, "Well, I'm going to go see my mother."

Just as the door closed behind her, it finally dawned on me that she was angry. And a phrase went right into my head: "I wrote a song for everyone, and I couldn't even talk to you." It was specifically true right at that moment! In writing the song, I made it less personal and more general. There were politicians during those days who were older and couldn't relate to their kids—the generation gap. Maybe his child was arrested for drugs or being drunk, and the public figure's thinking, *What am I gonna do with this kid? I can talk to the masses, but I can't even talk to my own son.* That seemed to be a worthy subject for a song.

We first recorded that on a day when we recorded four other songs at Wally Heider's. It wasn't hanging together, didn't groove—I didn't like how the drums felt. Wobbly. So we went back. Musically, on that version the band was tighter. But nobody had guitar tuners in those days, and the effect of the guitar being D-tuned made the strings floppy enough that my guitar's tuning on that second version really bothers me. I'd love to be able to hear the first version, but I don't think it exists. Even then, I was afraid that Fantasy would dig up the outtakes and put them out later, and I'd already begun erasing the other versions once we had the keeper down.

Musically, I was always trying to go somewhere new. Listening to the radio, you got the sense that some artists—early Elvis, the Stones, especially the Beatles—were restless and didn't want to repeat themselves. The Dave Clark Five did that same sound for four or five singles in a row. It's been said that AC/DC—whom I love—continues to make the same album over and over. I was determined that Creedence would go with its strengths—mid-tempo songs with a lead vocal, sometimes harmony—definitely no shuffle beats. What I told the band at the time was, "We're gonna show them what we *can* do well and eliminate what we *can't* do well." I also wanted different feels, different approaches, different guitar sounds. I thought it was boring to always sound the same. Boring! That was a one-way ticket to the land of the one-hit wonder for sure. "Proud Mary" and "Born on the Bayou" were two completely different sounds on the very same single. "Proud Mary" had that gospelly thing; "Bayou" was swampy. "Bad Moon Rising" was kind of rockabilly. I wanted to go deeper.

On "Green River" the guitar riff, the musical hook, was how I imagined James Burton would've done it. James would always find just the right part. I wanted that bluesy rockabilly sound rather than a pretty melody like "Proud Mary." It's almost as if, had I been lucky enough to be recording at Sun Records, this is what I would've come up with. Even though Stu played electric bass, I also had him play stand-up. They're both in that song. That's a real thought-out bass part. It isn't just, "Play whatever." I created that part because I *had* to.

You can go into a studio, and if you've got all the great Nashville session guys and everybody gets it, a song might happen in five minutes. Or it might never happen. I had been in my band long enough to know that it was going to be much more like the latter. What usually happened was, nobody knew what to do. These were not guys who could invent parts. That bass part on "Green River" could've been a country ticktack bass line, but that would've been lame. I love country, but we were not a country band. I had to figure out a bass rhythm that wasn't exactly Sun Records, because they weren't making this record—I was—and I can tell you it was thought out long before I showed it to the band, and certainly long before recording. Stu was not going to invent his own part, but if you gave him something that made sense, he could learn that and play it well.

Stu has taken credit for the distinctive (and relatively tough) bass line for a later song, "Down on the Corner." But that's not how it went down. Stu had a lot of trouble with that bass line in the studio. Because of Stu's large but fragile ego, I had been spoon-feeding that part to him. What that meant is I already had the parts figured out before I showed it to the band. It had to be that way. I was the one who solved the puzzle of what worked together to make a great arrangement for the song I had written. Then at our rehearsals I showed it to Stu a little bit at a time—"Here, try these notes." After a few minutes, letting that much sink in: "Okay, now try *these* notes." Then as Stu fumbled with what to do next: "Okay, how 'bout if you add *these* notes?" After a few days, Stu had been presented with the whole bass part. Eventually, we spent six weeks rehearsing the song, but Stu still couldn't do it when we got to the recording session. It was very tense. Tom was already sitting out because he couldn't keep the rhythm going all the way through the song, so we'd decided that later we'd over-dub his part a piece at a time. And now Stu was having a melt-down. Finally he yelled at me, "Well, this is no good! And besides, *this ain't rock and roll!*" And I'm thinking, *Right—because Stu can't play the part, he's gonna tell me what is and what isn't rock and roll?*

I remember this very clearly, as it was one of those times when I had to be...quiet. Very quiet. The thought in my head was, *I didn't come here to fight. I came here to make a record.* Looking back, I should've been like one of the Kinks or the Troggs, picked up a guitar or a hi-hat, and just horned the guy—"You stupid-ass bimbo, this is *not that hard*. It's just that it's got some *rhythm* in it, and you don't have any!" My job was to make a hit record, so somehow I defused the situation and we all conquered the song. Nope—I didn't hear "thank you" afterwards.

It's funny: of all the guys in the band, Stu's personality was the most negative. And vocal. In the fall of 1969, we taped *The Dionne Warwick Chevy Special* alongside Burt Bacharach, Glen Campbell, and George Kirby. We pulled up for the taping at the CBS building, and there was a long line of people dressed up in funny costumes, trying to get on *Let's Make a Deal*. I made the band stay in the car while I explained to them that I didn't want three or four different people voicing their dissatisfaction over this or that to the production staff. I said it would be much better if just one voice addressed the needs of the band. I said, "Bring your issues to me, and I will tell the appropriate people." By the time I got inside, Stu was already in the face of the director, Art Fisher, complaining about God knows what in a very unpleasant and aggressive manner.

The first time we went over to England to play Royal Albert Hall, Stu had issues with the promoter. When we got back to the States, he popped off about him in the press. The next time we were in England, I was standing at the hotel elevator and some guy goes, "Are you John?" And I got served with papers. If anyone was going to speak in the wrong place and with too much aggression, it was Stu. That personality was always coming at you.

CHAPTER 9

"We're with Ya, John!"

REMEMBER HOW QUICK everything was happening? "Susie Q" had been a hit single, "I Put a Spell on You" had been a radio hit, the first album had been a hit, and the next album, *Bayou Country*, was a hit, with "Proud Mary" and "Born on the Bayou." Both songs on the next single, "Bad Moon Rising" and "Lodi," had been hits, and now "Green River" / "Commotion" was climbing the charts, with the album *Green River* just about to be completed. It was right about this time that the guys in the band started saying, "Remember Saul said if we had a hit record we were gonna tear up the contract and get a bigger piece of the pie?" Well, we weren't hearing anything about this from Saul. He wasn't knocking on our door. By now he'd moved into a new building in Oakland and had several more employees.

So the band said, "John, you go talk to Saul." And they kind of pushed me out the door. Meaning *they* didn't want to confront Saul. I'm the leader of the band—at least in this instance—and they want me to go see him. So I went and sat in Saul's office and started talking about the meeting we had at his house and how we were promised a bigger piece of the pie. "We would now like you to honor that promise," I said. He ignored that and immediately started talking about how he's thinking of taking Fantasy public.

"What's that mean to me?" I asked.

Saul explained that he was going to let Creedence buy stock in Fantasy, and that this would add up to 10 percent of the company for us. I kept asking about his promise to tear up the original contract, but he kept bringing it back to the stock. He said, "So in return for letting you purchase part of the company, we want you to sign a ten-year contract with Fantasy."

We'd already signed a contract with options adding up to seven years, and other than what the casual, everyday, average American has heard about business and the stock market, I really didn't know what any of this meant. When I explained this to the band, I made that clear—"I'm not taking this on myself. I don't want to be blamed for this later." I wanted our professionals to sort this out and explain it to us. By this time we had an accountant, Edward J. Arnold, and a lawyer, Barry Engel, who was with the firm that Stu Cook's dad was a partner in. We sent them to meet with Saul's people.

When they came back, they explained that Saul wasn't offering 10 percent of the *company*—just the opportunity to buy 10 percent of the stock offering that represented 11 percent of the company. What it boiled down to was that Creedence, which was responsible for 99.5 percent of the records Fantasy sold, was being offered a ten-year contract, and in return we could buy 1.1 percent of the company ourselves. That didn't look very appetizing.

I want to stress that point, because in later years Saul Zaentz said, "We offered John Fogerty ten percent of Fantasy Records and he refused." And he sold that falsehood to at least two of the members of Creedence Clearwater Revival, even though we had all heard the real offer back in 1969. I know my brother Tom used to quote that one. And I've heard Doug Clifford quote that. Plain and simple, it's just not true. And in fact, Fantasy never went public, so there was no stock offer anyway, and no 10 percent offer.

There was a lot of tension between the band and Saul now. I'd still go in and talk to him, but the mood had changed. When Fantasy had their second annual company picnic in 1969, it was not so friendly. The executives sat away from us at one end of the field. I think that's where Saul told me he was going to give me back my publishing. He said, "By contract, I don't have to—I could have it for another three years—but I'm giving it back to you at the end of this three-year period."

I thought those words meant that he was giving me back all the publishing on the Creedence songs I'd written. No. What Saul really meant was that any songs I wrote in the future (specifically, after January 1, 1971) I would own. He was keeping everything I wrote until then and wasn't giving anything back. Unfortunately, by 1971 the band was on its way to breaking up, and I'd only get one more song on the radio, "Sweet Hitch-Hiker." Screwed again.

At the time, I started feeling actual physical pain over all this, although I didn't know at the time that this pain was an ulcer. At twenty-four!

Next, Saul started talking about offshore tax planning (first via this individual Harry Margolis, and then it changed to Chicago and this guy Burt Kanter) and how this would be his way of giving us a bigger piece of the pie. At the time, Creedence wasn't even incorporated, and we were getting taxed at 90 percent. So we were sold this idea that our royalties would be paid to an offshore entity so that instead of paying 90 percent of every dollar we earned to taxes, we'd pay something less than 10 percent. Our accountant and lawyer advised us to do it. We were told that this was all quite legal, that it had to do with foreign treaties, and that this was what the big, rich, old-money people like the Rockefellers and the Kennedys did. We were also told that Burt Kanter was a former IRS agent and had the inside scoop. It was only years later when we were preparing for trial that I found out this was a lie.

After much deliberation among all four members of the band,

Creedence entered into Fantasy's tax plan, which was tied to this outfit in the Bahamas: Castle Bank. I'll tell more of this story in a bit, but needless to say, it was a disastrous move. This was all part of a new contract dated June 5, 1969, that was marginally better than the last one. (I believe this contract was backdated, as we were still talking about all this throughout the summer of 1970. It hadn't been formally agreed to until late 1970 or even into 1971.) We'd get back ownership of our name, which Saul had claimed for himself in the first contract, and Fantasy was forbidden from sticking our songs on schlocky compilation albums without our consent. Yet we owed Saul 180 masters, which he'd own forever. So much for tearing up the old contract.

Later on I'd be blamed for these decisions, but they were made unanimously by the band with advice from our professional team. And the truth is that in the early days of Creedence—even going back to the Golliwogs era—Tom was considered our business leader. He was older, had a family and a grown-up job, credit cards, and a house. The situation was still this way when we signed our first contract with Saul back on January 5, 1968.

Soon after that, Tom talked us into hiring Max Weiss as our manager. I really didn't like that idea, but Tom felt that Max had been "left behind." There were other financial decisions that bothered me, but the capper as far as Tom goes was in the summer of 1968, after "Susie Q" had been released and our first album was doing well. Tom accepted an engagement for a fee that was far below what we were now worth.

It was then that I put my foot down. I said, "We should only have one voice talking to people about our fee. You don't seem to understand how our career is going." I could see that I had a much clearer idea about our career. Unfortunately, the worst damage had already been done: signing that contract with Saul.

Strangely, we weren't approached by outsiders, although the notorious Allen Klein met with us sometime in 1970. And get this—we told him about our horrible contract with Saul, and he looked it over and said these exact words: "There's nothing I can do."

There is some weird rock and roll irony about Allen Klein.

He met with the Stones...they broke up.

He met with the Beatles...they broke up.

He met with the Kinks...they broke up.

He met with Creedence...yep, they broke up.

There's long been a rumor that Creedence was the first band to sign on to play at Woodstock. We were by no means the first. In the spring and summer of 1969, we were playing up and down the eastern seaboard, and I remember seeing billboards from Atlanta to New York with that logo of the hand on the guitar and the little bird perched on the neck.

By the time Woodstock came together, we were approached through our new booking agency, Associated Booking Company. I know we wanted a headline spot on the best night. At that point we were obviously heading to be the number one band in the world—well, actually number two (behind the Beatles, of course).

Right before Woodstock, we'd been taping *The Andy Williams Show* all week in Hollywood, and we had to rush out of there and catch the red-eye to New York. We touched down just as the dawn was coming up—I remember because I was thinking about "Midnight Special," a Lead Belly song I was going to have us record. After a drive up to the Catskills and a few hours' sleep, some very shaky little World War II helicopter took us to Woodstock. I had visions of every rock singer who had died in a plane crash dancing in my head.

When we finally got up over the field, the crowd took my breath away. They say there were half a million people there, all between the ages of fifteen and twenty-five. It was humongous. I know I felt more than nervous: I was scared. I think I was one of just a few people who had that particular emotion.

I actually went walking out in the crowd. Had a little hat on, and kind of hid. Somebody was selling water—a gallon for five dollars. And I was aghast. That was so mercenary to me, that somebody was making money off water. So I came back to the guys even more nervous. I was worried that all these people would get moving in a stampede and that people would get hurt. Even though we were the so-called peace and love generation, we'd never been tested that way. I didn't want something bad to happen because all the naysayers—starting with President Nixon—would just go, "See? I told ya! Make no mistake about that: you people are just no good!"

Then it got dark. It was getting later and later and later, and the acts that were supposed to be on at six o'clock still hadn't been on at nine. I got the sense that the whole thing was being held together by the thinnest of threads, and I was just trying to be mellow, ready for whenever it was our turn.

We would be following the Grateful Dead. Finally the Dead went on and played for an hour or so, and then their equipment broke. After what seemed like a long, long time, they started playing—again. And they played for a good forty-five minutes or whatever. All I know is that we ended up going on way late in the night.

We came charging out like we always did, James Brown–style—*bang!* We started with "Born on the Bayou." By the second number I was looking around and I saw...nothing. Blackness. Shadow, but no movement. I finally looked closer, because you can really only see the first four rows or so, and it was like a scene from Dante's *Inferno,* the souls coming out of hell. All these intertwined young people, half naked and muddy, and they looked dead. The Grateful Dead had put half a million people to sleep.

So I walked up to the mic and said something to the effect of, "Well, we're havin' a great time up *here.* Hope you're havin' fun out *there!*" No response. Dead audience. Could've heard a pin drop. It was like Henny Youngman on a bad night. And finally some guy a quarter mile away in the distant night flicked his lighter, and I heard him say ever so faintly, "Don't worry about it, John! We're with ya!" So I played the rest of the set for that one guy. I was connecting with somebody—that's all I cared about. We definitely warmed the audience up for Janis. By the time she came out, everybody was up and rockin' again.

Creedence isn't in the movie. I was the one who vetoed that. Besides the crowd being asleep, Doug's drum broke, so it didn't sound good after a couple of songs. There were also issues with lighting and I think even with the monitors. I didn't look at the movie as being a historical document, the way I might now: I looked at it as a career opportunity. I think the promoters went broke immediately. Somewhere in the vague recesses of my mind I'm not exactly sure that we ever actually got paid for playing Woodstock.

My mind-set was, why should I show the whole world we're doing badly? I didn't think that was going to help us. We were doing great everyplace else.

I have great memories of all our supporting acts—Ike and Tina Turner, Bo Diddley, Wilbert Harrison, Booker T. and the MGs, Tony Joe White. We picked them. Coming from the R & B end of things, we certainly weren't seeking out the Cyrkle or the Cowsills. No, this was about payback. We were honoring our influences, people who were still out there making music. It was a cool thing to tour with them, and I thought it would be a great thing for Creedence's audience to see.

Bo Diddley put on a heck of a show. I felt like a sixteen-year-old seeing the Giants with Willie Mays: he's older maybe, but he still knocks it out of the park. At some point on the tour, he showed up in a shiny new green Cadillac convertible and drove from city to city in that. Wilbert Harrison—now that was a treat. He had a current hit, "Let's Work Together." Wilbert did a one-man-band thing. He'd play guitar and sing, and there was a big bass drum with a hi-hat that he'd play with his feet. It was loaded with shaker stuff so you'd think it was a tambourine. His kick drum said "Mr. Kansas City—WILBERT HARRISON!" It was almost folk art.

One of my favorite memories from a long career involves that drum. We were in an airport somewhere, waiting for our bags. Suddenly, I start to hear a clattering combined with a low booming sound, and it's getting louder. Then up from the basement comes that big ol' bass drum on the conveyor belt. No case. No cover. Up, up, *crish, crash, clatter.* Slowly, slowly... then over the top and *bang!* Down to the carousel with the other bags. *Boom! Boom!* Mr. Kansas City!

I had noticed Tina Turner early on, long before she and Ike did "Proud Mary." The Blue Velvets used to do "It's Gonna Work Out Fine." It was funny and funky and had this cool guitar riff dripping in tremolo. Flash-forward to 1967, and here are these singers getting lots of credit in the underground world, Janis and Grace Slick. I just thought, *Man, Tina could sing circles around them. (Or Mavis Staples!)* I was overjoyed by Ike and Tina's version of "Proud Mary." That was their most commercial mainstream hit up to that point. It felt like a really positive thing, that sense of paying back and honoring your influences. We played some dates together. Ike loved "Fortunate Son." He'd be up onstage and toss that lick into one of their songs. Can you imagine how that felt?

We played with them at the Salt Palace in Salt Lake City, which of course is the spiritual center of Mormonism. I'd go out in the audience to watch Ike and Tina, and this time I noticed all these monitors—older guys in civilian clothes acting like security guards. If anybody got up and started dancing, these guys would tap on their shoulder and lead them back to their chair. Tina went into her version of Otis Redding's "I've Been Loving You Too Long." She'd get real suggestive with the microphone, doing pretty much everything you could do with a mic, especially if it represented some guy that you were attracted to.

Now the elders in the audience were freaking out, just losing their minds, jumping up and down. I don't know if they thought they were going to stop the show or what. All I remember is Tina taking her sweet time with that mic. I'm loving every second of it. Back then I didn't know any of the stuff about Ike that we heard later. I'm an honorable guy and I love women—I love and respect my wife completely. We treat each other as equals. Therefore, I don't have much respect for Ike Turner.

One of my favorite memories of all time is playing arenas like the Oakland Coliseum with Booker T. and the MGs as our opening act. I'd go stand in the wings and listen. What a sound. You think the records are great? The way that organ spun around that big coliseum was magical to me. In the middle of "Time Is Tight" they hit the big crescendo of the bridge, and God! It certainly inspired my band to be as good as we could be, because those guys were watching us. Somewhere there is footage of Creedence and Booker T. and the MGs jamming together for a TV special. They filmed that show but turned the cameras off before we did "In the Midnight Hour." That performance was really special. You know why? Because of that thing R. B. King told us back in high school: "There's somethin' missing." Well, with Booker T. and the MGs helping us, it wasn't missing.

Willy and the Poor Boys was released in November 1969. The album title came from seeing an ad in the newspaper for a "Winnie-the-Pooh Super-Pooh Package." I just loved how that sounded, and I wanted to create a cartoonish Winnie-the-Pooh story in song, with a mythical group. I had started writing "Down on the Corner" when we were scheduled to be on *The Andy Williams Show*. We were staying in a hotel in Universal City, and I was in my room, duty-bound to come up with the next single, and I looked out my window and saw the fellas hanging out by the swimming pool, waiting to be picked up for the taping. Each character I name in the song is basically one of us.

I'm Willy, the guy in the front playing his harmonica and doing a little dance. Stu is Blinky, meaning somewhat myopic and somewhat nervous. Tom was Poorboy because he'd frequently sound like, "Poor me. I should be doin' this, I should be doin' that. This isn't good enough." Of course Doug was Rooster, a name that he had earned out on the road by looking for whatever female companionship he could find or pay for. Wilbert Harrison told me that the song was very popular in New York City with the Latin people, that they loved that rhythm, that sound. That made me feel good.

We shot the cover out in front of Duck Kee Market. I almost cropped its name out. I'm sure glad I didn't. The photo was taken by Basul Parik, who'd taken our previous two covers, but he showed up with only one roll of film, which un-got him the gig for our next cover. We were actually playing "Poorboy Shuffle" at the time. A bunch of little city kids showed up. That was a happy accident. Some of them ended up on the cover with us. Saul actually wanted to call the album *Down on the Corner with Willy and the Poor Boys* because he thought that including the lead single in the title would make the distributors, the rack jobbers, happy. I resisted that suggestion.

I loved the Lead Belly song "Cotton Fields." Pete Seeger had done it, and so had the folk group the Highwaymen as a B side in 1962. The guy sounded a little like Buddy Holly, there wasn't a bunch of folk attitude, and the song even had drums. Man, I loved that record. So I knew that at some point I was going to do that song. I wish I'd had a Telecaster back then, but I didn't. I played my Rickenbacker and used a lot of reverb.

Then there was Doug. Doug was a rock and roll drummer. It wasn't finesse, it wasn't jazz, it wasn't quiet and subdued—it was kicking you right in the face, which is what I wanted. He had pretty good tone most of the time. That's important. But it just wasn't real polished or professional, and sometimes I had a problem with his timing. The drum break on "Lodi" comes to mind.

On "Cotton Fields" the drums were just...bad. Tempo wasn't right. After rehearsing that song for probably four weeks, we recorded it at Wally Heider's in three, maybe four takes. It wasn't going to get better. I had to say uncle.

A little while later, when I put the vocals on, I had to confront that track, and it was not acceptable to me. The drumbeats were all late. Now, this was in the days before digital, when it wasn't easy to fly things around. We're talking about two-inch analog tape. I said to Russ Gary, "Russ, are you game for this? I want to edit a little bit out of each backbeat so that the beats will hit a little bit sooner." There were maybe thirty or forty edits. I knew the guitars wouldn't sound right after that, so I added two tracks of acoustic strumming to try to smooth out the edits. That kind of editing is nerve-racking, like holding nitroglycerin. Screw up and you ruin the master tape.

But we managed to do it. I sang all the background vocals, the lead vocal, played the acoustic guitars, maybe a tambourine, and mixed it. That was certainly a full day. When we were all done, there was a pile of all those pieces of tape we'd cut out lying on the floor. So I went and got an envelope. Because I was pissed. I put all those pieces of tape—a lot of pieces of tape—in the envelope, drove to Doug's house, and said, "Here's your drum track."

Years later, in the early eighties, Martha and the kids and I were driving down in Texas near the border, listening to the radio. Creedence was huge in Mexico back in the day, and sure enough, from across the border comes "Cotton Fields." Even in the middle of nowhere I couldn't escape that friggin' drum track! And it's *still* late!

"It Came Out of the Sky" was inspired by two things. As a youngster I read every science fiction book in the El Cerrito library, and I loved all the movies—*Invaders from Mars, Them!, It Came from Outer Space.* I saw every one. I was immersed in them. I must've seen *The Day the Earth Stood Still* 250 times. I'm also a fan of that old movie *Ace in the Hole.* Kirk Douglas plays a reporter, and somebody falls down a hole in a cave, and they figure out a way to milk the thing—to make his rescue take longer than it should. At first it's just happening out in the middle of nowhere, but soon there's catering trucks, film crews, and reporters—all the support that goes with people selling a story. That was the direction I wanted to go in with "It Came Out of the Sky." Walter Cronkite and Eric Sevareid are in there, big newscasters at the time. And Ronald Reagan—I call him Ronnie the Popular. I was trying to imitate a horn section with the guitar, but the background's kind of plunky, vaguely Chuck Berry. I wish I could go back and make a better record of it. The song is better than that record.

In "Don't Look Now (It Ain't You or Me)" I was just prodding my generation a bit—"Before we get to feeling holier-than-thou with all our grand ideas, let's take a look at what's really going on," who is really doing the work. I always considered myself right in the middle of my generation, not removed in any way, although I thought the "hippie" label was sort of a *Time* magazine manifestation. I've only ever met one guy who actually called himself a hippie—a fellow in the army who was going to move to the middle of Arizona and let everybody else take care of him, which I thought was immoral. We used to argue over that: "We need a police force! Aren't you gonna pay taxes?" "No, I'll just live off the land." "Well, you're living off of *somebody's* land."

Even though new ideas were being vocalized, and there was all this hopefulness and do-gooderness, and we'd accomplished a lot of philosophical things through demonstrations and protests, my generation wasn't working in the blue-collar mainstream yet, and we weren't doing the kind of stuff that the pioneers who built our country did. So I was saying, "Don't look now, but it's not you or me. Other people are the ones doing that stuff for us." But I'm not saying I hate hippies. When I said "hippie," I also meant myself.

"Effigy" was inspired by Nixon. What a schmuck. Nixon just didn't have a clue. I think the topper for me was in November 1969, when 250,000 demonstrators camped out near the White House to protest the war. Nixon came out and told them, "Nothing you do here today will have any effect on me"—he was going to go back inside and watch the football game on TV. It was like, "Your people have come to talk to you, King Louis XVI. They're upset." And he's telling them he doesn't care, he's going back in the palace to do what royalty does.

Watching the Watergate hearings on TV a few years later depressed me. I really wrestled with it. I felt so ashamed of America. Finally I came to a realization. I'm American. I love America—I love Daniel Boone, Abraham Lincoln, and the Grand Canyon. I love my country. But the crooked government—that's not my country. Every time Nixon's upper lip was sweating, you knew he was lying. Of course, the older we get, the more our history moves away from our forefathers. George Washington—you just have to admire somebody who turned down being emperor for life. A lot of people haven't been able to resist.

"Fortunate Son" wasn't really inspired by any one event. Julie Nixon was dating David Eisenhower. You'd hear about the son of this senator or that congressman who was given a deferment from the military or a choice position *in* the military. They seemed privileged, and whether they liked it or not, these people were symbolic in the sense that they weren't being touched by what their parents were doing. They weren't being affected like the rest of us. Usually I strive to make my songs more general, but that was one case where, when I said "It ain't me," I literally meant me.

With this kind of song, you're carrying a weighty, difficult idea. I didn't want the song to be pulled down into that "Now we're serious; everybody get quiet" place. If I was going to write a quote unquote protest song, a serious song, I didn't want it to be a *lame* song. It's funny: of all my songs that are more serious and have real intent, "Fortunate Son" took by far the least time to write — like I said, just twenty minutes.

As I told Dave Grohl once, there's a lot of genres and styles in rock and roll, but the one that's absolutely the hardest to do right is a driving, kick-ass rock and roll song. You hear a lot of songs with lame lyrics like, *"Rock rock rock! Yeah! Yeah!"* But something that's really valid and leaves you breathless at the end? Those are few and far between.

Doing "Fortunate Sun" with the Foo Fighters for *Wrote a Song for Everyone* was like a duck taking to water. It was just, "Man, this is *fun*." Really simple. Not complicated. We spent some time kind of twisting up the arrangement a bit, but basically the power of the band just jumped right in and made it really cool. The Foo Fighters have their own studio. When I first got there, I parked my car and came in the back. I opened the door, and it hit me like a big *whoosh:* "God, there's a *band* in here." I took note of that immediately. Their drummer, Taylor Hawkins, was sitting at the drums by himself, making a heck of a racket. There was a palpable sense of *a band*. It's an atmospheric thing. Just a group of fellows locked together, who think as one.

Made me remember I was in a band. A long, long time ago.

*　　*　　*

Creedence was invited to appear on *The Johnny Cash Show* in the spring of 1969 for an airing in September. We taped it at the old Ryman Auditorium, and Roy Orbison and Carl Perkins were also on the show, so I was in hog heaven backstage. These were people I really admired, and I was hearing fables of a time that I loved. At some point Roy says, "Oh, yeah, I had 'Ooby Dooby' out, I was just this kid, I do my show and figure I might end up at this girl's house, in a room with her." He said it kind of politely. "Yeah, then I found out Elvis had been there first." Roy said that like it was a common occurrence. I hope I'm not saying anything that offends anyone all these years later, but it was such a funny picture. Then he talked about recording "Ooby Dooby." Until then I had no idea that Roy had played lead guitar on the record. I thought it was some young hotshot—well, yeah, it was—*Roy!* Awesome!

I met Mother Maybelle and she gave me a big hug. I love that feeling I get now, all these years later, just knowing that my path crossed hers. June Carter Cash came over and sat down next to us, wearing shorts, her hair in a ponytail. God, she was great. And Johnny—"We-e-e-e-l-l-l, I'm Jo-o-o-o-hnny Cash." He really did talk like that. A little of that Mister Ed vibrato in the voice. When I first met him, I was so dumbfounded that I just blurted out, "I-I-I love you, Johnny Cash." That's all I could manage, because I *do* love him. He gave me a pat on the head and said, "I know, son."

In 1992, Johnny Cash got inducted into the Rock and Roll Hall of Fame. We were up there onstage for the jam. We played "Big River"—I kind of knew how it went. There are twenty-five rockers onstage, and suddenly Vernon Reid breaks into "Purple Haze." Johnny Cash was on one side of me and Keith Richards was on the other side—how many times in your life can you say that?

Johnny's got his acoustic guitar, and in the middle of "Purple Haze" he leans down and says to me in that warbly voice, "We-e-e-e-e-l-l-l, I think I met my match."

In November 1969, a small band of Native Americans went to Alcatraz Island. They were upset over various injustices and were taking a stand. Nixon's government pushed back, and the FBI was threatening to come, so it became more of an occupation.

Quite naturally, I took the Native Americans' side. It seemed apparent that the government was going to try to starve them out, so I wanted to help. First I talked it up among my bandmates, and they were happy to join me. We were able to purchase food and supplies for them. I was not trying to get any credit for it. I've always been really suspicious when a celebrity does something charitable, poses for all the pictures, and then puts out a poster. That wasn't my motivation. We pretty much tried to do it anonymously, and it was anonymous—until a few weeks later, when the Native Americans named their boat the *Clearwater*.

That story only got funnier when Fantasy arranged some sort of gold record presentation party on a cruise boat at around that time. We actually neared Alcatraz, and there was the *Clearwater*.* I knew what that meant, and so did the band, but the people from Fantasy didn't: "Hey, look! There's a boat named *Clearwater*!" They didn't have a clue.

That episode did not necessarily end well, like most things that happened between the Native Americans and the government. But I felt good about doing what I did. When you try to do something for the right reasons, you feel good. I always feel like I've done fewer benefits than many musicians—some people have a whole regimen. I do them as they come up, when it feels right to me. I

---

* It had been scuttled—sunk—probably by the FBI.

want to be genuine about it. I've been given such a huge bounty of success. It's the right thing to do.

I felt guilty about my success. I *always* felt guilty about it. I was kind of sheepish about having money after not having any for so long. I knew inside that I could buy things, but I also had a sense about not being flamboyant or showy. I was still wearing my flannel shirts!

When the rap guys started having big dollar sign chains and rings that said "money," I was taken aback. In my generation, if you stood up there and started talking about money, they'd probably have thrown rotten tomatoes at you. But I came to understand that it's just a different reaction to the same thing—a reaction to not having it.

One thing I did purchase back then was an MG sports car. I was driving down San Pablo Avenue, the main drag in El Cerrito, and the car just died. A week after I bought it! I literally had to push it off to the side of the road. There's a lesson to be learned there. I bought myself a fancy sports car, and here I was, being spanked for doing something like that.

The trouble with having stuff is that everybody else wants it. I was careful not to say anything about it, because people were starting to come up and ask for free money. And since I never had anything as a kid and already felt guilty, I was an easy touch—"Yeah, sure. I have way more than I'll ever need."

There was one young singer on Fantasy who asked, "John, can you give me five thousand dollars? My manager wants to put me on this tour of Europe. They say it's important, but I don't have any money. Fantasy said they would support the tour, but then they reneged. When we get home from the tour, I'll pay you back." I gave her the money, and then I never heard from her again.

That's kind of how it works. People come to your doorstep with bags full of their problems. They ask you for money, you give it to them, they give you their baggage, and then you open that little closet next to your front door, where all the other baggage is kept, and wait for them to come get their baggage and return the money. Because now the problem is yours. You have to wait to get paid back...you might be waiting a long time.

Saul actually said to me once, "Money doesn't change you. It *unmasks* you." No shit, Saul!

I played sax on "Travelin' Band," the Creedence single that came out in January 1970. Well, I just felt the urge to pay homage to that whole Little Richard sound. I had gone and rented a sax in the early sixties to play a song that Tom had written called "Watusi Lucy." I had practiced enough to play that little part, which is exactly what I did with "Travelin' Band." Of course, what I really should've done is get a real horn section. That's what the Beatles would've done, but somehow there's that thing in my head: "I'll do it myself." In a way, that made it sound charming, homemade.

I love horns, especially when they're used right. Stax had it down. I thought the horns in Chicago or Blood Sweat and Tears were too big, too much for rock and roll. I guess people feel, "Well, I gotta pay him for the whole time, so I'm gonna use him the whole time." Horns really ought to play a little bit, and then be quiet!

The flip side of "Travelin' Band" was "Who'll Stop the Rain." That's really kind of a protest song, but I imagine a lot of people don't look at it that way. I was going at it sideways. With "I went down Virginia," I'm talking about Washington, DC. "I watched the tower grow" is their Tower of Babel. I'm talking about BS, really. Political spin. I think that song was done enough like a fable that you don't necessarily have to know what it all means or even worry about it. (I remember sitting down and explaining "Who'll Stop the Rain" to Ronnie Milsap one night in Memphis.

This was before he was a big star. He was just a rock and roll guy singing songs like "Ball of Confusion." I know sometimes for lots of fans a song is a song—that's all.)

There's a lot of drumming on "Who'll Stop the Rain." Some would say too much drumming. It's sort of surprising in the context of Creedence, but I think the mind-set was to sound biblical or historical, like some of the old fables—perhaps Ulysses. I know I had the concept of "folk rock" in mind. The guys insisted on doing the background vocals on that one. This became one of three songs that they sang the background vocals on (the other two being "Porterville" and "Sailor's Lament"). They didn't insist with quite the same intensity as they did at the infamous "band meeting" at the end of 1970, but the shit was beginning to hit the fan.

The more success Creedence Clearwater Revival had, the more the guys started to grumble. For a group that was supposedly on top of the world, there sure were a lot of unhappy people. There was a big argument when I had gotten us a weekend's worth of concerts on the East Coast. One of the guys was mad because he was planning to take his boat out. I remember thinking to myself, *Do you realize we're in the middle of a whirlwind career here? We're basically conquering the world.*

Stu complained that we didn't have limos. Once, very early on, when we were to play the Fillmore East for the first time, we had to leave our hotel rooms and get there on our own. Well, I was pretty unsophisticated. I thought we'd just hail a cab. We ended up having to walk through that neighborhood late at night and saw some things that were fairly upsetting. In hindsight, we should've had our own car. At the time, I didn't know about things like that. I wasn't the one making those arrangements. To me, having a limo was pretty damn uptown. That's one of the times that Stu railed at me for being such a stupid leader, manager, whatever. He would come at you like a screwdriver, a knife out of his pocket, *bam!* So after that, we got limos. Then they weren't long enough. "So how big a fucking limo do we need, Stu?" I always heard about how his hotel room should be bigger, grander, blah, blah, blah.

We arrived in London for the first time to play at Royal Albert Hall in April 1970. That was such a big moment for us. We were just four guys from El Cerrito who had never been anywhere, and we're landing in merry ol' England, home of the Beatles, the Stones, and everybody else. We flew overnight, a long flight, and Stu's grumbling and grousing on the plane, complaining about the stewardess. Huh? Then we were getting off the plane, and there were two or three press people with cameras on the runway. And I hear Stu right behind me: "Where's the limo?! Hey, *where's the limo?*" I was thinking, *God, he's gonna wreck this thing. They're all gonna see this.* I was acting like that guy in charge, trying to keep the ship going, because we didn't have Brian Epstein; we had *us.*

There were other problems. We'd be going through an airport, and some kid would walk up and ask for my autograph. Right behind my ears I'd hear grumbling from the guys because the kid didn't ask for *their* autograph. He wasn't trying to throw acid in their face; he was just being a kid. But the guys in my band weren't big enough or smart enough to realize, "Wow, this is great! We're being recognized!" No, it was, "This is awful. *He's* getting recognized!"

Tom was such a storm. Before this, he was always the positive guy—mellow, happy-go-lucky. Then he got dark. I think Tom felt intimidated because there was a lot of stuff he couldn't play. Like "Down on the Corner"—he couldn't keep up with the rhythm, so we had to overdub it in pieces. He'd get mad. I remember when we rehearsed "Green River" for the first time at Doug's. I was standing out front with the guys, and Tom said, "You're getting quite a repertoire." This wasn't said cheerfully. He spit out the words with clenched teeth. I thought we should've been happy because we had a new, original song—which, by the way, he was getting paid for.

When we did the album cover shoot for *Green River,* I was giving direction, telling people where to stand, and Tom went, "Oh, now you're producing the photo shoots too?" You'll notice that in most of the posed pictures of Creedence after that I'm standing in the back. I made a conscious effort. I thought, *I better make sure I don't do anything that shows me off as a star, the front man.* But really, I was mystified for the longest time: *God, why are my own people mad at me all the time?*

All this made it hard to talk about things, fragile things, like the merits of one song over another song. It was less fun. As the negative energy got louder and louder, I would have conversations with myself: "Well, shoot, I wish *I* was in a band where some guy knew what to do and just did it. I'd be happy to tag along behind and play rhythm guitar or whatever. Man, we're on top of the world! This is *great!*"

In a sense we had outfoxed everybody. Here we were on this tiny label with no budget, no manager, no producer, no publicity. One by one I had assumed all the roles out of necessity. And now we were being called the number one band in the world after the Beatles broke up in 1970. We're about to play one of the most famous halls in the world, but instead of being happy, everybody is miserable!

In some ways, the English press was sort of a crotchety bunch, meaning they acted like they weren't part of the rock and roll world. They were more like the *National Enquirer.* As much as there was talk about the music, there seemed to be talk about other stuff that I didn't really care that much about—"Are you all millionaires?" "Do you have a fancy car?" I didn't want to tell them my MG had died in the middle of San Pablo Avenue.

We didn't play an encore at Royal Albert Hall in 1970. Creedence no longer did them. One night somewhere in the States I just decided that Creedence wasn't going to do an encore after the show. Or ever again. I seem to remember it was Philadelphia, but my brother Bob says Davenport, Iowa. I've read where Doug has said he was so mad about it he smashed a bottle of Pepsi against the wall, knocked me off the table I was sitting on, and then broke off the table legs and threatened me with them. I don't remember any violence, or a specific confrontation with Doug. I am not and was not afraid of Doug, and the idea that he had me cowering on the ground is a fabrication. Our road manager, Bruce Young, did say to me, "You should've warned us beforehand."

I guess I did spring it on everyone, but I'd been thinking about it for some time. Doing encores had gotten so expected and predictable. At the Oakland Auditorium, B.B. King would play a twenty-minute set and encores would start after three songs. It started to feel phony, Sinatra in Vegas, you know, showbiz shtick—and we were against that.

It was also a matter of safety. The concert scene had gotten crazier and crazier towards the end of 1969. I'd begun to see the frenzy at the end of each show when we came back out to play. It was like some kind of switch had been thrown—people who had been behaving themselves now weren't. There were a few shows where the crowd rushed the stage and grabbed some of our stuff and bolted. I daresay there were other people not doing encores for the same reasons—the Beatles, the Stones, Zeppelin...

The encore we didn't play at Royal Albert Hall is our most notorious one. We did our show, fifty-five minutes. And then we were done. (When they play "God Save the Queen," the show is over. I guess that's a showbiz tradition.) At the time, it was controversial and left a bad taste in some people's mouths. But there was a time there when the top echelon of showbiz was not doing encores, ending a show when it ended, and I was not the first to make that call. Of course, things have changed. I now do encores!

Putting together our next single was another one of those times when I just wanted to keep the music coming, stay fresh on the radio. I had already been working with the band for weeks on the music, but there was no time left, and I had to write the lyrics and, if necessary, rename the song.

We were leaving for our first European tour the next week. So we would have to go in the studio on Tuesday and do the basic tracks, and then I could come back on Wednesday and do all the vocals, guitars, and rhythm instruments, and then mix both songs. So I went home on a Friday determined to write these two songs: "Run Through the Jungle" and "Up Around the Bend."

Through the course of the weekend, I believe that one of the songs actually drifted away from the song title I'd had in mind for a while. In other words, I entertained the idea of changing what the song was about and writing a new, different song. Luckily, I resolved whatever impasse was causing this and came back to the original idea. That's pretty late in the process to be starting a new song. I worked feverishly through the weekend, staying up most of Friday and Saturday nights, and by Monday morning I had the two songs completed. After that experience, I said to myself, *Yep, you can call yourself a songwriter.*

"Up Around the Bend" was inspired by riding my motorcycle. I just remember riding along, and the title phrase came to me. Just the feeling of *going.* Movement. By now Martha and I had a newer house. I had a room upstairs that became a studio, but at the time it was just an empty room. This might've been the first song I wrote there.

I used to say that there were four ingredients to a great rock and roll record. First, have a distinctive title. Next, the overall sound of the record has to be cool. Almost as if you could take a snapshot of the sound and look at that photo. Picture the difference between "Smoke on the Water" and "My Girl." Different, but they both sound fantastic! Three, you have to have an exceptional song. And finally, the very, very best ones will have a killer guitar riff. That's the icing on the cake.

I think I was playing my Rickenbacker with the humbucking pickups, or maybe the Les Paul, and I was messing around with the guitar intro from "A White Sport Coat (and a Pink Carnation)" by Marty Robbins. I may have even played it wrong, because it's a little bit tamer on Marty's record. I was just widening the range, you might say. What was really fun at that time was that I had a little late-sixties all-tube Fender Deluxe Reverb amp that I had bought just for songwriting. The Fender Deluxe is one of the best amps ever made. It's like the Model T of amps. It doesn't have really high wattage, and turned up, it would distort in a certain way — not quite as good as a Marshall, but it certainly had a funky edge to it. The way that bridge pickup sounded coming out of that amp — especially when I played the lick that became "Up Around the Bend" — was just a nice edgy thing. It was so good that I said, "This isn't just a practice amp. I gotta make the record with this." Playing "Up Around the Bend" through that amp with the bridge pickup was a great combination. That sound inspired quite a few songs from me. Eventually, I moved up to a slightly more powerful amp — the Fender Vibrolux — and it's hard to tell which amp is on which song.

I've seen it written that "Run Through the Jungle" is about Vietnam, but that's not true. I was speaking about the landscape in America. I had been thinking about the idea ever since 1966, when Charles Whitman had gone on a rampage, killing sixteen and wounding thirty-two others, shooting from the observation tower at the University of Texas. That was the first time in my life I was confronted with the fact that a seemingly normal person can turn not only criminal but into an insane, raging thing that we can't even understand.

The song is really about gun control. Now, I'm a hunter. And I'm intrigued, even fascinated, by weaponry through the ages. But I am in favor of gun control. I don't think machine guns should be allowed—who takes a machine gun to go deer hunting? The Constitution says various things, but it doesn't mean that you can build a hydrogen bomb in your basement. I think there should be some psychological interrogation for gun buyers. If you can't get through that, you're probably not the right guy to have a gun anyway. They shouldn't make it so easy. And anybody with a gun should get some training—it shouldn't be, "Hey, I hear a burglar." *Bam!* Lord, people shoot themselves or their own kids when they don't know what they're doing.

Remember the 1989 shooting at the elementary school in Stockton, California, that left five kids dead? George Bush had just been in office a little while, and Barbara Bush came right out and said we should ban assault rifles. Whoa—the rest of the Republicans were immediately like, *"Shut her up! Don't ever let her say anything again!"* Boom! Gag! She said stuff that made sense, so they didn't let her talk anymore. We could've gone after gun control then, before the countless shootings that came after and still continue to happen. But once again, it boils down to the fact that somebody's making a big profit, and I daresay those somebodies are rich corporations that are conservative by nature.

Now there is one more thing I would say about this complicated subject of gun control. The founding fathers thought it was important that us citizens have "the right to bear arms." Since 9/11 (or perhaps because of it), our government has passed a lot of legislation that further diminishes our rights as ordinary citizens. With the revelations of Edward Snowden, we see the specter of parts of our government spying on its own citizens. Therefore, I think it is important that our citizenry is armed. I believe this acts as a deterrent—whoa! Deterrent? Against what? Let's just say that the fact that there are millions of armed people ready to defend their homes probably acts as a huge roadblock against those who would try to seize the country for their own ends.

So guns and gun control were on my mind writing "Run Through the Jungle."* At the same time, it was all mixed up in the fearmongering of Richard Nixon that had taken hold in our land. "Over on the mountain, thunder magic spoke / Let the people know my wisdom / Fill the land with smoke." That was my arch inspiration—Mr. Nixon. Mr. "We'll let them know how powerful I am. We're gonna crack down on all you bums!"

With the "storm clouds" that open and close the song, I was trying to go beyond the usual start-stop. I think there's some backwards guitar and piano on that, plus a couple of tambourines. That's the Rickenbacker into the Kustom. One of the guitar tracks was a pick slide with slapback echo. The overall effect was ominous, spooky. I was getting a lot with just a little. It wasn't Hugo Winterhalter or Hans Zimmer. I was just a kid in a rock and roll band trying to add some color.

It's funny how our cover of "I Heard It Through the Grapevine" came about. One day I was down in Los Angeles, maybe Sunset Boulevard, in a hippie clothing shop where they had a lot of leather, vests, and hats. They had an FM radio on and the

---

* The line "The devil's on the loose" came about in a funny way. Phil Elwood, a Bay Area writer, had written about "Down on the Corner" in the paper and misquoted the words: "Willie goes into a dance, the devil's on the loose." (The actual lyric is "Willie goes into a dance and doubles on kazoo.") I read that and thought, "That's a cool line!" Into "Run Through the Jungle" it went. I believe I thanked Phil for that one.

speakers were really far apart—one was in the front of the store, another way in the back. I liked Marvin, especially his early stuff, but I really hadn't paid attention to his recent, very produced recordings, and "I Heard It Through the Grapevine" came on. Motown always had all that production and echo covering everything up. Because I was back there near one speaker, I was mostly hearing his voice—clear as a bell, with all his cool gospel inflections. Suddenly I was smiling—I was hearing Marvin really sing. I heard a guy really cutting it, singing his rear end off, and I was knocked out.

I took it as a challenge, a throwdown—"That's kind of my territory. I could do that song." I got the single and just started working on it. I'd play the cool riff. One day I just had one of those epiphanies—"Wow, this could be a guitar song." I changed the piano riff to guitar and did the tuned-down thing with the vibrato guitar with that low string always droning. Since it was a cover, I thought it would be cool to make a jam out of it, turn it into a fun thing to play. I took it into the swamp. Duane Eddy could've done that song. Beat you to it, Duane!

"Ramble Tamble" just came to me one night when I was lying in bed. The melody, the guitar, the whole vibe of it, from stem to stern. I had no idea what it was about, but I could hear the sound of the guitar and the way the record would sound. That was a true gift—"Here, my son. You might need this. Pay attention." Every once in a rare while, it works that way.

The cover for *Cosmo's Factory* was funky, just all of us hanging out at the Factory. Stu's nickname for Doug was Cosmo—it had something to do with the Cosmo Topper character on the old TV series *Topper*. That cover made him famous. I told the guys I thought it would be cool if we took a shot of us with our favorite things near us at the Factory. I thought it was a way of fleshing out the personalities in the band. It was sort of anti-showbiz. I told my brother Bob, "Go buy a camera and we'll take some pictures."

I wasn't the final judge of that cover shot. We had four or five test prints and we settled on that one. Unanimous vote. I remember thinking that wasn't the one I would have picked. I thought Doug looked a little funny. I wasn't judging it like, "Is this great art?" No, it was more like, "This is who we are."

Nineteen sixty-nine. No one had a better year that year than me. Three hit albums in one year. It was like winning the World Series, but in music. Nobody's bigger than the Beatles, but I'm told that worldwide we outsold them that year.

Cosmo's Factory came the next year. I felt this was a culmination. The record is just chock-full of good music—even on the album cuts, like "Ooby Dooby" and "My Baby Left Me." Six hit singles, and this was not a greatest-hits album. I thought that we would make some sort of turn after that. And we did.

CHAPTER 10

Tom Leaves

THE NEXT CREEDENCE single was "Lookin' out My Back Door" and "Long as I Can See the Light," which we recorded around May or June of 1970. I'm somewhat surprised that I came up with such a cool metaphor in "Long as I Can See the Light." I'd never heard of a candle being described as a beacon, a safe haven that you come back to. It's about the loner in me. Wanting to feel understood, needing those at home to shine a light so that I can make my way back.

I'm not sure if I realized what a beautiful song it was when I wrote it. Other people did. I didn't do that song for years. I didn't feel that natural with it. Now I do it all the time, and it resonates. I'm not sure I ever really felt at home until now. Home is what I've experienced with Julie.

"Lookin' out My Back Door" was the first time I played Dobro on a record. I'd gotten it in Nashville, and learned enough to play a little part.

That song came because of my young son, Josh. I wanted to write a kids' song. One inspiration was *And to Think That I Saw It on Mulberry Street* by Dr. Seuss. Another was a children's book by Margaret Wise Brown, *The House of a Hundred Windows*. My mother would read that book to me and sing this folk song, "Pretty Kitty," by Josef Marais and Miranda. The only character I remember in the book is a kitty cat. He's in this enormous house, looking out all the windows. He sees a train going across the prairie. Then he sees a parade, and a harbor with a ship. At the end of the book, he comes to the front door and it's open. The kitty cat is sitting there, looking out the door. Does he walk through it? I don't know if it's happy or sad. That memory chokes me up. Somehow that kitty is connected to "Lookin' out My Back Door."

Some little kids came to visit us in the studio after we recorded that single, and we played the songs for them. They were from a school for the blind, which was rather ironic given the titles of the two songs. After they left, I went to talk with my brother. Tom was on rhythm guitar, and he was supposed to be playing with the pickups in the middle position to make a full, more acoustical sound—a bed for what was the lead guitar and vocal. But Tom put his guitar on treble and it sounded jarring, spiky, like fingernails on a chalkboard. Real...*bright*. He did it on both songs and it was very noticeable.

Tom had kind of sucker punched me. I have rabbit ears and I notice everything. It made me nervous, because it was a change from the way the records had been arranged. Afterwards I brought it up: "Hey, Tom, your guitar is really bright. It's *too* bright."

Tom said, "Well, I can't hear my part. I did that so I could hear myself more."

But once you do that, it's too loud for the bass, so you turn that up. Now you can't hear the lead guitar or the vocal, so you turn *them* up. Now you're back where you started, except that *everything* is louder. I'd never forgotten what that guy had told me in his homemade studio way back in tenth grade: you can only put so much water in the glass before it spills out. Plus, that's just insurrection, chaos. If you're on a football team, you can't just have everybody runnin' off and making new plays. It's not good for the team.

Tom was more vocal in his mutiny. At around this time, the rest of the band started meeting at night down at the Factory and playing without me. I was always telling the guys that we needed to be tighter as a rhythm section, like Booker T. and the MGs. They were trying to improve, and it was working. But something else was happening too.

My brother Bob was about seventeen then. Back in '68, it had been my idea to hire Bob to work for the band. My motivation wasn't nepotism at all—it was just a good thing to have smart people around. And Bob has been at my side ever since, helping get stuff done. Years later, he told me that during these rehearsals Tom would start complaining about how the rest of the band should be writing songs and singing them. Bob called it "Tom's rant." I found this out only a few years ago. To learn from one brother that another brother was at least the partial instigator of all the turmoil ahead just makes me shake my head.

At the end of October 1970, we were just about to start recording our next album, *Pendulum*. I arrived at the Factory, and the guys were looking real serious and tense—more than usual. They said, "We want to have a meeting."

We went back to this little area where there was a conference table that we'd gotten from Stu's dad's law firm. And they started in. It was a confrontation. "This is the deal: we want to be able to write songs. We want to be able to sing those songs. We want to be able to have more say in the music and in the running of Creedence Clearwater Revival."

I can only say that by this time I was worn down. Throughout the life of Creedence, there was quite a bit of tension. It had started with "Proud Mary," when I insisted on doing the background vocals myself. Since then, the tension had continued to mount. There had been many times when I just had to keep my cool and get the job done for the good of the band. I was just tired of taking it on the chin and not fighting back.

Now all three of them were voicing the same opinion. I could see that to go forward, this band was either going to do it this way or not go forward at all. I thought, *If I'm still gonna have this dream of mine, this rock and roll band, I've got to compromise. We'll stay alive by doing this.* So I caved.

I said, "Okay, how do you want to do this? What do you want to do?"

"Well, we all want to write songs."

Tom had written some songs before Creedence, but Stu and Doug had never written a song before — and they wanted the first song they ever wrote to be recorded by the number one band in the world. Well, you're supposed to work your way up, aren't you? That really did bother me.

As I have been quoted as saying, the worst thing that ever happened to my band was the Beatles, because the guys in my band thought they could be the Beatles. Not only did the Beatles have three of the greatest ever songwriters, they had two great singers plus another pretty good singer — and actually a fourth guy with so much personality that it worked for him too. We didn't have that. And then comes all the arranging, producing, and the rest. These guys had no clue about what was necessary. A vision. That's just the truth.

Early on I thought maybe somebody else might write. Tom had written in the Golliwogs, but he didn't want to push to find better words or a better place for the melody. Once, sometime in 1970, Tom said to me, "I have some songs here," and he handed me a cassette. I went home and listened, and there were no instruments, no vocals, just Tom humming. Humming! It was almost comedy. Can you picture this? You're listening and after a minute, for emphasis, he hums louder. Then *softer*. After five minutes I turned it off. The truth is, it was up to me to write the songs. And produce and arrange them. To my mind this new concept was shaky—career suicide.

I explained to them that we were trying to get a record out by Christmas. "It doesn't have to be right now," they told me. And they continued on about how they wanted to have much more say—it wasn't going to be a dictatorship anymore. It was going to be a democracy.

At that moment I felt like one of those characters in some movie where everybody is deciding the future. There's the one guy who knows what's really going on, and he's saying to himself, *God help us now.* Because that's certainly how I felt. I didn't think, *Hooray! Let's do this!* I was like, *Wow, this is going to ruin our band.*

But I didn't say that. In order to keep the band from breaking up, I capitulated—"Okay, from now on you guys can be singers. You can write the songs." We all still had the unanimous-vote rule going, though everyone seemed to have forgotten. There really wasn't much else to say. I just wanted to go forward and get the next album done.

Do I feel like I was a tyrant in Creedence? I don't feel that I was, even now. Was I sure-handed, a perfectionist, even bullheaded about what I wanted? Yeah, you bet, sometimes. And sometimes not. Those moments when I had to teach a song or an arrangement, explain why something didn't work—I think I was pretty gentle and supportive. Part of a team. I didn't sit there and berate or belittle someone in front of everybody else. That just wasn't in my makeup.

You know, bands and marriages are similar in some big ways. At least my band and my marriage—but in marriage, I'm on the other side. There are some moments in a marriage when you don't necessarily agree with your spouse, when you get into this place of

"I don't see it, I don't get it." When I don't, I don't kick and scream about it. I just tell myself, "Y'know, it has all worked out really great so far."

There's times when Julie just knows something so clearly. And my wife has a better track record than I ever had as the leader of Creedence: 99.999 percent of the time she's just really right. When you have a great marriage and you're with somebody that you have ultimate faith and ultimate trust in, you just go with their sense to know stuff, even when you don't see it right then. It's happened with us over and over and over.

Are *those* moments tyranny? I don't look at it that way. The difference is trust. All I know is that I trust her, and that the result of that trust is the best of all possible worlds — for me and for her.

And I think that's what wasn't happening between the band and me during the time when Creedence was actually recording and making hit records. I was darn sure of what we should do. I was darn sure about my songs, darn sure about the arrangements, and I sure knew when I heard a clunker — "Hmm, no, that's not right. Do this." But the trust wasn't there.

As I said, a band is like a marriage. A brotherhood. And at least in the good times, people are professing their love to each other, which is certainly how I felt. But there can come a time when people don't have faith in you anymore. They're not trusting you. They're wanting to do something else and they're letting you know.

It's a very volatile situation. When you're in the middle of that, I'm sure you're not seeing everything clearly. It's like being lost in the middle of a stream: you're splashing so hard, you don't know what's swimming by or where's the shore. You're just trying to stay afloat. You're freaking out.

I was not perfect. I was not always totally at ease and calm and open and everything else that you would hope. At some point I really couldn't talk with everybody else. I just kept thinking, *Well, if I could just work harder and make it better, then they'll under-stand. One more hit, one more success, and then they'll see.* I even thought Fantasy would see the light, that Saul would honor me. In that sense, I was probably delusional, desperately hoping that all the success from my music, my leadership, would convince them to do it my way. But in the end, they didn't care about that.

Pendulum certainly wasn't made the way we'd made the previous albums. The idea was that we'd go into the studio for a month, experiment, jam, make *Sgt. Pepper*. *Sgt. Pepper* was the curse of every other rock and roll band that ever lived. The Beatles could do it because they were the freakin' Beatles. No one else could, including Creedence.

The guys didn't want to do the work. They just wanted to go into the studio and come up with songs by osmosis, spontaneous combustion. To me that was scary...a disaster...can I go as far as to say catastrophic? After all the years of growing up, through the Blue Velvets and the Golliwogs, we had finally evolved into what really worked, and now we were going to blow that up, just go hang in the studio like the Grateful Dead?! In reality, what happened was that there was a lot of rambling and, "Well, I don't know what to play here." Basically, nothing was going to happen if I just sat there.

My song "Born to Move" was on that album. There was a place in the track where the bass part was missing something, a hole there. Just a space of, I think, four bars, right? At this point I felt like the old graybeard shaman that the young bucks had banished to live outside the village. So I had Stu come in to play something in that spot—just a transition to fill the space between the two pieces of the song.

Over and over we went, finally spending two hours of a four-hour session, and he never did come up with anything. Finally, I showed him what to play and we moved on. It wasn't in him to ever create a part. Stu is a Top 40 jukebox guy. You know that guitar part at the beginning of "Green River" or "Up Around the Bend"? Musicians call those things riffs. They are a specific set of notes and rhythms that catch your ear. A lot of songs have riffs—"Day Tripper," "Satisfaction," "Louie Louie," "Smoke on the Water." In all the years I was around the guys, I never heard one of them come up with an original riff. None of the guys could play a solo.

So here we were in this studio that we'd booked for a month to make an album. Facetiously, I began to say, "Well, we've got a *month*." But in my heart I knew we could stand there and stare at each other 'til the cows came home and we would still end up with nothing. At some point after a few days, I started to go home after the daily session and write. I grew up with these guys and I'd learned how it worked—and how it didn't.

The only thing we ever really collaborated on as a band was the six-minute-plus instrumental with sound effects called "Rude Awakening #2." (Which begs the question, what was "Rude Awakening #1"? Maybe that was the fight we had over the "Proud Mary" vocals.) The Beatles had done this "sound collage" called "Revolution 9"; that type of thing was in the air. I'd recorded a beautiful fingerpicking song that I did with a split pickup guitar. I liked the song, but the stuff added on after it is just free-form nonsense. Doug farts on the track—that was his contribution. So that's the one and only Creedence collaboration. A masterpiece? No. Much of the rest of *Pendulum* was me going, "Okay, I'll go home, write a song, come back, and we'll record it." The meticulous preparation was gone.

Pendulum happened during a period in my life when my head started to feel really dry. I don't know exactly how to describe it or what it means, but my head felt physically dry. I still worked as hard on *Pendulum,* but there aren't as many great songs. "It's Just a Thought" wasn't necessarily my best effort. I could've possibly made a better song out of "Pagan Baby." During my short career in Catholic school, we were always having a collection for the pagan babies. There was a tin can bank in class, and you'd bring in change and drop it in for them. Pagan babies—what a wonderful phrase. With some sarcasm I wanted to turn that into rock and roll, with implied sex and all the rest—maybe that pagan baby isn't so unfortunate after all! I was almost a little too serious about it, but it was a cool idea, and I probably could have made it better with more time.

I concentrated on the single, "Hey Tonight" backed with "Have You Ever Seen the Rain." One of the complaints the guys had was, "We don't like it when we rehearse the two songs for the single for six weeks." Ironically, the band was tighter than ever due to the time they'd spent rehearsing on their own and all our touring. There was nothing specific behind "Hey Tonight." You have car songs, food songs, beach songs. Every once in a while there's a "tonight" song, like "I Gotta Feeling" by the Black Eyed Peas.

"Have You Ever Seen the Rain" is about the breakup of the band. I was feeling, "Man, we achieved all our dreams. And you guys are only talking about negative stuff." By your own volition, you bring in a huge rain cloud and cause it to rain. On your own perfect dream. That's the way I saw it. I was watching the band disintegrate right in front of my eyes.

There was a guy hanging around at the time named John Hallowell, who was writing a book called *Inside Creedence*. The book was far from great, but he was around. And when he heard "Have You Ever Seen the Rain," he cried. John knew exactly what the deal was from hearing the song. The other guys didn't seem to know *at all*. But he knew it was over. He came to me after hearing it, and the first thing he said was, "John, really?" The other guys in the band had no idea about how I wrote the songs. They have no knowledge of the inspiration or personal motivation that led to all those songs!

*   *   *

The disastrous direction Creedence had taken was symbolized by an event that I dubbed the Night of the Generals. That title came from a movie about Hitler's Third Reich as it was crumbling. No one was following orders anymore. Everybody's in charge, everybody's a general. On December 12, 1970, Creedence had its own Night of the Generals.

The rest of the guys in the band were very, very concerned about our image. I used to chuckle to myself when the press said, "Creedence—they're just a Top 40 machine." You'd read quotes by Bay Area musicians like Jefferson Airplane, saying things like, "Y'know, we're really not trying to have hits. We just want to have quality music." "We don't want to be commercial"—it was a catchphrase, like "What's your sign?" I thought, *Yeah, right—you just want to play in an attic where no one hears you, and maybe your mother will buy one copy of your record. Why make a record at all if you don't want to be commercial?* I could see through all that crap—"I'm an artiste, I'm too good to ever be on Top 40 radio."

Some people put us down because we had hit records, but I didn't give a whit about that. Why? *Everybody* I ever loved was a Top 40 band. The Beatles, Elvis Presley—Top 40. I just never worried about it. But my band certainly did. I thought, *Aren't you smart enough to realize they're jealous? Not everybody can do this, y'know! The Grateful Dead can't do this.* Even Led Zeppelin couldn't do it. Great band, but they were only on underground radio. I knew all that then.*

But the guys in the band were paranoid. They wanted more respect. And they also wanted to be seen as hip. They really

---

* I'll admit that I was a little jealous of the Band. I admired their music and felt we were mining similar territory, yet they were the ones who landed on the cover of *Time*. Plus they recorded "Long Black Veil" before I could get to it!

worried about it—"Oh man, we're not hip enough!" I remember we went to a radio station, and Stu had to say very loudly as he was drinking his Coca-Cola, "I'll have another *hit!*" They wanted to appear more relevant, cool, dope smokers. The guys wanted to hire somebody to create that image for us to tell the world how hip we were.

Tom wanted to hire Colonel Parker—Elvis's manager. I thought getting the Colonel would ruin us. Up until then, we'd been pretty down-home, handmade, homemade...and we were number one. The guys wanted to go the slick Hollywood route. Some of their complaints were probably well-founded, but I do think it was also a case of, "Take that away from John. Don't have John do that." They just wanted to dilute my position. And so, at their insistence, we hired Rogers and Cowan, a big publicity firm, and had a big press event with a listening party for *Pendulum* and a showing of a Creedence TV special. We flew in rock critics from all over the country. I don't remember the final tally, but it was costly.

I didn't say much that night. I was pretty uptight. I sat in a corner and didn't do much interviewing. The guys sure did. "Everybody has the most fucking respect for the Beatles," Doug cried to *Rolling Stone*. "Well, we're the biggest American group....We shouldn't be taken lightly." They talked about their new plans to sing and write their own songs—that sort of thing. John's tyranny is over! Stu said, "We're tired of that riff about John Fogerty's backup band....We all contribute now."* (Years later it would always bother me when the guys would say I forced them to sing and write their own songs for our next album, *Mardi Gras*—"This was all John's idea. We never wanted all those things." I thought, *Well, gee, we had a big party and you told the world that was what you were gonna do!*)

_____

* Stu Cook and Doug Clifford quotes from "Creedence Gives Serious Party," *Rolling Stone*, January 7, 1971.

The press people I talked to that night were confused by it all. As one of them told me, "We're just surprised that you're doing this now, after two years of enormous success. This is how you announce a brand-new band." I just muttered, "Yeah." They were wondering what all this hoopla was about, since we'd already released five hugely successful albums!

Maybe the lowest point of the night was when our publicity person Bobbi Cowan asked me to stand up and make a speech thanking Saul. That really stuck in my craw, but being a good soldier, I did it. I got up and said the only thing I could think of: "Thank you, Saul, for buying my Kustom amp."

Which of course later came out of our royalties.

A few weeks after the Night of the Generals, Tom did a remarkable thing. He left the band. I was stunned. I had given the guys everything they'd said they wanted. And now, Tom just quit. We never talked about it directly. Tom was in a bad mood. He was real tense about it. There was a whole long interaction with Bruce Young acting as a go-between—Bruce was our tour manager, and a guy we had known from the very beginning. Tom would tell Bruce something, and Bruce would come and tell me what Tom had said, and I'd tell Bruce to go back and tell Tom something.

Bruce was saying, "Tom wants to leave the band. He just wants to leave." I'd say stuff like, "Well, he got everything he wanted. I *agreed*." I remember telling Bruce, "Look, tell Tom the band can just stop. We can take a break! Tom can make a record on his own. We can all just do other things for a while—it doesn't have to be Creedence. Tell Tom it's okay. The band doesn't have to break up."

Bruce came back with, "No, Tom's gonna leave the band. He wants a clean break, wants to be on his own." Truthfully? I think Tom was being more honest than Stu or Doug at that point. Tom was so overwhelmed with the prospect of writing, singing, and arranging that he left the band. He thought, *Oh my God, what do I do* now? Because I had said yes, you can do it, instead of saying no, like all the other times.

There's a quote Tom gave in 1971 to *Rolling Stone*. I didn't see it until I was working on this book. He said, "Here I was, John's older brother, yet not really leading." That kind of says it all, doesn't it? You read that, and you understand what Tom's point of view was. His motivation. I didn't understand that until much later. Had it simply been that I had been the older one, maybe it would've been different—I don't know. He also said later, "I didn't want to just be the guy standing there playing rhythm guitar." I thought his playing was solid, often great, and that it was the coolest thing in the world that we were in this band together. I may have been trying to include him in the music way back when, but we were in this now. I didn't understand that Tom was jealous of me until Julie pointed it out.

I couldn't figure out any of it at the time. I really couldn't. I was a very mixed-up guy. I didn't know how I was supposed to act towards Tom, y'know? He was still my brother, I'm going to see him here or there, but he was taking a big dump on our band. We were the jilted ones, right? The ones left at the altar.

Losing Tom—that was tough. I didn't like that. The divorce of a well-known band is a really, really public thing. You might say that was a fatal blow to Creedence Clearwater Revival. *Bam!* to the solar plexus.

CHAPTER 11

Three-Legged Stool

TOM LEAVING THE band took the wind out of my sails. That was early 1971, and outside of one single, there were no plans to record until a year later. We had been putting out three albums in one year, so a year without making any records felt like a lifetime.

What did I do in that time off? I moved out of my house and lived in Denmark. With a girl named Lucy. We were just two people who happened to meet each other.

Martha and I separated. I was very serious about moving in with Lucy. I thought this was going to be my life. In my heart I was gone for good. Lucy was a deejay in a discotheque, working all night. Lucy was a wonderful person, energetic and positive in the time that I knew her. Social, outgoing, gregarious, full of life. I found that very intriguing and wanted to be in that energy. She had a very different personality from my wife, Martha, who was kind of introverted. Lucy's energy was something that I needed in my life at the time. There wasn't much happiness or love at home between Martha and me. So this was an escape from reality.

Over the course of the time I was in Denmark, I began to realize that what I had been so attracted to there was probably not real life. In other words, it was unsustainable. At some point you have to settle down. You can't be going out every night having a party 24/7. You begin to long for some sort of stability again. At least I did.

And it seemed like the more time that went by in that relationship, the more problems we would have. Fights, squabbles, disagreements. Besides all the happy fireworks, there were fireworks of conflict. I can't quite put my finger on why. It's all kind of trivial now. And I'm assuming as much responsibility for it as anybody else. Perhaps I was not really being a grown-up. I'm not trying to protect myself: my behavior certainly isn't textbook perfect in all of this. Hopefully I'm perceived as a person trying to do good, although maybe not always doing the best job of it.

But the arguments with Lucy would happen more and more. And I'd find myself not understanding the squabbles. There would be times when I'd literally feel like I didn't know what language I was speaking. That suddenly the normal laws of physics weren't working. The furniture just wasn't sitting the way I'd always thought. My frame of reference was just really upset, and eventually it became too much.

The relationship lasted a year or so. Even though I look back on that relationship very fondly, not with any blame or faultfinding, there were parts that were just unworkable. As I've told Julie, in the years after I left Lucy, I thought about a relationship with energy like that in a longing kind of way. But where everything between us was good.

There's a line in the song "Rocky Top" that I always remember, because back then I would wish I had it. And the line is, "Wild as a mink, sweet as soda pop." You can name all the great thinkers who have said wonderful things about humanity—and to me that line by Felice and Boudleaux Bryant is as good as it gets. I'd hear that lyric and remember something I'd experienced once, but that had gone wrong. And when I met Julie, when things calmed down and I really, really got to know her, that's exactly what I found: "Wild as a mink, sweet as soda pop." Julie's my dream girl. Dream *woman*.

While I was in Denmark I had a dream. I saw my infant child, Laurie, who was just a few months old, and I was filled with guilt. Absolutely filled with guilt. I was having the emotions of a man who felt that he should be taking care of his family. So I went back. Came home, got back together with Martha, and stayed for another fourteen years or so. But after that, she didn't want to hear anything about music. Or touring. She just really didn't. Who could blame her?

In other words, I had ruined it. The truth is, you can never go back. At the time, I did the best that I could to try and care for my family. Martha and I have three wonderful children together: Joshua, Laurie, and Sean. But I was a terrible father—terrible. Just inept. It's a shame for those kids, because they had a dad who was loving but wasn't very nurturing, in the sense of realizing what my role was. I was not a very involved dad. I was just sort of existing, if that makes any sense. Being. I really didn't understand the responsibility, the things you're supposed to do. I didn't do any of that kind of thinking, as far as I know. I pretty much wasn't aware of it.

I'm not trying to excuse myself or anything like that, but it's pretty clear to me, looking back, that I didn't know anything about living back then. I couldn't even take care of myself, let alone a wife and children. I didn't know who I was. I was just doing the thing that I loved, which was music, but in my personal life—I don't know how to say it—I just had a big lack of understanding about everything. I didn't feel a sense of being in control of my life outside of my songs. I spent so much of my life being noncommunicative.

I really didn't want to have my family suffer through a divorce. But Martha and I were the wrong two people to be in a long-term relationship together. It was what you'd call a dysfunctional relationship. I hung in there trying to make it work. But it just couldn't.

When we finally divorced, I took it badly—beat myself up, especially over the kids. I hated the whole thing. But I think there is some truth when kids tell their parents, "Yeah, we were really glad when you finally resolved it. Life got a lot more peaceful, less stressful." I remember that my daughter Laurie wrote a paper for school when she was quite young and mentioned, "My dad is always angry." When I read that, it just opened my eyes. I'm sure it's the truth. It's a shame to put your kids through that. A lot of it had to do with my career and Fantasy—and a lot of it just had to do with being in an unhappy place.

I wandered around all of 1971 thinking over the future of Creence. We'd recorded a single in the spring, "Sweet Hitch-Hiker." The B side was a song written and sung by Stu, "Door to Door"—really the first true labor of Creedence's "democracy"—and the results were, to put it mildly, underwhelming.

I remember getting out of my car in Emeryville and walking around an estuary, watching the speedboats and water-skiers. I just needed to think. I was arguing with myself because I was hurt and angry about the whole situation and not sure I wanted to get back together with Doug and Stu. I was in turmoil. I thought about blowing Creedence up: "Forget it—I quit!" But this band was my dream. One side of me said, "No, no, no! Don't let 'em do that. Just take over and be the way you always were." Then the other guy in my head was arguing, "Yeah, but you already said you'd stop being like that and let them have a chance." The phrase that kept playing over and over in my mind was, "I guess they deserve a shot."

I've never told anybody this, but Elvis had something to do with this decision. When Elvis hit the big time, his manager, the Colonel, picked him out of the little group he was in with D. J. Fontana, Scotty Moore, and Bill Black. That was his original, classic band. And Elvis went off and left them. It was a big deal to me when Elvis turned his back on the other guys, went on without them. I thought it was against the stars in the heavens, against the laws of nature. I just felt he screwed his band, and I didn't want to do that.

The Elvis situation was in my head when I made my decision—"Okay, we're gonna do this."

After the guys and I hadn't communicated for a long time, we had a meeting. I said, "Look, we're gonna record again, but this is how it's gonna be: you guys are going to sing and write your own songs. That's what I agreed to—and that's what the world is waiting for, because you told everybody that's what we're gonna do. Stu, you'll write, sing, and produce three songs. Doug, you'll write, sing, and produce three songs. And I'll write, sing, and produce three songs. The deal is we're gonna do it now. Right *now*."

I relinquished being the guy in charge of the music in exchange for being just one part of the music—"Okay, I'm in charge of my part. Here's my three feet of space. Don't invade it. You guys do your part." And that's exactly how *Mardi Gras* was made.

Doug and Stu were happy with this arrangement, but on my *Mardi Gras* songs, there's a certain melancholy, a kind of resignation. Listen to the way the album opens: "Lookin' for a Reason." The writer Robert Hilburn busted me during an interview at that time—"Is this about the band breaking up?" "No, no." I didn't put up a very good facade. I think he knew. I referenced that honky-tonk style in the song because the words seemed to sound good that way. I had a little Sho-Bud Maverick steel guitar that I was painfully learning how to play.

I wrote "Someday Never Comes" when I left Martha. It was written right out of my gut, for better or for worse. I was really pining over our children. I was seeing the unhappy thread. I had been in a family where the parents had divorced and I really took that hard. Now here I was, a grown man, doing the same thing to my children. That just seemed really sad. If you want to say ironic, I guess so, but I wasn't comfortable enough with it to look at it that way. It was more just seeing the pain of, "Wow, here it is again." For a long time I tried to hide and not really talk about how painful that is—and painful for those kids from that marriage. I'm trying to just face everything and be as honest as I can.

I think Lucy was there when I was recording it, yet I was on my own with that pain. That's kind of...revealing. No matter what's going on all around, each of the partners breaking up is doing it alone. Obviously you're not calling your ex and asking, "Oh, how do you feel? Don't feel bad." Somehow we don't do that. We wish that some older and wiser person would call and help us out. Breaking up relationships is one of the sadder things we do, and putting children through that is just about the saddest thing we can do.

I'm a little angry in the song. Bitter. The record doesn't really have the force I would've loved it to have, because the band couldn't do that, especially as a trio. When I get to the part that goes, "I'm here to tell you now each and every mother's son / You better learn it fast and you better learn it young / 'Cause someday never comes," there's supposed to be fifteen Marshalls on eleven in the background going *r-r-r-r-r*, just angry as hell. Then it should come down, down, down into the pathos of the chorus. We weren't quite good enough to do that, on an album where we were not really talking to each other much. I felt very sad about that situation too.

I think the version I cut with Dawes on *Wrote a Song for Everyone* actually surpasses the Creedence track. It's much closer to the original vision that I had of the song forty years ago. You feel that

Dawes is pissed off, as young people are. It's the disillusionment we all feel when we come of age. When you're four years old, you think the adults have everything in hand. Then you start to inherit the world and realize that the generation before you kind of screwed up—"Why the hell didn't you guys do a better job?" Don't worry, folks, the same will be said by your kids about you, and on down the line.

When we were in the studio doing *Mardi Gras,* Stu and Doug's material was sounding like…well, what it sounded like. I remember that Doug would always be walking around singing some song he was working on—"Eco-nomics! Eco-nomics!" Doug and Stu thought their stuff was really great. They weren't sitting there at rehearsals or in the studio going, "Oh God, this is awful. We're terrible! John's forcing us. We're not going to do this!" They were saying, "Man, this is really cool—listen to that!" They were high-fiving each other in the studio.

I'd play on Doug and Stu's songs, and when it came to the guitar solo, I'd give it my best shot. But at some point Stu perceived a problem with one of his songs. This wasn't a great situation for me in the first place, and now Stu was coming to me and saying, "Here's my song, John. But will you fix it like you did before with Creedence? Make it better?" Now, you *can* take a really lackluster song and orchestrate an arrangement and have it sound, at least on first blush, pretty good—ever heard "Fly, Robin, Fly" by Silver Convention?

But in this particular situation, doing something like that struck me as wrong. Stu was crossing into my territory. I shouldn't have been asked to prop up this thing I didn't believe in in the first place. That wasn't what the agreement was. I said, "This whole thing, this insurgence, was about you guys getting to do your own stuff. And now you want me to *fix it* for you, and then you take credit? It's not fair. I can't do that." I refused to do that. And the end result is what you hear on *Mardi Gras*.

The album was released in April 1972. It was about as bad as I'd thought it would be. But remember: I let them do it. It was their idea. I didn't twist anybody's arm or hold a gun to their heads. Stu and Doug were proud of *Mardi Gras*. They thought they'd written some good songs. It was only six months later, after everybody tore it apart, that they started saying, "Oh, no, John made us do that."

The best commentary came by way of Lucy, who was there when the album was being recorded. She had a phrase when it came to food: you see something funny on your plate, a bunch of fat on the meat, it doesn't look like something you'd better eat, and she'd say, "Looks like there's something extra in there." That's what we said about Doug and Stu's tracks: "Sounds like there's something extra in there."

I know that some critics called the album "Fogerty's revenge." I didn't make it with any sense of revenge. I don't even think there was any sense of, "See? I told you so," or any of that. I was doing my darnedest to give my best performances and to have it be as good as we could make it under the circumstances. But the damage had been done.

A few years later I was talking to some fan, and he made the statement, "The big change in Creedence was when Tom left the band." He'd brought along the single off *Mardi Gras*, "Sweet Hitch-Hiker." On the label it says, "Produced by Creedence Clearwater Revival," which isn't how previous singles had been credited.

I said, "No," and pointed to that credit. "The big change is right there."

Eventually Creedence had to go back on the road. We'd been touring as a trio since Tom left. There was talk about adding Duck

Dunn from Booker T. and the MGs, but we decided not to bring in a new person. My guitar was loud enough that you didn't really notice anything missing. But that addressed the practical problems rather than the emotional ones. Doug and Stu couldn't supply the solutions. I didn't have my brother there and it really wasn't a band anymore. It was back to being the Blue Velvets. You have to understand that Doug and Stu are joined at the hip. Whatever Doug says, Stu agrees; whatever Stu says, Doug agrees. They were the Corsican twins. Even though Tom and I often differed, I could count on him to be an independent vote. Without him, we were a three-legged stool.

The vibe on this tour was different because of it. When we were a quartet, we didn't have a zillion groupies hanging around, people offering joints to everybody, all the rest of it. One night as we were rolling along from city to city, either Stu or Doug said, "Yeah, the backstage was really boring back then." After we became a trio, it was like a three-ring circus backstage. The whole thing was just one long party.

The groupie thing was almost being done with a vengeance, and it wasn't like I was still some sort of Boy Scout. Doug and Stu were talking about all these conquests. It was ego, like guys with motorcycles — "Who's got a bigger engine?" It became more of a challenge, a rivalry: "I'll show you."

Backstage on the trio tour, you could probably see three or four of the seven deadly sins going on at any given time. There was something out of kilter, to be doing things for those sort of reasons. In the Beatles, Paul and John would challenge each other to come up with a great song — I would've loved that, some guy sitting there who was my songwriting equal. That's cool. But this sort of one-upmanship wasn't healthy.

Particularly as the group went on as a trio, it seemed even clearer to me that other stuff was more important to Doug and Stu than the music. The debauchery, the imbibing, the groupies, even destroying property. One of Doug's favorite things to do while bored or drunk in a hotel room was to take room-service cream, turn on the television, pour the cream down inside the TV, and watch the television boil and blow up. I didn't understand that.

It wasn't in my nature to just destroy things for the heck of it. I never really got it. I came from too meager beginnings. My parents were Depression-era people, and I knew about breadlines, soup lines, and one set of clothes. I saw how my parents behaved: they hoarded and saved compulsively.

I'm actually that way myself. If something has value, even if it's a plastic bag, I have a hell of a time just throwing a perfectly good thing in the trash when maybe my brain can invent some use for it. I just can't light a match and watch it burn for entertainment. Maybe I can use that bag as a trash liner, instead of going to the store and paying three dollars for a box of trash liners. I'm quirky that way. It might be a little compulsive. My kids don't have that unless I remind them of it—"You gotta turn the light off! That costs money!"

I was just another guy in the band at this point. The other John had been more of a leader. I saw myself as a Brian Epstein, but after the band meeting I stopped acting like that. I couldn't tell them how to conduct themselves anymore because they didn't want me to. So when the guys acted like buffoons, the best I could do was laugh nervously about it and try to get along.

We met the guys in Led Zeppelin on that tour. I think it was in Adelaide, Australia. Jimmy Page and I stayed up very late together having the best of times! We love rockabilly and Sun Records, and I think we both were excited to talk about what got us into this crazy music biz in the first place. Funny thing: the day before Zeppelin showed up, the security guys in the hotel came to each of our rooms. They were checking everyone in the Creedence party to see what damage we might have done. Well, our rooms were just fine—no damage—but as security was leaving, I couldn't help but think, *You guys have* no *idea. Don't you know who's coming here tomorrow? Hide the women and children, it's* Led Zeppelin! *These guys* start *by knocking out the walls between the rooms... and then it's every man for himself.*

I met Jim Morrison at the Fontainebleau Hotel in Miami. He had that indecent exposure trial going on and he showed up in the wee hours at a party in my suite. I remember being in the kitchen there, saying stuff like, "Yeah, man, I really think the machines are gonna take over," stuff I halfheartedly believe. And Jim's like, "Oh, I don't feel that way at all. The human spirit will always find a way to *continue!*" I'm going, "Is this the Jim Morrison I've heard about? The guy who sang about killing his dad?" He was all cheerful. I was the one talking gloom and doom!

Tony Joe White opened for us throughout 1971 and '72. Just Tony Joe and a drummer, really sparse. He really has a musical style and presence unlike anybody else. Funky guitar player. And his songwriting territory is so unique. "Polk Salad Annie" is one of the best records ever made. I was tighter with him than with our other opening acts. He had a real friendly, open, sunny face and that Southern thing. I used to say. "Man, Tony Joe, if only I had your looks and my brain, we could be a big star."

We'd hang a lot after the show—go to a bar, sit and drink and tell stories, or, as we used to say, "tell lies." I spent a day fishing in the Arkansas River with Tony Joe and the photographer Jim Marshall. Jim was a character. He couldn't glue together a sentence without seventeen expletives. We had rented our own Lear Jet for the trio tour. Our pilot was a guy named John Chaddick, who had been a B-52 pilot in Vietnam. To escape Russian MiGs while under fire, he'd loop-de-loop that B-52 and end up behind the MiG. He used to barrel-roll the Lear for us going across the Atlantic, and suddenly we'd be upside down. Jim Marshall turned green, white, red, and yellow, ready to puke. We did that to a lot of folks, including the governor of the Bahamas. Did he turn green!

Tony Joe would jam with us. I had bought a little three-pedal steel guitar, a Sho-Bud Maverick. I bought an instruction book and slowly and painfully learned how to tune it and use the pedals. I loved country music, and the Sho-Bud was a way for me to take on that persona. We'd rent an extra hotel room that we called the Mondo Bizarro Room and play. After those shows, I felt like doing something different from what I had done onstage.

So I was doing rock songs in a country way or country songs with a little more rock in 'em—"Jambalaya," "Rollin' in My Sweet Baby's Arms," the Fats Domino song "Poor Me," done Hank Williams–style. And I'd do this song the actor Sal Mineo did as a kid in 1957, "Start Movin' (in My Direction)." It was a cool song, especially if you put it into Hank Williams mode. I could tell that Tony Joe appreciated my "Jambalaya." He'd always go, "Awww, John, that funky ol' voice..." He'd be sitting there with his guitar or beating on a beer can or playing a tambourine. We were making a heck of a racket. Nobody ever taped this stuff; we just did it for fun. This was all pointing in the direction I'd take on *The Blue Ridge Rangers,* my first solo album. Turns out I was already rehearsing—sort of living out—this thing that I was going to do. Not that any of us knew it at the time.

That tour felt like dragging the flag through the mud. Because what had been the proud vision I'd had of Creedence was being desecrated. Our last live show was in Denver on May 22, 1972. It was pretty bad.

You felt like you knew these kids in the audience. You'd be looking down and they'd look at us like we were their compadres. They had adopted us. Kids at eighteen, nineteen, adopt some new band and that band becomes exalted. But the audience saw us a little differently on this tour. During that Denver show, I looked down while Stu was singing "Door to Door" or Doug was singing "Tearin' Up the Country," and there was just a big question mark on their faces. We'd been Elvis, but suddenly we'd turned into Pat Boone.

People literally threw money at us. The audience was telling me what I already knew: this sucks. It was one of those moments when you're standing there taking it for the team, but you understand why completely. Yet the other two guys still thought what they were doing was great.

After the show, I reached down and picked up one of the quarters, and later went to the local jeweler and had him make a necklace out of it. The guy put it on a dog tag chain and I wore it for a few years. A reminder—"This is as bad as it can get." Eventually I put it in a drawer and finally just lost it.

I was really feeling like quitting. The trio was just so contentious. It had probably started to dissolve the moment Stu asked me to bail out his song. That was the beginning of the end for me.

The public would naturally like to think that Creedence was a band, four guys like the Beatles. That's not really true. The minute I didn't supply the music, we were lost. It was even more evident in the trio than it had been in the quartet. And it got harder and harder to keep this dirigible afloat when the guys were doing everything they could to poke holes in it.

Finally I just said to myself, *I'm not going to do this anymore. This is dumb.* I went over to Stu's house, sat down, and just told him. I can't remember if I talked directly to Doug. I think I tried and he wasn't home, so I asked Stu to tell Doug. I wanted to get it over with that day. I was tired of holding it in. Sometimes in life you arrive at a situation that calls for an unpleasant confrontation. You know you have to face it and take a stand, but it makes you very uncomfortable. So you force yourself through it to get to the other side. That's how I was feeling with this. I sure wasn't happy about it. A lifetime's worth of dreams and all the joy of my musical soul had been poured into Creedence without reservation. It had simply gotten too hard to go forward this way. I was sad. I think Stu was sad.

By this time I was living in an apartment in Emeryville, so I headed back there.

Alone.

CHAPTER 12

Hoodooed

CREEDENCE HAD FINALLY called it quits, and not long after, I was down at Saul's office—I'm not sure why, because I wasn't really that friendly with any of them by now—and he asked me directly, "Well, is there any chance you and the other guys will get back together?"

Just talking about it felt like delivering a news report after a catastrophe. I felt horrible inside.

And then Saul looked at me and said, "You're *sure* there's no chance?" I told him no. I could tell the wheels were turning in Saul's head.

Now, we had signed a contract as a band. I thought that now that the band no longer existed, it would be null and void. But after that little discussion with Saul, I received a notice in the mail: Fantasy was informing me that they were exercising their right to renew their option on my contract. This is when I discovered that they could hold on to us individually, even though Creedence had broken up. At about that same time, they let Tom, Doug, and Stu out of their contracts, so they no longer had any obligation to Fantasy and Saul. Fantasy and Saul kept me.

It actually played out this way: within a few months of Creedence calling it quits, both Doug and Tom released solo albums. They did not sell well. *Then* Fantasy released Doug, Stu, and Tom from their contract with the label. Even though Fantasy had made millions of dollars from Creedence, I guess they figured there was no sense wasting any money on *those* guys. It now sank in that I owed Fantasy a lot of product. Per the contract, we owed them twenty-two masters a year in 1969 and in '70. For the years 1971 through 1974, it jumped to thirty-four masters for each year. In 1969, we'd recorded three albums, but even that amounted to only twenty-six recordings, four of which were covers, which didn't count. In 1971, we had recorded just one single, "Sweet Hitch-Hiker," and in 1972 came *Mardi Gras,* which contained eight more new songs (plus "Sweet Hitch-Hiker" and its flip side). Everything else was owed. And the unfulfilled numbers slid into the next year. And the next. The band was gone, but the obligation remained. For *me,* not the other guys. They were free and clear. I was not. I saw a lawyer. And then another lawyer.

Obviously I still wanted to make music, but at the same time, I owed it all to Saul. I couldn't give it to anybody else. I began to work on *The Blue Ridge Rangers,* which was released in 1973. This was my first solo album and the first of my one-man-band projects, where I played every instrument on the record. I chose to do an album of covers because, as with "Susie Q," it entailed doing other people's songs instead of trying to write songs. The reason I had to do it that way was my brain was locked. Frozen. I couldn't create new songs. I was under Saul's thumb, and I was trying to keep my sanity.

The thought behind the one-man-band thing was, "This will be quite an achievement if I pull it off, and it will take enough time that maybe there will be a solution to all these problems." Because

I really couldn't figure it out. And it never got better. But I started down the road of, "Okay, I'll play the drums. I'll play the bass. I'll do this all myself." I'm sure that at the time I thought, *I'll make records that are just as good as Creedence*. But it was really sort of a split impulse: yes, I wanted to have success, but at the same time, I didn't, because Saul would own my success.

The songs I chose for the album were country songs from the fifties and sixties, plus a couple of old gospel numbers. Songs I knew growing up. The hippie country of the seventies just bothered me. Rockers who can't play guitar well enough to play the real licks doing "Okie from Muskogee," singing with fake, exaggerated accents—I thought that was an abomination. I revered the people who had to be good enough to actually make it in the world of country music. This other stuff was a homogenized supermarket version that could never hold life on its own. I was working too hard trying to be actually *good* at country music. I could never make fun of it.

I actually had a hit with my version of "Jambalaya," which went to number sixteen. I liked my version of "Hearts of Stone" and especially "Blue Ridge Mountain Blues," but I felt that some of the other music was not quite good enough. It didn't feel as relaxed or as authoritative as a real band of musicians would have made it. And it was hard for me. Perhaps I'm not as talented as Prince or Stevie Wonder (who played every instrument on "Superstition," which was also a hit that year), where it just flows like honey off the beehive.

That album, plus the Fantasy singles "Comin' down the Road" and "You Don't Owe Me," as well as the recordings I'd do next for Asylum Records, all embarrass me now. They're missing the mark, not as good as they could be. In some ways I think I remembered them being more inferior than they actually are. I recently heard a couple of things from that era, and I was surprised that they were better than I thought. I may have been too hard on myself. If you don't really know how they were made, don't have all those emotional memories about how you were feeling, then maybe they're okay. I was always like, "Man, I don't want people to find out about these records. I just want them to stay buried!" So I was being pretty harsh.

Because of Julie, I'm healthy and would never pursue doing things that way now. She helped me learn a lesson: it's way more fun to be in great company, and that includes playing with other musicians, especially *great* musicians. That's what I seek out now. I want to cross paths with as many great players as I can for the rest of my life—and I sure don't want to play all the instruments.

But back then, unfortunately, I was a one-man band. I kept pursuing that method for years, even when you didn't hear about me. I had a little office and studio in Albany, California, and I spent a lot of time there, working on my own. It's not like I was off in the woods sitting under a tree, not knowing what day it was, or in South America on a drug binge. When all the doors were slammed in my face, I kept working, kept trying. It was the same process as *The Blue Ridge Rangers;* I just got better at it. But in my mind, not good enough. I wouldn't work on my own music with an actual band in the studio again until *Eye of the Zombie* in 1986, but that's a whole nother story.

The Blue Ridge Rangers had been out a month or so when this eight-year-old kid and his dad came to my door for an autograph. The dad pointed out that their copy of the record had a defect in the grooves. He pointed to a walnut-size "bubble" and sort of drew a circle around it with his finger. When I got out my copy, I saw the same thing. I couldn't believe it. Consumers were erupting in the streets over the quality of the product, and who were they coming to? Not Saul, but me. I went down to Fantasy and told Ralph Kaffel (the president of Fantasy), but he wouldn't take ownership, nor redo the pressings. And I was mad. If they're going to make millions, shouldn't they check the product? They never did.

Fantasy had their own mastering outfit, and the assistant there was a young guy with an Afro named Mike. He heard my story, took it upon himself to investigate, and went on a stealth mission to the RCA plant that pressed all of Fantasy's albums.

He found out that there were four grades of vinyl used at the plant, and therefore four levels of quality and cost. Elvis was on RCA and got the top grade. Guess what grade my album got? The cheap shit. Number four. That's why there was a bubble in the vinyl. But nobody was going to tell me that information. Mike was the whistle-blower. I do believe the poor guy lost his job.

This was my breakaway from Creedence, my first album on my own, and Fantasy couldn't have cared less. They had enjoyed all the riches from what I'd done and acted mystified over my defective album, like I was nuts. When *The Blue Ridge Rangers* came out, none of the executives were even around. Not a one. Everybody was on vacation now. What a bunch of losers.

Of course, I learned from this experience and vowed never to let this happen again. As usual, I seem to have adopted another job—that of quality control—as part of my lifelong quest to improve and try to be the best that I can be. Remember, this was in the age of vinyl. One of the things I did was to get my own rather average record player to test all records that I would make from now on. I wanted a record player that would represent what a kid would have, not the audiophile equipment of a millionaire. So I got a simple portable player from Sears. I named it "Skip Tracer."

After the *Blue Ridge Rangers* album had been out awhile, Al Bendich, one of Fantasy's attorneys, arranged a meeting with me. He told me that Fantasy wasn't going to count my new album.

I said, "What do you mean you're not going to count it?"

Bendich said, "You know the masters you owe us? We're not counting this album."

"Why?"

"Because it's country."

I was stunned. I couldn't believe they had that power. I could record for them for the next twenty years and they could reject it all. I was a prisoner in Saul's dungeon. And I couldn't escape.

Here I am in my little apartment, trying to come up with songs, and I was just a blank. It was almost as if I wasn't that guy who wrote "Proud Mary"—I was working but no songs were coming out of me. To say I was having a tough time with all of this is putting it mildly.

So I decided I would call a meeting with the people at Fantasy. I wanted to go and plead my case. According to their oppressive contract, I owed them a mountain of material, and I needed some relief. They had a nice new, big building with their own studio and had started making feature films. One of the receptionists used to call it (not within earshot of Saul) "The House That John Built."* They also owned the whole city block. I went to the meeting by myself, didn't have an attorney or anyone else with me.

When I got there, I was led into a side room. Later, I would think of it as the Roomful of Soulless Men. After a moment, they filed in. Saul was there, Fantasy president Ralph Kaffel, attorneys Al Bendich and Malcolm Bernstein, plus the writer Ralph J. Gleason, who was now a board member of Fantasy Records, with his own office. Shit, I never had an office. Right at this same time, Ralph was writing articles for the *San Francisco Chronicle* about downtrodden musicians—I remember reading one about a sax

---

* I went into Saul's office one day, and above his immense desk was a huge, five-foot-tall picture of the Beatles. The Beatles! Aren't you supposed to be proud of your *own* racehorse, your number one band in the world?

player from the thirties who'd been screwed out of his royalties. Given that, I thought in this situation Ralph might be my advocate.

We sat down and made small talk for a moment, and then I said, "Look, I'm having trouble coming up with anything. My brain is just not functional. I'm not able to write my songs. I'm not able to move forward, this contract is so oppressive. All I can think about is how it's weighing on me all the time. I can't seem to create anything."

Immediately Saul said, "That's not true. The whole history of art shows that the greatest art is created under conditions of oppression and depression."

This is, like, a minute and a half into the meeting. "That's not true." That was a curious phrase. I'm explaining why this huge contract, this huge obligation is harming my artistic efforts, making it almost impossible to create, and he says "That's not true"?!

I was stunned, shocked. I looked into the face of each guy. There's Ralph Gleason, defender of the downtrodden. Moments go by...

Nothing. Not a word is said. Not one word. I realize that even though there's a bunch of people in the room, really it's just Saul. So I say to him, "Look. I'm going to get up. And I'm going to walk to that door. And if nobody says anything to change this, I'm gonna walk out that door. If I go out that door, I'm never coming back."

It was like time stopped. I walked to the door as slow as I could. I'm waiting for Al or Malcolm or Ralph to say something. Silence. I'll never forget it.

I went to the door, slowly turned the knob, and walked out. I never went back.

Some people think Saul was a smart and shrewd businessman. I think he was an idiot. Think about it: you've got a guy who can do what I did for them the previous four years, and this is the way they treat me? Was that really smart business? Imagine what it could've been. What could've been accomplished.

When I was recording *The Blue Ridge Rangers* there at the Fantasy studio, the Creedence gold records were on the wall, up a grand staircase. And this little, dare I say, *fantasy* would cross my mind, where I'd just run up those stairs with a baseball bat and smash all those gold records. I wish I had done that.

Right when I felt I had nowhere to turn, David Geffen entered the picture. He was a delightful guy who was dating Cher at the time. I explained my dilemma and he said, "Maybe I'll just buy Fantasy." That would've been great. I think things would've turned out way different.

What happened was this: Geffen bought the rights to have me on Asylum in the U.S. and Canada for one million dollars. In the rest of the world, I was still on Fantasy! The way they arranged it, the money was paid to *me,* and then I gave it to Saul. So I had to pay the income tax on $1 million that I never saw so that Saul could receive the money. The whole thing was just totally fucked. As part of the deal, I did get back five or six reels of unfinished music from Fantasy's vaults, which included an out-of-tune version of "Long Black Veil" and a cover of John D. Loudermilk's "Break My Mind."* Things I didn't want them to put out.

John Fogerty came out on Asylum in 1975. I call it the Shep album because my dog is on the cover with me. I remember playing my version of "Sea Cruise" for the Asylum executives. David blurted out, "Well, that's a hit song!" They were all looking at him like he was crazy. I think they were kind of kicking him for

---

* You'll note that on all the Creedence albums (except on *Cosmo's Factory,* where Fantasy screwed it up) my writing credit reads "J. C. Fogerty." That was inspired by John D. Loudermilk.

signing me. They had one of those little record players and they couldn't quite manage to work it. I thought to myself, *Oh man— executive turntables.*

Oh jeez, I was such a boob. My brain was really fractured by then. I had on a brand-new cowboy shirt with large red circles, maybe some stripes. It kind of looked clown-like. And a brand-new pair of not-quite Levi's—more like Haggar pants that had a little crease. I looked stiff as a board. David, who looked quite relaxed in his jeans with stylishly frayed fringe at the bottom, even commented on my look. I said, "Well, I wanted to look like a million dollars." I actually said that.

The Shep album is not my best work. I was having flashes of brilliance in the middle of the incompetence. "Almost Saturday Night" and "Rockin' All Over the World" are good songs, and it would've been really great if somehow I'd fallen in with a producer I really trusted and had written eight more songs as good as those two. But the rest just aren't good. "Dream/Song" doesn't even seem finished, but there it is—it's on a record. I hate that I allowed that to happen.

I wrote "Almost Saturday Night" and "Rockin'" on a tuned-down Telecaster in my Albany studio. I actually recorded a demo of "Almost Saturday Night" when I was still at Fantasy. I had been moved to a different room because they'd grown weary of me having the big room tied up. That's the one-man band again. On "Almost Saturday Night" I added a glockenspiel for a little color.* There's all kinds of moods you can put yourself in, and one of my favorites is the one where something is just so wonderful that you're caught up in the excitement, feeling the urge to scream out loud. Sometimes I feel like that when I'm writing, and

---

* I distinctly remember that, because as I did it, the great keyboard player Merl Saunders stuck his head in the studio and flashed me a big smile. There, in the midst of the sinister evil that was Fantasy Records, was a fellow artist giving me encouragement.

that's what I was trying to capture with "Rockin' All Over the World" — "I like it, I like it, I like it!" I loved that Status Quo had a hit with that. It was like, "Go get 'em, guys!" It made me feel that I was surviving in spite of all odds.

My next album for Asylum was going to be *Hoodoo*. A single managed to escape in 1976 — "You Got the Magic." It's dreadful. Stiff and angular, not smooth and nice. Some of the words are cool, but the musical style to me is foreign. Foreign. It sounds more disco than anything else. And disco sure did suck. That was a silly era in rock and roll.

Punk was a reaction, a rebellion against disco. I liked the Ramones. Bad Religion's "Sorrow" is one of my favorite records *ever*. The Sex Pistols I didn't get at all. It wasn't singing. I don't know what it was. What do you mean you're not going to tune up? Don't you have to tune? Spitting? It didn't appeal to me. They weren't disciplined. They were making a whole shtick out of being undisciplined. I guess that sounds funny, huh? Saying "discipline" when talking about rock and roll? What I heard was chaos to me. Not good chaos — just chaos.

The thing I found lacking with much of my own music during those days is not so much that I wandered off into other styles. It's that the songs weren't quite…finished. If I repeat a phrase or a word over and over in a song, it's not me on my game. I heard "You Got the Magic" not long ago and was cringing — "Don't say that again! You already said that in the last verse! Find a new word." My best songs do that. But my brain wasn't functioning like it did in the good times. I'd go to do something musical and it was like…*lobotomy!* There'd be nothing there. Like forgetting how to ride a bike. Weird.

Joe Smith was now the head of Asylum, and just before my new album *Hoodoo* was to be released, he requested to meet with me in Los Angeles. Very gingerly, he said, "This isn't very good, John. We'll put it out if you want us to. We just kind of feel like it's not up to your level." You can't be any more generous or diplomatic than the way Joe Smith handled it. That was hard for him to do. You have to be able to be brutally honest if you're ever going to be worth a crap.

It was hard for me to hear it, too. Nobody likes to hear, "You stink!" But they didn't really have to twist my arm too much. I kind of knew it in my heart. "On the Run" was one of the songs on *Hoodoo*. I could never quite get all the words to make sense. Funny: about a week before I wrote this chapter I was still trying to write that song. People under duress will do stuff because of a deadline, let it go, call it finished when they really don't think it's finished. My head just wasn't right. I was in a bad way. The one-man-band thing was really hard. And the stuff with Saul was eating me up. Those were the hardest times I ever went through up to that point.

Joe Smith was right, of course, and I knew it, so I went back home and instructed my engineer, Russ Gary, to destroy all the *Hoodoo* tapes. Some things in life it's better not to get snagged by. It's better to move on. I didn't want to have this come out after I'd died in some plane crash. One of the things Joe said to me was, "Why don't you go home and fix whatever it is that's bothering you?"

I'm sure glad I don't feel now like I felt in those times. The hand I was dealt was shitty, a really bad hand. In many ways, I was far worse off than I had been before "Susie Q." Music, my career—it all seemed to be in the rearview mirror, with every avenue blocked off. And it took me a long, long time to get through it. I was a pretty frustrated guy, a miserable person. Completely immersed in all this bitterness, anger, and confusion. At least mentally, I'm forever asking forgiveness from anyone who knew me then. I sure was a shithead. And my gift was gone.

Members of my own family were so weird about it all. It was always, "John's goin' off again." No one wanted to know the depth of it, to understand how blatantly unfair it all was. I was pretty much alone in the struggle.

One day I went into Capwell's, a store in the little El Cerrito shopping center, to buy socks. I was trying to talk to the girl behind the counter, and suddenly I was just neutralized. I didn't know how to go forward—I was so lacking in self-confidence that I couldn't do it. I couldn't explain to the salesperson which particular socks I was trying to buy. So I turned around and left without buying anything. It seems so pathetic now, that feeling of just being completely stuck, unable to engage.

It didn't help that I was not sleeping well. There was actually one time when I was awake for three days straight. *Three days straight*. By then you're a zombie. I was so bothered. And so angry. I couldn't shut it off! It would *not* shut off.

Eventually I began to self-medicate—a pleasant phrase that means drinking as much alcohol as possible....Such a horrible decision. It kind of worked, although I was a bum. That's the John who's a horrible guy. When Martha and the kids would go to bed, I'd just stay up and get drunk. I'd drink, sometimes smoke cigarettes, and finally fall asleep. I don't like publicizing this. Certainly it's not a time I'm proud of.

At some point I went to a sleep clinic in Berkeley, where they teach you how to get into your alpha state. You're supposed to slow way down and go, "Ohm, ohm." I never really did learn that, but in the course of these sessions, I'd sit in this reclining chair and start telling this nurse my situation—almost like that person was a shrink, but of course they weren't. I'd sit down in the chair, and out would pour all this *"Arrrrgh!"* pain.

It was now 1980, and some rather earthshaking things had occurred. I had come to feel that the whole Castle Bank offshore financial plan was a scam. And even though I had been led into it with the guidance of some of my own advisers—making it sort of their fault—I felt that every day I *stayed* in the plan was *my* fault. It would be my choice to stay or go. So I had tried to withdraw from the plan, which I will explain in another chapter of this book.

The result was that as of 1980, *all* of my life savings had been stolen, *and* several years of royalty payments from Fantasy that I had never received were now being claimed to have been deposited *directly* into a defunct bank. Fantasy had steered the band into this thing in the first place, and this financial plan was basically Fantasy's baby. (The Castle Bank owner-director, Burt Kanter, was on the board of Fantasy Records. Saul had told me personally that he had given Burt "carte blanche" to run his affairs.)

When I left Fantasy for Asylum, I still owed Fantasy four albums—not in the U.S. and Canada, but in the rest of the world. That's what stunk. I got away from Fantasy, but I was still *on* Fantasy. The Shep album was only the first under that deal. I remember blurting out to the sleep nurse, "I still owe them three albums! *The Bee Gees' whole career is three albums!*" I didn't mean that in a derogatory way. I meant, "Look how much great music can be contained in only three albums."

When I blurted that out, I realized I had to fix this situation. Fantasy had cheated me out of my own songs, had paid a pittance of a royalty and then had *stolen it all back. Stolen my life savings.* And I was supposed to give them *more music?* I never got any good at the sleep alpha thing, but I knew I had to take care of owing Fantasy more material in *any* part of the universe if I was going to survive.

I decided to give up my artist royalties in lieu of having to give Fantasy any more music. Because in my mind I was getting paid a pittance for the Creedence stuff anyway—one-quarter of our very low royalty rate. I'd get a foreign royalty statement from Fantasy that said earnings were $480,000, and by the time they took their deductions they'd whittled it down to $30,000. So I swapped those royalties for freedom. If you don't think it was a good deal for me, remember: Saul would have owned *Centerfield, Eye of the Zombie,* and *Blue Moon Swamp*—which came out in 1997! And I would *not* have been paid correctly.

My brother Tom made it clear that he didn't think this was a good idea. Saul must've told him I did it. I'd get letters from Tom trying to convince me that I'd made a mistake, bragging about how much he'd made in royalties, how he and Saul were pals and wasn't I a dumb schmuck. Tom bragged that he'd earned a million and a half dollars in ten years of Creedence sales. For probably twenty million albums, that's a rather paltry rate!

I may have been giving up money, but man, I was free.

Two things helped me keep my sanity during this time: running and going into the woods. I had taken up running in 1974. I'd seen a picture of myself on a fishing trip and my gut was hanging out, and I thought, *My God! I've got to do something about that.* In my world, no one really knew about conditioning, so I thought, *How about if I just run?* My place was a few blocks away from Albany High School, so I went over there and ran around the track: run a lap, walk a·lap. A few days into this I decided I was going to sprint all the way back to my office. I got one block and I collapsed on a lawn.

This is when I was still smoking. Since high school I'd smoked about a pack a day. I was disgusted with myself over how out of shape I had gotten. I thought, *What a pathetic old man you are! You can't even run one block?* I was only twenty-nine! It was at that exact moment when I became a runner.

And I stopped smoking. The running thing filled up whatever desire there was in my lungs. And in my head too. I do an awful lot of thinking while I'm running—I've had a lot of inspirations for songs, inspirations for things to do with my career and my life. Through a lot of hard years, bad years, the best I ever felt was while running. There were so many things in my life that were out of my control, but running I could do something about. I was in charge. I've been running for over forty years now.

It's good to have an image in mind, a goal to keep you inspired. I can remember turning a corner on the sidewalk near my office way back around 1974, and I had a picture in my head of the way Jackie Wilson had moved onstage at the Oakland Auditorium. That was perfection, and how I wanted to be. I thought, *Yeah, that's why I'm doing this! Jackie Wilson!*

Hunting wasn't as much about having an image in my head as it was an escape. Jake Rohrer ran my office, and in 1974 an old friend of his invited him up to Troy, Oregon, for a pack trip, and I came along. I hadn't been around a dad or an uncle to show me how to hunt, and here I was, getting up to this place right in the middle of nowhere. I brought a fishing pole, met a couple of local characters. We stayed up late the night before, singing songs, drinking beer. Jake and I caught a whole bunch of fish. I enjoyed it so much that before the weekend was over, I had decided to buy some property there.

First I bought a place in town that was being rented to loggers, which was a mistake. I was really glad when I was able to sell that. The actual day my Asylum album was released, my hands were in a toilet in Troy. I had to fix it all. Then I bought property on the other side of the Grande Ronde River and built a house there. I'd fish in the Wenaha River, the best water in the world. It was a place for my family to vacation, and I went hunting there until 1990. The longest I was in the woods was a month nonstop. Without a shower.

At this point in my life, I am ambivalent about hunting. I could go either way. If somebody were to say to me, "Oh, how can you kill Bambi?," I totally get that. Or "Guns are so evil!" I understand that. And when another person says, "Man, you must really enjoy getting out in the woods with the fellas, roughing it and being lucky enough to get an animal," yeah, I get all that too. In my whole 1950s view of the world and masculinity, there was stuff that was considered part of the package of being a guy. Hunting was a reference point of manhood. And I really enjoyed it.

I was fortunate to have Harvey Graham as my hunting buddy on these trips. He was a carpenter by trade, and we had met when he did some remodeling work at the Factory. Harvey was twenty years older than me and had served in World War II. He had lived in places like Grand Junction, Colorado, and various small towns in South Dakota, and was an old-school mountain man. Even as a kid, living in rural areas, he was the go-to guy that folks relied on to find people (or livestock) that had gotten lost in the mountains. And he was perfectly able to exist in the wild for extended periods of time.

I learned a lot out there just by watching Harvey's example. One big lesson was that we humans can endure much tougher conditions than we think. I would see Harvey, sometimes sick as a dog with the flu, just forcing himself to "keep going"—hiking over the mountains in a blizzard. One time, he stumbled and fell on the side of a mountain and his elbow got lodged in the crook of a tree, dislocating his shoulder. He was alone and in pain, so he reset his own shoulder! I was a city slicker by his standards, but I like to think that some of Harvey rubbed off on me.

When you go hunting, you're obviously going to have a gun with you. Although I've already mentioned that I'm in favor of gun control, I really like guns. Yes, I acknowledge that a gun is a tool whose whole purpose is to kill. But as a kid, long before I ever thought about hunting, I thought about the Wild West and the Colt Peacemaker, the guns of the Civil War and the Revolutionary War. Historically, it's part of who we are. And I'm attracted to and fascinated by that. Since I was fourteen, I've daydreamed about being part of some sort of landed gentry, or a rich, idle play-boy. You'd step into my library and there would be a collection of flintlocks—"Here's a blunderbuss from the *Mayflower*."

Hunting is just a game where you try to be very stealthy and quiet for hours and days and nothing happens. And then for about three seconds, all hell breaks loose and everybody jumps around for a few minutes. Then it's over. And we all go back to being stealthy and quiet again. But for the rest of the time, we're thinking and talking about those three seconds. That's the absolute truth.

The hunting is such a tiny part of "hunting." I think in twenty years of going, I might have been successful getting an animal five or six times. That's about it. So hunting is the excuse. I'm a hard-working person, and I'd work right up until I left for the trip. After being out in the woods for three days—it was always three days—the same thing would always occur. Something would just click. Suddenly the clock slows down, the mind opens up, and you're really self-aware. It just sinks in: all the smells, the sounds and the pace, the trees and the stars and the mountains and crea-tures.... You're watching the squirrels, owls, all the critters. That's when I'd find myself saying, "Imagine—they do this every day. Even when I'm not here!" You certainly believe that you are with God.

You start to become very appreciative of all life, especially your own. Being so introspective gives you a chance to worry about the things you've done wrong in life. When you're in civilization you're too busy; you don't worry about the negative scorecard. I think it makes you more soulful. Unfortunately, the situation I was in was unchanging: Fantasy Records and Saul Zaentz. It was good for me to go into the woods. I would come back feeling like tackling things again.

Those problems didn't always leave me. One year an elk came right up to me and I shot, but he got away. I was so pissed off—I

was stomping through the woods, kicking rocks, yelling, "Fuckin'
lawyers, fuckin' Fantasy, fuck, fuck, *fuck!* God, John, you're such
a loser!" By now my heart was thumping. I put my pack down
right where the elk had been, took my rifle and went down about
a hundred yards, aimed at my pack, *bam!* I came back, looked at
my pack. Nope, I didn't hit it.*

Troy was great for me during that time, but of course things
change. One day in the early nineties I was starting to get busy
with my *Blue Moon Swamp* album, and I hadn't been back to
Troy in a while. Julie was in my life now, and I mentioned it to
her. Kind of matter-of-fact, not with any sort of attitude, she just
said, "Well, I don't want to go to that house. That's a different
life. It's a sad place to me. You had to escape and get away, and it
just hurts me that you felt that way. I don't want to go there."

So after that, I sold the place in Troy. I was looking right at her
and I thought, *Yeah, right—we'll create our own new place that's
just for us.*

---

* The next year I put a scope on that rifle.

CHAPTER 13

Springtime in the Bahamas

IN 1977 CAME another blow: I lost just about every dime I'd ever made from Creedence. Remember that offshore tax plan that Saul Zaentz led the band into rather than pay us more money or tear up our contract? That "bank," Castle Bank in the Bahamas, was run by Burt Kanter and a former CIA agent named Paul Helliwell— two lawyers that, I learned while researching this book, had "direct ties to organized crime," as one author put it. Kanter was involved with mobsters Moe Dalitz and Morris Kleinman; Helliwell had ties to Meyer Lansky and Nixon bagman Bebe Rebozo. (In fact, an IRS investigator claimed that Nixon's name was on a computer printout of Castle Bank clients, although that's never been completely verified.) Nefarious dealings at the bank would lead another writer to describe Castle as a " 'dual purpose laundromat' serving both the CIA and the mob."*

---

* The first quote is from *Masters of Paradise: Organized Crime and the Internal Revenue Service in the Bahamas* by Alan A. Block (Transaction, 1998). The second quote is from *American War Machine: Deep Politics, the CIA Global Drug Connection, and the Road to Afghanistan* by Peter Dale Scott (Rowman & Littlefield, 2014).

I knew none of this then. In fact, I was told at the time that Kanter was an ex–IRS agent, which years later I learned was a complete lie. (And guess what? Kanter just happened to be on the board of Fantasy Records.) At the time, we asked our accountants and lawyers and everybody else I could think of to ask, "Is this thing legal? Is it okay to do this?" All of our advisers assured us that it was. By the latter part of the seventies, when there was more and more evidence that this Castle Bank thing was hokum, it really started to bother me.

I'm not a big guy for business meetings. It's not something I was good at in school. My eyes glaze over when people start talking numbers. But even I had started noticing things. Ed Arnold, my accountant, would show me a page that supposedly represented my account, my own personal money in Castle Bank. And on this page I'd see a couple of withdrawals that I hadn't made—a few thousand here, five thousand dollars there. Over the course of months there were repeated withdrawals. I had thought that once we were in the plan there were no monthly bank fees. It wasn't like borrowing money, where I had to pay interest—this was my own money.

I asked, "Who's making these withdrawals?" Ed kind of fumbled. He said, "It's just maintenance of the account. It's normal." I thought, *The money just sits there. Why does it have to be maintained?* I couldn't really have my own money. Say I wanted to buy a car—I had to call Ed. Then some time would pass and it would be okay for me to buy one—but the car had to be owned by the trust. The whole thing was cumbersome and strange.

Then I saw a report on *60 Minutes* on Bahamian trusts and how the U.S. government was taking the position that they weren't really legal. I don't think it mentioned Castle Bank specifically, but that's when I started saying, "It may not be illegal, but it sure feels unethical to me. And immoral."

I entered into this whole thing like some Boy Scout. I hadn't gone into music to escape paying income tax and become shady. I'd heard stories of Elvis sometimes paying taxes when he didn't have to. He would donate to charity and not take the tax write-off he was entitled to. Elvis felt deeply about giving back. I don't know if those stories are true, but I'd always go, "Oh, wow, cool." Now that may sound naive, but that's how I felt then. I wouldn't lie to people to make myself look good or to get out of consequences. If my country says I'm supposed to pay this much tax, well, by God, then that's what I should do. I was very proud of my honesty.

I didn't want to be Richard Nixon sobbing to the camera. But this looked like something I was going to have to back up, maybe lie about. And that wasn't me.

It all came to a head when I was talking to Joe Smith on the phone one day. He called in 1976, a few days after that meeting where it was decided that *Hoodoo* wasn't coming out. He was probably worried that he had totally devastated me, because that was a hard pill to swallow. Not everybody would have followed up. He was a good guy and could tell I was in a bad way. At our meeting, he'd said, "Why don't you go fix what's bothering you?" That's what moved me to get out of that whole Castle Bank thing. I took a stand. I'm the guy who said, "Y'know, this is wrong, and the decision to stand up is going to cost so much of my life and money, but I'm a man. I'm not a wuss."

I called a meeting with Ed, my accountant, and my lawyer, Barry Engel. I called it "the Shoe Box Meeting." I said, "Look, I don't really know what my finances are. I want to understand this. Creedence sold all these records. Picture a shoe box, an empty shoe box. Take everything I've ever earned, put it in the shoe box. And everything I've ever spent, take that out of the shoe box. Show me what's left in the shoe box. What's the number?" I really pushed it because no one could or would tell me. Every time I would ask, I'd get, "Well, we have to move all of this to this column..." It was like the shell game at the carnival.

I said I wanted out of the plan. They tried to talk me out of withdrawing. Ed turned to me and said, "If you get out of the plan, you may have to pay one hundred and ten percent of everything you've ever earned."

I said, "What do you mean?"

"You'll be receiving all of your income in one calendar year," he responded. "And they could penalize you for every single year that you didn't pay taxes. If they throw the book at you, they're going to charge you one hundred and ten percent."

I'm thinking, *Here I am, this kid from El Cerrito who went on to create the number one band in the world, sold millions of records, and now I'm going to owe more money than what that whole journey earned.*

I said, "Okay. I want to do it anyway."

I had given a specific directive: "Get me out of the plan." Nothing happened. Barry Engel, who was also representing the rest of the band, says, "John, if you start doing all this you're really gonna harm the other three guys."

I go, "What do you mean?"

"If you start telling the government all about the plan, and that you're taking your royalties out of that plan and paying the taxes on it—well, Uncle Sam is gonna know that the other guys are in this, and you're gonna hurt their position." The threat Ed relayed about owing 110 percent wasn't working on me, so here was another nudge—you should feel sorry for the other guys and consider staying in the plan, because you're going to hurt everybody else.

So I did this: I said, "Barry, I won't talk about it for one year. I won't say a word to anybody. For one year. After that, whatever anybody has to know about this I'll have to explain. Because you and I both know this thing looks shaky. I'll keep quiet one year. And by then you better have something figured out." The other fellas really didn't want to get out of the plan. I know some of the guys thought about transferring their money to some Swiss account in Geneva.

Still nothing was happening! Looking back, I would say they were stalling. A few days went by. I finally had to call another meeting, at which I pointed at my advisers and said to them directly, "Get me out of this plan!" My people contacted the mysterious Castle Bank, telling them, "John wants to withdraw completely from this plan."

They got back a telegram. It was February 14, 1977. I know because the attorneys and accountants dubbed this the Saint Valentine's Day Massacre telegram. I didn't find this out until many legal fees later, when we had to reconstruct the events. They were all having a big laugh on this little point in history. The telegram said that Paul Helliwell, the president of the bank, had died. In a sauna. (The telegram claimed that he died the day before, but it appears that was just a stall tactic. He died on December 24, 1976.) Because of this, the bank was closing until further notice. All assets had been frozen. Access to my money stopped right then.

I'd seen enough old movies in which the mob traps some guy in the steam room by sticking a broom through the door handles, turns the heat up to four thousand, and he's cooked like a lobster. I started looking under my cars for wires. Something that looked like it might blow up if I started the car. I was scared. I checked under every car for months. Here I was, the whistle-blower on a shady bank, and all of a sudden, I'm locked in the sauna with my money on the other side.

Weeks and months were spent searching for my money, pursuing any trails. Finally my office manager, Jake, came to me. "The trail has gone cold," he said. "In Panama. Your money has disappeared without a trace. There's no more places to look. It's gone."

I went to my studio to regroup. I told myself, *You're zero.*

You've lost your life savings, everything you've earned from being the number one band in the world. All that income from your songs, songwriting, records, concerts—it's just all gone.

Now, in my own kind of stumbling way, I kept trying to stay current in music, and I had bought an ARP 2600 synthesizer. It bothered me that you could play only one note at a time on this mono keyboard. Suddenly, right in the middle of this terrible day, I had an epiphany. I should approach the synth like an orchestral composer, blending single notes into chords. It was just like what I was doing as a teenager in my bedroom with that add-a-track tape recorder and my guitar. And I created this delightful—I mean delightful—little piece of music. It sounded like little birdies, little crickets, and all sorts of little animals singing together. Kind of like a Disney cartoon. It was fully formed and realized, right there after I got the news about my savings disappearing. And I named this piece of music "Springtime in the Bahamas." I don't know where the heck that recording is now. I'd like to hear it.

Despite the beautiful music, I was pissed off. Completely enraged. And I grew resolute: "They ain't getting away with it. Whatever it takes." I decided I needed a symbol. I suppose van Gogh would've cut off an ear. In my mind, I pictured myself as a pirate standing on the deck of a ship, fighting overwhelming odds, brandishing my last two swords and one of those little flintlock guns, yelling, *"Arrrrgh."*

A pirate has earrings. So I went to the local mall and got my ear pierced. In 1977 you didn't see guys walking around wearing earrings. Nobody had an earring then. Nobody. When I came home, Martha and the kids were like, *"Ooooh-kay."* Everybody thought that the earring was pretty strange. But I was all by myself going through this. I was doing this alone.

After my initial action to have my funds withdrawn from Castle Bank and the ensuing anxiety that the money might just go missing, I had been instructing my own attorneys and accountants to take action...to "find the money." Slowly, it began to dawn on me that I had a bigger problem than just my life savings being missing. The IRS was going to insist that I pay income tax even though the money was missing. And they were probably going to demand taxes on money that had gone (supposedly) straight into Castle Bank—without *ever* having been in my possession. *Yikes!*

I was really worried about the consequences of this plan. If it was not legal, did that mean I would go to prison? What if I didn't have enough money to pay the taxes? I didn't have much money at the time—would I have to earn more money in the future to pay taxes on income from the past? I thought about Joe Louis, the former heavyweight champion of the world. Things had gone so bad for Joe that it took an *act of Congress* to forgive his debts. Was I going to end up like him?

I wasn't sure how I should feel about the professionals that I already had working on this. After all, many of them were *also* representing my ex-bandmates, and those guys didn't want to get out of the plan. I decided that I needed to be represented by a "Tall Building"—meaning a law firm in a big, fancy building. I didn't know where to start, so I called Joe Smith at Asylum Records. It was Joe who had suggested that I go fix whatever was bothering me.

Joe recommended Werner Wolfen at the firm of Irell and Manella in Century City. Werner was absolutely wonderful to me. The way I feel, looking back on it now, is if I hadn't had Werner Wolfen in my corner from this point on, I *never* would have survived this mess. Werner had me come down to his office and pour out the whole dismal, awful story. Over the next few weeks he took me under his wing and just went to work. He felt it was really wrong, what had happened to me, and he just wanted to help. At this point in my economic life, I never could have afforded the representation that Werner and his firm gave me. Basically, he provided me with Ferrari performance for the price of a Kia. I will always be grateful for his generosity.

A day or two after the Saint Valentine's Day Massacre telegram, I suddenly remembered that a separate account had been set up for my songwriting royalties. To their credit, BMI had refused to send payments to some obscure entity in the Bahamas.

I didn't know where it was or how to get at it—that's how naive and out of touch I was. I told Jake to go down to my accountant's office and camp out there until he had the details. Because Ed was acting more and more nervous and evasive about this thing.

We found out that the BMI money had gone into an account at the Royal Bank of Canada. I instructed Jake to tell Ed, "Get that money back!" The check arrived and it was made out to "Fred Fogerty." Ed was going to send it back, but I said, "*No, don't do that!* If it goes back, I'm sure we will never see it again!" I signed the check and deposited it at my bank in El Cerrito. At that moment that was all the money I had in the world. The IRS, of course, contended that I owed taxes on the income that had been deposited in Castle Bank. (The whole point of "the plan" had been to avoid paying income tax.) So this check that was made out to Fred Fogerty? That money went straight to the IRS.

The other guys in Creedence were represented by many of the same lawyers and accountants as me. When they learned about my decision to leave the Castle Bank plan, their reaction was, "John is crazy," and they went about trying to salvage their funds while staying in the plan. Tom went so far as to fly to Geneva with one of the professionals, hoping to transfer his account to Switzerland. The three of them stayed in the plan for another year or so without taking action to withdraw from it, even though their accounts were frozen too.

I was now suing Saul, Fantasy Records, my accountant, my

lawyer, and mastermind Burt Kanter. So did Tom, Doug, and Stu, in a separate action. They had lost their life savings like I had, but they got wind of the fact that I had actually rescued my songwriting money. They started going, "Well, John saved some money. Maybe we should get some of that." So they not only sued everybody I was suing: they also sued me.

At some point—more than a year and some months later—my new lawyer, Ken Sidle from Irell and Manella, came to me and said, "John, the other guys have hit a brick wall with their case. They waited too long to take action, and the statute of limitations ran out." More than likely, the judge would throw their case out. Ken said, "I've heard from their attorney, and they're wondering if they can attach their case to your case."

This gave me pause. So many times I had bit my tongue and kept the band moving forward despite what I thought was foolish and very self-destructive behavior. So many times I had kept quiet while they were hurling insults at me. I said, "Geez, they want me to save their butts...again. Wow."

But I didn't think about it for very long. I looked at Ken and said, "I guess it's not their fault that they lost their money." (I thought to myself, *Yeah, because* crooks *stole our money*, but I didn't say that out loud.) I let Tom, Stu, and Doug join my case.

I didn't have to do this. Given how they had treated me, that might've been one of the most generous things I've ever done. Not that anybody ever said thank you. Meanwhile, they still had their suit against me—so if we didn't prevail together in the one case, they could still come after the one thing I'd managed to save: my personal songwriting royalties. The fact that they were both joining my team *and* suing me at the same time is a curious piece of rock and roll history.

Tom was living in Hawaii then. He'd made a couple of records, and I just thought they were bad. He'd done the Elvis song "Mystery Train," and it was a mess. I remember thinking to myself,

Y'know, it would be really cool to help Tom make a better album. Maybe I could be his producer. We were pretty estranged then. I'd get all these weird letters from him full of rants about what a crook Saul was, plus wacky ideas like how Creedence should just reunite and cover some old pop tune. I would read his letters and immediately burn them. They were so weird and delusional. I didn't want to ever be tempted to release them to the world.

Then Tom got back from Hawaii, and what do I hear? He'd gone to several labels looking for a record deal, and no one would sign him. So he went back to Fantasy Records! I couldn't believe it; I mean, Saul stole *Tom's* money too. This was the way that Saul bought Tom's allegiance so Tom wouldn't sue him. What's a couple of recording sessions to him? Sure enough, Tom dropped out of the lawsuit against Saul (although he still profited from it in the end). It was such a Machiavellian thing for Saul to do. Saul Zaentz really poisoned my relationship with my brother. There's no doubt in my mind that things would've been different without Saul in the picture, that Tom and I would still be making music together today.

Despite all the people we had originally sued, the trial wound up being solely against our accountant, Ed Arnold. His insurance carrier thought they could beat the case, so we went to court. We had settled with Burt Kanter and the others for pennies on the dollar. Fantasy had been dropped from the case altogether. This fact has always bothered me. How in the world could Fantasy be dropped from this case? We were four kids from El Cerrito. We didn't know anything about "international banking." The label that we recorded for, Fantasy, had gotten themselves into this Castle Bank plan. Then they insisted that we be in their plan. Obviously, we didn't make that decision without Fantasy Records. Burt Kanter, the owner of Castle Bank and director of the plan, was on the board of directors of Fantasy Records. I have always wondered if there wasn't some kind of relationship between Burt, Saul, and the people who were handling the case in the legal system. Some kind of "cocktail party coziness."

The trial was surreal. There were some weird characters on the stand. One day this person showed up to testify. We called her the mystery woman because we didn't know anything about her. And the day she's there to testify, four or five of the biggest guys you ever saw walk right in and sit down in the front row. They were in suits, had no necks, and looked like human torpedoes. They were very interested in the mystery woman's testimony. Then they were gone. That was scary.

One of the witnesses was a guy named Elliot Steinberg, and he is a prime example of the weasel mentality among these guys. My attorney Ken Sidle questioned Steinberg on the witness stand, under oath, about a particular meeting involving the professionals representing Creedence and some of the people from "the plan."

> **Sidle:** "Mr. Steinberg, who did you represent at that meeting?"
> **Steinberg:** "No one."
> **Sidle:** "No one?"
> **Steinberg:** "That's right, no one."
> **Sidle:** "Well, who did you represent before the meeting?"
> **Steinberg:** "Saul Zaentz."
> **Sidle:** "And who did you represent after the meeting?"
> **Steinberg:** "Saul Zaentz."
> **Sidle:** "So, that being the case, who did you represent *during* the meeting?"
> **Steinberg:** "No one."

At this point, my brother Tom—who was seated about four feet to my right—said, "I believe him."

A whoosh of disbelief and almost laughter enveloped the rest of us, who were all seated closely in a group. Tom's former wife,

Gail, turned around towards our row and said, "Mashed potato brains."

When Steinberg was finished testifying, he walked directly out of the courtroom and down the hall. I got right up and followed him out. I found him in a phone booth. I poked my head in and said, "Elliot, how do you sleep at night?" I just shook my head, staring at him. He just sort of looked down. I was very angry. We had really been screwed over by those people. I turned around and there was my old tour manager, Bruce Young. I asked him what he was doing there. He said, "I didn't know if you were gonna kill him."

Burt Kanter's receptionist testified. She had a Bahamian accent. At one point my attorney asked her if the bank was actually solvent. "Oh, we got plenty *moooooney*," she drawled. Everybody cracked up.

In May 1983, the jury decided in our favor. The headline in the San Francisco paper said, "Creedence Wins Case, Gets 8.3 Million." That might sound like a lot to you, but considering the fact that we sold millions upon millions of records, it was pathetic. And it all came from Ed Arnold's insurance company. Saul Zaentz and Fantasy never paid a dime. They got away with it. They took our money, and they kept our money.*

Let me add a final dismal detail: Fantasy was always years behind on their payments to us. In 1973, we'd still be after them to pay what they owed for 1969. When Castle Bank was frozen and closed, they suddenly claimed that they'd been very timely in depositing our royalty payments into the bank. But the deal was, according to them, that they were somehow depositing checks into a defunct, insolvent bank after it had been shut down. Right?

---

* In 1987, the IRS opened a case that went on for years, investigating Fantasy, accusing it of diverting $28 million in profits from the Zaentz-produced *One Flew Over the Cuckoo's Nest* to offshore trusts to avoid paying taxes. I believe the eventual settlement was in the neighborhood of $15 million.

Who was there at the "bank" to *receive* the checks? How could anyone disprove it now? It was a devious and despicable move on their part, since it allowed them to appear current in their payments without sending us checks. Our money, and whatever records that went with it, was all gone.

You know that phrase "art imitates life, and life imitates art"? In 1984, I took Martha and the kids to see *Pinocchio*. Disney had rereleased the animated feature to theaters, and it was playing at the Albany Theatre on Solano Avenue, where I'd gone as a kid. We got to the theater and they'd converted it into two screens. The fact that I was planning to watch *Pinocchio* wasn't even the funniest part, because what was playing in the other theater? *Amadeus*—the story of some greedy, heavyset guy who takes control of Mozart and takes all his money. Who produced *Amadeus*? Saul Zaentz.

Gritting my teeth, I took my wife and kids to *Pinocchio*. If you're not familiar with the story, Stromboli, a greedy, heavyset guy with a beard, takes possession of Pinocchio and keeps him in a birdcage, only letting him out to sing and dance onstage so people will throw money.

There's a famous scene where Stromboli is counting all the gold he's made off the puppet. "My little wooden gold mine," he calls Pinocchio, to whom he's only given one measly silver coin. "One for you, two for me! One for you, *three* for me!"

I had felt pretty much alone in my struggles with Saul. Going hunting, getting the earring, and all that. But life can learn a lot from art too.

A few days after watching *Pinocchio*, Martha came to me and said, "I finally understand what you've been trying to tell me."

CHAPTER 14

Put Me In, Coach

SINCE THE FAILURE of *Hoodoo,* I'd been locking myself away in my tiny garage studio on Key Route Boulevard in Albany, California. I had my mixing board in there, a professional eight-track tape machine, some amplifiers, and a big speaker that I called Godzilla, which eventually damaged my hearing. I'd start at ten and work all day. Sometimes I'd come back after dinner and a run and play some more. No weekends off. Day in, day out, all I did for years was work on my playing, trying to perform better so that I could somehow present this one-man-band thing.

I had to be good enough on all the instruments to sound authoritative. The music had to have a certain swagger to it. The drums continually held me back. I wish now that I could take the ten years I spent playing drums and have that time invested in the guitar. I guess I can say that I got good enough, but I never really got great. There's a scene in *Pinocchio* where he believes enough and he's a good enough boy that all the puppet strings fall away, the Disney music comes up, and he says, "I'm a real boy!" Well, I'd be on those drums just waiting for the day when I could say, "I'm a

264

real band!" I deluded myself into thinking that it might even come true at some point.

You might ask, why didn't I just go find other people to make music with? I guess I'm persistent. Or stubborn? Depends on how you look at it. I'd been on this road for a long, long time, and I'm no quitter. It seemed to me that I should fulfill this dream, accomplish what I'd set out to do. I don't let go of an obsession so easily, especially then. I was pretty tenacious. I'd lock my alligator jaws onto an idea and never let go. Until maybe I collapsed.

Or until it worked.

At first I wasn't capable of writing songs, so I'd do covers — "Break My Mind," "Stood Up," all kinds of songs out of the past. I was basically making a recording every day, but the real point was to get better. I kept busy. Whatever flicker, whatever ember was alive down in my soul, I was protecting that with the last Viking armor of the ages. In a sense, the one-man band was a kind of therapy. I'd just keep going to my garage, practice drums and work on arrangements, try to stay sane.

People would come visit. All they had to do was mention Fantasy Records or the band breaking up or Saul Zaentz, and it was like pushing a button. This involuntary anger would erupt out of me. It was not coming from a position of strength. I was a sorrowful person who felt that he had no recourse in life. I would see reflected in their eyes what they saw looking at me: "Man, they look at me like I'm dead. They talk to me like I'm dead." To them I was a has-been. It was a terrible mirror.

There finally came that day when I said, "Okay, I have to write a song." This was a very big deal. It had been a long time. So I thought, *I'll go fishing*. It was spring of 1984. I rented a boat, took my fishing stuff and a pad and a pen, and went to the San Pablo

Reservoir in El Sobrante. I thought, *Well, I'll just see if I can* think *about writing a song.* I knew that somewhere in my DNA was the ability, because I'd done it once upon a time. You have to understand: I had been so far away from songwriting for so long that I was sort of scared of it. But I got in the boat, started fishing, and started thinking.

I started remembering when Eisenhower had been elected. They sent us home from Harding School so we could see the inauguration on television. This was early '53. All I could see on the screen was a bunch of big black Cadillacs. I start thinking about that. And other things I saw on TV then: the Yankees, the Mickey Mouse Club, and Elvis on *Ed Sullivan*. All the things I had experienced while watching TV.

The words started to come. And then a melody. Instead of thinking about the process of writing a song, I slid into *actually* writing a song. But I didn't know that. If you become self-aware, you break the spell. It's really true. So I just stayed with it. It was stuff I knew.

A few hours went by. I'm not sure if I got a nibble as far as fishing went. I paid for the boat and packed up my stuff, just as I had done a zillion times before. I walked to the car, opened the door. I was sort of in a trance. I put my pole and tackle box in the back of the car, and as I was closing the door the realization came to me: "Damn, *I wrote a song.*" It had been since *Hoodoo*—1976!

It was overwhelming. I had gone on that trip with the hope, "Maybe I can think about what it would be like to write a song. Maybe I could make an outline. Maybe I can come up with an idea or a direction." *Maybe.*

And now I was on the other side of that hope and I had a song: "I Saw It on TV," which would be on *Centerfield*. It's like suddenly becoming Willie Mays. And I thought, *Okay. Here we go! I can write songs again. We're gonna get down the road now.* If life were like the movies, this would've been one of those times when the emotional soundtrack music gets real loud and the whole audience bursts into tears.

I wrote a lot of *Centerfield* in my car. I had to find a place where I wasn't going to get tapped on the shoulder. Where I could concentrate. At first I'd try to get away to somewhere in the Bay Area. I'd drive over to Berkeley and to a BART station and park. Then I'd get pissed off—too many cars, people staring. I couldn't find that perfect place. Finally I just decided, "I can't get away from 'em. There's nowhere to go." Necessity over comfort—you just have to *do* it. So I'd drive over to El Cerrito Plaza and literally park right between two cars. Nobody notices you then. Or in front of somebody's house. I'd listen to a little music, maybe smoke a bit of a cigar, pull out my notebook, and get myself into the frame of mind of whatever song for *Centerfield* I was working on. People would be walking by and I'd be writing "Big Train (from Memphis)." I was so friggin' focused.

After Warner Bros. Records took over the Asylum label, I worked with Mo Ostin and Lenny Waronker, two of the best guys I've ever known in my life. Lenny is one of the truly great rock and roll people, a great record man. He really loves music. You'll never know all the different suggestions Lenny gave people that led to hit records. That was a good time in my life—being with a real record company in the real record business doing real stuff. That's the only time that has ever happened in my life. I'm sure I made it a little difficult for them at times, me being the kind of sporadic artist that I have been since my heyday with Creedence. It wasn't meant in any mean way, it's just that I kind of disappeared at times.

Lenny and Mo treated me—and my music—with so much

respect. They put that company behind me. With Fantasy, the budget was always ten cents and they never did anything. The Warner Bros. building was so full of life, the energy was so great. It was swinging. It was smokin' hot. People had ideas, they were all working. It was very artist-friendly. Looking in the rearview mirror, those were the days. We all didn't know how good we had it.

And these were the guys who were going to be hearing my new songs.

I remember writing "The Old Man Down the Road" like it was yesterday. I was in my little room in Albany, playing this Washburn Falcon guitar. I had special-ordered it. Later I got a couple more and they weren't the same. This one was exactly right. It's the guitar on the album.

The first time you pick up the guitar on any given day, you're not all warmed up. Your brain is off somewhere else. You're in standby mode. So you noodle. I had the guitar plugged into a cool little tube amp that had a slightly overdriven sound. And I'm doing my swamp stuff. Suddenly I went *dear dear dernt dernt dernt*. There are lots and lots of guitar players and writers in the world. Great ones. I've always thought one thing that sets me apart is that I can recognize a good riff, a good line, or a good melody from just a little snippet.

Let's say I'm off somewhere jamming. You play something—and you recognize that it's something you can sink your teeth into. You know it's strong enough to do again. It's a statement. You restate it, to let everybody know that you know. (Albert King was the master of this.) If you play it a third time, you alter it a bit to let everybody know that you can edit yourself on the fly. In a nanosecond you make the decision: "Yeah, that's not the whole thing—that's the beginning of the thing." It needs the comeback, the response, the answer. Are you going to play the same notes or something new? All the while you know you're never going to feel like this again. There's only one time that's the first time.

You're also hoping the next thing you do on that guitar is the right move. The wrong thing and you're probably going to have to come back tomorrow. You lose the immediacy of the moment, and maybe the whole thing.

When I came up with "The Old Man Down the Road," my brain was cooking before I said a word. The first thing I played might've been an accident, but my brain knew immediately that it was crying out for that something extra to make it a great riff. I'm suspended there. I'm waiting, hoping that the next thing I do will be the answer, the one-in-a-million group of notes that is *just right* to complete the riff. And suddenly it comes, I play...*dernt dernt dear dear dear dear.* I've got it! It's a riff! Finally I played a little rhythm on my special E7 chord and I thought, *Okay, maybe this could be a song.*

My title notebook was right there—I'd never stopped jotting ideas in it—and I thumbed through it and saw "Somewhere Down the Road." I don't know how quickly I went away from that one after I'd first seen it written it down—was it right then? Five minutes later? A day?

Coming back to it, something in my brain still said that it was a little lame. That it seemed too generic. Vague. Not ominous. So, *what* was somewhere down the road? The old man doesn't have to be human. It can be the devil, it can be evil, it can just be a bad wind. The old man. And he's down the road, for sure. So I was off and running.

The curious thing about it is, I went back to my notebook months later, and "Somewhere Down the Road" is not written in there. I went through it page by page. It's just not there. So weird. Same with another song, "Change in the Weather." Maybe I have one of these notebooks full of shape-shifters, where whatever I need to see, it's there. Then I close the book and it's gone! That certainly blew my mind. How else to explain it?

People thought "Old Man" was about Saul Zaentz. Not when I wrote it, though there were times when I sang it later that I thought of Saul—but not the way you might think. One day I was driving down the freeway and "The Old Man Down the Road" came on the Top 40 radio station for the first time. There are no words to describe how I felt besides overjoyed. After being chained to the rack in Saul's dungeon for so many years, I was so happy, like a little kid. The song ended and I said, "*Ha!* Take that, *old man!*" Okay, it wasn't as clean as that. "Take that, you *fuckin' old man!*" It was a catharsis. As I told one writer at the time who asked, "This is more than a comeback. This is a triumph over evil!"

"Rock and Roll Girls" was inspired by watching my twelve-year-old daughter, Laurie, and her best friend hanging out. That's what I'd call them—the Rock and Roll Girls. I was writing about teenagers, how they have their own world that they're not telling Pop about. It was all fairly innocent. I'm quite sure people thought of that other vision of rock and roll girls, the ones you might find in a Mötley Crüe video, but for me it never was. Musically, I was referring to "Wild Weekend" by the Rockin' Rebels. I don't think of it as stealing—more a case of honoring. I still had to make a real song out of it. I'm a sucker for that sound. At the end of "Wild Weekend" the drummer gets lost—he's hitting the backbeat on the downbeat. That poor, unfortunate drummer. Maybe he got better later.

"Searchlight" came from a trip to Lake Havasu on the Arizona-California border. Driving down the highway, I saw a road sign: "Searchlight nine miles." So I wrote that down in the book. It was also one of those first-thing-in-the-morning inspirations. I remember playing it on guitar in my studio and going to that place where you concentrate and relax at the same time. I hit this swampy, mournful chord: "Oh, the midnight / Need a searchlight." Mo

Ostin liked how I pronounced it "soichlight." He got a big kick out of that. I liked how that sounded. I didn't know what it meant. Still don't. In "Searchlight" there are lyrical and emotional references to one of my favorite songs, "Endless Sleep." But my song, it's about being lost. The metaphor was me.

The one-man band was so difficult to do. There were times when it felt literally impossible. Once I'd finally nail an arrangement, I'd really have to know how long the parts were going to be. I couldn't just nod at some other guy and go, "Take it!" Nowadays, with digital recording, you can edit very quickly. In those days, you were stuck. If you were wrong or changed your mind, you had to start all over again—which I did many times. It was so unwieldy. Cumbersome. In the back of my mind I was still hoping that somebody would just walk in with a great producer, and boom, it would all be done for me. I'd be like Sinatra and I wouldn't have to do anything but open my mouth and sing.

There were a total of nine songs on *Centerfield,* and at one point I had six pretty much done. I was really having trouble with the song "Centerfield." The drums weren't good, which was always the sticking point. I had gone so far as to use a drum machine but have my real snare vibrate along with it so it sounded more lively and real than a stinkin' machine. I went through that process, made a drum track that way, played a guitar to it, and in the end I listened and said, "Ouch...that sucks."

At that point I thought, *I've got to go down to Burbank and see Lenny. I need to know if I'm on the right track or not. Is this one-man band going to work when I get it done, or is it...stupid?* So I took working tapes of six songs, leaving out the three songs I didn't feel were finished. I know that "Centerfield" and "Zanz Kant Danz" were two of them.

That trip was nerve-racking. I still remember that I flew out of

San Francisco from gate 35—a lucky number for me. I thought, *Wow, okay—it's an omen.* I was hanging on to any glimmer of hope. Turns out I really did have my game together, though I didn't know it quite yet.

I went to Warners with my hat in my hand. I didn't know what the reaction would be. I was ready to get kicked in the teeth again, like the *Hoodoo* rejection.

Lenny was the perfect guy for me to see that day. He's very demonstrative, and he really liked what I played for him. You could see it in his reaction. He let you know! And at some point at the end of the meeting, Lenny said, "Oh man, this is really in the ballpark." At that point he didn't even know the album was going to be called *Centerfield*!

Centerfield was okay after that. I went back home with happy vibes and got it done. I recorded the album tracks at the Record Plant in Sausalito. They gave me a rate because I was in this room they really didn't use a lot. It had been Sly Stone's. They called it the Pit. The cost of making that whole album was $35,000.

Jeffrey Norman (or Norton, as we called him) was an incredibly great engineer. We had the room set up like a band was actually there—bass, drums, guitar—but I was the only one playing. I'd go in each day to make a basic track, and they just fell down one at a time, just like if a real band had walked in. I had two different kick drums, each for a specific kind of song. I had tried every drumhead I could find on each of those drums, searching for the best sound. No, I wasn't a great drummer, but I sure was into tone. I realize now that I was probably over-anal about everything, but God, so much was at stake then.

Recording that album went by in a whoosh. I was so prepared, down to having notes on the different amp settings I used. I had gone through all that in my studio in Albany so I wouldn't have to worry. I knew each part that needed to be played. On "Search-light" I was the horn section. We set 'em all up and I played 'em. As I laid down the third horn, Norton said, "Man, this is awesome—you could hire out as a horn section!" At least to his ears it was sounding good, which made me feel fantastic. I wasn't a great horn player or a great drummer. I got good enough to carry the song—but that's all. It never went past that, y'know?

Making a record the one-man-band way is like slow-motion photography. It takes thirty-seven days to get two seconds of film. I don't want to do that anymore. I really don't. I wouldn't play drums now either. Although I got very good at tuning them.

There was a time in the seventies and eighties when recording in the studio, with all the layering and overdubbing, became almost scientific. The records people made then sounded perfect. As a one-man band I was always thinking, *Oh, it's got to be precise.* That was the approach then by everyone. When I play *Centerfield* songs with my band now, they're looser, have more personality. I like that better, since to me that's the songs coming alive.

I thought I was really tempting fate by doing a rock and roll song about baseball. It hadn't happened before. Okay, there was a song called "Say Hey (the Willie Mays Song)" by the Treniers, but that really wasn't about baseball. It was about Willie. The two don't fit, never did. I wanted to do it anyway. I deeply love both. I love the way that old times are revered in baseball, all the record keeping....The first book I ever read was *Lou Gehrig: Boy of the Sandlots.* Because I could run, I was an athletic kid, but I didn't hit the ball a long way. And I couldn't throw a lick. In the third grade we had to write an essay on what we would do if we were president. At the end of mine, I said that I wasn't just going to throw out the first ball at the World Series: I was going to pitch the first three innings!

The fact that "Centerfield" became an actual radio hit was great, but watching the song get adopted by baseball fans and Little Leagues was incredible. When my boys were in Little League, we got to hear it during our warm-ups. Awesome. I remember being up in Troy on a hunting trip in the fall of 1985. There's only one commercial business there, a little café, and I was sitting there pretty much anonymous in my hunting garb, getting a burger. The World Series was on the TV, and as it went into the commercials they played "Centerfield." More than once. I was looking around, kind of happy and kind of hiding at the same time. The waitress came up and said, "John, isn't that your song?" And I whispered, "Pretty cool, huh?" Nobody knew but us. I could hardly contain myself.

And then in 2010, to have the song honored by the National Baseball Hall of Fame in Cooperstown? Unbelievable. I didn't want to look like an interloper when I was onstage with all those guys. I was so unworthy! My family got to meet Willie Mays, who I mention in the song. And Mr. October, Reggie Jackson—to actually meet him? He was so nice! For a day I'd gotten to live the dream. I even loaned Slugger, my baseball bat guitar, to the hall of fame. It's been such an amazing journey for that song, that album—and for me.

I was vehemently against music videos then. It's still all so weird to me now. I was like the guy standing in the doorway, trying to keep computers out—"No! *No!*" I just felt that a music video told people what the pictures in the song are. They have no chance to imagine. Now, most musicians like me would kill to have millions of people watching a video of my song. It's what you call a marketing tool.

I've only made a handful of videos—I kind of missed the wave. The video for "The Old Man Down the Road" was just one shot following my very long guitar cord through the woods, past all these various characters. You didn't see me until the very end, and then only briefly. Pretty cool.

Jeff Ayeroff was the guy at Warners in charge of that project. I could never quite figure out what he did. Jeff was an idea guy. I actually told Jeff that making a music video was like polishing a turd. He didn't love that comment. What a smart-ass I was then.

John Fogerty's All-Stars, the special I did for Showtime in 1985, was really my first concert since Creedence. We did that in front of a small, invited audience. I handpicked the band, utilizing some of my favorite players: Booker T. Jones, Duck Dunn, Prairie Prince, Albert Lee, and Steve Douglas. It was so great bouncing ideas back and forth with Lenny.

Doing the zydeco song "My Toot Toot" with its author, Rockin' Sidney, down in Crowley, Louisiana, was my idea. That was absolutely wonderful. Sidney was cool. He was really a keyboard player, not an accordion player. He had made that song (and that album) in his bedroom with a drum machine. He did it just like I did it — "Okay, I need an accordion part." Necessity *is* the mother of invention.

I remember walking into a Safeway grocery store in Bullhead City, Arizona, after *Centerfield* came out, and they had a little sign taped up. Instead of "Rutabagas, ninety-nine cents," it was a homemade blurb for *Centerfield:* "It's a wonderful thing that John Fogerty has been able to make this album after many years of struggles." I was reading this and thinking, *Where did this person...find out about all that?* A lot of people seemed to understand what it had taken to get across the finish line. *Centerfield* was a wonderful vindication, and a big success. The album went to number one, which is unbelievable. There were three hits on that album and it was critically acclaimed. It was one of those moments, like the Boston Red Sox finally winning the World Series after a hundred years.

*　　*　　*

I enjoyed the *Centerfield* euphoria, and then, out of nowhere, I started to get really...angry. Instead of being happy and over-joyed, I was pissed off and sad. Disturbed. And unhappy. To the point where somebody could say some little thing to me and I would break down in tears. Have a meltdown.

I thought to myself, *I should be enjoying this. Everything I have prayed for, I finally accomplished.* I didn't even understand it myself. Imagine you were wrongly imprisoned for years and years and years, wasting your life away. Then one day they discover the mistake and set you free. You walk out into a beautiful, enchanted meadow. The birds are singing, the little animals are frolicking, sweet music is playing. But then you turn around and see the hor-rible dungeon that kept you imprisoned for so long. And you think about the people responsible. The anger is almost overwhelming. Because the whole imprisonment thing was just so wrong.

Looking back, I think the obvious thing that triggered my unhap-piness was that Saul was suing me. Not once, but twice. I found out about it one day at Warner Bros. By that time I had set up a little rehearsal space there. Lenny said to me, "That guy at your old record company is making waves about 'The Old Man Down the Road.' They're saying it's too much like 'Green River.'" (At first they were comparing it to "Green River," not "Run Through the Jungle," as they did later.) Since Saul owned the copyrights on the Creedence songs, he was suing me for plagiarizing myself. Lame. Yeah, it's swamp rock and has the same feel, but it's a different song! Most people *liked* the fact that "The Old Man Down the Road" reminded them of Creedence. Fantasy just wanted to own anything I did that was successful, period. I didn't take it seriously at first. I just thought that Saul was being vindictive.

Saul was also suing me for $140 million over defamation of character, due to the last song on *Centerfield*: "Zanz Kant Danz," about a "little pig" named Zanz. The lyrics go, "Zanz can't dance / But he'll steal your money."

I actually wrote it in the aftermath of *Hoodoo*. Joe Smith had called to check on me days after rejecting the album. I was telling him about my troubles with Fantasy, and he mentioned how the Kinks had written a song about some guy who screwed them, and they got it out of their system that way. We said good-bye, and as I went to hang up the phone, the words "Zanz Kant Danz" popped into my head. I ran to my studio and wrote it down. It was as instantaneous as that. Thanks, Joe. It was therapeutic. Warners actually made a Claymation video for the song (done by Will Vinton, who did the California Raisins commercials). This video featured dancing pigs.

Warner Bros. seemed to be taking the suit seriously—to the extent that they wanted me to change the song. Saul was demanding that we remove it from the album. No way was I going to do that. Warners felt that by changing the song slightly I'd be avoiding a major headache; otherwise, a court might prevent any more copies from being sold before the suit was settled. You never know how some judge is going to rule, and I'd had enough of that crap in my life, so I listened to the lawyers. I can be bullheaded at times when I really think I'm right. Stubborn. But there's times when I'm also easygoing—"Yeah, you guys are probably right."

Now the first 250,000 copies of the album, which have "Zanz," are collector's items, since I went back and rerecorded the vocal parts so it was "Vanz Kant Danz" instead of "Zanz."

After *Centerfield,* I began feeling the urge to write new songs and make a new record. My office at Warners was downstairs in the basement, where I wouldn't bother anybody. It was a little room, and I brought in some recording equipment, had a guitar and a couple of synthesizers. At night, after everybody went home, I could make all the noise I wanted. It was very liberating. I wrote an awful lot of the music for *Eye of the Zombie* right there. Strange location, but creative.

At the time, I was worried about being current. You have the nagging suspicion that your kind of music has been passed by, and on the radio there's these new things that have come along, and you're saying to yourself, *Yeah, I suppose I should keep up with that*. There's some truth to that, or at least it's a common feeling, but I'd also say you should throw that feeling out and never worry about it. There's a knack to knowing how much of it is useful. I'm sure Bill Monroe didn't worry about it too much — although when he heard that this Presley guy had rearranged "Blue Moon of Kentucky," he went back and rerecorded it.

So I messed with my sound. To see if I could be more current, including drum machines, synthesizers. I bought new gear, I read tons of manuals. I was infatuated with all the machine junk.

People like records made with machines because they have a certain vibe to 'em. They don't sound human. It's robotic, and so is the music. The opening instrumental of *Zombie*, "Goin' Back Home," was actually played by a human being — me. I had first programmed the whole thing to play by itself and it was absolute crap — disturbing, inhuman, robotic crap.

I've had to relearn that same lesson a couple of times. In the first part of this millennium, I started forgetting and got into Pro Tools and all that. For a while I was convinced that I could make a drum machine sound like a human being. Stupid. It's like trying to turn lead into gold. Classic rock and roll does not sound good if the drummer sounds like a robot. You can't make a drum machine do Al Jackson Jr., the drummer with Booker T. and the MGs!

For years I had been doing the one-man-band thing. With Creedence, some of the tracks are very, very good musically. You can't take that away from us. There are other tracks where we were outside our comfort zone, and they sound a little shaky. I thought that was because we weren't good enough.

And with *Eye of the Zombie* I thought, *Screw the one-man band and the machines: I'm gonna get the best. I'm gonna get studio musicians.* People who really had chops. *Chops.* I was envious of studio musicians—guys who knock out everything fast and can play circles around anyone. I asked Lenny Waronker who to use, and he named a few top people. Berklee College of Music graduates. I went to meet them. That all seemed good.

We did it at the Lighthouse, the same North Hollywood studio where I would record *Blue Moon Swamp*. I had the songs written and demoed on my equipment. We'd learn the song and then record it that day. In the old days I had always counted on the process of developing the song in a room with the band. That's what I had done all through Creedence. These guys were studio musicians, and they were so spot-on it happened rather quickly.

But the final product? I had been led to believe that studio hotshots can play anything, any style. Sacre bleu—it's not true. It's an entirely different way of making and presenting music. These guys were ever so accomplished, but they didn't play with my feel. You think this person who grew up in Encino is going to sound like Clifton Chenier?

Eye of the Zombie is not a very good record. But I can't blame it on anybody else—it was my design. After all, I'm in charge of the ship. I picked those guys to do that music, which wasn't my style of music. I can't stand here and try to defend it. If some guy was in line at the music store holding *Zombie,* I'd try to talk him out of it: "Hey, don't get that one. It's not very good." "Change in the Weather" (which I rerecorded for *The Blue Ridge Rangers Rides Again*) and "Sail Away" are great. The rest of the songs might be all right with someone else doing them, just not me. They're just...sideways. How the album is shaped and played just doesn't seem like me.

Centerfield was this liberating record full of good songs, good performances. And then the next album is this dark, spooky, and not even well-realized thing, messy and artistically screwed up. There was an almost uncontrolled anger in the music, stemming from all that stuff you'd think I would've gotten over. It's a disturbed album because I was disturbed. It seems bizarre to me now, but the fact that I wanted to do something like that then is a litmus test of my own psychological health. I was not a happy guy. You might catch me calling that album *I Am a Zombie,* because that's exactly how I felt.

This is one time when you can even judge the album by its cover. For the art I wanted to do my face with a Papua New Guinea tribal tattoo, but Warners said David Lee Roth was already doing one for his cover. So I went for zombie. It ended up looking fake. Nothing hit the mark with that album. I think the label was embarrassed even before it came out. I'd heard that Mo Ostin had looked at it and said, "This is all wrong." And of course he was right. In fact, after it was out awhile, Lenny Waronker said, "John, why don't you make another album like *Centerfield,* where you play all the instruments?" I thought he was crazy. I didn't want to do that again. But now I see what he was saying: at least that was *me*.

I hadn't toured since Creedence, but I was set to go out on behalf of the *Zombie* album. For my nearly fifty-date Rockin' All Over the World tour of the U.S., I used the same guys on the record plus a few more musicians. The first date of the *Eye of the Zombie* tour was at Mud Island in Memphis on August 26, 1986. I was overjoyed to be in Memphis, thinking about all the great music there.

The day before the concert, we were at Handy Park, looking at the statue of W. C. Handy. And one of the dudes in my new band

Coverdale Lake, Union, Michigan. This shot was taken after Julie's grandpa Ray and I caught a fish together. The joy on his face (and mine) was priceless and so pure. He was a wonderful, wonderful man. The best man I ever met. I will remember this incredible day for the rest of my life. He gave me the knife he used to clean his fish. I cherish that knife.

Julie making fun of how it feels to have a big belly. It was the most beautiful time for me.

I was showing Julie I had a belly too.

This was the dinner we had with our friends Bruce Jackson, Betty Bennett, Patti Scialfa, and Bruce Springsteen. Julie was expecting our first child. Bruce S. and Patti had just had their first child together. Bruce was sharing how wonderful being a father is. He also was happy for me, knowing what I'd gone through. He was, in his own way, sayin', *It's all right, John. Look what you have now.* He is my friend, and I will always remember those times, hangin' out in L.A.

My love—one of my favorite photos. It's from the *Blue Moon Swamp* days.

Christmas at my house in L.A. That's my kids Sean and Laurie.

Rock and Roll Hall of Fame, 1993. It's here in the book what happened and why. (Photograph by Gregg DeGuire, courtesy of the Rock and Roll Hall of Fame Foundation, Inc.)

Julie took this on the steps of the Supreme Court. A historical moment but a sad day. In the courtroom Julie had noticed the legal team from Fantasy snickering and pointing at me. They seemed to be having a great time watching me go through this. She was deeply upset by their behavior. Something I had to endure from them for years.

Me and my two boys Shane and Tyler. They were born a year apart, Irish twins! My face says it all.

Almost finished *Blue Moon Swamp*.

The day *Blue Moon Swamp* came out, I drove Julie to Tower Records. She wanted to go in and buy it, see for herself that this day had finally come. It had been a long, tough time for sure. Wow!

A shot of us at the House of Blues. I think Julie was so happy for me. I love this picture!

Blue Moon Swamp tour, when I started doing my CCR songs again. That's me, Julie, and Kenny and Liz Aronoff. I've been with Kenny ever since. The best drummer out there.

Blue Moon Swamp hit number one in Sweden. This is when I said, "If I'm going to do this, I want my family with me." I signed albums in a store in Stockholm while my family sat in the café. Pretty special moment for me. Julie was interviewed by the paper.

My one and only Grammy arrives in the mail. Julie snapped this shot of me taking it out of the box.

Just one of the many sights we got to share with our kids on tour.

I was nominated for a Grammy for *Revival*. Julie and I are getting ready to see Tina Turner sing "Proud Mary." Behind us is Yoko Ono. Fun night for sure. (Frank Micelotta/PictureGroup)

This is what life is about—nothing better than this. My little girl Kelsy and Daddy taking a nap.

Me and Kelsy. She has good taste in shirts.

Teaching Kelsy to fish at one of my favorite places, the Kern River. She is hooked, and I must say Daddy couldn't be happier. This is where I wrote most of the songs that ended up on *Blue Moon Swamp*.

Julie and me more recently at the Rock and Roll Hall of Fame.
(Lester Cohen/WireImage/Getty Images)

My son Shane graduating from USC. That little boy grew up into a fine young man, and I am darn proud of him. Grateful I had a second chance. Life is wonderful.

Three Fogerty men, Shane, Tyler, and John.

Singin' "Proud Mary" in my favorite city, New Orleans. (© 2014 Willow Haley, Willow's World Photo)

I just love Florence. Spending time with Julie in such a romantic place is the best!

said, "Who was W. C. Handy?" If you could've read the little balloon over my head at that moment, it would've said, "Man, we in trouble now!" Don't they teach you guys anything in music college? And were they overpaid! I was a doofus. I thought they deserved a big payday because they *said* they deserved a big payday. One of them even mentioned royalties from the record. I thought, *Really? After all the years that I've been screwed out of my royalties, now I've got to give 'em to you too?* That didn't happen.

The *Zombie* thing just seemed so misguided. Yeah, I really stood onstage and sang "Eye of the Zombie" and "Mr. Greed" instead of my Creedence-era songs. I heard that people were yelling for the old songs and booing me. I don't blame them. Clearly the guy who made the decision to not play his most famous songs out on tour has some stuff bothering him. At least I wasn't standing onstage stoned or drunk or throwing up. I'm not saying the music was much better than that. Maybe it wasn't!

Of course, there's a perfectly appropriate way of playing that might have been better—and it's painfully obvious looking back now, as it was to some folks even at the time. After the tour was over, Bruce Springsteen and I went to see Steve Earle. One of the guys in Steve's band said it straight out, clear as a bell: "I heard that *Eye of the Zombie.* Why didn't you just get you some guys from Texas and play the blues?" Ain't *that* the truth.

The *Zombie* album marks another dark period in my life. If you're idle and not financially obligated to go to a job at 8 a.m., that's a recipe for a lot of bad behavior. I was well aware that I was marking time, spinning my wheels—enough that I was saying to myself, *John, you're not going forward. You're just getting drunk, sleeping all day, and thinking about hooking up with a female companion or figuring out how to get a pizza delivered.*

It wasn't just that my music wasn't working. Saul Zaentz was torturing me again. Lawsuits. Depositions. I was really pissed off and very unhappy. Drinking enough to sink a battleship, and doing it with a vengeance. The odd thing about it was that I desperately wanted things to change. I kept trying to figure out something that would change my life. All my life I'd been looking for something and just hadn't found it. I just seemed to have a kind of emptiness.

I was a freight train of sorrow. I only weighed about 120 pounds, drank too much, smoked too much.... Ever seen that movie with Tyrone Power, *Nightmare Alley*? He starts out on top of the world and by the end of the movie he's the geek. Locked in a cage, being thrown a raw chicken bone to gnaw on. That was me.

Sometimes I wondered if I would make it out of the eighties alive.

And then I met Julie, and everything changed. You're probably used to me being the storyteller thus far, but now I'm going to have Julie join in. She can tell you things I can't and add depth to the story. She knows the truth—and isn't afraid to say it!

CHAPTER 15

Wild as a Mink, Sweet as Soda Pop

JULIE: I was born Julie Kramer. I grew up in a small town in northern Indiana. My parents were blue-collar: my father served as a marine, my mother worked in a factory. She was secretary of the union and she worked there until it closed down and they moved all the jobs out of the country. President Kennedy was a big star in our house. Those values and beliefs were important to us. We were right smack-dab in Middle America, red, white, and blue.

There were four girls in our family. Much of my childhood was spent at my grandparents' lake house, where my grandfather would fish every day and my grandmother would cook the daily catch. It was a very ideal life for sure at the lake. But my parents divorced when I was five, and their relationship was similar to John's parents'. They could never get along and they sure didn't handle the divorce well with us kids. I think this is why John and I both try to protect our kids from things they shouldn't be a part of or worry about. Childhood shouldn't be filled with all of the adult stresses. We feel very strongly that childhood should be pure, simple, and joyful.

I met John on September 24, 1986, in Indianapolis, Indiana. I lived in South Bend, Indiana, at the time. Indianapolis was about four hours south of where I grew up. I had a sister who went to school down near Indianapolis in Terre Haute. She had been having terrible trouble in a relationship, and we were all very worried about her. She asked if I would help her move out of this house she shared with her boyfriend at the time. She was scared, and I offered to get her things and move her back home. We both decided on the way down to Terre Haute that we would stop in Indy and have some fun together. We left South Bend a little later than planned—I think we got to Indy at around 10 p.m. We stopped off at a gas station and changed clothes, since we both were dressed in jeans, and put on fresh makeup—something girls do.

We walked into this club in Indianapolis called Don't Ask. I don't really know how we ended up there, but we walked in and sat at the bar. Wow—this place was crowded and seemed to be happening. There were the usual dudes trying to pick you up. My sister and I were just having fun, chatting and laughing. Entertaining the dudes…

I was recently separated and was getting a divorce from my husband. I married at twenty-three and I had a little girl at home, Lyndsay. This trip was intended to be a little break, and we were going to make the best of it, even though the next day we would be facing some very serious stuff.

One of the "boys" hanging at the bar with us noticed John walk in. He said, "Hey, that's John Fogerty over there!" Now, I wouldn't have known that was John unless he pointed him out. I was a casual music fan, and I'd worked in a large independent record store, so I had knowledge of who he was, but I never would've recognized him. I had seen a music video on MTV starring John, "The Old Man Down the Road." I'm really not sure why I remember that, looking back.

This was not my nature, but I walked over to John—maybe it was a way to get away from the dudes, or maybe it was just a dare of sorts. I was going over there to shake his hand.

John: I'd just played a concert in Indianapolis. We were staying at the Canterbury Hotel and some of the fellas in the band said, "We're going around the corner to this bar. Why don't you come on over there?" I was looking for adventure in those days. I walked inside and around the whole place and determined that I hadn't really seen anything I was interested in, and decided to leave.

But this group of shadows in the corner caught my eye. The shadows parted, and it was as if a light was coming out of the sky. There was this beautiful girl in a red sweaterdress. I said to myself, *That's the most beautiful girl I've ever seen.* I'm just standing there dumbfounded and suddenly she starts walking towards me. It was the strangest thing. It was like one of those slow-motion dream sequences. And she walks up and says, "Can I shake your hand, Mr. Fogerty?" I talked to her a little bit, eventually asked if I could buy her a drink. She said, "Peachtree on the rocks." I'd never heard of such a thing. I said, "Say that again?"

Julie: John was a little rough around the edges. He had on a pearl-snap Western shirt, baggy Levi's, wore a scarf around his neck, and his hair was long and shaggy—to this Indiana girl he resembled a Willie Nelson character, a broken-down cowboy. We chatted in the back of the bar for hours, and even danced to the song "Sledgehammer," if you can believe that. John ordered quite a few drinks. I think I stopped at four. He kept ordering straight shots of tequila and chasing them with a beer. Then he'd tear off the filter on his cigarette before smoking it. This was something I had never seen before, except maybe on TV. It just sent a message that somehow this guy wasn't caring about himself or didn't have anyone to care for him.

He asked about my relationship and I told him I was getting a divorce. I asked him if he was married, and his reply was, "Well, sort of, but it's not really a marriage. It's not at all what marriage is supposed to be." I wondered what that meant, being only twenty-six and newly separated myself. I thought, *Maybe that's a normal way of life for a Willie Nelson character, for a broken-down cowboy. That's just how they live.* Looking back, it seems a little funny but that's truly how this twenty-six-year-old felt.

It was time to leave, as my sister and I had a job to do. She had a really old car at the time, and all three of us piled into the front seat, and we drove John back to his hotel. He invited me in and told me that my sister could sleep on the couch. It was that Willie character again. I said, "Thank you, John, it's been wonderful to spend time with you, but that isn't in the cards for me." I will never forget dropping him off at his five-star hotel. There was a really long red carpet and I watched John walk very slowly to the door. My sister and I looked at each other and felt bad for him— John looked so sad and alone. We both remember that walk to this day. I never gave John my number and I never thought I'd see him again. We just drove off.

Days went by and I couldn't help but think of him. Something in him, I don't know what, connected with me. There was just something about John.

John: There was a gap in that tour, between the first and second time I saw Julie, and I checked myself into rehab. I was ready for whatever it was—because I needed to change. I always blamed myself for drinking. I didn't try to blame somebody else. Of course, in rehab they don't let you outside. I wanted to go running but I couldn't, so I was doing all the calisthenics and exercise in my room to get my heart rate up. Finally, on the third day, the doctor checks my pulse, and I guess all my physical signs weren't what he was used to. He said, "Why are you here?" I said, "I have a drinking problem." He said, "Really? Look, if you really want to stay here—and you beg us—we'll let you stay. But we don't think you *need* to." That was helpful: "Here's the steering wheel. You're in charge of what you do." I think that, luckily, I was not physically addicted. And when Julie saw me the second time, it was like I was a completely different person. I wasn't drinking or smoking at all.

Julie: John played a show in Merrillville, Indiana, on November 13. This was close to my home, and I decided I needed to see him. I had no idea how to contact him other than by going to his show. My friend Bev came with me, and outside the venue I saw this guy who looked like a crew member. His name was Slice and I gave him a note to give to John. Slice went off, came back out, and informed me that John would meet me after the show, which was just about to start. After the concert, there was John—wow, did he look different! He was all cleaned up, wearing a leather jacket. He looked quite handsome and healthy. We talked again for hours. John didn't drink or smoke that night, although he served me so many drinks I should've never driven home. I had no idea where this crazy thing was headed—if anywhere—but I felt something special happening. I remember walking with John to my car. It was freezing cold and the snow was falling.

John: Julie says, "Why don't you just come to South Bend with us?" And I'm thinking, *That's impossible. I'm out on the road, I'm in a bus, I'm traveling here and there.* But here's this beautiful siren, this temptress, trying to get me to jump ship, leave the tour and fly away with her to South Bend, Indiana.

The windshield was frozen over solid. I'd never seen that in my life. So we were scraping away. And then Julie kissed me—the first kiss. And...oh my. I started having second thoughts about not going to South Bend. I thought she was the most beautiful creature. She seemed to be everything that I hoped in my heart I would find someday. I had no way of knowing something like that so soon, but she just seemed...perfect. And delightful.

I said, "How do I get in touch with you?" She wrote her number inside a matchbook and I put it in my pocket. Next day I dig out my matchbook to give her a call, and it was just a bunch of scribble. Let's just say Julie had a bit to drink. My hopes were dashed. All I knew was "Julie from South Bend."

Julie: Time went by and I was finding myself thinking of John often. With a divorce coming and handling all of that, I had been through quite a bit. I needed a getaway, a break from everything I had been going through. I booked a trip to California—my aunt and uncle lived in San Juan Capistrano. While there, I rented a car and drove to Los Angeles. I went to Universal Studios since it was my favorite place to visit when I was a kid on vacation there. And then—either I read it in a newspaper or saw it there on the Universal Amphitheatre marquee (this was pre-Internet)—I learned that John was going to be doing a show while I was there!

So I went home to my aunt and uncle's and called the Universal Hotel. I remember looking it up in the phone book, and there were two hotels by that name—I figured it must be the nicer one of the two. So I called the hotel and just asked for John Fogerty—what did I know? Well, they put me right through and he picked up the phone! Now I know how rare that is, since he *never* answers the phone—even today!

John: The hotel had quite specific instructions not to let any phone calls for John Fogerty come through. So I pick up the phone and hear, "Hi, John, this is Julie," and I literally fell down on the floor, laughing. She said, "Why are you laughing?" I said, "I was sitting here, feeling really lonely and forlorn, about ready to tie one end of a rope around my ankle and the other to a big rock and toss it off a pier. And just sink to the bottom. And there you are!"

Julie: John came to visit me on New Year's Eve, 1986. He had been trying to reach me where I worked. My coworkers had been telling me, "Someone keeps calling you. Someone with a *very soft voice.*" Funny. I really didn't put together who this was until after we connected on the phone.

So he came to visit, pulling up in a subcompact budget rental car. I wasn't expecting a limo, but that was a bit funny and cute. John wiped out on the ice—being a California boy, he wasn't used to the weather. It was winter and he had on Reebok tennis shoes with peach socks. My friends and I were all in our twenties, and they were looking at me like, "*Huh!?* Who is this guy? You mean *the rock star* John Fogerty?" I wasn't too sure about the whole thing. John was in his forties and I was just a twenty-six-year-old girl. He was kind of funny, kind of cute. (I felt so sweet towards John and his innocent, non–rock star self. He was just so *John,* and this has been the man I have loved for over twenty-five years now.)

After spending time with him I'd see so many things in him that I'd never seen in anyone I dated. He just wanted to know everything about where I was from, South Bend. He wanted to know all about the Saint Joseph River—I had driven past that river my whole life and not paid much attention. The Studebaker automobile factory had been in South Bend, and my grandfather had sold them. This just fascinated John, and he'd go off to the Studebaker museum and get all the books on the subject. John found so much beauty in simple things. We'd have so much fun together. We'd head to Chicago quite a bit. He took me to ball games, blues clubs, dinners in the city. Some of the blues clubs were in rough neighborhoods, and I was the only girl most of the time—this little blond girl stood out for sure. Looking back, it was a great thing to have done and experienced, even if it wasn't on my list of things to do while in Chicago! It was just so fun with John.

We took Lyndsay to see *Cinderella*. John and I had been dating for eight or nine months. I knew he really cared for me and we were getting closer and closer. I was just sitting there watching this beautiful love story with my daughter. The relationship with John was new—we were just getting to know each other. Cinderella was trying on the glass slipper and I suddenly felt my chair shaking. I looked over and saw John sobbing. I was just so overwhelmed with his reaction. How sweet and beautiful this was. It just melted my heart.

John: The story of *Cinderella* is very important in the journey of John and Julie. When I was young, like many people I thought the idea of finding and marrying a beautiful princess was the best thing that could happen in life. As I grew older—again, like many people—I began to hear the superficial wisdom that this was unrealistic and delusional and that a real-world marriage would probably be somewhat less than the fairy-tale version. As all of the horrible, nightmarish results of my musical career began to drown me, I became massively unhappy....I seriously wonder if even the best marriage in the whole world could have survived those torturous years.

During the time leading up to my decision to leave Martha, I began to wonder if that long-lost fairy tale could actually come true. I knew I wasn't happy and that I wasn't making Martha happy. When I just looked at that head-on, it seemed that I was supposed to figure this out, to *do* something about it, to make a choice. I decided that it was worth a try, this notion of fairy-tale happiness. When I was gathering up the strength to actually leave,

I said to myself, *I don't know where I'm going, but it's got to be better than this.* What that really meant was this thought: *I know I don't have it now, but I'm going to take the chance that out there somewhere I might find unconditional love…*

Well, I found it. Julie is my fairy-tale princess, and it will always be that way for the rest of eternity. Unquestionably, this marriage, this union, was meant to be, and I feel that with every fiber in my consciousness. So when I see the story of *Cinderella,* I always break down and cry.

They made a new version of *Cinderella* with live actors, and I went to see it with Julie and our daughter Kelsy. I had thought that nothing could touch the way I feel about the original Disney animated version, but about two minutes into this new version, I knew I was in trouble. I said to Julie, "I don't think I'm gonna make it through this one" (without breaking down)!

I made it to the end, and it was beautiful. There are so many—*too many*—moments for me to describe, so I will try to let one beautiful scene explain my feelings. The moment when the handsome prince puts the glass slipper on Cinderella's foot, thus identifying that he has found his true love, is *everything.* The whole universe, the meaning of life. Of course, I lost it right there, broke down (again) and cried. In the car on the way home, I finally blundered into the words I'd been searching for to explain my heart. Referring to that moment, I said to Julie (and Kelsy), "I'm just so grateful for my life."

I started traveling east to South Bend more and more. And more. Pretty soon I was hardly leaving at all. By that New Year's of 1986, I knew that Julie was the one. But we didn't move in together. I'd been in a marriage for a long time and was a little scared of any kind of permanent relationship. Something in my brain was telling me to proceed cautiously. I was like a penniless prospector who had found the biggest gold nugget of all time—I didn't know quite what to do now that I had the bounty in my hands. I just knew I didn't want to lose it! Somehow I realized that this relationship was the holy grail, my salvation.

I had also promised myself that I was going to live out all my bachelor fantasies and be a Hollywood swinger like Errol Flynn, going to parties with a different babe on my arm every night, partying all the time. I had told myself, *Yeah, now that I'm single, that's what I'm gonna do!* Even had me a brand-new blue Corvette!

So, trying to be a wise man, I said to Julie, "Let's be apart for a year"—meaning let's date, but not cohabitate. Probably six minutes into this situation I knew: this ain't what I was meant to do. I was just a raging failure at *all* of it. Certainly I partied—a lot of it by myself! I was drinking alcohol like water again and I was not happy. I dated a bit, went to a couple of parties. I was utterly miserable—and miserable being away from Julie. From the moment I met Julie, my life had begun to get better. Instantly, just like that. So all this bachelor stuff was suddenly meaningless.

But I was afraid to say I loved her. We were having dinner at this fancy restaurant in South Bend, Tippecanoe Place, inside the old Studebaker mansion, and I said out loud, "Well, I don't know about marriage..." Her eyes got real big. It's a look I've come to cherish. I'd said a word we'd been careful not to talk about.

On another night separate from all those, I held her real close and said something like, "I really, really, really *like* you." She knew what I meant to say and thought it was cute, but she also knew I was afraid to admit my feelings. *Of course* I loved her, so that became a joke between us. At some point during the televised concert for the Vietnam vets on July 4, 1987, I went to the mic and said, "Really, really, really." Julie wasn't there and that was my little message to her.

Julie: On these visits to Indiana, I would take John to Coverdale Lake in Union, Michigan, to visit my grandparents. I was very close to them and spent much of my childhood at the lake with them. My grandparents had an amazing marriage and life. They looked out for each other and loved each other so much. They had a beautiful, pristine home on the lake — "perfect" is the only word that describes that place.

John had bonded with my grandfather. He really enjoyed spending time there with him and my family. Grandpa played guitar and wrote songs from time to time. John really noticed how Grandpa treated Grandma. So much respect and love. As our relationship grew, John would say to friends (about me), "The better I treat her, the better my life becomes."

John: Grandpa Ray was probably the best man I have ever met. I could just tell that the relationship between Julie and her grandpa was really special. Ray was kind and wise and dignified. Calm. You know how people who are just comfortable with themselves can't be hurried or rattled by anything? That was Ray.

He had a little pier on his property that sat on the lake, and he invited me fishing. So we rigged up a pole for me. We were just two dudes in two chairs sitting there looking at the lake. The women are up in the house. And I catch a little bitty sunfish. Ray says, "There's a big bass down there I've been tryin' to catch for days! Let's use your fish for bait." So we rig that fish as bait, and lo and behold, I bring in the bass.

Now, Julie had dated other guys, and her sisters had too. I don't know if Ray had any use for a lot of 'em. But at that moment I was in the club. We went in the garage and Ray cleaned the fish, and then gave me his special knife that he'd used for years. When he handed me the knife, man, it was like he was giving me the keys to the kingdom — "John, you're all right. You can be with Julie. You're accepted." That was really important to me.

Julie: John reached out so fast and so hard. It was very sweet. He'd call me up at work from Los Angeles all the time and send me flowers. One time John called while I was at work and asked me to marry him. I wasn't sure if he was drinking, or what was going on. He had been drinking quite a bit then. I didn't know what to say to him. I was unsure of what was happening, but I felt that maybe he wasn't thinking clearly enough to be doing this on the telephone! I told him to call back when he wasn't drinking. John claimed he wasn't. He would not hang up until I answered him. Finally I exclaimed, *"Yes!,"* although I was unsure of what I was actually committing to at the time. John later proposed in a very romantic way.

Finally he asked me to move to California. He did not want to be apart anymore. Lyndsay and I moved in, in early December of 1987.

John had a place in Beverly Hills. I remember walking in and seeing this beautiful house. He'd hired a designer to help him with his pad, and it was really nicely decorated. Everything was white — white carpets, white sofas. I remember thinking how it didn't feel like anyone lived there, since everything was so perfect. It looked like an art gallery. I looked at that new white everything and wondered how a three-year-old was going to do in this house.

I didn't quite feel at home. It was very quiet, and lonely. It was difficult. We didn't go out much, and the place felt pretty dead. It was very different than what I was used to—I missed my family and my friends. John didn't have any friends or family around. He'd sometimes stay up all night and drink quite heavily, sometimes for days. John was drinking to check out, gallons of it. Like pouring gasoline down your body to burn it up, to fade away. He would share so many painful things with me, so many things that I could not understand. I was only twenty-seven but I wondered why he had no family or friends who cared—no one. Not one.

Sometimes John would sit and not say much at all. He was so kind to me and very loving, but he didn't have much life in him.

Just a depressed man sitting in a chair. Not talking, not happy. My family is a pretty crazy bunch. I'd take him to visit and he'd sit there for hours, not say a word, not mingle, nothing. They always thought that he didn't like them. He couldn't smile a lot. He just wasn't feeling good.

Music wasn't even his friend. It was so much of who he was, and yet he wasn't able to create. John just did not have music in his life anymore. I would try to encourage him, but this was a man who wouldn't let me turn on the radio—when I did he'd turn it off, call it noise. He had no interest.

The music he'd created had caused so much trouble for him. There were so many lawsuits, so many battles he had to fight. Every time he turned around there was another lawsuit or negative thing to deal with. He'd lost who he was.

John would find other distractions, like being a pilot. He'd immerse himself in flight training and reading about flying an airplane and whatnot. Then he was into the computer world, so he'd read computer manuals all night. These distractions kept his mind active. But I knew it was really killing him inside.

I'd escape to my family and friends, because I led a pretty social life back in Indiana. And John would be back in California by himself reading books. I was getting ulcers and not feeling well at all. At one point John told me he couldn't stand to bring me into all of this and that he couldn't have a relationship anymore. I think he knew he was so messed up, he was hurting me and didn't want me to go down with him. I was heartbroken, but I knew that he was probably right. Interestingly enough, this was happening in Indianapolis, where it had all started. Sadly, it was going to end there.

I just knew it was probably for the best. It's hard when you care for someone so much but you don't know how to fix it for them. I drove the four hours home to northern Indiana. So many emotions came over me on that drive. At first I just cried, and then I started to feel strength from the idea that this was the right decision for all of us. I cared about John so much and worried about what was going to happen to him. I loved John, in spite of all of this.

As I got closer to my mom's house, I knew that I had to pull myself together and figure out my life. I was saying exactly those words to myself as I was turning the handle on my mom's front door. And then, walking up the stairs, I heard the phone ring. It was John. He told me not to go anywhere, that he was coming. John cried to me that he couldn't live without me—he loved me too much. He arrived in less than three and a half hours, speeding ticket in hand.

John: It was a blizzard. I was going 105.

Julie: I remember trying to protect him so many times. John would drink so much in public and—sadly—at home that he could hardly walk, talk, or function. I remember walking him off planes and trying to keep him out of the public eye. In February 1988, John was producing Duke Tumatoe and his band, so we went to a club in Chicago, DeSalvo's, where he was recording them live. John had been drinking quite a lot and the band wanted him to perform with them. I told him no, but he wasn't thinking clearly. They fed him so much alcohol onstage that by the end of the performance he was barely able to stand, and his singing was barely recognizable. This was a very sad moment for me.

John: I was drunk onstage, which really goes against my rules. I was recording Duke Tumatoe at three different venues, and it turned out the engineer hadn't recorded the vocals at the first venue. So in typical Irish fashion, I was like, "Well, fuck, I guess I'll get drunk!" I think I did "Susie Q." We were recording, so I'm the guy who had to listen to what I did. I was lucky I was not living in the Internet age, because this would have been on everybody's computer. I'm thoroughly ashamed of this. Especially given how many years I fought to respect music and myself. And here I am, the guy that's not trying. That poor guy who's too scared to dig to where the real stuff is, too afraid of it. Used to be an artist.

Julie: I went up and told him it was time to go. I had to practically carry him out of the club. I remember trying to hold him up, and a glass broke and some shards went into my foot. (To this day, it's in my foot, maybe as a reminder to be grateful for how great things are now.) I couldn't stop to get the glass out because I had to get him the hell out of there. I remember John falling in the street. This was symbolic of almost giving it up. I picked him up right in the middle of Michigan Avenue and carried him into the hotel. I have no idea how I did that.

John: I don't run away from these memories. I'm not proud of them, and I don't necessarily want to relive them. I cringe thinking about them. But one thing I've learned is that you can't be in denial. Denial is your enemy. Denial is where you don't get better. Julie didn't have an easy time of it. Through any of this, really. I was that broken-down cowboy. Julie kept saying, "If we're in a relationship, aren't we supposed to *have* a relationship?"

I was a pretty closed guy. I could be very distant, aloof. I honestly didn't know any better at the time. Obviously that didn't get better overnight. The transformation took some time. Didn't get better in the first year, or the second year, or even the *third* year that we were together. But I was healing. I don't think it was any one step. It was like a ramp. I could just feel that we belonged together. Every day I just felt a little better, because *we* were better. The more days that passed with Julie, the more I had the sense that everything was going to be okay—maybe it didn't feel okay right *now,* but I could look down the road and know in my heart that it was going to be okay.

I don't think I was romantic at all before I met Julie—she made it okay for me to be that way. I was normally such a doofus about these things that what happened really came from left field. It's pretty romantic, actually.

We were back in South Bend, and I wanted to go running. Of course, Julie's ex-husband lived there. She worried about setting him off. I decided to go running anyway. And as I run I'm thinking about Julie being with her girlfriends, and how when they ask about our relationship she's got nothing to show them. No ring. You know, girls really get excited about "He asked me to marry him...and look at this ring!" It's a girl thing; it's romantic. So I finish my run, get dressed, go right down to the mall, and find a jewelry store. And I make a reservation at Tippecanoe Place.

When we got there, Julie went off to the powder room, and I gave the ring to the waiter and explained that he should put the ring in her glass of white wine. He arrives with our glasses. Julie has a little sip, puts it down. I say, "Why don't you have another sip of your wine?" She's looking at me. I say, "Maybe I'm trying to seduce you." She takes a big gulp. Finally she sees the ring. That was one time I truly shocked her.

The debt I owe Julie is for her sticking with me after she began to see what a lot of baggage there was, what a lot of work I was going to end up being. And I know I was. All I can say is, thank God she saw something and she hung in there.

Julie: The ring in the wineglass—that was the moment I knew that John was really, really starting to show signs of healing. I just knew that he deserved someone who cared deeply for him. Someone who could celebrate his life, love, and talent. He never had anyone even pat him on the back or give him thanks. Although his mom had been very helpful to John in certain ways, she never gave him affection. He had never had that in his life. To this day, John and I hold hands as if it's 1987.

Everybody thought I was crazy, but I felt that John needed help, regardless of how I felt and how bad it got. And it got bad. I remember how his guitars just sat there unplayed. I would go in the studio and see some of his instruments covered in dust, not having been touched for years. They just glowed to me. I felt the energy coming off of them. There was a spiritual connection between those instruments and John, but he couldn't get back there. The music was there. It was just locked up, frozen in pain. I knew in my heart that I had to help John. The songs he had given us needed to be heard again.

CHAPTER 16

Zanz Kant Danz (But He'll Steal Your Money)

IN OCTOBER 1988, the plagiarism case went to trial in federal court in San Francisco. Saul Zaentz was claiming that my song "The Old Man Down the Road" was an exact copy of the Creedence song "Run Through the Jungle." Which Saul owned.

By this time I'd already been through the 1983 Castle Bank trial, which stretched into three or four months. I'd been giving depositions day after day for Saul's lawyers. I actually had to go on tour for *Eye of the Zombie* before the album came out because of the trial date. The day before the first show, in Memphis, I was tied up giving a deposition. One group of depositions went on for a week straight—eight to five every day. This was Saul saying, "I'm going to make John very uncomfortable." Just because he could. Because he had the money.

Being deposed is one of the most stressful things ever. They try real hard to break you down. The way lawyers can attack you is unnatural, at times cruel. All day long you're terrified at what might come out of your mouth, because it can and will be used against you. When you're done, you go home, conk out, and then you come back and do it again the next day. At one point I was so stressed I couldn't even remember my own address. My lawyer tried to pass it off as, "Being a celebrity, Mr. Fogerty does not want that information in the public record," but the truth was, I was so flummoxed I couldn't even remember where I lived! I was in a state of perpetual anxiety. I felt that my life was at stake in all of this.

During one group of depositions, I had actually developed a strategy of taking as long as possible to answer. Deposition transcripts don't note time passing—there's just the questions, and then the answers. So I'd sit there holding a baseball that I got in Cooperstown. It reminded me of my childhood, and all the wonderful things that came out of the song "Centerfield." I found solace in that little ball. The lawyer would ask something like, "Mr. Fogerty, where were you the night of the seventh of January, 1978?" And I'd just sit there for ten minutes, playing catch with myself, before answering. I'd think to myself, *The hell with you, mister! They just sent you here to spin my wheels and help my attorney get rich.* There was some Pyrrhic solace in doing that, but the whole thing was exhausting.

In addition to this, once the lawsuit was filed, Fantasy just stopped paying me. For three and a half years I didn't get paid any songwriting royalties, not just for "Run Through the Jungle"— for all my songs, *everything*. That was illegal: the other songs weren't in contention—only that one song. They were trying to starve me out. Luckily, I was frugal and lived pretty simply. I had saved my money...otherwise I probably wouldn't have been able to fight back.

I didn't have Julie come to the trial with me. That was a mistake. Julie's so beautiful—I didn't want that jury looking at her and going, "Look at his wife! Oh man, John's doin' all right. He doesn't have any problems at all!" I didn't want anything outside of the events and the facts to sway their decision. I regret that. I should've been there proudly with my wife. I could have used her support a lot more than that little baseball!

There was a lot at stake in this case. We're talking about two songs that had been on the radio and earned a lot of money. Everybody knew these songs, including members of the jury. Fantasy was suing to dissolve my authorship of the newer song—it would not be a sovereign, separate song. Legally it would just be "Run Through the Jungle," and therefore they would own this new song just as they owned the older one.

Fantasy was the publisher on "Run Through the Jungle," and in theory I should get 50 percent of the earnings as the writer of the song. Early on the judge in the case ruled that if Fantasy won, not only would they own "The Old Man Down the Road," but 100 percent of the proceeds would go to Fantasy and nothing to the writer—me. So where in the world does that sort of ruling come from? That is just patently unfair. Thank God they didn't win, because that would've been a pretty horrible precedent for us songwriters.

Fantasy really had no case. One of the music experts we'd hired was on the stand, and he'd gone through all my music and was pointing out the similarity in style between all my songs, the places where I tended to do things in a similar way. And Fantasy's lawyer asked, "Well, why didn't John change the parts that were similar?" And the guy answered, "Because it wouldn't have sold a nickel's worth." Everybody laughed because it was the damn truth. It was my style that was on trial.

There were so many ridiculous moments during the trial. I had used the word "thunder" in both "The Old Man Down the Road" and "Run Through the Jungle." So of course they wanted to claim ownership of the word "thunder"—"John, you can't write another song with that word. That's unique to our song. And it appears in no other songs anywhere ever in your whole career—just 'Old Man,' which obviously came from 'Run Through the Jungle.'"

For about a week the only "music" we heard in the courtroom was computer-driven beeps that supposedly represented the melodies of the contested songs. Then they put on my *John Fogerty* album, and suddenly there's actual, real music with drums and guitar. Everybody in the courtroom got kind of peppy. And this song I'd written called "The Wall" starts, and the very first line references "thunder." I could see the whole jury going, "What the...?!"

Saul was just out to discredit my music, and me. When we sat down in court the first day, Al Bendich was twenty feet away from me and caught my eye. I could tell he was embarrassed. This lawsuit was clearly vindictive. Near the end of the trial, Saul got on the stand, and my lawyer Ken Sidle asked him, "Mr. Zaentz, isn't it true that this whole trial is just a vendetta against John Fogerty?" And before he finished the question, Saul exploded, "It's an *answer* to a vendetta!" He just had a meltdown. You could see his face turn red and steam come out of his ears. Seeing that was *nearly* worth the price of admission.

Fantasy's lawyers had hired a couple of nerds to try to make their case for them. The thing that really went bust happened the first or second day of the trial. They had programmed both of the songs through a computer. This was their big lab test. First they played the two songs separately, with all their parts. (They never played the actual records for the jury—just crappy, computerized, beeping versions.) Next they stripped the songs down to just their melodies and played snippets of them separately. Then they announced that they were going to play the melodies together and instructed us that the places where you're just hearing one note means the songs are the same, and anytime you hear two notes means the melodies have diverged and are separate, different.

After about three of these awful computerized notes—*beep beep boop*—the melodies started separating. To put it mildly, it didn't help their case. I'm thinking, *Didn't they test this* before *they did it? Because they are making the case that these are two distinctly different songs. I spent years of my life to get here?* I'm watching the jury, and everybody's squirming in their seats.

On October 31, I had to testify. I was there to explain the differences between the two songs. Because I'd let my emotions run away with me three days before the trial, I had a cast on my arm. I had been sitting in my office, thinking about what was to come, and I just got really, really angry. I saw Saul sitting there grinning, with all my money and all my songs—and getting away with it. It felt like a volcano was welling up in me, and *bam!* I hit this office chair as hard as I could. I broke some bones in my hand.

So I took off my cast in front of everybody and played my Washburn guitar through a little amp. Obviously the people in the courtroom were somewhat entertained. It's rare that something like this occurs in a courtroom. But this was not a performance. I didn't have an Elvis jumpsuit on. Everything in a trial is under a microscope. Any little nuance—your facial expressions, or if you happen to say the wrong word at the wrong time—they can hold that against you. So you're being very serious.

I explained that there is a certain chord I play that's really kind of swampy. You play an E7 chord at the seventh fret on the guitar. You have both a low-E and a high-E string ringing out. They are open, not held down like the other strings. This gives the chord a chimey, sustaining sound with a bit of dissonance or mystery to it. Then if you kind of smash or slur your fingers over to the next strings, you get sort of a sustained A chord with elements of the E still there. You don't hold it there, you just accent it there. It gives the music an eerie feeling. My colors, kind of my invention. At least I feel that way about it. Basically, this trial was all about style — my style of music, swamp rock. And if one guy can own another person's artistic style for the rest of his life, it would be a horrible thing — for every artist.

Before this, their expert had played a melody on the piano: "Rudolph the Red-Nosed Reindeer." Then he played another: "Rock of Ages." Exact same notes, different timing. He was trying to say that even though my song "The Old Man Down the Road" had different timing, I was using the same notes as in "Run Through the Jungle." Yeah, but the point is that they're different songs! So when I was on the stand, I sang a little bit of both of my songs. And I sang a little of Bo Diddley's "Bring It to Jerome" — another song that had the same notes as my two. We're talking about the blues. You've only got five notes anyway, so somewhere in your blues song you're going to have those notes.

Their expert also labeled certain notes as "pickup notes." These were notes in the songs that came before or after the bigger beats in the music. He tried to imply that they were spontaneous, unintentional, as if they didn't count. So I hummed this melody that was unrecognizable to everybody in the courtroom until I sang it with the so-called pickup notes: the song was "Mack the Knife" — and those in-between notes are important!

At one point I was on the stand explaining how I'd learned about the lawsuit, and that I'd heard they were basing the plagiarism on "Green River," not "Run Through the Jungle." And in the course of my testimony I mentioned how an engineer at Wally Heider's had heard "Green River" as we were working on it and called me at home — this was somebody I didn't even know — and how he'd quoted the line "Pick up a flat rock / Skip it across Green River" and told me, "That's such good writing."

I was being grilled by Fantasy's longtime lawyer, Malcolm Bernstein. And he said, "Well, that doesn't mean it's any good. That doesn't prove anything." I really wanted to stand up and scream at that guy, "You no-good so-and-so, the only thing your client has ever done in life is rip me off and steal my songs." I didn't, of course.

Bernstein was this very distasteful guy. His voice grated on your nerves, and at that moment he was holding my private songwriting notebook, the one I'd written all my titles in. They were allowed access to it because of the trial, and here this creep was thumbing through my personal songbook like it's nothing and talking about me like I'm nothing. I'm looking at him turn the pages in my songbook — that is my soul. I was completely disgusted by this.*

I don't think anyone noticed, but after the trial I heard from the jury foreman, whose name — believe it or not — was Robbie Robertson. He sent me a Christmas card, and on the front was a picture of Rudolph the Red-Nosed Reindeer, along with the music notation of the song. Mr. Robertson had drawn little arrows pointing to the notes, which he had humorously labeled "pickup notes." Inside the card he wrote that the most telling moment of the trial was Malcolm Bernstein standing there berating me with my songbook in his hand.

During the trial, the moment that really knocked me for a loop came during Saul's testimony. My lawyer asked, "Why did you decide to do this, anyway?" And Saul answered, "Well, that bass

---

* One morning back in 1973 I was on my way across the Fantasy parking lot to work on the *Blue Ridge Rangers* album. I was met by Malcolm Bernstein, who seemed to want to talk to me. "John," he says, "I wonder if you would do something for me? Could you write down the words to all your songs? We get requests..." I looked at him with *total* disbelief at what I was hearing. Now, you *know* I was not happy that Fantasy owned all my songs from the Creedence time. And here I'm standing in the building that was paid for with those songs that *they* own and this flake, this flunky, is asking me to write down the words? *They* are the publisher; it's *their* job to write down the words. They are making a fortune for doing nothing (except stealing). I just shook my head and walked away...what a creep...

player in Creedence, Doug Clifford"—you'd think that Saul could at least remember that Stu Cook is the bass player in Creedence, since the band had made him a fortune—"came to my office with John Fogerty's new album, and he played John's new song 'The Old Man Down the Road,' and then he played 'Run Through the Jungle.' And he said, 'John is ripping off Creedence! You should sue him!'" So, according to Saul, that's where he got the idea to sue.

I had no clue that this had transpired. And to learn by way of Saul was really offensive. You'd think that in the course of depositions and evidence this would've come up, but here I was, finding out in the courtroom that someone could be so shallow, so heartless. The whole thing was a shock. It just knocked me out. How could Stu have done this?

I felt that I had been stabbed in the back. To intentionally go see Saul—a person who'd cheated and lied and really treated *all* of us like crap—and do that? I'm the guy who actually provided you with millions of dollars, Stu. So *that* strange bedfellow is the one you climb into bed with—against *me?*

After the trial, it took me years and years to be able to write a song anywhere near the territory of "The Old Man Down the Road," because some part of me down deep inside worried that I was going to get sued again. Finally, in 2007, I was trying to write a swamp rock song for my *Revival* album. I was up in my little writing studio, and as I started to make that certain chord that I'm very familiar with and am known for, I began to play that funky rhythm. A little devil-lawyer figure appeared on my shoulder. And as I'm doing that swampy-feeling music, this critter says, "You can't do that!" This had happened many times before—that same little devil would rise up, say those words, and my inspiration would just fizzle. That's how vulnerable I was. But this time I willed it away. I said, "You go away! You don't belong here!" And I proceeded to write "Creedence Song."

This didn't happen in some big, heated battle in the middle of a courtroom with a bunch of people. It was a very quiet moment alone in my room. I finally knocked that fear out of my life. That was a moment of victory for me — artistically and emotionally.

We ended up prevailing in that trial. The six-member jury deliberated for only three hours. But Judge Samuel Conti refused to hold Fantasy responsible for my legal fees, which were in the neighborhood of a million dollars. I had to go all the way to the U.S. Supreme Court, and I won there on March 1, 1994. It was nine to zip in my favor. I was far from done with Saul Zaentz, however. There was still the matter of the $144 million defamation suit over "Zanz Kant Danz."

The trial had ended late on a Friday afternoon, so I flew home to Julie in Los Angeles. The next Monday, I went back up to San Francisco. I wanted to meet with the judge and ask him man to man why my attorneys' fees weren't being paid. I went to the courthouse and spoke to his assistant, who said, "The judge will not see you."

At the plagiarism trial, Saul Zaentz's ex-wife, Celia, had testified for him, which I thought was remarkable considering she went through a bunch of crap with him too. (Celia told me that when they split, she and the kids left the family home completely vacant save for a big picture of Creedence, to remind Saul where his money had come from, and a football. Why the football? I don't know.) After the judge dismissed everyone that day, I made a point of walking back and saying to her, "Celia, how in the world could you testify for that bum?" And she said, "Oh, John, you and Saul should've resolved this years ago." For some reason that stuck in my head. So after the judge turned me down, I went to a pay phone and called Saul. I wanted to have a meeting with him right away, that afternoon. But he was out of town. So that failed, and I went back home empty-handed.

A couple of months later, on February 25, 1989, I went to the

Bammies in San Francisco. Bill Graham was there. I hadn't seen much of Bill in my years away from the music business, although we'd run into each other at Rock and Roll Hall of Fame inductions. Bill always made a point of inviting me up to the famous jam that just kind of started up spontaneously at the first hall of fame inductions in 1986. I'd been away from music for a *long* time at that point, and it made me feel really good that he wanted me there.

Since *Eye of the Zombie* I'd had trouble writing anything. At one point Julie and I were on vacation, staying in a Chicago hotel. I was trying to write a song on a little pad. She looked over my shoulder, and every word on every page was negative — "hate," "anguish," "pain," "venom."

So when I saw Bill standing there at the Bammies, I went over to him. I figured, with his experience, he'd seen it all and could help, so I said, "Bill, I'm not being productive at all musically. I can't write. I'm not being me — I'm stuck. And a big part of this is because I have all this unresolved crap with Fantasy Records and Saul Zaentz. Would you help me try to figure it out, try to resolve it?"

He said, "Yes. I'll do it." I pictured that Bill would judge both sides, come up with what was actually fair, and make a recommendation. I was going with what Celia had told me to do... as if it was that simple.

A few days later, I get a call from Bill — he's working on a meeting between me and Saul. Within a week he has me fly up there. Bill himself meets me at the airport gate and drives me to his office.

I lay out the whole history to Bill and his assistant, Nick Clainos. I go home. Bill arranges our first meeting with Saul at Bill's house in Marin County. Saul says his stuff, I say my stuff, and Bill is in the middle. It's all quite correct, almost like teatime in London. Two well-respected, honorable gentlemen discussing their issues.

It really boils down to two big issues: Saul thinks I've slandered him and wants restitution. And I want to buy back my own songs.

At one point Saul says, "We really honored John. We offered him ten percent of the company, and he just rejected our offer." Saul actually says this. Which is, of course, a lie.

Then out of his mouth comes the phrase, "First the lawsuit, then the publishing." And he makes it very clear that he wants a check for $600,000 for slandering him. It's going to take that to make the suit go away. He puts his fist on the table and says, "Not negotiable. Not negotiable."

So Bill talks more with Saul and gets him to acknowledge, "Well, in deference to John and the respect our company has for him, we will sell the songs to John at a fair price, lower than we would sell to anyone else. I'm not gonna give away the store" — that was one of Saul's pet expressions — "but in deference to what John has meant to us, we will have other attorneys and experts look into this, determine a fair price, and then we'll sell the songs to John. But mind you, first the lawsuit, then the publishing."

First the lawsuit, then the publishing. That was a phrase I was to hear a lot in the days to come.

At the end of the meeting, Nick Clainos said, "I think you both need to get new attorneys for this negotiation to work. Not the same old attorneys fixed in their positions. We need some fresh ideas."

So then we adjourn. I went right home and got a new attorney. I'd find out soon enough that Saul didn't.

Bill Graham — what a guy. He had an AIDS benefit at around this time in Oakland, and he asked me to be part of it — that's how I wound up playing with members of the Grateful Dead (in addition to Steve Jordan and Randy Jackson). We had just played a really wonderful set. I come offstage, I'm getting my guitar off, and Bill is looking at me with a strange expression on his face. He says, "You really paid a high price for your principles, didn't you?" In that way that was Bill, he laid it on me in just one sentence. Bill didn't have to say any more. It meant a lot to me to know that he understood.

These negotiations with Saul dragged on for a long time. While this was going on, my brother Tom passed away in 1990. This was sad and personal. Running into Al Bendich—Saul's second in command—at the service for Tom didn't make it any easier. I found it offensive that Al or *any* of the crooks from Fantasy would be there. This was a family matter. On top of that, by this time I had been calling Al Bendich at Fantasy for months in an attempt to further the negotiations that we were supposedly trying to resolve. Al would just "go missing" and be unreachable...over and over and over. If I called on a Tuesday, they would say, "Call back on Friday." When I called on Friday, they would say, "Call back on Tuesday." This happened dozens of times...too many times to have an accurate count. So now, at Tom's home after the funeral service, "unreachable Al" was standing there in front of me.

I said, "Al, I've been trying to call you."

He said, "I hardly think this is the time or place. I'm going to take the high road." He actually used that phrase. I was ready to kill him.

What I didn't know then was that Julie had bumped into Bendich outside. She told him what effect all of this was having on my life, and she got so upset that she actually got on her knees and begged Al to call me.

He swore to her that he would.

He never did. That's Fantasy Records in a nutshell.*

---

* The January 2015 *Los Angeles Times* obituary for Bendich included this lofty quote by the man: "If poets reveal the deepest truths of ourselves to us, they also reveal what prevents us from realizing our humanity....And so poets must be free to think and feel and express themselves; and we must be free to hear them." To which I'd add, "Unless you're John Fogerty and signed to Fantasy Records."

*　　*　　*

In early June, Bill Graham calls: we're having another meeting. I pull into Bill's circular driveway, and before I go in, Nick comes out to my car and says, "John, at the last meeting Saul said they offered you ten percent and you rejected it."

I said, "Yeah, Nick, but it's baloney." It hadn't been 10 percent of the entire company.

"Well, John, we were all there and he told us. So now let's tell him we accept!"

Sure enough, Saul arrived, we all sit down, and Nick goes right into the 10 percent offer that Saul had made. "We'd like you to know that John now accepts the offer."

Saul blustered, gathered himself, and said something like, "Well, it's too late now." So no matter how many people Saul told that he offered me 10 percent of the company and that I turned it down — sorry, it's a crock of shit.

Next we got to the slander suit. We agreed that I would come up with a check to satisfy Saul — and he would sell me my songs for a price that was going to be less than they could actually get out in the world. In deference to who I am.

In the months and years after that second meeting, I spoke with Bill a few times, but many more times with Nick. Bill was a busy guy. During this time Bill had several meetings and phone conversations with Saul, and Bill (or more often Nick) would give me a report by phone.

At some point after several phone calls with Nick on this subject, he was pushing me to write Saul a big check and accept his promises. So finally I said, "Nick, this guy's a crook. You're asking me to jump off this cliff into the darkness — *'Jump, John!'* — and you're telling me there's a safety net down there, but I don't see the net. This guy's a crook."

And Nick said, "No, John, you just have to have faith in Saul's word—he's an honorable man, and he has promised to sell the songs to you."

I kept saying over and over, "Nick, this is the guy that has screwed me for thirty years. He's a crook. As far as I know, he's never told me the truth once in his whole life. Why am I gonna give him a big check?"

"John, Saul's a man of his word. You need to give him a check, and then he's going to sell the publishing to you."

Right.

So we divided the payment between three parties: myself, Warner Bros., and, if I remember correctly, my insurance company. Mo Ostin did not want to pay Saul. He told me he wanted to get that guy—"I don't wanna settle. No matter what it costs, he should be made to pay." But I felt that this was my only path to getting my songs back. So Saul got his money.

And despite his "word," he never sold me my songs.*

At that point, once you've done what you've agreed you'd do, you start trying to negotiate the other half. But what are you supposed to do when both sides have agreed to play with marshmallows and suddenly the other side fires a cannonball through your windshield?

Years went by—lawyers sent letters back and forth that hemmed and hawed, with a "whereas" and a "what for"—and a price was finally put forward. With a publishing company, one common way to declare its value is by multiplying its yearly income by ten.

---

* Nick Clainos had this to say: "Saul was charming. He played the role of the simple, easygoing businessman who had the law on his side. John was the fanatic who was complicating things. At least initially, Bill and I fell for it hook, line, and sinker. We had been scammed by one of the best—this guy Saul Zaentz. Saul did in fact agree to an arrangement; he did receive money. Ultimately he reneged. Saul just stopped taking our calls. He'd gotten what he wanted: his pound of flesh from John. Saul screwed John Fogerty—again."

The value that Fantasy declared was...*twenty* times its yearly income! Unlike what was promised, there was no allowance made in deference to me, the one who actually wrote these songs. I couldn't afford the price. No one could have.

I even went down to Warner/Chappell publishing in Century City and had a talk with the head honcho there to see if there was some way I could buy the whole thing, give it to them to manage, and maybe the fees they would earn would help me pay for it. Maybe they could loan me the money to actually purchase it in the first place, and I could pay them back as the songs earned royalties.

And he just told me it was not sustainable.

Not sustainable.

I really had thought that somehow there was a way we could make it work.

But Saul had put such a high number on the price he wanted that Warner/Chappell just couldn't do it.

That was one of the more crushing days of my life. I drove back home to see Julie. After all this time and effort, this was really like the end of the world to me.

During this period of time, Bill Graham had gone from being the man in the middle to being my advocate because Saul had reneged on his side of the deal. At one point I'm talking to Bill on the phone and he says, "John, I can't believe your attorney let you give a big check to Saul." Jeez. It was *Bill's* guy, Nick Clainos, who'd convinced me to do that, right? That's how crazy this thing was. Of course, I didn't have the bad taste to tell Bill that.

Bill was so disgusted after one meeting with Saul that he related what he had told my nemesis: "Saul, one day I'm going to be traveling across the Sahara Desert with my camel train, and I'll come upon you. And you'll be buried up to your neck in the burning hot sand. You'll say to me, 'Bill—please, Bill, just give me some water.' I'll ask, 'How much money do you have, Saul?' You'll say, 'Eight dollars.' And I'll say, 'Okay, Saul. The price is nine dollars.'"

Unfortunately, Bill died before he could take his camels across the Sahara. I would've loved to have witnessed that.

The negotiations to buy back my songs dragged on for years. It was excruciating. One day, in 1994 or so, I'm jogging in the Valley on a Saturday afternoon. There was this radio shrink named Dr. David Viscott that I used to listen to while I ran. He's talking to this woman and she's been living with some guy for nine years. She's got kind of a mournful, whining sound to her voice. David says, "What's the issue?"

"Well, I want him to commit. I want to get married! He just won't commit."

"Has he told you he won't get married?"

"Yes, he says he won't marry me. I want him to marry me."

"How long have you been together?"

"For nine years."

He's been telling her he's not going to marry her for nine years.

I'm jogging along, and I'm hearing this. Even for me it's beginning to sink in.

I'm really starting to pay attention here.

David keeps saying, "Well, he's told you he's not going to marry you. Isn't that right?"

"But I want him to marry me."

By now everyone in the listening audience can hear how pathetic this poor woman's position is. She wants what she wants so desperately. And she is so invested that she just can't see it isn't going to happen.

And all of a sudden I just go, *"Oh!"* There was an epiphany. A revelation. I'm running along and I'm laughing. I laughed so hard I couldn't run anymore. I fell down on the grass, laughing.

It was all clear as a bell.

"It ain't gonna happen, John! Saul ain't gonna sell you the songs.

Ever. It was all just words. *It's never going to happen,* and if you don't hear it, you're gonna be like that poor woman."

After that, I realized that Saul was just evil, pure evil. But at least finally it wasn't like a sore you keep making worse because you pick at it all the time. It was time to say, "Leave it alone! Stop it!" Because nothing was going to change. It's not right, but that's what I have to live with. Saul Zaentz was a schmuck. Lying there laughing on the ground was me *not* being a schmuck anymore. Or dancing with a schmuck. Perhaps that was the beginning of my healing.

Eventually you get stronger. I could not have accomplished this without Julie. And I could not have lived through all of it without her. There's been a lot of great moments since I met Julie. Things like that were impossible before I met her. In the morning when I wake up, now it's, "Wow, life is good." I don't go, "Ah shit, I gotta pay another lawyer."

But I also know that the day I gave up on Saul was the day I moved forward.

I guess Saul passed last year, same day as Phil Everly. I always used to say that I'd dance a jig on Saul's grave, and throw my half-gold record from "Susie Q" down the hole in the ground with him.* Instead, when the day came, it really didn't affect me. I thought Phil's passing was much more important.

---

* None of the gold records we got from Fantasy were officially issued by the Recording Industry Association of America. Saul didn't want that kind of attention—he didn't want anyone looking at the books. When Fantasy sold half a million copies of "Susie Q," they took a 45 and dipped it halfway down with gold paint. We didn't get real gold records until twenty years later.

CHAPTER 17

Crossroads

SOMETIME IN 1990, I was standing at the grave of one of the greatest bluesmen of all time: Robert Johnson. And I was talking to him. Either out loud or in my head, I can't remember. I was back behind an old Mississippi church. It was a hot, humid day, and this was a turning point in my life.

There had come a time, starting in 1972, when I made a conscious decision not to sing Creedence songs anymore, meaning the music I had created during the Creedence era. The inspiration for this extreme action came from a conversation I had had with Saul shortly before I walked out of Fantasy for good. We were discussing some other artist who was having a squabble with his label—it might've even been Elvis. Whatever beef the musician had, it didn't matter to Saul. His position was that, no matter how bad the situation, an artist would create. "It's in you," he said to me. "You would have to keep doing it anyway." Saul thought an artist would put up with any indignity to record, have a career. "Keep doing it anyway." His words stuck with me.

Once I realized just how bad I'd been screwed by Saul and Fantasy, I had to take a stand and be a man. *Do* something. And one

317

thing I decided to do was not sing those songs anymore. The situation tortured me. If "Proud Mary" came on the radio, I'd change the channel. Creating that song was one of the greatest moments of my life, but hearing it was no longer a happy occasion. I could picture myself in some dive in Vegas, sloshing my way through my oldies, bitter over having been screwed and numbing myself with booze. So, to save the rest of me, I decided to cut off my legs—stop singing my own songs. To some extent, it worked. Living was better than dying.

For about fifteen years I kept that vow.* But on February 19, 1987, a funny thing happened. Taj Mahal was playing at the Palomino Club in North Hollywood. I think he's an American treasure, so I went. I was sitting there a little while when I noticed someone kind of hiding in a corner—it was Bob Dylan. He'd come down to see Taj too. And he told me he'd brought George Harrison with him.

Taj got wind of this and had Bob come up and play. Then George. Usually I'm kind of shy at such events. Instead, I was chomping at the bit to join them. Taj called me up, they found a guitar, and we played a couple of songs. I could see pretty quickly that most everybody had been, let's say, imbibing. It was a little wobbly. And a whole lot of fun.

Somebody yelled out, "Bob, do one of your songs!" So Bob did. Then somebody pointed to George. As if turning a switch, George broke into a strong version of "Honey, Don't!" I could feel the noose getting tighter. We did "Twist and Shout," and for three minutes I sang "Ooooh" directly across a mic from George Harrison, like the Beatles on *Ed Sullivan*. That was an amazing feeling. Bob said, "All right, John, we've all done a song. Do 'Proud Mary.'"

---

* Outside of playing those songs for local dances in Troy, Oregon. That's where I hunted and fished—my soul getaway. I didn't really consider those professional gigs. More like family reunions.

"Sorry, Bob," I told him. "I'm not doing my old songs. I don't do them anymore." I was being kind of difficult, and I knew it. And instead of arguing about it, Bob Dylan, in his genius and ever so influential way, said, "If you don't do 'Proud Mary,' everybody's gonna think it's a Tina Turner song."

There was no way out now. I thought, *Bob Dylan just told me I'd better play my song or it's gonna turn into a Tina Turner song.* It was something only a musician could do—get out from under all the crap and find a way. So I played "Proud Mary." And enjoyed it. Immensely. "Eat your heart out, Tina," I told the crowd. This event didn't change my mind about doing Creedence songs, but I had certainly done one of them in public now.

A few months later, on July 4, 1987, I was in Washington, DC, playing the Welcome Home show for Vietnam veterans. Producer Ken Ehrlich had called and told me about the concert, which was being televised on HBO. This show was about publicly honoring our veterans. The government didn't do it, and culturally we didn't do it. It was like, "Hey—wake up! We should honor our veterans!" I was proud to be invited. Ken didn't really ask what I'd play, but I informed him, "Well, Ken, I don't play my old catalog." He said, "That's all right. I just want you to be part of it."

When Ken asked me to do that show, I fully intended to just do new material. But I began to feel that I owed the vets more. Whatever I did, I wanted to be deferential to them, in the hope that they'd understand that I personally recognized what they'd done for us. The most special thing I could think of was to do my old songs from the Creedence era. Just for the vets. For that one day, I'd get over my own embargo.

I'd been playing with a Los Angeles band called the Boneshakers, and one night at a local club we took my idea for a road test. I'd had a recent hit with "The Old Man Down the Road," so I started playing the riff, and then slipped into "Born on the Bayou." I hadn't even started singing, but every person in the room reacted. The crowd went wild. It's amazing what a few seconds of a riff can do. Donny Gerrard, one of the background singers, said after the song ended, "Is that gonna work or what?"

We went to Washington, DC. I didn't tell anyone what I was doing—other than my band, and they were sworn to secrecy. I gave a vague instruction to Ken, the producer: "If something happens, be alert."

We did the intro to "Old Man," but soon lurched to a stop, faking the audience out. I held that chord, and then started into the swampy menace of "Born on the Bayou." The roof came off the place. It just erupted. I'm not even sure what happened for the next forty-five minutes—I just know it was a good thing.

"Happy" is not exactly the right word to describe it, because these brave, neglected soldiers were carrying a lot of baggage. And I was right there in the lifeboat with 'em.

Before one song I addressed the vets personally. I looked out there and said, "I myself have gone through about twenty years of pain—and I finally faced that pain. I looked it right in the face and said, 'Well, you've got a choice: you can do it for twenty more years, or you can just say, 'That's what happened.' You can't change it...

"So I'm telling you guys—that's what happened. You got the shaft. *You* know it, *we* know it, it's reality....In fact, send me a letter—Berkeley, California—but promise me somethin': drop it in the box, and then drop all that shit you've been carryin' around. Is that a deal? Get on with it, buddy!" (I do wish it were that simple...it isn't.) I went into "Who'll Stop the Rain," a song very much inspired by those times we'd lived through together. I was amazed by their reaction. It turned out to be a very emotional day, and a really great thing to be part of.

After I left the stage, this guy came up, telling me how much my music had meant to him and his soldier pals. He had his war medal in his hand. "Would you wear it?" he asked. I was taken aback—he'd earned that fighting for our country. But I wasn't about to turn him down. "You betcha," I said, and he pinned it right on my guitar strap. I still wear it proudly when the occasion calls for it.

Fantastic as it was, the Welcome Home show was an isolated event. I still had no intention of singing the Creedence songs in public again. And then in 1990 I started taking trips to Mississippi. For a few years, I'd been thinking about musicians I love—people like Howlin' Wolf, Muddy Waters, Jimmy Reed, Bo Diddley, John Lee Hooker, Elvis, and Jimmie Rodgers—and how they all came from Mississippi. I was thinking about the blues, the Delta. And I realized I didn't even know what the Delta looked like.

I kept having this pesky thought: *Go to Mississippi.* At first it was an annoyance. I'd brush it away, but the urge got stronger and stronger. It wasn't like obsessing over a cool car. This was more like, "I have to figure this out before it drives me crazy." I felt like Richard Dreyfuss building the mashed potato tower in *Close Encounters of the Third Kind.*

At this point I'd been with Julie for just a couple of years. One day I came to her and said, "Honey, I have to go to Mississippi."

She looked at me with those big blue eyes—Julie knows I'm not whimsical; I'm a fairly serious person—and says, "Okay. Why?"

"I don't know."

"Okay. When?"

"Now."

Off I went. I took a total of six trips, each about a week. Eventually I took a camera, bought myself a laptop. I made a lot of notes that first visit—too much time with the stupid computer in the hotel room. Next time, I flew into Memphis and had more of a plan. I was very serious about these trips. I visited the plantation house that Muddy Waters had lived in, visited the site of Dockery

Plantation, went to a couple of juke joints—tiny little one-room clubs that had names with big aspirations, like "Rainbow Disco." It looked like you could buy the place for fifteen bucks. One joint had a crude painting of Michael Jackson on the outside wall.

Entering the digital age—I'd been resisting the whole damn thing—I bought my very first digital boom box on that second trip, not to mention my first CD, Big Bill Broonzy. The CD player didn't have shocks, so I couldn't listen while I was driving, since the boom box would skip.

I also got ahold of a book about Charley Patton while I was down there. One of the greatest Delta blues singers—and a guy I had totally missed. I went and bought a cassette, put it in the player, and when he started to sing, the hair on the back of my neck stood up: "Oh my God, he sounds like *that?*" It was like hearing Moses.

Charley Patton was before Howlin' Wolf. At times I'd imitated Wolf, more or less. He was one of my guys. The way I say my "woids" in some songs had to have come from him, although it wasn't something I was doing on purpose. So to hear Charley Patton, I thought, *This is where it all starts.*

I wanted to find where Charley Patton was buried. I had the name of the town, Holly Ridge, and after talking to a few people I found this guy, Coochie Howard, a cemetery caretaker who'd been taken to Patton's unmarked grave as a kid. I was amazingly bold for a guy who wasn't even writing a book. I was just seeking knowledge.

Coochie took me to a large field, and we walked right up to a place on the edge. Very assuredly, he pointed to a spot in front of us and told me, "Charley Patton is buried *right there.*" Coochie told me that his mom had pointed out the spot to him when he was four or five years old, and I can only imagine that he'd been looking at that spot for many a decade, because on that day he looked to be in his mid-sixties. I think he said there had been some kind of temporary marker, like a flag or small piece of wood, but that it disappeared long ago.

Later, through Skip Henderson, another blues fan I met down there, I had the opportunity to put a headstone on Charley's grave. I really don't like making a big deal about it, but it sure brought some wonderful memories my way. They had an official ceremony, unveiling the headstone on July 20, 1991. They had a service, with a real preacher. It was moving. One of Patton's relatives was there. I had a little guitar slide in my pocket, and so, hoping that a little Patton mojo might rub off, I talked her into holding it for a few seconds. It was hotter than blazes that day. I sat next to Pops Staples, who was wearing a breezy, all-white linen suit. Me, I had on a dark blazer and tie. Guess who didn't grow up in Mississippi? The intense heat from days like that was one of the inspirations for my song "A Hundred and Ten in the Shade."

That brings us to Robert Johnson's grave—well, one of Robert's purported resting places, of which there are three (I may have visited all of them). This one, which is currently said to be "the most probable," is in a little graveyard behind Mount Zion Missionary Baptist Church, outside of the little town of Moorhead (Johnson's death certificate lists only a "Zion Church," which is part of the problem). You go to the post office, ask the postmaster, and he directs you: "Be sure to look for the big pecan tree. Robert was buried under there." As with Charley, there was no marker. (Blues researcher Stephen C. LaVere would put a headstone there not long after my visit.)

It was humid as all get-out in Mississippi that day. There was a swampy, tropical feel. I was dripping wet. There are those of us who will tell you that when you're in Mississippi, you can feel a rumble happening in the ground, electricity in the dirt. It feels like the place is buzzing.

I found the church. This was my first visit to Robert's burial site. There had been a bad storm, and the ground was completely flooded. A few ancient tombstones were scattered about. I was determined to touch that tree. There was a lot of undergrowth and weeds, making it a bit tricky, but I'm a fisherman. I waded into the water, which was up to my knees, and put my hand on that big old tree.

At that moment Robert Johnson was suddenly a pop star. Sony had released a box set of his work on CD, and it had gone Top 10, eventually platinum. It was a current seller. Even though I was there for earlier, long-lived desires, I realized that there was renewed interest in Robert.

And there I was, staring down at his lonely grave, wondering who owned his songs now. Being a bit cynical due to my own experiences, I pictured some tall building in which sat a crooked lawyer sporting a big cigar. Some guy who had as much to do with this music as the man in the moon was probably making millions off of it. I was disgusted at the thought.

I said, "It doesn't matter, Robert." I was literally talking to Robert Johnson at this point. "Those are your songs, Robert. The whole world knows those are your songs." I don't know if I was actually saying it out loud, but it unfolded like a conversation. I was sticking up for this guy who was a particular inspiration for what I do.

It doesn't matter. The whole world knows those are your songs.

Suddenly it was like an explosion went off in my head. I thought, *John, that's* your *story too.* The parallel was inescapable. Some disgusting guy with a big cigar *did* own my songs. I stood there a moment, mulling that over.

And I thought, *Dammit, John, you gotta start playing your songs before you're lying in the ground like Robert. Everybody knows they're yours. It doesn't matter who owns them.*

It was clear as a bell.

As I've indicated, I think of myself as a principled person. I couldn't just go, "Ha! Never mind. Forget your vow." Something would snap in my head. I'd feel that I broke a promise to myself, a promise to respect myself, and one that I took seriously. But I recognized this as the way out.

There was still a long journey ahead, but thanks to Julie, I was able to do these trips. And thanks to a little help from Robert Johnson, I'd seen a glimmer of light.

I made several more trips down to Mississippi. It felt really good to learn about all that music, not to mention take in the energy that comes from it. And I came back home and started playing Dobro. This all led to the *Blue Moon Swamp* album. But first things first.

I must confess that, outside of this or that obligation, I hadn't picked up a guitar in any serious way in ages. Years of litigation and disappointment had left me spent. I didn't want to hear anything about music, and I certainly wasn't making any.

When Julie came home and saw me with a guitar in my hands, she stopped dead in her tracks. She'd never seen that happen before. I get emotional remembering it, because she said it was one of the happiest days of her life.

CHAPTER 18

"This Is Only Going to End One Way"

JULIE: John had a music room in the house. He had converted a bedroom into a small studio. The room was soundproofed, and John had studio gear and instruments in there. Every time I walked into that room, I had this overwhelming feeling of joy—and sadness. The guitars sat there so proudly on their stands. These were the guitars that played on "Proud Mary," "Fortunate Son," "Green River," and so on. They were so beautiful to me, and I was so proud of him. Knowing that those guitars were played on those songs and what those songs meant to John—well, it just knocked me out. I couldn't get over the feeling of loss for John. Those guitars sat untouched for years.

Then one day, around 1990, I came home from shopping with Lyndsay. Coming through the front door, I heard guitar playing. I saw John with the guitar in his hand, and it just got to me. I stood very still so I wouldn't interrupt this beautiful moment and draw attention to it. Tears ran down my face, and joy filled my heart. This was the first time I'd heard John's music in our home. It was a big symbol for me, a very emotional one. I remember standing there by the front door thinking, *John is coming back.*

John: I was getting the will and the energy—to try. To create something new. I don't just mean opening your mouth and regurgitating some old song that was a hit twenty years ago; I mean daring to dig. I wanted to record a new album. I knew instinctively what that had to be. I was *not* going to make any more records like *Eye of the Zombie* or *Hoodoo.*

I wanted to get back to being that guy I was in 1969, and I hadn't been him for a long time. When you're young and bulletproof, the music rolls out of you. Then, for whatever reasons, you reach a plateau in your life where layers accumulate—money, success, lawsuits, heartbreak, everyday life—and you're not doing your art anymore. The very idea of scratching around in the pile of baggage that has become *you,* especially when you're an older person, is the scariest thing you can imagine. Let's face it: most rock and roll artists lose it when they get older. It's just too hard, too painful to walk the high wire like you did when you were young and fearless.

Frankly, I'd rather go digging around in some other guy's crap! Digging around in my *own* crap, the idea that you're really going to face that—it's, "Oh my God, what am I gonna do to myself? How disgusted, how unhappy am I gonna be? How frustrated, how repulsed, how disappointed in myself am I gonna be when I rip all my scabs off?"

You may have noticed that I'm the type of guy who doesn't take commitments lightly. You see, I just seemed to know instinctively that I would *never* be any good again unless I was willing to dig through all the layers of protection, all the layers of pain and hopelessness, and scratch my way through the stupid, drunken, and evasive years that had accumulated like reptile skin around my heart. All the while staring it right in the face without blinking. I knew it was gonna be rough, and it was. I had made the decision to dive in and go for it. And I could only go into that emotional place by realizing, "I got Julie, I got me, and we're gonna do this."

Several things happened around that time. There were the trips to Mississippi. And I'd bought a Dobro. I was just drawn to the sound.

For three and a half years I played Dobro. I got really manic about getting good, because I knew I wanted that thing on my record. So much so that I called Julie the Dobro widow. I'd be practicing in my little room and she couldn't tell if I was getting better, so she would comment every now and then.

And I started buying albums that had Dobro. All paths of the Dobro eventually lead to Jerry Douglas if you're serious and trying to learn. How he sounds when he plays the Dobro hits me right in the heart. It touches me very deeply. I just love his music. He's my favorite musician of all time. He could've been a zither player—the instrument doesn't matter. It's the sound, the emotional content and the technical ability. So listening to Jerry gave me a big boot in the butt. And it made me rediscover a promise that I'd made to myself as a kid.

I was listening intently to a Jerry Douglas record and savoring the playing of the other musicians around Jerry. I was just smiling in wonderment. I'm sure I said something like, "These guys are just so good—*all* of 'em!" It was as if a little flashlight in my head suddenly shined on this little molecule that was my promise to grow up and be like Chet.

When I was fourteen or so, I thought about Chet Atkins a lot. He was probably the best guitar player on earth. And I said to myself, *I'm gonna grow up and I'm gonna be really, really good. Great. Like Chet Atkins—a great guitar player.*

I had total recall of that memory. Then my conscience kind of woke up and I went, "It didn't happen!" It was like cold water in my face. "Oh my God—it didn't happen!" This was 1993. I was forty-eight years old!

I daresay most sane people would have gone, "Oh well—too late now." Or "You're good enough." I just thought, *I gotta get really busy! That's who I am. That's what I'm supposed to do.*

And so I started practicing—seriously.

And it all went into the Dobro first, and then from there to guitar. And right in there is where I gave up the idea of being a one-man band. Consciously and for real. The moment I started thinking about guitar again is the moment I said to myself, *It takes a lifetime to get good on one instrument—to be world-class. That's what I'm gonna do. All the rest is taking me away from that.*

During this period I would go to the Kern River and stay up there for a week or so. During the day I would find a quiet place by the river and just think about what I wanted to do. I had a writing pad, a recorder, and, back at the cabin, a little drum machine. At night I'd pick up the guitar and come up with ideas for what I'd been thinking about that day. Being near water seemed to be a really good thing.

It's no secret that throughout my life I have paid close attention to drummers. With *Blue Moon Swamp,* I certainly wasn't going to play the drums. I was done with that. I knew I wanted real musicians. I wanted the joy of people playing in the same room and having that feel. It was a long evolution.

I tried out thirty drummers. Jeff Porcaro, Chris Layton, Eddie Bayers—great, great musicians. But nobody could do it all. The guy might be the top of the mountain as far as players go, and yet he might not be the guy who best understands how to play a particular thing I'm trying to do. I would bring in more and more musicians. It went on and on.

I'd be in the studio with this famous guy or that famous guy, and they wouldn't be able to play a certain feel, so I would edit the drumming by cutting up the two-inch master tape. This was a long, long process, not like it is now with Pro Tools, where you just push a button and—*whoosh!*—the drums get lined up. Maybe we would do two songs in a six-hour day, and then I'd edit the best pieces of those sixteen takes—part of the verse here, another part from take eleven—but you still have places where it's shaky, and so you're literally down to snipping three-sixteenths of an inch out of the track. John Lowson, my engineer, would lay it out when we got to that point: "Okay, we're gonna cut the two-inch. There's no goin' back." It's a little like brain surgery. Because if he screws up...Editing the master was always stressful.

On *Blue Moon Swamp* there was an incredible amount of editing. It took a lot of patience. We'd spend all day on a verse and a half, just trying to get the drums right. Then we'd have the bass player come back and play his part. I'd play along with him, but mine was just for reference, for inspiration. I'd have to edit some of the bass part, too. That's the way everything was going on that album—edit, edit, edit. There were a lot of parts that I recorded myself. That's another thing I want to get away from in the future. It was a lot of work, time-consuming, a lot of stress. I was in the studio for five years starting in 1992. John Lowson kept track of all that. Thank goodness he was a really calm guy. I'm told that there were five hundred analog reels of tape and twelve digital by the end.

Julie: We had gotten married in April 1991. Three months before the wedding, I'd discovered that I was pregnant. And John and I had not really talked too much about having a baby. I had to tell him about this surprise.

Interestingly enough, after I took the test I found John in the kitchen reading some article in the newspaper about Paul Anka and his song "(You're) Having My Baby." True story. John starts talking about how he hates that song* and starts singing it at the top of his lungs. I couldn't believe it. How was I not going to tell him this news at this exact moment? I just sat down and handed him the pregnancy test. He didn't know what it was. I said, "I'm pregnant and we are going to have a baby. I can't believe you were just singing that song." This was certainly a gift that neither one of us knew was coming. It was a blessing.

At around this time, John and I had dinner with our friends Bruce Springsteen and Patti Scialfa. Bruce talked to John and told him that he had so much going for him now—a wonderful relationship and a baby on the way. That he should focus on all of this and try to live within that. Bruce mentioned to John that when he and Patti were going to have their first baby, he went to all of Patti's doctor's appointments and said how he'd loved every minute of it. That went right into John's soul, and he, too, didn't miss a one. We have three kids and he's been at every appointment.

John: I was really, really worried at first, because at that point I was going to be forty-six years old—"Oh God, am I gonna be able to roll around on the floor with my kid? Am I gonna be a good daddy, or am I gonna be like some professor who comes in the room, sees the kids, and then leaves?" I needn't have worried. The instant that Shane was born, it was like all the switches in my head just went *click!* There was no hesitation. I was in it.

We learned that we were pregnant early in 1991. Shane was born on October 15 that year. Then pretty quickly we were pregnant again, and Tyler was born on October 26, 1992. The boys were fifty-three weeks apart! Lyndsay had started first grade in September 1989, and it just seemed like Julie was always pregnant.

---

* **John:** The rock and roll guy in me thought this song was sappy. The family guy in me loves the sentiment.

So many of our family pictures from those days show a mommy-to-be. I absolutely loved that time in our family. Julie became even more beautiful to me. With joy in my heart, I took to saying, "She is that most beautiful of all creatures...a pregnant woman."

That might surprise most people about me: I love babies—absolutely *love* babies. If we could have seven more, I would do it. Julie wouldn't! I just go all goofy. I really enjoyed that part of our experience with each baby that came: Shane, Tyler, Kelsy. I got every single second out of it that I could. Seeing the world through their eyes—it just keeps you in that place. There's still wonderment in everything.

When Tyler was an infant, he would wake up in the middle of the night. I was trying to help Julie as much as I could. I'd get the bottle ready and we had this cool little papoose thing he'd lie in. He'd have his little bottle, and I'd sit with my Dobro and practice. I figured I had to get up early if I wanted to get good. Before that, I stayed up partying and got up late. The babies changed that.

Julie: The doctors let John help deliver Shane at the hospital. And as soon as Shane was born, that boy never left John's arms. Shane would fall asleep on John at night. It was such a beautiful thing because I knew that somehow that love was something John really needed and wanted.

And now when John performs his show, that little boy Shane is by his side. How great is that? No one can ever take or steal that away from John. Shane might never know what that means to his father or his mother, but I can tell you that this is a wonderful, beautiful gift we have been given. It's a big, big deal. We pinch ourselves every night knowing how lucky we are to have Shane up there with his father, playing his heart out while John and I just melt with pride, joy, and pure happiness.

So John was getting better and better, but he was not quite well yet. He was still struggling with his music. There were times when he would disappear into his music room. I could hear him yelling through the soundproof walls. I knew he just wanted to make music, this music man who'd had his soul ripped out of him. He was fighting big-time to get it back.

He felt so frustrated when he would try to write a song—he still didn't have that back. John was really struggling to make music. I knew that if he could just get through making *Blue Moon Swamp* it could make all the difference for him.

Unfortunately, the drinking had continued, and although it was not as often or as much as before, it tied in with moments of despair when John was trying to work everything out. I just didn't know if I could go on watching him drink himself to death.

I was pretty torn up after going through years of this. I had a gallbladder attack while I was pregnant with Tyler and wound up in the hospital. And I ended up getting myself home. Because when I was released from the hospital, John didn't even pick me up. I had to take a taxi home. He just couldn't handle it. That was sad for sure, but it was real. This is something he feels very bad about today, but it shows he really wasn't functioning normally then.

John wasn't well enough inside to handle anything else. He took sleeping pills at night, and I knew he wasn't going to answer the phone. It seems really sad now, looking back, but it was the truth, and I was deeply troubled by all of this. At times I felt really alone. Half of John was there but the other half wasn't, and I knew it.

One day I poured out several bottles of alcohol on the floor of the garage and told him that he had to stop. John was on a mission to destroy himself. At that time, the lowest of low, when I had really had it with all this chaos, he said to me, "Once you become perfect, then I will." That statement was very hard to hear. When someone says that to you, the message is, "I am not going to get help and I am lost." That stung pretty hard. I hung on, but by a thread. There was part of me already gone. I had joined group therapy for support, and everyone in the room would look at me and wonder why I was still in the relationship. In many ways I wasn't. I just couldn't figure out what to do.

There was a moment when I really thought I couldn't emotionally handle all of this. I ended up in some lawyer's office, and that was a low time for sure. That *Blue Moon Swamp* period was hell. It took ten years to make that record, not just the five in the studio—it was over 3,650 days before we saw another song from John. What made me hang in there was that, number one, John is just a wonderful, beautiful man. I saw the pain he was suffering, and it just broke my heart. But John always let me know how much he loved me and cared for me in his own way. As he put it, I was the joy of his life. How could I leave John? I just couldn't do it.

I saw the innocence in John: Imagine a little boy with a bicycle. This boy loves to ride his bike everywhere, and it brings him so much joy he rides it every single day. Then one day he suffers a horrible fall and he stays away from that bike for years. He won't even go in that garage where the bike is, nor does he feel he wants to ever get back on that bike. It had hurt him so badly. He's scared of what might happen to him if he climbs on that seat. Until one day he gets up enough courage and self-determination to get back on that bike, trusting that he can do it again and that bad things won't happen.

John now knows that someone is holding the seat and running alongside him. That I'm cheering him on while he rides down the road. He understands that I'm always there for him. That I have his back. John never had that before in his life.

This beautiful man just wanted to play a guitar and write songs and live a happily-ever-after life. I really, really felt that John would be okay if he could just make this record. I may have seemed naive, but I was committed to seeing him through this, no matter what. John was *going* to make that record. I came so close to leaving, but I just couldn't walk away—I needed to see him through it. I cared for him so deeply. Not knowing how it would end up, I believed in John and wanted to be there to do anything I could to get him well enough to finish that record.

I know that John wonders how I got through it all. It was personally very traumatic and crazy, for sure. Looking back, it was as if I was guided to do this. I don't know how else to describe it. It was just meant to be.

John: I wasn't fully a grown-up then. I was keeping some of my old habits—I'd still go down a hole, get drunk, be rather quiet, say something I shouldn't. So it was remarkable that Julie had as much patience with me as she did. Julie had a lifesaving grip on my hand and was pulling me out of that hole one step at a time. And it was...hard. It was hard on Julie because I was such a pain in the ass to be around.

Julie: John worked on that record year after year. No days off. No lunches.

As someone on the sidelines, I found it really hard to understand how it could go on for five years. Or how you can be in the studio for all that time.

John isn't difficult, but rather critical. He knows what it should be. John won't sign his name under the picture until it's just right.

At the time, I wasn't involved in really helping John with music because I didn't know how. Had I been involved, I could've said, "Drummer's no good. Next!" John kept hoping. He doesn't like to be that guy.

There were a lot of tears over *Blue Moon Swamp*, a lot of strain on our relationship. Hard times for sure. John wouldn't leave the house all day or night. I'd leave to get away...to stay sane. I wasn't sure of anything. If the kids and I were around, it would mean that he was distracted. I'd leave him Marie Callender's TV dinners so he'd at least have something to eat. I'd send my friend Betty Clearmountain to check on him, but he wouldn't answer the door or the phone, except to talk to me a few times daily. It took *everything* that John had—and more—to get *Blue Moon Swamp* made. He was so hell-bent and focused.

But we'd still go to dinner every Thursday night and have our date night.

John: I said to Julie, "This album's only gonna come out one way—and that's *great*. It's not gonna be lame." So I would tell her again and again—I would tell *myself*—"This is only going to end one way." But there was just one obstacle after another, and it dragged on and on.

Julie: On January 17, 1994, two days before John was supposed to be in New York City to induct Duane Eddy into the Rock and Roll Hall of Fame*, the Northridge quake hit California in the wee hours of the morning. We were home. John is the calm one; I'm not. I was running down the halls with two babies in my arms, yelling, "It's the big quake! It's the big quake!" We fled our shaking home, wall and glass crumbling all around us. Just hours before, I had moved Tyler's crib away from a huge TV in case of an earthquake, as I did every night, and it had landed right where

---

* **John:** I had been invited to induct Duane Eddy, and I was pumped for the opportunity. Duane had been my hero since "Movin' 'n' Groovin'" in 1958. But the quake had intervened. With my home in shambles, I called the Waldorf Astoria in New York City at about 7:00 eastern time. I asked for Duane Eddy. I'd had my speech ready for weeks! I knew he would be in his tux getting ready to go downstairs to the ceremony. Happily, Duane picked up the phone. I offered my congratulations and then I read him the speech I was supposed to give that night. Wish I could have been there. Rock on, Duane!

his crib had been. Our house was demolished and we had to rebuild from scratch. John was so focused on *Blue Moon Swamp* that you couldn't ask him to do anything, like turn on a light switch or get you a cough drop. *Any* distraction was too much. I was so exhausted by it all that I escaped with the kids to Indiana.

After the quake, the house started to flood, and John stayed there, surrounded by buckets catching the water. At the time, we barely had any money because of the court cases and Fantasy withholding royalty payments. But we were grateful to be alive. Ninety-five percent of the house was destroyed, right down to the framing. And then my grandfather passed away.

John: In the middle of all this, Julie threw a fantastic surprise party for my fiftieth birthday. She'd even prepared a movie about me, with the kids talking about Daddy.* We played music and really had a ball. I drank out of a moonshine jar. Bruce Springsteen got up and sang a few songs. And Julie was on tambourine in an unforgettable white dress.

Blue Moon Swamp wasn't going well. I was going to work every day and didn't even have one good track yet. Have I ever met a deadline in my life? I hate 'em. But I'm good with getting Kelsy to school on time.

If there's anything I've learned, it's don't let a deadline force you to put out something inferior. By 1995, I'd been in the studio for four years. I'd spent a lot of money, because I'd been there every day. There was a point when Julie really wanted me to get done. A long time ago I took to saying, "I married a real woman. I didn't marry a doormat." Sometimes it felt like I was in the principal's office.

---

* **Julie:** I ended the video with a beautiful picture of John, and the soundtrack was the Tom Petty song "Wildflowers." That song described how I felt about John and how things should have been for him earlier in life. There wasn't a dry eye in the house—including my husband's.

The music wasn't living up to what I wanted until Kenny Aronoff came along. I think he was the last drummer I auditioned. Once Kenny arrived, I didn't have to make any more phone calls. I think the very first song we did was "Rambunctious Boy." I thought, *Wow, he gets this. I'm gonna have him come back.* Kenny did everything I threw at him.

I consider him the best in the world. If you've got a great drummer, you've got more than 50 percent of it right there. It's like the frame of a house. Kenny keeps really good time—at times it's perfect time. But his style, his feel—he's a little bit ahead, yet the hi-hat is right on the money. That feel is what I love. It's got kind of a lean to it, and that's what rock and roll is.

Kenny's also got a photographic memory. I'll go, "Hey, try doin' this." We'll go listen, it'll work, and then after that he'll always do it every time we get to that point in the song. Even though that sounds a bit like science, it never comes off that way. As far as technique, just handling the drums, Kenny is an amazing and wonderful drummer—but he's also an *emotional* drummer, meaning he understands the music. I've played with him longer than I've played with any other musician.

Blue Moon Swamp all came together in the last year and a half. Usually when people work on something for a long, long time, it kind of sounds that way. This was the opposite: in the beginning of the five years in the studio, it sounded labored, and in that last year and a half, it sounded free and lively. I think the closer the horses got to the barn, the more they could smell the oats—"Man, here we go! C'mon!"

Now when I hear it, *Blue Moon Swamp* is one of my favorite albums. "A Hundred and Ten in the Shade" took a long time to write. I had the title since the seventies. I made a couple of different attempts but never quite got it. It finally came together on one of my writing trips out to Newhall, California. I'd take this beat-up route they called "the old road," which took you to the first commercially successful oil well in the state. I'd sit out there all day and never see a soul. Now it's all built up, developed. The place I went to doesn't exist anymore. I remember working on "Rambunctious Boy" and "Southern Streamline" out there as well.

The great Eddie Bayers played the drums on "A Hundred and Ten in the Shade." He understood the feel of that one really well. But we didn't have one complete take where everything was perfect, so I spliced that all together. Once you finally have a good song, you want the production to live up to what the song is. I wanted stand-up bass on the song. It's bluesy, very Southern, but I wanted somebody who understands musicals—*Show Boat* and *Porgy and Bess*. Quincy Jones recommended John Clayton. That was so right. He brought his gut-string bass and played wonderfully!

Then I wanted to find background singers—gospel guys. I kept saying, "I'm looking for a sound that's as old as the dirt." Jerry Douglas suggested the Fairfield Four. There's actually five of them. A true gospel group, they have a real bass singer—the whole thing. The guy I took to calling Little Joe was a big guy with a big, high voice. Incredible.

These guys don't use headphones. We just put live speakers in the room, and what that meant was that my guitar parts—which I had chopped up from different versions to make this one master take—bled into the vocal mics. So later, when I decided to get the guitar part really clear and strong, there was no way to get rid of the original guitar on the recording—I had to play it again and exactly match what was there. That track was a privilege to be a part of.

With "Blue Moon Nights" I was thinking about Sun Records. When I'd explain the song, I'd say, "Imagine if some kid walked in off the street to see Sam Phillips, and he's got a sackful of songs, and one of them would go like this." There's such an affection coming from me about that music, and I just really wanted to get all that in the track—and it wasn't by playing it eight million times. It's more about thinking about it a lot ahead of time. To get yourself into that emotional and mental place. I love doing that.

"Southern Streamline" started with the melody. I love train songs, probably because of my dad. I'd hear this melody and this urgency—"Mama, I'm on fire!" I wanted to get better at guitar, specifically Telecaster—country Telecaster. So this was a way to get some of that on this record. I played my custom Telecaster, which at one point belonged to the Eagles. (They had a hollowed-out place behind the pickguard that they used when they needed to hide something. I'm sure that was a long time ago.)

I used an old Vox AC30 amplifier with that guitar. You can fry eggs on top of them, they get so hot. When I was a Golliwog, this guy let me use his Vox and I blew it up. I wasn't very impressed. But as I got better on the Telecaster doing the chicken-picking, string-bending thing, I began to adopt the Telecaster-AC30 combination as a really cool sound. (Turns out Brad Paisley's in love with Vox AC30s too.) That sound is all over the record—"Rambunctious Boy," "Southern Streamline." I wanted it to be really smokin' guitar. I'd play it until I had a solo worked out, and then stick to that and do it ten or twenty times because I wasn't really good enough yet to just whip it off. That's how my earlier records were made: I'd hook onto a part and practice it over and over, and with scrupulous editing it could come out pretty good.

We did a lot of experimenting. Like for the lead guitar on "Rattlesnake Highway" and the Telecaster on "Southern Streamline," we used the room the old-fashioned way, placing different room mics, hearing what that sounded like: "Here's the Vox AC30 with a mic in front of it. How about if we do it on hardwood? Carpet?" We were trying all kinds of stuff to get as exquisite a sound as possible. "Bad Bad Boy"—that's where I discovered the Gibson Goldtop. I use that all the time now. It's just got the coolest tone. The only song on *Blue Moon Swamp* that I don't like much is

"Walking in a Hurricane." I worked on that for years and years. To my mind, it didn't really come off completely.

"Joy of My Life" is very conversational. It's not like a regular song. In fact, sometimes I think it's so personal, I even wonder if I should perform it live. I always have a good time playing it—I don't know if everybody else enjoys it when I do!

That one has an obvious influence. Due to my interest in flying, I'd go to the Oshkosh aviation show. I'd gotten friendly with this young couple, and Elizabeth, the wife, would ask me, "How's Julie?" My answer was always, "Well, she's the joy of my life." One day Elizabeth said, "You're always saying, 'She's the joy of my life.' You should write a song."

That was in 1991. Later, when I started getting serious about the Dobro, I kind of wrote this cool little Dobro riff. I thought, *Wow, that could make a neat song.* I was at the Kern River, trying to write.

So I came home, I'm with Julie, things are peaceful and great. We put the kids down, go to bed, and I'm lying there next to her in the night, thinking about my family, and the riff just starts playing in my head. And the words start coming.

And instead of writing a song, I'm just telling a kind of narrative of right now. Especially when Julie was pregnant, it would be 7:30 p.m. and she'd say, "I've got to have my rest." That's almost the first words of the song—the remainder is just the story of my life with Julie. It just flowed. And fittingly, the song written for the Dobro widow was played on one.

"Joy of My Life" is truly my first love song. And it really is a love song. Through my career, through the whole Creedence time, there just weren't any. Because I didn't write that way. Those kinds of songs seemed generic and meaningless to me. I was trying to write something that mattered. I'd written some love songs as a teenager, but in the Creedence era I just stopped because I didn't believe in that. This one I believe in. I can write about feelings, intimacy, relationships. This does not scare me because these are things I know about now.

Once *Blue Moon Swamp* was basically done, I thought we were going to mix it right there at the Lighthouse. But mixing is a really special deal, and I wasn't convinced that it could be done there.

Bob Clearmountain is my buddy. He got wind that I was done, and he said in the sweetest way, "John, I'd really like to mix your record." Now, in my head I've kind of pegged him as Mr. Digital (and that is not true, he's Old Skool)—he's worked on Bruce's records, Bryan Adams....I knew he was great. I just didn't know if he was the right "great" for me.

Bob says, "I tell ya what: let me mix one. For free. No obligation."

I gave him "Bad Bad Boy." When I came back at the end of the day, he had gone in there and found the essence of the song. I'm pretty sure what you hear on my record is what he did that day. I don't know how he knew to do it that way, but he did.

That's when *Blue Moon Swamp* was taken off of me—"We're done, we got a real mixer, he's gonna do it."

Julie: One day John came in and asked to take me to lunch. *Lunch?!* I looked at him like he was crazy. Then it hit me: he's done with *Blue Moon Swamp*. A great warmth went through my body. He's actually done. We are actually going to be together and not have this cloud hanging over his head! John had crossed the finish line. Man, was that a huge moment in our lives. I felt such a burden lifted at that moment! It was beautiful and unforgettable.

Off we went to share the record. John put it in his little brief-case, and we were going to play it for Warner Bros. I came along—I wasn't going to miss this moment. I wanted to be there for John. There were a couple of folks in the room who knew what the record was, senior vice president of Warners Carl Scott being one of them. Bob Merlis, John's publicity agent, knew it big-time. I can't say the reaction was that big from the rest of the group, but when they started getting letters from the fans once the record was out, I think they all got it. It's too bad that they delayed the marketing, because they had to play catch-up after that. The fans knew, but the label had to be told.

After all that pain and suffering I had been through with him, I wanted to be there, and I was excited for John because I knew what this meant. It was the rainbow at the end of a very dark road.

Blue Moon Swamp came out in May 1997. It was nominated for a Grammy—Best Rock Album. I'll never forget the night John won. John and I were in New York City at the Rihga Royal Hotel, and we're getting all dressed up and ready to go to the awards show. I think John was having trouble with his cuff links, and he had me helping him. I knew the telecast wasn't going to air this particular award—it was at a preshow event. Bob Merlis said he would go for us.

Well, the phone rang right before we headed out the door. And Bob said in his sweet voice, "You got it! *You got the Grammy!*" I just screamed with joy for John and ran over and grabbed him and gave him the biggest hug. John wasn't quite sure what had just happened. It was a vindication of that long period that was so hard and impossible for John, but he did it—and he did it against all odds.

John: Maybe the best part came the first time I played "Joy of My Life" for Julie.

This was before the album was out. Every year at our kids' school there was this thing called the Dads' Club Variety Show, and I would always do something for it. This year I had a plan, but nobody else knew about it. After we played a few songs, I turned to the other dads in the band and asked them to leave the stage. This was an outdoor amphitheater, at night.

I was there by myself with my Dobro, and I launched into "Joy of My Life"—for my wife, who was sitting in the audience and had no idea. I was really just singing it for her. It might've been a little shaky—I'm not the world's greatest musician. It was more from the heart. I got through it, and it didn't turn out too bad.

Julie: Tears were rolling down my face. I am not sure I took it all in at the time. I had two small boys and a daughter I was caring for. Not to mention the fact that a hundred people were staring at me! It was such a beautiful gift from John. Knowing everything that it took for him to make that record, I knew that this moment was a big one for him. And for us.

One lyric in particular from that song really hits my heart. "She says, 'Come lay beside me / I been waitin' since you left.'" That's a true story. John came home from making *Blue Moon Swamp*, it was very late and I knew he had given it his all, and I said those words to him. After all the roads we had traveled, those words rang so true. "I been waitin' since you left"—before *Blue Moon Swamp*, John had left himself behind. He couldn't get past that dark cloud. And now he was free.

CHAPTER 19

Why I Didn't Play at the Rock and Roll Hall of Fame, or *They Don't Care About the Music; Just Give 'Em the Money*

THERE IS ONE event that happened in the middle of the *Blue Moon Swamp* period that's a story unto itself: the induction of Creedence Clearwater Revival into the Rock and Roll Hall of Fame on January 12, 1993. I refused to play with Doug and Stu at the ceremony (Tom had died on September 6, 1990, which I'll also reflect on here). I played Creedence songs with Bruce Springsteen and Robbie Robertson instead.

Stu and Doug made a big stink about this and sold their case to the media—and at the same time acted like there was nothing more to the story. To the outside world, it just looked like I had snubbed them. Stu wrote a letter to the hall of fame, which was leaked to the *Los Angeles Times*. I responded to that, but my response was unclear, not definitive. I didn't give much detail. I didn't like saying something mean or one-sided, so I pulled back and spoke in general terms. Nobody had bothered to ask me in any depth. Was I just being a jerk, or had someone done something that made me feel this way?

I was confused by the reaction. I thought people would understand, but I guess I didn't explain it very well. That's sort of been a defect in the way I've talked about these conflicts.

Over the years, people had certainly gotten the idea that I had taken a stance with Saul Zaentz: "Yeah, John's angry. Yeah, Saul ripped John off." But they don't really know the absolute betrayal I endured. I didn't use that word until, at the insistence of my wife, I spent a little time in front of a shrink. When I told him what had happened with Saul and my bandmates, he told me, "Well, John, that's betrayal." The shrink gave me that word, and yes, that's exactly what it is: *betrayal*. Hopefully I can explain it once and for all, right here.

The very last time Creedence Clearwater Revival played together as a quartet was at Tom's wedding, on October 19, 1980. Playing the wedding was stressful. Don't get me wrong: I was happy that Tom was getting married, moving on with his life—even though at the time I was still pretty upset with Tom, and with Doug and Stu. I was there because Tom was my brother. There was a pretty big distance between us, but I knew that Tom would want us to play, so I did it. It wasn't great. It didn't really prove anything. Afterward, I felt like I'd compromised myself—that other people would look at this and say, "See? You're all together here! If John had any objections he should've stood up at the wedding and said, 'No, I won't play with you guys.'" Well, you don't do that at a wedding. That's not very nice or polite. Family sticks together.

So we weren't exactly pals throughout these years. From time to time, Tom or Doug or Stu would call up and kind of ask for a favor, and later I'd always regret that I did it. Because I would usually get poked in the eye after doing the favor. And then in June 1989, I was on my way to Bill Graham's house for my second meeting with Saul concerning the libel case and song ownership matters. I turned on the radio in the rental car and heard this Shell Oil advertisement. It was a promotional thing. If you bought five gallons of gas, for another dollar you could get this hits compilation album. It named a couple of the songs—I think the Four Tops was one of the artists—and right there, along with them, was "Proud Mary." I went, *"What?!"*

We didn't have many rights at all as Creedence, but one of them was approval (or disapproval) of compilation albums. The Beatles didn't appear on them, nor did Elvis. I thought they were tacky and lowered the stature of our band. This was very important to me: there was a specific clause in our 1969 contract that stated that we had the right to say no to that. And here was my song being peddled by a gas company on some schlocky cassette called *Cruisin' Classics*. Soon after this, other things began appearing—like some paint company used "Who'll Stop the Rain." ("Who will stop the rain? Our paint thinner will!")

I had to go face Saul at that moment, so I decided to deal with it later. Back home, I told my brother Bob to find out about it. He called up Doug Clifford, who pretended to know nothing about it. This went on for ten days. For a couple of weeks, it was a complete mystery. Finally Doug fessed up, and it was a whopper. My three bandmates, including my brother, had sold their group voting rights to Saul Zaentz.

As I've stated previously, we had decided from the very beginning of Creedence that everything got decided by way of a unanimous vote—not a majority vote, a *unanimous* vote. It was even written into our contract. Fantasy could not compile our songs with other artists without the approval of Creedence. This was something that we all owned together. It's our vote collectively; it isn't something I can give to somebody walking down the street—"Here, buddy, go vote in Creedence now!" It doesn't work that way.

Apparently Saul felt that if he *bought* three of the four votes, then he could do whatever he wanted. And behind my back, Tom, Doug, and Stu went along with the plan. It had happened in 1988, before the plagiarism trial started. Saul bought each member of the band—first Doug and Stu. They got $30,000 each—that's right, thirty pieces of silver. Tom got wind of this, and he wanted more money. He got $50,000. Now Saul was the majority vote of Creedence—even though we had all agreed that no matter what we did in the band, it had to be a unanimous vote. I don't even think this was legal, to sell such an intangible thing.

To me, the selling of the votes was the final betrayal. From that day in the eighth grade, in Mrs. Starck's class, right up until the moment I found out about this, I still thought of Creedence as a band—yes, the band broke up in 1972, but the music from the time that we created it was something we were still in together. I'd always think, *What is the best light that our band could be shown in?* I fought Saul on their behalf—a lot of times at my expense and not theirs, by the way.

I was so protective of Creedence. And I certainly couldn't and wouldn't suddenly concoct a secret plan with Saul in 1988 and say, "Hey, guess what? You don't have to pay those guys as artists anymore—just pay me. And they won't get a penny." That can't be done. Not by me, anyway—that would be immoral and wrong. But they sold out, the same way you'd sell out your country by selling atomic secrets to the Russians. Yeah, it was that big a deal to me. A band is a sacred thing. You don't betray that.

When I found out about the selling of the votes, I thought, *Wow, why was I protecting these guys? They certainly weren't protecting me.* And remember that this happened at the same time that I was meeting with Saul, trying to actually get a better royalty deal from Fantasy—not just for me, but for Doug and Stu and Tom.

This Shell Oil thing happened a matter of weeks after the *Exxon Valdez* disaster. The world was rightfully mad at these oil companies, and here my band had put us right in their back pocket. It was very distasteful to me. So I sent out a little group of packages, each containing an empty can of oil and a newspaper article about some oil tanker that had run afoul down in Southern California. Over the tanker picture I wrote the word "whore." I sent one package to each guy in the band and one each to Saul, Al Bendich, and Ralph Kaffel at Fantasy. In my cynical way, I put everybody on notice that I wasn't happy.

Sometime after that, Stu let it be known that he wanted to talk to me. He came to my office out in San Fernando, and a couple of nervous pleasantries were exchanged.

"Well, Stu, what's up?"

"I've done things to harm you," he said. "I've done things that are wrong, and I want to say I'm sorry about that. I apologize."

I was not in a conciliatory mood. I looked at him and said, "Sorry. Don't get it. Yeah, you've done some things to harm me. But you gotta go fix the things that you've done that are *still* harming me. You undo all that stuff—then maybe I'll listen."

And then I asked him, "How in the hell could you sell your vote to Saul? We were a band. We had a bond. I had your word of honor as a man. Sell your vote to *Saul?* How could you possibly do that?"

His response: "I just got tired of them asking me what to do with this song or that song—should it be in this movie or that movie? It wasn't gonna happen anyway. You'd just say no. Besides, I don't care what they do with the music—*just give me the money!*"

Those were the exact words he said. Just give me the money. *Just give me the money.*

People in a rock and roll band very much feel like it's them against the world. Your parents think you're wacky—"Why don't you get a real job?" The social structure thinks you're wacky— you're not earning any money and you look funny. All you have is a dream. You're like guys in a foxhole. You don't know what the future is, but those present are basically vowing, "Until the day I die, I'm in this thing with you." Way back in 1968 I had made an agreement with Tom, Doug, and Stu to be equal partners. I let them share in my songwriting money. At the time, I thought I was dealing with people who understood the responsibility of what we had. But to say "I don't care what they do with the music—just give me the money"?

I couldn't believe anybody would be so knuckleheaded.

I was disgusted. We certainly didn't have much to talk about after that. If you want to know why I wouldn't play with those guys at the Rock and Roll Hall of Fame, Stu said it right there: *I don't care what they do with the music—just give me the money.*

And I made that clear to the hall of fame when they called in late 1992. They said, "We are going to induct Creedence Clearwater Revival into the hall of fame. Would you perform with the other band members?" I said, "No." I had gone to every ceremony except one, so what I did tell them was that at the end, when everybody's onstage, jamming, if we all happen to be onstage, that's fine. I'm just not going to stand on a stage with those people, three in a row, play our songs, and be presented as a band— particularly because these guys just sold their rights in that band to my worst enemy. I also made it very clear that if I didn't play at all, that was fine too.

It wasn't like this hadn't happened before. After Bill Clinton was elected, they wanted Creedence to play the inauguration in January 1993, and I had rejected it. I said, "I'm not playing as a band with Creedence. I don't play with those guys. We will never play as a band again."

Prior to 1993, there had never been a ceremony where the actual inductees played their songs. When Bo Diddley and Jerry Lee and James Brown got inducted, they didn't perform at all. It just wasn't done that way. The year that Creedence got in was the first year that the inducted artists actually got up and performed. So this was a new concept. After I made it clear that I wasn't going to play with Stu and Doug, the hall of fame came back to me with another way of looking at it: they wanted the songs to be heard, so they proposed getting other people—including Bruce and Robbie.

I expected to have fun that night. But Stu and Doug were playing a role that they had concocted. Had I known they were going to pull that, I would have made a different speech. Instead, I sidestepped saying anything about group haggling and the chicanery that had gone on, and I talked about the great music we had made. The truth was, they had turned their backs on our group, dishonored the music, and sold out to Saul Zaentz, taking money and making a side deal that didn't include me.

I didn't want to get into that, but they acted to the public like they were victims, playing for sympathy! It was phony.

I had run into Doug and Stu the day of the ceremony, or perhaps the day before, in the very room where the inductions would be held. I wanted to be very clear about my intentions and their expectations. I told them, "Considering what you have done, I will not play with you. You guys went and joined with my worst enemy."

Stu said, "Well, we did kinda leave you twisting in the wind."

They knew this, but during the ceremony they still pretended to be shocked. As if they were pure as the driven snow.

Anyone who has ever been in a band knows how disgusting it is that these guys sold their voting rights to an outsider. They have shamed themselves forever. Nothing will ever change that.

If the fans were disappointed with what happened at the Rock and Roll Hall of Fame ceremony, I regret that. I'm very sorry about that. To the fans, all I can say is, things in the real world change. Particularly if things that are unpleasant happen between the members of a band, you've got to understand that they may not be happy to see each other again. But if you asked me a hundred more times, when the conditions were like this, I would do the same thing. I didn't—and don't—respect these people for what they have done.

The year before Creedence got in, the Yardbirds got inducted. I was there. That was funny. Jeff Beck is the world's greatest rock and roll guitar player, and of course he was in the Yardbirds. When it was his turn for his acceptance speech, he said, "They kicked me out [of the band]....Fuck them!" And that was that, ha ha. My mouth dropped open. And then my brain caught up with his words. That was absolutely right. What other emotion could he have? He stuck up for himself.

I had tried to reconcile with Tom long before he died. I'd think about Tommy and Jimmy Dorsey, how they had a feud for years and didn't speak, but they reunited, and their mother was so happy.

I wanted to do that with Tom for our mother. I mean, "How hard can this be?" That picture of the Dorseys was in my head: *The two brothers reconcile and their mother is so happy.* So I started a dialogue. I think I wrote him a letter—"It would be a shame not to do this for our mom." We talked on the phone at least once.

I said, "Tom, I think we should each write down all our issues, the things we think we're mad about. Write it all down, get it out in the open, and we'll talk about 'em."

I'm trying to do this the right way. Face it. Deal with reality.

So I write a letter. The very first thing I say is, "Number one, Tom, you sued me"—referring to the lawsuit that he and Doug and Stu initiated against me over the songwriting royalties in the Canadian bank during the Castle Bank era. "Two, you sided with Saul." And so forth. There were probably about eight points on my list.

I get a letter back and he says, *"No! I didn't sue you."* Tom's reasoning for why I couldn't say that he sued me was the fact that on the morning of the Castle Bank trial, he walked up to my attorney and said, "I'm not suing John *anymore.*" That was in 1983. But I'd already had to deal with the lawsuit since 1978! That meant going to depositions, meeting with and paying my attorney to prepare a defense, and dealing with all the anxiety that goes with the legal system. Many thousands of dollars later, Tom decided to drop the lawsuit. In his mind that meant he didn't sue me.

So I sent him the cover page of the lawsuit filing, which said "Tom Fogerty vs. John Fogerty." I don't think we got any further than that. Unfortunately, our mom passed away.

I'd still get crazy letters. When Saul sued me over "Zanz Kant Danz," Tom wrote to me, taking Saul's side and ranting about how the "Kant" in the song's title stood for Burt Kanter, one of the Castle Bank heavies. He ended the letter, "Saul and I will win."

In the late eighties, Doug was proposing that Creedence re-form even though Tom was very sick. (The world didn't know that he had AIDS then, and I sure wasn't at liberty to be talking about it. It was family business. Until his son, Jeff, started talking about it openly after Tom passed, I wasn't going to break that trust.) All I could think was, *Oh, great—Doug and Stu want to drag Tom around the world in a wheelchair.*

I thought they really wanted to do this for themselves. It was bizarre and disgusting to me. Immediately you get cynical—"Okay, c'mon: what's the angle here?" Maybe I'm just sticking up for my brother. I wouldn't think he'd want to be carted around in a wheelchair for some concert.

I went to see Tom a couple of times in 1990, shortly before he died. He was very thin and fragile-looking. Always wearing sunglasses, even indoors. And still kind of detached, in that way he had been, going all the way back to 1969 or 1970. After I won the plagiarism trial, I ran into Tom. He said, "Congrats on the trial." Like it was a science project. He had become so aloof, maddeningly detached.

Even the very last time I saw Tom, he told me, "Saul's my best friend. I can count on him."* He came out with that out of the blue. Tom forced you to suspend reality. His reasoning wasn't based on the laws of the universe, like gravity and how light travels. You had to abandon logic to have a conversation with him. We just made small talk, like two old-timers at the country store watching the log burn: "Yep, it's gonna be a tough winter, don't you think? The leaves need to be raked..."

I'm not good at BS. I see no point. Time is precious to me. But what could I say? He was fragile, dying. So I was the good soldier, the dutiful brother.

Tom passed away on September 6, 1990. I was sad that life had been taken from Tom. And that sadness was mixed up with all the other emotions. I was pissed that Saul had mangled our relationship, because he certainly messed it up. Tom was an unwitting pawn. But all that sure doesn't mean anything wherever Tom is now. I used to say, "I can't wait. I'll meet him again. I'll yell at him. We'll have a showdown in space."

But I've forgiven Tom.† I'm not angry anymore. Tom may have been motivated to get money for his family because he was dying.

---

* Saul Zaentz did not attend Tom's funeral. So much for being Tom's "best friend."

† Apparently sometime recently, Doug read in the paper that I'd said I'd forgiven Tom. "Forgiven him for what?" was Doug's response. Oh, I dunno, Doug. Maybe for calling the guy who stole *our* life savings his "best friend." Doug is clueless.

I can see how that would hinder a person's judgment. I don't carry that around, and I think that's important to say. I love my brother. I sure loved the old family days, the way we were as kids. I don't have to chew on a bunch of perceived infractions from the dim past that don't affect anything anymore. It's resolved, and somehow Tom knows it's all right, wherever he is.

In 1995, Stu and Doug formed an outfit called Creedence Clearwater Revisited to go out and play my songs on the oldies circuit. You can probably guess how I felt about this. Just imagine: you're driving down the road one day, and you see a sign next to the Walmart—"Tonight! One night only: the *Beatles!*" Yeah, right. You know something is wack. Then you drive a little further down the road and you see a Kmart, and the sign says, "Tonight: Creedence!" Sadly, that could actually be true.

I never thought we'd be a K-tel compilation band. Acting like one-hit wonders, so desperate in their old age that they've got to get together and fool the public into thinking this thing is somehow the remnants of Creedence Clearwater Revival. Which it's not. Man, I never intended to be in a band that turned into *that*.

As I've explained, we even talked about it specifically. We had agreed long ago that any version of our group that called itself Creedence Clearwater Revival would have to include all of us, or else it just couldn't be.

How did this happen? It turns out that Stu and Doug had pounced on Trisha, Tom's widow, a couple of years after he died and gotten her to sign over her well-wishes—not her vote, because Tom had already sold *that*. I'm going, "Well, wait a minute. They sold all their votes to Saul, so shouldn't it be up to him?" I can't tell you how disgusted I am with Doug and Stu. You've got to be a pretty slimy, sneaky person to do that. And I'm pretty disappointed in her for signing it away.

Why and how was that ever allowed? People say, "John, you oughta sue them!" At first I took it to court. To my way of thinking, these guys were trying to rip off the public and confuse them. I won, and then it went to a higher court and they reversed the decision. I thought it was wacky. I daresay judges who actually understand what rock and roll bands are about are few and far between. Stu and Doug had a letter from Trisha giving Tom's vote to them; it gave them a majority, and in business a majority vote wins. But we're not IBM; we're four guys who made a vow, a pact. Try explaining that to a judge. And then there was that feeling of, "There's John again. This guy does nothing but file lawsuits."

Finally, around 2000, I thought, *Why is it my job to make sure there is truth in advertising, and purity in rock and roll? Why am I the guy who's got to go spend the rest of my life battling this crap so that this stupid charade that calls itself Creedence Clearwater Revisited won't be allowed to foist its phoniness on an unsuspecting public? This can't be my job anymore.* Instead, I worked out a way to charge them a royalty, but these two guys are so devious that they've refused to pay that—and it was a very tiny amount, let me tell you.

And right now they are suing me because I've advertised the fact that I'm doing Creedence songs when I present an album like *Green River* in concert. The distinction? I don't pretend that I'm Creedence: I say I'm going to play some Creedence music (all of which was written by me). I wouldn't bat an eye if Stu and Doug decided to tour as "Stu and Doug."

I hope it'll all get sorted out at some point. I just hope that people don't go to see them expecting something good. There is an old truth in the world, I don't know who said it first, Plato or Socrates: When you have no taste, you can do anything.

Reporters always ask me if Creedence will ever reunite. A few years ago, someone asked again, and I was surprised that I didn't have my usual reaction, which is not until hell freezes over. But

I'm not angry anymore. So my answer was this: while it isn't something I'm actively trying to make happen, maybe there's some situation where it *could* happen. I don't know.

This of course got back to Stu and Doug, and their reaction was something to the effect of, "We would never have a reunion, it's too late, and besides, we have Creedence Clearwater Revisited and we're doing so well. Why would we want John in our band?" Oy.

I guess they're still angry. In early December of 2014, just as I was finishing this book, I learned that I was being sued by Stu and Doug over trademark issues. This came right after I'd done a tour of Canada focused on all the songs I wrote for Creedence in 1969. Unlike those guys, though, I didn't claim to be some version of Creedence; I was just doing the songs I'd created.

Y'know how it is when people act overly paranoid, and you realize they don't have much?

I could get into all the details, but you've read enough about this stuff already. I won't inflict it upon you again. The important thing to understand is that this time, it didn't really get to me. In the past, the people around me didn't want to deal with this stuff. I had to fight it by myself. Now I have so much support from Julie. She just rolled up her sleeves and got into it. This time I wasn't alone.

CHAPTER 20

Revival

WE LIVED IN Nashville for about a year, from the summer of 1999 to the summer of 2000. Ricky Skaggs was doing a tribute to Bill Monroe, and he asked me to join him on "Blue Moon of Kentucky." What a great experience! We recorded at Ricky's studio with his band and the legendary steel player Kayton Roberts! As if that wasn't enough, I also got a guitar lesson from Ricky. Later, I had a private lesson with his incredible guitar player, Clay Hess.

On another day that could only happen in Nashville, I was going into a Starbucks on Franklin Road, and who do I meet but Randy Scruggs coming out the same door? Turns out he's doing a tribute to his dad, Earl Scruggs, and asks if I would like to join in. "Sure," I say, "but you gotta give me a guitar lesson." We arranged for the lesson to be on a different day than the recording session, and that was some great instruction. The session itself was wonderful. Earl and Randy were there, along with Jerry Douglas on Dobro, Chad Cromwell on drums, Glenn Worf on upright bass, and Glen Duncan on fiddle.

During a break in the session, I had tried to impress upon Julie that even though Earl was now in his eighties there was a time when his playing "would rip your head off." After the session Randy invited Julie and me to come over to Earl's house for a little visit. Of course, Earl is the inventor of "Scruggs style" banjo picking—a revolutionary leap in the world of acoustic music. So at some point I asked him to tell me about the beginning of it. He said he had discovered the technique as a boy and was practicing to get it perfected when he was twelve years old. He was chomping at the bit to show his older brother, who was married and lived about a mile away. It was his brother's custom to walk over to Earl's house on Saturdays. So one Saturday when he was ready, Earl was outside with his banjo waiting for his brother to come walking down the road. (As a musician I'm relishing the idea that his brother is going to be the first person in history to hear this mind-boggling technique.) I said, "Well, Earl, did you show off?" And he says, "I hit him with both barrels!"

One day in early 2000 I had an electrifying thought. I realized that I was living in the midst of some of the greatest guitar players on earth. I was dying to figure out a way that I could somehow get a peek into this very high level of musicianship. I called my friend Joe Glaser. Joe is a world-class luthier and all-around guitar doctor. He had worked on some of my guitars, but more important he was a guru to all the guitar heavyweights in town. I talked to Joe about wanting to get really good, especially on Telecaster-style guitar. What happened next was pretty darn cool....Joe arranged for me to get lessons with some incredible guitar players, and the experience was amazing! I want to thank these guys who were so generous with their time and their knowledge:

Bill Hullett, Ray Flacke, Jimmy Olander, Tom Hemby.

Thank you, fellas. It is still much appreciated.

It was years before I could play the things they showed me...

Julie: John is a very simple man. He isn't about fanfare or celebrity. Sometimes he can be a bit quiet. Some might think he's withdrawn. Not really, though. He would be happy to play music on his porch with his family beside him, and never step outside of that world.

John doesn't use a cell phone much. It took him forever to learn how to read a text. He doesn't answer a door, or a phone. Although this can be annoying at times, I like that guy. It's pure, wholesome, and just plain simple. He is truly happy that way. Sometimes we all chuckle at Dad, but we get it.

I wasn't really involved in John's career. I was the mom. Then slowly I ended up taking more responsibility because I could see that he needed help. It just evolved into the big job. Now I'm trying to get out of it! I'm not his manager. I'm just helping my husband and making sure everything is okay. I enjoy making fun opportunities for John. He can manage himself. But he does need someone to prod him along a little bit.

John: Among other things, there were financial shenanigans going on with lawyers, and Julie got to the bottom of it. I began to respect Julie's counsel so much that she became my manager. She doesn't like me to say that. Very late in life I had finally tried to have a manager, and it didn't work out. I'd be talking to Julie—"Go call up X and get him to do such and such"—and then one day I just looked at her and said, "Let's cut out the middleman." But what I really meant to say was: Let's keep the middleman (Julie) and fire X (the manager).

Having Julie in my corner has affected my life in so many ways. I've really been working hard on getting better as a guitar player for close to twenty years now. It was something I'd always wanted, but I'd stopped going after it long ago. I didn't have the confidence, the self-assurance. You don't make long-term plans when you're not quite certain if you're going to be around very long.

Committing to something like that is huge. Julie and I—*we make plans*. I like living life that way. I know that "Yes, I can work on it today, and I can work on it a year from now." It's not going to get pulled away from me. My life isn't suddenly going to be in a suitcase on its way to Singapore—or Sing Sing. I'm a routine kind of guy. Julie says things like, "John eats the same granola every day for seven years, and then he changes to oatmeal." I like routine. That doesn't mean I *get* routine! I'm chasing her all the time, running around and trying to figure her out. It is far from boring.

We have always had an incredible relationship. So what is the secret to that? A wise man said it this way, and I really agree: equal parts lust and respect. We have a very happy and healthy love life. The way I would put it is: "I envy no man."

Julie: I drive him crazy. John moves like a turtle sometimes. I've gotten him to do so much more than he would ever do on his own. I'm the one who can nudge him off the porch to hit the road, attend some dreaded awards show, make an album, or even write a book. He needs to be out there. I'm working on him all the time. Sometimes I have to use "You are *doin' it!*" in a loving way. John is not one to "just wing it." It's just not him. He's very particular and knows exactly what he wants. We are pretty connected and I know what he needs. We won't do anything we aren't 100 percent committed to.

What do I do? Well, everything. I mean everything. The set list, John's wardrobe, hiring personnel, booking the tour, working out offers, coordinating John's schedule, doing artwork, doing ad mats, coming up with album titles like *Revival* or *The Long Road Home* for the greatest hits compilation–live DVD. Those titles are all personal. The truth? I even iron John's clothes before he heads onstage. Yep, the plaid flannels. The crew gets a big kick out of that. I'm onstage making sure the sound's good and the show is running the way it should, and that John knows I'm right there beside him. If something goes wrong, he'll come right over and tell me. I'm just there to push away the clouds so the star can shine.

After *Blue Moon Swamp* was done, John was willing to start touring again, but there were many things to learn. There was a lot of waste. We struggled to find the right crew, and there were many shows in the beginning that I didn't think he'd get through. But John brought all of us with him. John wouldn't tour without me—and I couldn't leave the kids, so he brought the whole family.

We had three kids twelve and under when we started, and then Kelsy came in 2001, which made four. Two of which were rambunctious boys one year apart! I still don't know how I did it. I think we had thirteen suitcases. On one European tour, we were in Frankfurt, and one of our sons decided to pack his toy gun in a carry-on. We didn't know it was there and went through security. Well, you can imagine the terror on the faces of the security guards. John almost ran away and let me deal with it—thanks, John! We got scolded pretty bad.

Many times after the show, we'd drive to the next town to break up the travel time. John would do a two-hour sound check, and then the show, and we'd get on the bus and arrive at the next hotel in the wee hours of the morning. John would pick up sound-asleep Kelsy and carry her into our hotel room. His energy amazed me. The truth is, we were a family on the road. Not your typical rock star life, I am sure. We felt we could have it all: our marriage, our kids, and John's career, all in that order. So when he jumps on the bus after a show, he has his family at his side. He knows we climbed over the mountain (one step at a time, maybe), and we're okay.

I don't think John realized the impact that his old songs had on the audience, what those folks had missed hearing. I would see grown men high-fiving each other and crying. I was proud of my husband, that he was back out there. So happy and excited for him.

John: I am oh so lucky to be here in the world at this time in my life, and to have fans loving songs that I wrote forty-five years ago and still smiling when they look up at me at a concert, singing the words. I probably don't deserve that, being a guy who's been so difficult and hard to find. I recognize that my long, dark age had to have been difficult and mystifying to normal people. Lord knows it was for me! To have survived long enough to get happy and healthy again, to still be able to enjoy their company....In some secret way, that's why I'm working so hard, putting so much effort into being a guitar player. I'm a fan myself of many artists, and I realize how precious that is. You hate when something goes wrong, or their last album didn't sound so good, but you stay with them and love them from afar. I'm lucky that I have those fans who have stuck with me from the beginning. It's what I dreamed of as a little boy. You don't always get to have your dream come true. To those fans I say, "God bless you."

Déjà Vu All Over Again came out in 2004. The drummer played to a click track. My engineer convinced me to do that, even though I'd learned not to do that with *Blue Moon Swamp*. It robbed some of the feel of *Déjà Vu*. In fact, around the year 2000, I got a Pro Tools rig, and after *Déjà Vu* I actually thought about making *another* one-man-band album—with a drum machine. If you're competitive, you get obsessed and try to beat something. Even though I'd already learned my lesson, I spent way too much time on this stuff. I just don't think in my lifetime a machine is going to sound like a human.

The title song "Déjà Vu (All Over Again)" was written about the Iraq War.

As usual, the rich white guys were not happy: here's this place over in the Middle East loaded with oil, and here's this bad guy, Saddam Hussein, who doesn't do everything we tell him to do, so hey, we have to get rid of him. Which is what they always do— Noriega, the Shah of Iran, blah, blah, blah. Saddam's thumbing his nose at America, and lo and behold, you start hearing talk on the radio about invading Iraq. I thought, *We're too smart, aren't we? We've all heard this stuff before. We're not going to let this happen again.*

I was renting a house where I kept all my recording and writing stuff, and I was driving over there one morning, like I did every day. I get out of the car, my keys in my hand, and walk to the front door, just like I always do. I'm actually on a mission that day: I've commissioned myself to write a swamp rock song. So I put the key in the lock and I hear this song in my head—the melody was there, I think some words were there. All I know is, the sound of it was the saddest thing I've ever heard in my life. It had this atmosphere, like echo. It was just sad, sad, sad.

I push that away. In my brain I remember I'm here to write a swamp rock song, so I close the door and drop the keys on the table. It happens again.

Did you hear them talkin' 'bout it on the radio...

Now I realize it's calling me. I had tried to deflect it, but now I realize it's one of those times. Like *other* times. But never quite like this.

Somebody really wanted me to hear this. That's how it felt. Somehow even my bumbling morning brain realized that I was receiving. I wasn't creating. It was simply, "Your radio station's picking this up. We're sending this to you. Please don't push this away."

So I ignored my normal routine. Got my acoustic guitar, found the chord, and just followed it.

It's like déjà vu. What? *It's like déjà vu.*

And the rhythm to complete it was right if I said "All over again." I know that's a Yogi Berra line. But I go past that. And then came,

Day after day I hear the voices rising
Started with a whisper like it did before

I think, *Oh shit, that's what this is about? Vietnam?* Because the new war hadn't happened yet. So I stood there keeping the guitar on me for maybe an hour and a half. I didn't want the inspiration to slide away. I was doing it over and over so I could remember it, and then I finally wrote it down. I didn't have it all, but I had the chorus and the first verse before I ever put the guitar down.

This was clearly just tuning in. I wasn't cleverly crafting a song. It took my breath away — "Where did I just go? What happened here?" I wasn't there to write an important song. I wasn't even in the mood to be important. I hadn't been important in a while. I'd been a silly rock and roll guy. And now I was writing about something I felt very deeply about. I can't even tell you what that feels like. It had really never ever happened like that before. Or since.

When I got to the part about "stumblin' across Big Muddy," I was pretty damn happy. That's a reference to a Pete Seeger song. I wasn't stealing from Pete — for all I knew he was sending it to me. Artistically, "Déjà Vu (All Over Again)" is one of the highest moments of my life. Commercially, it probably didn't even make a dent, ha ha.

For the next two years I sang that song on the road. At some point I started doing it acoustically in my show, and I wish I had recorded it that way for the album. Because the song doesn't need all the stuff that's on the record.

Trying to get the populace upset about anything these days is a challenge. The times were a lot different when I was young. Things were more visible and we were a lot noisier then.

But there have been times when I've done "Déjà Vu (All Over Again)" and people in my audience have booed. People who came to see *me*. I thought most of the people who come to see me are a little on my side politically—I take it they've heard my other songs. I guess these folks were my fans, and I grew up thinking that booing was a bad thing. So I felt it the way it was intended: critically.

That particular summer, I was touring with Willie Nelson. (Willie Nelson is an amazing musical presence: absolutely unique and hugely influential on all of us who came after. I was thrilled that my family got to meet him when we both performed for the veterans in Washington, DC, during the October 2014 concert that I describe in the introduction to this book.) We were playing at some casino, and I was sitting on the bus with Willie and his sister, Bobbie. One of them said, "Are you doing 'Déjà Vu'?"

I said, "I don't know if a casino is the right place..." I'm thinking alcohol, drunks, cigars, gambling—the whole thing. To me it just seemed atmospherically incorrect.

And Willie said, "You should sing that song"—his voice got extra deep—"*everywhere.*"

I thought, *Yeah...you're right. They're human beings; they've gotta hear this. I'm sorry if for three minutes it's a little uncomfortable.* So I kept doing it.

And long after feeling embarrassed, I felt glad that those boos had been there.

When we started to go into Iraq after 9/11, it was a confusing time in our country. I think we all may have learned a lot since then. I'd love to see if those people who booed me then have changed their minds, because a lot of the smoke has cleared and I think more of us see the motives. I would like to hear from some of those people who felt that strongly, who thought I was singing against the soldiers who were doing that impossible mission. Obviously I'm not. I have respect and praise for those kids. I'm talking about the policy. Greedy corporations trying to make a lot of money off our suffering.

I have the feeling I'll be singing that song again.

Julie: Steve Bing had been reaching out to John for a couple of years to play on this Jerry Lee Lewis album. He just kept at it, and finally he flew out to meet us in this small town in Iowa, where John was performing, and recorded John's part. He mentioned that he'd been to see the remake of *The Manchurian Candidate* and heard "Fortunate Son." We explained that John had nothing to do with it, that because of Saul Zaentz and Fantasy, he had no input into the use of his songs. Steve thought that was terrible. Norman Lear's company Concord Music Group had bought Fantasy. Steve said, "Norman Lear? He's my buddy. I'm calling him right now." He did, and told Norman that he needed to meet with John.

We went to the Concord offices, spent a couple of hours with Norman, and eventually made an agreement to do an album for them. John told about how he had to sign away his artist royalties in order to get out of the contract with Fantasy. Norman Lear and his colleague Hal Gaba felt that was wrong and said, "First thing we want to do is reinstate your artist royalties."

So we walked away feeling pretty good. That was a nice gesture. After all, it was incredibly wrong that John did not get paid for all those Creedence albums.

We start negotiating the contract, we're just about ready to sign, everything's set to go, and literally two days before, our lawyer John Branca calls and says, "I'm really sad to tell you this, guys. Concord's written a letter and now they're saying they're only reinstating John's artist royalties for the length of his contract with them. I'm going back to them to tell them the deal is off, and how dare they do this to John Fogerty."

Long story short, John Branca called Concord and let loose. He was furious that they were putting John through this. In the end they did the right thing. I think they had good intentions, and then the money people and the lawyers got in the way. I have to thank Concord, because they pay the royalties—and that's the right thing to do.

If there is one thing I still hope for, it is that John Fogerty will be able to own his songs again. That they are put in the hands of the author who wrote them. They need to come home. "Someday may come," and I will never give up hope. When that day comes, oh boy, get ready for the biggest celebration ever.

John: For my 2004 album, *Déjà Vu All Over Again,* I wanted to write a song for my daughter Kelsy. I started it the day she was born. I had this idea: "I Will Walk with You," meaning, "I'm going to be with you every step of the way." Kind of a daddy's promise to take care of his baby. It's a pretty serious thing to me.

The doofus in me started writing some sort of big arena-rock ballad. At that point you're not singing to a little girl; you're singing to some *big* girl in a Mötley Crüe video. So I left the song alone for a while.

Before Kelsy was born, I'd get up early and practice my acoustic guitar in her room. Then, once she arrived, we had a little tub in there so Julie could give her a bath. So one day she's in there giving Kelsy a bath, I'm playing the acoustic guitar, watching the two of them. I'm looking right over the headstock of the guitar. And it dawns on me: this should be an acoustic number. I don't do a lot of those. From then on, I knew what to do. It sure took a while—2001 to 2004.

Kelsy is musical. Maybe she'll grow up to be a rocket scientist, but music is what she really loves right now. We talk about music in the car. I take Kelsy to school and back, so we have a lot of time to listen and talk about it. Basically, that means listening to Taylor Swift, because Kelsy is a big fan. I've even done Taylor's song "Mean" with Kelsy onstage.

We went to see Taylor in Los Angeles and scored a couple of

backstage passes. It was maybe one day before the event, and Kelsy says, "Dad, do you think you can bring my guitar to the meet and greet for Taylor to sign?" You have to understand: this is my little girl. I will walk through the fires of hell in a gasoline suit for my little girl.

But I'm thinking, *Yeah, but when we get to security, they're gonna think it's a machine gun. And maybe Taylor will feel insulted—maybe she's not supposed to sign stuff like that.* But we made some calls and Taylor graciously signed it after the concert. That's pretty doggone special, for both of us.

I was so impressed with the instrumentation on Taylor's records that I looked up Nathan Chapman, the producer of her early albums, and had him play mandolin on my version of "Wrote a Song for Everyone" that I recorded with Miranda Lambert. I'm very impressed with Taylor. As Kelsy hears me say all the time, "So many great songs, so many great songs."

In an indirect way, I have to thank the Wiggles, the Australian band known for their kids' TV show, for three of the songs on my 2007 album, *Revival*. I had recorded "Rockin' Santa!" with them. That was as much for me as it was for Kelsy. We'd listen to the Wiggles in the car all the time. What a hoot: one moment they're doing a mod song, the next they're surfers or doing some sort of French cabaret chanteuse number. Outstanding.

The Wiggles gave me a guitar made by Maton, an Australian company. Over the years, Australia's become a very familiar and fond touchstone in the life of the Fogerty family. We've toured there and like to cruise around. So I visited the Maton facility down under and had them make me a guitar, a hollow body electric guitar with little sound holes.

Working on songs for *Revival*, I had about four guitars sitting in my room, but the one that was speaking to me was the Maton.

I was in a certain kind of mood, and that kind of melody I associate with Southern music came through me. "Proud Mary" is from that place. There's a certain shuffle to the melody, like Allen Toussaint's "Southern Nights." I'm playing the Maton and out comes "Don't You Wish It Was True." I started strumming those chords that same sort of lilting way. When you write a new song and it seems to be a fresh, defined idea—not just "I love you, moon, June, spoon"—you really feel good about it.

A few days later, I was trying to get into a song and looked around my room and over at that guitar. I picked it up and almost immediately wrote "Broken Down Cowboy." The next time I picked it up, out came "Gunslinger." Basically, I picked up the guitar three times and out came three songs. Three good songs. Three for three. I actually sent Maton a note: "Did you guys know you built a lot of really good songs in your guitars?"

Writing "Broken Down Cowboy," I saw that guy instantly—kind of a rawboned, lanky guy sitting in a cantina at a little round table. He's got shot glasses of tequila, a cigarette, a deck of cards, and he's playing solitaire. He's wearing a straw cowboy hat, what used to be a nice cowboy shirt, kind of frumpy jeans, boots. Has that leathered, weary look to his face, fifty or sixty years old. I could just see it. And eventually I realized it was me—the *old* me. "Saddlebags full of pain / Carries 'em around just like a middle name." I was writing the song and almost breaking down. I literally had tears in my eyes—"Fuck, this is good shit. This is *me*."

My brain was just racing to play it for Julie. I was beside myself. But real life intervened—I had to go do other stuff, and that opportunity slipped away. It wasn't until about a month later that we were at a rehearsal place and I was teaching the song to the band. Julie comes walking in with her girlfriend. I didn't know she was there at first. She just stopped dead in her tracks. I saw her and could hardly finish the song—I was bawling and trying to sing. Julie realized this was kind of for her, because it's about me. And us.

Jeez, that was quite an experience. Some healing took place there because I was releasing that pain — owning it, writing about it. "If I was a gamblin' man / Never would've let you play your hand / With a broken down cowboy like me."

In 2009, I made my second Blue Ridge Rangers album, *The Blue Ridge Rangers Rides Again*. The big difference, of course, is, you guessed it: on the first one I played everything myself; on the second one I had *a band*. On *Rides Again*, there's a lot of really great playing, some superlative musicianship. Not on the first, because it's me overdubbing everything. The first one is more rock and roll, the second one's a bit more hillbilly, honky-tonk. On *Rides Again*, instead of songs I knew from my childhood, I just chose songs that I love, like John Denver's "Back Home Again."

I had been at the very first Farm Aid doing a press interview when suddenly I heard John Denver singing "Back Home Again." I didn't even know he was on the bill. I'm afraid I wasn't so polite — I bolted from that interview and ran a quarter mile to the stage just to hear him do that song. I know that at times John Denver sounds kind of sappy — to me too — but after you let it all settle down, the really great songs go beyond any genre. It's amazing how authoritative, how complete, how powerful he is. All from just standing there strumming a guitar. I think of him as way up on the mountain, commercially and artistically. Another song I did on *Rides Again* is John Prine's "Paradise." I learned that one from John Denver's cover. That's the version I love. Both of these songs remind me of my Troy, Oregon, days and the logging trucks coming down the switchback, their air brakes echoing across the valley.

Doing "When Will I Be Loved" with Bruce Springsteen was fun. I hadn't really checked in with Bruce before I recorded the track, and I put it in the key of D. I have a fairly high voice, and that song's in a place that's hard even for me. I was singing the melody, and the harmony was above that, so it was high for Bruce too. He's a trouper, though, and we got it. When Bruce sings hard, with an edge, it's really good — "Born in the USA."

Bruce is my friend. A really great guy. It might surprise some people, but Bruce is a pretty self-deprecating guy. We were onstage together at Hyde Park and I called him "the greatest American rocker of all time." Off mic, he said, "Whoa! What an introduction!" I think he was a little embarrassed. But if you think about the number of years and amount of impact, yes, some candles have burned brighter for a short period, like Elvis. But Bruce is still going strong. I hope to do more things with Bruce. It's always really exciting and really good. And fun!

Julie: I am always bugging Bruce to make music with John. I think it would be great if they toured together, but Bruce doesn't tour with anybody. He always seems to chuckle when he sees me. I think he knows it's coming — "Oh no, Julie Fogerty again!" When we were set to play the New Orleans Jazz Fest last year, Bruce was playing the night before. I told John to call him up and suggest that they play a couple of songs together, but John is too shy. He never wants to intrude on anyone's show. So I had John's brother Bob call and set it up. John's so cute. When I told him that Bruce said yes, he said, "I have to get my show together. I don't think there's time!" I said, "Don't worry. You're doin' it. You have to." He didn't say another word. Smart man. John worries too much about perfection sometimes. I try and have him be in the moment, unrehearsed and wonderfully him.

CHAPTER 21

Wrote a Song for Everyone

THE IDEA CAME from Miss Julie. We were sitting together, having family time. Julie has these really intuitive, cool ideas—I'm kind of used to it now. She plugs into these mystical concepts. In some ways Julie is far more plugged into the mojo-voodoo thing than I am. She said to me, "Why don't you get a bunch of the people you love and sing your songs?"

I thought, *Wow, I can call up people that I don't really know, like Brad Paisley, and say, "Hey, man, I have admired your work. I'm going to make this album of my songs. Would you like to join me?"* That sounded like Christmas to me, so I jumped right in with both feet.

The first priority was to get the artists on board. Scheduling was the hardest part. Once they said yes, I'd say, "Okay, pick the song you'd like to do." I wanted the artist to take some possession of this idea. And then I'd say, "I want you to think about an arrangement or a vision that you have that makes it personal to you." I didn't want them to just copy what I'd done years before. I wanted it to be a collaboration.

And most importantly, I wanted to be in the same room with

each artist recording my song. That may sound basic, but in this digital world, a lot of these "duet" albums are made by musicians sending files to each other through the ether. My psyche just cringes at that whole idea. I wanted to make music, and music is really made between two or more souls sitting there in the same room and vibing off of each other. And I sure didn't want to call my album *Duets*.

"Wrote a Song for Everyone," with me and Miranda Lambert, was the first thing that we actually recorded for this album. Several years ago, I felt that I had discovered Miranda Lambert. I heard this wonderful voice one night on my little radio that I sometimes fall asleep with. She's singing this incredible song, "More Like Her," and I thought I was the only one in the world who knew this magical artist. About the third time I heard the song on the radio, I learned her name: Miranda Lambert. Now I'm off—I went online, found the song, made my own CD of it, and listened to it in my car over and over. I'd just get goose bumps when I heard her sing. It was like some exotic food—I had to have it again and again. I went back online, all ready to tell people about this song...jeez, I'm such a geek. I learned that eight months before, she'd won the album of the year. The whole world knew about Miranda—except me.

Eventually I met her at the Academy of Country Music Awards show in 2010. Later I asked her to be on my album—I think her exact answer was, "Hell, yes." Julie enters this story again. She thought "Wrote a Song for Everyone" would be a really cool vehicle between a man and a woman. I hadn't really pictured it that way.

She is such a trouper, Miranda. She sang every single take that we did with the band, and then all her vocal tracks, from which we made a complete master. We were listening together for her best performance, and as we got to where the middle instrumental solo would be, she blurted out what she thought was needed: "A face-melting guitar solo!" It was such a jolt to me. I wasn't sure if she was joking. I never really thought of a country record having a face-melting solo. When I think of face-melting, I think of Van Halen, big hair, and spandex. I had envisioned more of a hippie guitar solo for the song. I could almost smell the patchouli oil and see the flower children twirling in their rainbow dresses and beads.

Later on, I was finishing the song, trying to do my hippie guitar solo. Miranda's vocal was so great—she's just killer. I kept thinking to myself, *Oh man, I've got to live up to that. This solo has got to be just as good. I can't lame out and just throw something on there.* I could just sense that what I was doing didn't measure up. And Miranda's words keep coming back to me: a face-melting guitar solo.

I thought of Tom Morello because I'd seen him with Bruce at Madison Square Garden. And for a nanosecond I thought, *Yeah, I'll play something like Tom Morello.* Then the real guy in me took over—"No, I'm going to *call* Tom." I did, and he said, "Where? When?"

We met in the studio. He plugged in his very simple, direct rock and roll rig: an amp, one little special pedal that he uses, a speaker box with old Greenback speakers in it. I was still sitting there in the studio, didn't even have my headphones on, and he was already playing solos. I thought, *Whoa, I better get back there behind the glass.*

Tom says, "Give me some direction."

I said, "Soaring!" And then I added, "Heroic!"

Tom did it a few times and was basically done. He stayed for the whole editing process. He wanted to hear it all together—y'know, "What are you going to do with me? Will I recognize myself?" These were true artists I was working with, people with passion. They really care. And when it was done, Tom looked at me and said, "John, I think that sounds heroic."

I'm so proud of the result. It may be a little unusual for Tom and Miranda compared to their other records. Me, I don't think it's unusual at all. Whenever I play that track for people, I turn to them and say, "This is why I did this album in the first place."

I had been hearing about My Morning Jacket for some time, and I knew there was substance to their music—it wasn't just some flavor of the month. They wanted to do "Long as I Can See the Light" and record it in Nashville. I must say, this was kind of an out-on-the-edge session. Before a session I would usually discuss the specifics of the recording with my engineer, Kevin Harp, who did a great job on the project. In this case, I had been touring and hadn't connected with Kevin, so when I arrived in Nashville, nothing had been set up. All the equipment was just sitting on the floor. I'm used to having things more pinned down.

Then, when the band started to play, I thought, *Uh-oh*. It was a little vague-sounding. I had to remind myself that that's what jam bands do. I decided to be the wise, old professor looking in the mirror: "Well, this is exactly what you set up. This is what you wanted. So don't go ruining it now by saying something that screws it all up." I had been telling everybody on the project, "Don't be me. Be you."

The clock was ticking. I was hearing sounds that I wasn't used to, seeing things that seemed precarious, and as you might guess, I am a bit of a control freak. What that really all means is, My Morning Jacket was out of my comfort zone. My first instinct was to go, "Uh-oh, we better change this." I had to really step on my tongue and tell myself to shut up.

I was watching, waiting, learning. And it turned out so great— and so different from what I would've done. Jim James plays guitar in a really different way. His style is so angular and jagged. The track ended up being great, really cosmic. I can't really take any credit artistically, other than as the patient parent. I have to admit that I could have messed that all up, turned it into just a studio musician sort of thing. Instead, they made a great record, and I learned a lot about artistic expression.

I love Bob Seger's voice. "Night Moves" killed me, as have all the records he's made since "Katmandu"—I just thought, *Wow, that man is kicking it!* He's got one of the greatest voices in rock and roll history, and I knew I wanted to have that on my record. So I called him up. It turned out he likes my music. Singers tend to collect other singers, so fortunately for me, he liked my voice. In the eighties, Bob recorded a live version of "Fortunate Son," and when I heard it, I thought Fantasy Records had gone and snuck out some bootleg version of Creedence. He actually fooled *me!*

Bob says, "I want to do 'Who'll Stop the Rain.'" He puts down his cell phone, and I hear him pick up a guitar, and he starts strumming into the phone, "Long as I remember..." And he sang the whole song to me over the phone. My jaw dropped, it sounded so great.

Bob has a unique way of strumming the guitar. He does it with his thumb. So that sound that you hear on "Night Moves"—it's not a pick. It's not like me or Bruce or so many other singer-songwriters: when we're strumming that big chord it makes kind of a percussive sound. Bob's thing is almost a thump. Which is very personal.

We're there in the studio, and Bob goes off by himself because he wants to make sure his game is on. He's over in the corner alone with his guitar, going over the verses, going over his approach. I had been busy producing things, and suddenly I just hear that guitar thump and his voice: "Long as I remember..."

And I go, "Whoa!" The producer—no, the fan—in me heard another artist really doing it. This record was about taking chances, which didn't necessarily mean making a Top 40, two-minute song that fits some record company genre in a nice, neat little box. It was about being artistic, and I had all these wonderful artists. So when I hear something that cool—like what Bob Seger was doing—the artist in me says, "I've gotta have that."

I had met Alan Jackson back in the nineties, around the time of "Mercury Blues." I'm a huge fan. I started with his first album back in 1990, and I have loved them all ever since. Incredible voice, incredible taste. I feel he has much in common with the golden age of country music.

One day I got word from my record company: "Alan Jackson has heard about your project, and he wants to record a song with you." I was floored. Of all the times in my life, this was one that kind of took me aback. I didn't dare hope that this could ever happen. It really meant a lot to me.

I went down to Nashville, and we recorded "Have You Ever Seen the Rain." Alan is the friendliest, nicest guy. He didn't act like God, even though I think of him as one. In fact, I told people it's like having Lincoln on your record, because that's the bearing he has for me. I knew I wanted some of that cool left-hand piano stuff that Joey Schmidt does on Alan's records, like "Small Town Southern Man." And, of course, I had to have some great Brent Mason guitar! Brent has been one of my heroes for years, starting with the great solos he does on so many of Alan's songs.

So all these wonderful musicians were part of this session—plus a subliminal ingredient that you would never know about unless you were there.

The building where Alan records is a weird-looking old house from the thirties that they call the Castle. The band is sort of in the main room, and Alan goes into this side room where he always sings. We set up facing each other, each with his own microphone, and I was a kid in a candy store. Alan is singing with that awesome voice of his, and every once in a while he rears back to sing a line and you could hear it echo off the walls in that room. It made the hair stand up on the back of my neck. I knew that sound from listening to his records. Any other place in the universe, you would never get that sound. It's part of all his records, and it's not some button you can push. You can really hear the sound of that room, and this extra bit of magic just took my breath away.

Jennifer Hudson and I were both at a benefit a couple of years ago. We didn't actually meet, but I stood and watched her performance. She has a one-in-a-billion voice, for the ages. If I had a cannon like that, I'd be showing off all the time. I would stand on the street corner and stop traffic.

So I got up the courage to ask her. I wasn't even sure if she knew who I was. She chose "Proud Mary."

One night around this time, I was at dinner with Julie and we were having a gentle conversation about many things, including music. I started to talk about my song "Don't You Wish It Was True" and perhaps rethinking the arrangement. I mentioned that maybe it would be cool in a New Orleans setting, and I described some of the elements that make that city's music so great. Suddenly, Julie's eyes get real big and she blurts out, "Proud Mary."

I look at her as if to say, "No, honey, you misunderstood me."

She says insistently, "Proud Mary."

I go, "What do you mean, honey?" Now I realize that I'm hearing an idea.

She says, "Proud Mary. All those things you just said: the gospel feel, the zydeco, the wonderful fiddles, the washboard, the triangle, the horns..."

I'm hearing this and I say, "Yes, yes, yes, you're right. This is a great idea."

I was starting to get excited, and she adds, "It's got to be a musical journey. It's got to show the history of New Orleans. And we have to go to New Orleans and do this."

The first thing I said was, "I'm gonna need help—I should call Allen Toussaint."

So I did. We had met two or three times over the years. And I must say, Allen has a very special presence. Not someone I would walk up to, slap on the back, and treat frivolously. But there is one thing that is quite interesting. The first time I met Allen Toussaint was at the 1998 Rock and Roll Hall of Fame ceremony at the Waldorf in New York City. I was inducting Gene Vincent. I was sort of in my own world, trying to do a good job for Gene. But I look over and see Allen Toussaint.

Allen was being inducted that night. I'm a big fan and offered my congratulations. And then I said, "Allen, have we ever met?" His face gets a little curious, quizzical. He is a wonderfully suave, beautiful man—the way he speaks, just his manner, is so elegant. He goes, "No, I don't think so, John." And I go, "Oh, well, then I must have dreamed it." And then I just shook his hand and excused myself.

Well, what had happened was, years before, I'd had a dream and it was so real that I thought I knew Allen. So when I walked over there that night, I felt like I knew him.

Finally we're down at Piety Studio in New Orleans, tracking with Jennifer Hudson and the Rebirth Brass Band, from the streets of New Orleans. We had gotten a lot of the music recorded, so we felt pretty good. Allen was kind of sitting over by himself at the piano. So I came over and sat down next to him, kind of like the son to the father. I said, "Allen, I want to tell you something. Do you remember when I walked up to you at the hall of fame and said, 'Have we ever met?'"

He said something like, "I found that curious, John. Yeah, I remember that. But it was just sort of strange."

"Okay. I want to tell you about a dream I had. In that dream, you and I were in New Orleans working together, coming up with arrangements. We were doing this because we were producing a very talented girl singer, and the song that we were working on was 'Proud Mary.'" And that's the God's honest truth.

He looks at me and hits a strange chord on the piano. Kinda, *bra-ang!* And he says, "That's weird."

I said, "Yes, sir, but that's exactly what happened, and here we are."

"You know, Brad, you are just one of my favorite guitar players of all time. Can you show me how you make that sound?"

Guitar players collect other guitar players that they love. And Brad Paisley is at the top of a very select few. I know of other players who are virtuosos and all that, which I respect. But I wouldn't want to play like that—it doesn't do anything for me. In Brad's case, I hang on every note. I am an idolizing, genuflecting groupie. He plays the Telecaster like a violin player, ripping out stuff that is just so lyrical, musical. He is obviously one of the most talented guitar players that has ever lived.

We were backstage at an awards event when I asked him how he "made that sound." He just pulled me over to his amp and went immediately into guitarspeak. Now, we were just two guitar geeks talking gear. (With Brad Paisley? The Ultimate!) In the midst of that, I blurted out how I'd always wanted to do a record like his album *Play*, and he suddenly says, "As long as you let me play on your album." I was speechless. I didn't think anyone knew about my plans for an album. I think I said, "Yes...please."

When we got on the phone to talk about it, Brad wanted to do "Hot Rod Heart." I thought that was an unusual choice, but he said he loved *Blue Moon Swamp*. Then he told me about being a thirteen-year-old kid and singing "Centerfield" at a huge outdoor festival. He said, "I didn't do it in G. I did it in E." E is the guitar player's key. I just laughed and said, "Oh, you made a guitar song out of it." He goes, "Heck, yeah." Even at thirteen, Brad's voice was lower than mine.

We got back to "Hot Rod Heart." And Brad says, "I'm picturing two guys having a guitar duel out on Main Street." That was his vision. So I pictured an old Western duel. I thought, *Oh my God, he's Clint Eastwood, and I'm already dead.* We met in a studio in Nashville (on Main Street), and I knew immediately I was in the presence of the Yoda Master. Man, what fun that was! Back in the control room listening to Brad just ripping it out had me and everybody else cracking up at how great he plays. (Little-boy voice: "How do you make that sound?")

I admire Brad a lot, and it's more than just his incredible music. I love how he lives his life . . . how he is as a person.

I thought it would be really great if I could have my sons, Tyler and Shane, on the album with me. They've grown up in music, and they're both accomplished guitar players. They have their own band called Hearty Har. Julie and I are really proud of them, and these days we can support them by going to *their* shows! How cool is that? I'd really like people to know that our kids have figured out a lot of this on their own. I really can't take credit. I'm sure some people will assume that Dad showed them all this, but I didn't.

The boys wanted to do "Lodi." Their generation seems to be into classic rock. I had heard them out in the garage taking "Lodi" in a folk-rock direction. It was good, but it just wasn't ringing my bell, because for years and years I'd always thought I would like to bust out a kind of roadhouse version of "Lodi." I'd never quite had the right situation because the original is so well-known. I didn't want to confuse my audience. But, you know, being past sixty means I can get away with stuff. I've seen other guys do it (and it always made me scratch my head—*wha...?*). So I talked my kids into it—"Hey, why don't we try kind of a blues-rock version?"

I was back on tour again, and it turned out we were going to get to record at Abbey Road, home of the Beatles. I knew we really had to have our game on for this wonderful opportunity! We didn't actually get to record in the Beatles' room, but we were close enough. (Yes, we did get to sneak in for a peek. That room was full of orchestral instruments, waiting for something. We stood by *that* piano, under *that* clock...from those famous Beatles photos. Whew.)

We had a limited amount of time and hadn't gotten to rehearse, but I wanted to make sure we nailed the song while we were there. I don't like stuff where later you have to put it into a computer to fix it and it comes out all twisted. I wanted to be *done* on that day—at least the raw tracks—because we were in the shadow of the Beatles and George Martin. (Whoa, now—so much to say about *them*.) It was certainly a long day, but we did capture a funky roadhouse feel. Man, it's great to set out to do something and then *do it!* Looking back now, I hear a similarity to the Beatles' "Get Back." It wasn't intentional—maybe something was seeping through the walls.

Young people are competitive by nature. It's just the way they are, but I want Shane and Tyler to enjoy making music. That's what I hope for. I have been given such a bounty in this industry, and it's really not fair for anyone to judge my kids' efforts against that. That's the reason I never named any of my children John Jr. Could you imagine being Elvis Presley Jr.?

As far as the record business, what record business? When I was a young boy there seemed to be so many independent regional record labels. It was a really cool American dream. There were kids everywhere with little bands in garages who could make a record as good as "Henrietta." And it was quite possible for that record to be a hit on the radio. Now you make a record on your smartphone. And so can a hundred million other people. We thought the competition was pretty strong back in the day—now it's like locusts! Yet the playlist has shrunk. You have a much smaller chance of having an independent song played than you did before. And you won't make any money from your song anyway, because the instant somebody downloads it, it becomes free to everyone if they so choose. That's a huge change. I have to restrain my kids from dumping all their songs on the Internet without even copyrighting and protecting them. Everything seems to be so instant and so disposable. If you can get something with the press of a button, it seems to have a lot less value.

I had fun making *Wrote a Song for Everyone*. I think it's my greatest achievement as a producer—besides my kids, that is. I certainly think of it as a high-water mark in a very long career. I put my whole life into it. And a lot of those artists did too. It was hard work, but if something's worthwhile, there's probably going to be some work to it. I'm just so lucky I get to call that my album.

One person I just can't thank enough is Jann Wenner at *Rolling Stone* magazine. During the early stages of *Blue Moon Swamp,* I found myself completely stuck, artistically frozen. I was so frustrated—so overwhelmed—with the Fantasy Records battle that I thought speaking out publicly might help save my sanity. I got on the phone with Jann and just poured out my feelings about the situation. After hearing me out, he said something like "We've got to tell this story. I will help you." He had spoken just a few words, but for me it was huge. I started to go to work on songs and music. I started to move. It seems to me now that just know-ing I *could* tell the story was enough to get me unstuck. In the end, I didn't do the article, but I sure am grateful for the helping hand. Thank you, Jann!

Julie: We sent the CD to Jann. We didn't hear anything back for about a week or so, and then we got a beautiful note—he said he couldn't stop listening to it. That was really great for John to hear. He'd been in a cave. He didn't know.

Then Jann invited John to lunch. The record company set it up. We got there a little late, and we're a bit rummy because we overslept. And suddenly we're in this kind of school cafeteria with all the employees of *Rolling Stone*. What we didn't know is that they have this casual lunch where from time to time they have a guest speaker.

Jann introduced John and said some very flattering things. The next thing you know, Jann is asking John questions, and he has to stand up and speak like he's been called on in class. We weren't really prepared, but John's just a natural. Only I notice that the price tag is still on his shirt. So I jump up and tear it off, and the whole place roars.

Afterwards we were in Jann's office. And all of a sudden he goes, "Oh, have you seen the new *Rolling Stone,* with the review of your album?" He goes over to his desk, grabs it, and points at it—five stars. John had never gotten a five-star review in his whole career. I started sobbing. I was just so happy for John.

John: I'm in a happy place when it comes to music and how it relates to me. I have a band that's actually quite accomplished but that can also play simple... have the variation. Be as wide or narrow as you want it to be. For some reason, I can live in both worlds. I have some big plans rolling around inside my head but, you know me, I'd rather not say what they are until they're here. Don't talk about it—*do* it!

How would I like to be remembered?

I don't have it all wrapped up in some tidy phrase. How about, "John Fogerty was a simple guy—an ordinary guy. And as much as he could be, he tried to be a decent person. He dearly loved his wife and children. His greatest desire in life was to take care of them—and have them love him." I sure hope Julie and my kids know that. That's what is important to me.

I truly love music, but I'm not disappointed with my life if I'm not doing that just this second. I've already had an amazing journey. After where I've been, I know how incredibly lucky I am to have been given this chance. A short while after I had met Julie, as I started spending more and more time with her, I began to say, "You know, honey, it was worth twenty years in hell to spend one day with you."

Pretty much every day I say thank you. I'll say it all the way to the pearly gates—the most important thing that you can find in this world is love. It's worth far more than any of the other things you may think you want, and if you attain love, you've got everything. I absolutely mean that. I realize I sound like one of those goofy guys on TV, but it really is the secret of life.

I consider myself the luckiest man in the world. Because I found Julie.

EPILOGUE

Flying

THE OTHER MORNING I got up at about 4 a.m. I picked up my guitar, went in my library, and turned on the fire. Everybody's asleep, the house is quiet, it's still dark. The guitar was cold, so I put it in front of the fire. It takes a while to get warmed up.

Since I'd gotten up that early, I had a lot of time. The first hour was pretty good... getting better at some of the stuff I'm working on. But the second hour was "Oh boy, here we go!" I was really in heaven because I'd gotten to a place I'd never been before. Where it was just effortless, it just comes out of you, and you're no longer concerned with technique.

Yesterday I could fly.

There is one last song I want to tell you about: "Mystic Highway." It's on *Wrote a Song for Everyone*. If a little green man arrived from Mars and requested to hear just one John Fogerty song, this is the one I'd play for him.

It's the song I'd been working on the longest. I had written the title in my little songbook maybe thirty years ago. It was alluring.

A good group of words. Most people are going to go, "What the heck is that?" But it wasn't a phrase that was meaningless, like "Proud Mary."

It's a concept that really resonates with me. Even way back then, I just saw a highway, a road, a thread through time and space. I can see a group of travelers, a small band of people, maybe a family, kind of shadowy, with their faces looking up towards the sky. They are traveling. Weary, but not broken, not defeated. They've been doing this for a long time. I clearly see a man there, a dad, a father figure—it's me, not some other guy. He's got a cowboy hat on. They are not in a big hurry. They are expected on this journey, on this "mystic highway." And eventually they're going to get there, wherever it is they are supposed to get to, and it may be another twenty minutes, and it may be another twenty years, or it may be another twenty thousand years. Who knows? This is their destiny.

"Mystic Highway" is certainly a deep and ongoing subject. That's why it took so long to write, I guess. It took me forever to wrestle it to the ground. A lot of times I'd look at it and say, "Man, I don't understand that." It just seemed way too big.

But as this album was taking shape, I said, "Doggone it, I'm going to do 'Mystic Highway.'" I knew I wasn't going to write, "Oh, yes, the Mystic Highway is forty-two miles long and turns left at Tutwiler, wacka-doo, wacka-doo." No, you have a lot of emotion about it. And a lot of wonderment.

It had to express my beliefs, and it had to be general enough that anyone could believe it—*if* they wanted to listen and buy into it. I didn't want to be specific and go, "Well, I'm a human being here on earth, and about nineteen galaxies way over there, in a different dimension, there's another little planet, and there's some beings named Ward and June there with their young'uns, and I'm connected to them." Which I believe we are. You might think things work some other way. That's fine.

I started the song like this:

Lately I begin to wonder / How it's all gonna end

Yes. Isn't everybody at my age? Or anybody at any age? I wasn't doing it with any sort of pandering—you could be fifteen and asking the question. A kid sitting there on the side of the river with his little fishing pole: "How's it all gonna end?" We all do it.

It's one of those things no one can tell you about. You're just going to have to experience it yourself, like the first time you touch fire. You may hear someone say, "Listen, my friend: after it happens, I'll come back and tell you." But nobody ever has. Except Jesus, I guess. That's why we still don't know.

Without knowin' where I'm goin' / Probably get there anyway

That lyric is hilarious to me. And so true. "Mystic Highway" is very spiritual. Reverential. There's a whole lot of God in there.

Why fight the idea of God? Wouldn't you even want to hedge your bets? I don't have to think of it just one way: "Oh, yeah, I go on Sunday, kneel down, and God's that guy with the big white beard and lightning bolts..." No, I believe there are all kinds of different ways for people to think of what God is. And it's all good as far as I'm concerned. They don't have to contradict. Personally, I think God is the whole thing—everything. Assemble everything in the whole universe to infinity. All of it together is God.

Everything is connected / Everything and everyone

That's not too complicated. I happen to think that the entire universe is God. Therefore, we are God.

We're all connected. There's a lot of science pointing to the idea that living things like plants have awareness and feelings.

We who live together on this planet are all one.

Smooth city slickers and loaded dice / Take your money in a pig's eye

Maybe some of the reason I feel so good now is because I was trapped for so long in a horrible place. Where I felt really bad.

One of my constant companions then was frustration, which is a terrible emotion. And feeling lost, which we've all experienced from time to time. When you feel that way, it's a nightmare.

I don't feel like that anymore, and man, I'm really grateful that I don't. Yet I am thankful for the journey. Well, yeah, I wish I didn't have to take some parts of that journey, but it's just there— part of me. The way I see it, I had to go through all of that stuff to get to Julie.

I wish there had been a shortcut.

But even the hard parts of the journey seem to be important, because I wouldn't be me sitting here now without them. I'm not going to forget about what I've been through. But I don't sit around worrying about it, or spend a lot of time trying to rearrange it.

God wants you and every little other part of him to do well, be happy and healthy, and be with him. It's all about being positive. At peace, content. That describes me right now.

Tomorrow I'll get up early and play my guitar, just like I do every day before I drive Kelsy to school. Maybe this time when I play, I'll fly.

I will certainly dream…

Because my dream came true.

INDEX

ABOUT THE AUTHOR

JOHN FOGERTY IS one of rock's most influential guitarists, singers, and writers. He is a member of the Rock and Roll Hall of Fame and one of the only artists on *Rolling Stone*'s list of top 100 guitarists *and* top 100 singers.